RESPONDING TO SPECIAL EDUCATIONAL NEEDS: AN IRISH PERSPECTIVE

Second Edition

Sean Griffin and Michael Shevlin

D1512901

GILL & MACMILLAN

Gill & Macmillan
Hume Avenue
Park West
Dublin 12
with associated companies throughout the world
www.gillmacmillan.ie

© Sean Griffin and Michael Shevlin, 2007, 2011
978 07171 4998 8

Index compiled by Cliff Murphy
Print origination in Ireland by TypeIT, Dublin
Printed by GraphyCems, Spain.

The paper used in this book is made from the wood pulp of managed forests. For every tree felled, at least one tree is planted, thereby renewing natural resources.

A CIP catalogue record for this book is available from the British Library.

Dedicated to Kathleen O'Leary and Mary Cooney

Contents

Acknowledgments   viii

Chapter 1: Identifying the Issues   1

Section 1: Setting the Scene   9

Chapter 2: The Experiences of People with Disabilities: Marginalisation,
    Recognition and Rights   11
Chapter 3: Historical Emergence: The Irish Experience   29
Chapter 4: Developing Policy and Provision in Special Education   47
Chapter 5: Moving towards Schools for All   73

Section 2: Beginning the Process   93

Chapter 6: Addressing Core Issues in Special Education   95
Chapter 7: Identification and Assessment of Special Educational Needs   119
Chapter 8: Individual Education Planning   138

Section 3: Developing Classroom Strategies   153

Chapter 9: Accessing the Curriculum: Models of Differentiation   155
Chapter 10: Examining Difficulties in Literacy and Numeracy   172
Chapter 11: Understanding and Approaching Behaviour Difficulties   195
Chapter 12: Strategies for Specific Special Educational Needs   215

Section 4: Sustaining Collaborative Approaches   237

Chapter 13: Developing Collaborative Relationships with Parents
    and Families   239
Chapter 14: Creating and Developing Partnerships within Schools   255
Chapter 15: Conclusion: Mapping the Road Ahead   267

References   271

Glossary   291

Index   296

Acknowledgments

Many people have encouraged us in writing this book. Our families, friends and colleagues have assisted us through their advice and support. We are grateful to our colleagues in St Nicholas Montessori College Ireland and the School of Education, Trinity College Dublin, who stimulated our thinking about how teacher education can contribute to the development of inclusive learning environments. Over the years of our involvement in special education, the commitment and insights of many educators, student teachers, parents and children and young people with special educational needs have influenced our understanding of how critical issues in special education have a profound impact on the lives of the people of central concern – children and young people with special educational needs.

Our greatest thanks are for the people closest to us, who bring us joy, read our work, encourage our thinking and are always there for us – Kathleen O'Leary, Mary Cooney and Emma Griffin.

Chapter 1
Identifying the Issues

This is a very challenging time to be involved in special education in Ireland. Over a relatively short period of time we have witnessed enormous changes in how we think about special education and how we believe special education should be delivered in our schools. In the past, special education was seen as the exclusive preserve of dedicated professionals who looked after the needs of children and young people who had disabilities. These children were often educated separately from their peers in separate schools and institutions. As a result, there was little contact or interaction between these children and their peers in the community or even between professionals in special education and their counterparts in mainstream settings.

In our introduction we will outline how this situation has been dramatically altered through significant changes in special education policy and provision in Ireland. We will explore the implications of these changes for policy and practice, and the principles underpinning special educational provision will be examined. The language used to describe special educational provision and the children and young people who receive it will be analysed. Finally, we will provide an outline of the contents of the book to mark the starting point in the process of introducing special education to our readers.

Background

In the last 20 years or so there has been an upsurge of interest in special education policy and practice. This has been influenced by a number of factors. In particular, the worldwide concern to promote more inclusive forms of education has been recognised and endorsed in international agreements, legislation and government policies. Within an Irish context, a number of official government reports and policy documents have helped to change the face of special education.

The *Report of the Special Education Review Committee* (Department of Education 1993) represented the first serious attempt since the 1960s to address the complex issues involved in policy and provision. The *Report of the Commission on the Status of People with Disabilities* (Government of Ireland 1996) has also been pivotal in promoting an awareness of inclusion. With the introduction of the Education Act 1998, for the first time, all schools and all teachers have to take responsibility for all children, including those with special educational needs and/or disabilities. Every school is legally obliged to develop and publish its policy on responding to children who have special educational needs in their local community. The Education for Persons with Special Educational Needs Act 2004 put into place local support structures to deliver special educational provision. The legislation will require schools to implement individual educational plans for children and young people with special educational needs, involving proactive parental participation. This enabling legislation represents a significant shift in government policy towards the creation of inclusive learning environments. There is no turning back from this vision, even in times of economic constraint, and educators are challenged to respond.

The historical isolation of special education from mainstream education has facilitated the persistence of certain myths about children and young people who have special educational needs. There was a widespread belief that children and young people with special educational needs were qualitatively different from their peers and that their social and learning needs were significantly dissimilar to other children so that they required separate education away from their mainstream peers. It was also assumed that children with special educational needs could learn very little and needed substantial teacher time in order to make any progress. Also, it was often assumed that because a child had a physical/sensory disability, then they automatically had difficulty learning. These assumptions tended to generate low expectations for and an overprotective attitude towards these children. In addition, schools and teachers often struggled to overcome chronically inadequate resourcing and official indifference. However, since the 1990s, official government policy and provision have been more responsive, and pressure from parents, teachers and advocacy groups has resulted in significant changes.

Today within special education there is a strong emphasis on creating inclusive learning environments that can cater for pupil diversity. This represents a great challenge for everyone involved, including teachers, parents, children, special needs assistants, administrators and health professionals. Responding to this challenge involves a fundamental re-evaluation of our beliefs about education and prompts a number of searching questions. Does everyone have an equal right to education? Does everyone have the right to an opportunity to participate meaningfully within our education system and later within society? Do all children in the local community belong in the local school? Who is of value within our education system? How do we guarantee access to a balanced curriculum for all pupils? Do we really believe that children with severe learning needs can actually benefit from education? What are appropriate educational outcomes for children with profound learning needs?

As we can see from these questions, special education policy and practice raise serious issues around human rights, equality and participation within society. One major task of childhood is becoming educated and knowledgeable about our world and developing the capacity to participate as a valued member of the local community. However, in the past and today to a certain extent, this possibility is denied to children and young people for a variety of reasons, including disability, poverty, gender and ethnic background. These issues, by their very nature, are complex, multifaceted and need to be addressed by society at large.

Responding to diversity involves challenging previously held assumptions about children and young people from non-traditional backgrounds, listening to new voices and attempting to construct an equitable education system. Traditionally, special education addressed one aspect of that diversity – the education of children who had disabilities and/or severe learning needs. To an increasing extent, these children are in our mainstream schools and have become the responsibility of everyone in the education system.

Principles

The principles underpinning mainstream education do not differ markedly from the principles embedded in special educational provision. It is true to say that the beliefs and values that inform mainstream education rarely have to be stated explicitly, as few would argue, for example, that children should not receive an appropriate education that enables them to fulfil their potential. However, this is not always the case in relation to special educational provision. Children receiving special educational provision were not guaranteed access to a balanced curriculum and to nationally recognised certification. The type of education on offer was often dependent on the nature of the disabling condition presented by the child and the implicit assumptions about the capability of the child. Many children with disabilities were subject to stereotyped perceptions and lowered expectations for achievement. As a result, there continues to be a debate around what an appropriate education for particular children entails and where this education should take place. Due to a combination of these factors, the principles underpinning special education policy and practice need to be stated explicitly.

Education is recognised as a fundamental human right and 'no young person should be denied that right on grounds of disability any more than they should be denied it because they are female or members of an ethnic minority' (Hegarty 1993a: 9). This right is expressed in the United Nations Declaration of Human Rights and restated in many national policy documents. While this fundamental right has been acknowledged in Ireland, serious issues remain around what constitutes an appropriate education for children and young people with special educational needs. Economic arguments are often advanced to support this position, and helping these young people to become independent and employable would be a valuable outcome, but whether or not this can be achieved does not take away from the fundamental right to an education.

Equality of opportunity is widely accepted in principle as a fundamental right, though translating this into practice remains difficult. This principle is often misunderstood as involving treating everyone in the same way. However, to treat people equally means taking account of the diversity among children: 'Since children are different from each other, they must be treated in different ways in order to reach common goals' (Hegarty 1993a: 16). Differential educational treatment of this kind will succeed or fail at the practical level of pedagogy and resource allocation. Decisions at this level can be difficult when resources and expertise are in short supply. However, allocating sufficient resources and developing appropriate pedagogy are the minimum requirements needed to move beyond the rhetoric of equal opportunity towards meaningful participation for children and young people with special educational needs in our education system.

Children and young people with special educational needs also have the right to meaningful participation in society. In practice, this means these children and young people have the right to attend their local school, have access to the range of curricula and certification available to their peers and not experience needless restrictions that limit their participation in ordinary school activities alongside their peers.

The fundamental right to education, equality of opportunity and meaningful participation within society for children and young people with special educational needs is encapsulated in the preamble to the Education for Persons with Special Educational Needs Act 2004:

> ... to provide that the education of people with (such) needs shall, wherever possible, take place in an inclusive environment with those who do not have such needs, to provide that people with special educational needs shall have the same right to avail of and benefit from appropriate education as do their peers who do not have such needs, to assist children with special educational needs to leave school with the skills necessary to participate to the level of their capacity in an inclusive way in the social and economic activities of society and to live independent and fulfilled lives.

Terminology

The language we use to describe particular recognisable groups of people often reveals our attitudes towards this group and their status within society. As we will see, the language used in relation to people with disabilities has almost always been negative and reflected their marginalised status within society. As a result, many of the terms used to describe people with disabilities and/or particular disabilities have become discredited. In the past, terms such as 'idiot' and 'imbecile' were regularly used in reports (often medical) to describe people with learning difficulties, and so they became closely associated with negative stereotypes of people with disabilities. More recently, the term 'spastic' (or 'spa' for short) has become a term of abuse, especially among young people. This recognition has prompted concerted attempts to find acceptable terms that describe the disabling condition and the population affected and avoid negative labelling.

The language used in special education has often reflected the socially devalued status granted to disabled people. For example, in the United Kingdom, schools for children with learning difficulties were once referred to as Educationally Sub-Normal (ESN) Mild/Moderate schools, depending on the level of difficulty these children experienced. Later, this population became known as the 'mentally handicapped', which often became confused with mental illness in the popular imagination. We have often been overly concerned about categorising and labelling children with disabilities and assigning them to a particular type of education based on their disability category. This often led to unwarranted assumptions about the learning capabilities of children with disabilities. For example, it was assumed that if you had a sensory or physical disability, then you automatically had more evident learning needs than your peers. These issues will be discussed in more depth in Chapter 2, which explores societal awareness of and attitudes to people with disabilities.

There is an intense debate around acceptable terms to use in relation to people with disabilities. 'Mental handicap' is no longer considered an acceptable term to describe people who have learning difficulties. In Ireland the advocacy group formerly known as NAMHI (National Association of Mentally Handicapped Ireland) has, after a sustained campaign by people with learning difficulties and their advocates, changed the name of the organisation to Inclusion Ireland. If 'mental handicap' is no longer appropriate, what term should be used? Some would say 'learning disability', others 'learning difficulty' and yet others would favour 'intellectual disability'. In Scotland more recently the term 'additional learning needs' has been used in policy documents.

In this book we have decided to principally refer to children who receive special educational provision as having a 'special educational need'. For the sake of clarity and to avoid unnecessary confusion we will also, when referring to particular populations of children with a disability, use the terms currently employed by the Department of Education and Skills. This is not to say that we necessarily agree with these terms and where concerns arise about the appropriateness of particular terms, this will be pointed out. The concept of 'special educational need' will be explored further in Chapter 6.

At this stage, we can say that a child is deemed to have a 'special educational need' if s/he requires substantial additional educational provision in comparison to his/her peers. The Department of Education and Skills classifications in relation to sensory and physical disability are relatively straightforward, though children with a wide range of distinct physical disabilities are grouped under the general title of 'physical disabilities' for educational and administrative purposes. Children with identifiable learning difficulties (formerly known as 'mentally handicapped') are classified under the designation 'general learning disabilities' and further subdivided into 'mild', 'moderate', 'severe' and 'profound', depending on the level of difficulty experienced by the child. Children with emotional/behavioural difficulties are referred to as having an 'emotional/behavioural disturbance', a medical term that unfortunately can convey a very negative picture of these children. Children who are identified as having dyslexia/dyspraxia are classified under the umbrella term 'specific learning disabilities', which distinguishes these children and the nature of their difficulty from the children in the 'general learning disabilities' category.

Children on the autistic spectrum are classified as having an 'autistic spectrum disorder' (ASD). This is another medical term that has the advantage of indicating the range of children within this category and the drawback of suggesting that these children have psychiatric difficulties.

It is important to make a distinction between the terms 'disability' and 'special educational need', as in the past it has often been mistakenly assumed that once a child has a disability, s/he automatically has a special educational need. This is not so. Essentially, 'special educational needs' is a school-focused term that refers to difficulties in learning experienced by a number of children. A child with a disability may require technical support to access the curriculum and/or reasonable accommodation in taking examinations. This is clearly not a learning need, but rather highlights an access deficit. Our traditional way of categorising children with disabilities and providing separate education according to category of disability has undoubtedly contributed to this confusion.

Who are we writing for?

This book is principally designed to introduce primary and post-primary student teachers to the whole area of special education. We also believe that this book will have relevance for newly qualified teachers and teachers facing the challenge of creating inclusive learning environments for the first time. It will also be helpful to teachers undertaking professional development courses or further studies. We think that parents of children and young people with special educational needs will find this book a useful starting point in understanding systemic and school responses to special educational needs. This book could also be an important reference point for special needs assistants and professionals involved in supporting special educational provision in a range of settings.

The challenge of change

Special education knowledge and practice tended to be confined to those practitioners directly involved in special schools, institutions and classes. This was very convenient for mainstream education for a variety of reasons. Mainstream schools were not expected to deal with children and young people with disabilities. 'There was a place for them' and it certainly wasn't within the local primary or post-primary school. Generally, mainstream education remained blissfully unaware of special education policy and practice, as it rarely impinged on their lives. As a result, special education expertise and knowledge were restricted to special settings. Meanwhile, a significant minority of children and young people in mainstream schools were failing to achieve national certification, dropping out of school early or being asked to leave. For many years, 'blaming the child' became the dominant explanation for these outcomes and little further investigation was required. Dissatisfaction with the existing systems of special and mainstream education became apparent both at national and international levels. Rather belatedly, there was an increasing realisation that mainstream education urgently needed special education expertise and knowledge to respond effectively to the children experiencing difficulties in learning in their own schools. This knowledge was also essential within a context of developing inclusive learning environments.

Because education policy developed an inclusive focus, all schools are now expected to build their capacity to respond effectively to diversity among children and young people. Consequently, all teachers are expected to become capable in the design and delivery of a broad, balanced curriculum. These radical changes have implications for all facets of the education system. For example, special schools, through experience and commitment, have developed valuable expertise that is an important dimension of the continuum of special educational provision. It is therefore vital that structural links between special settings and mainstream schools are established and maintained. Teacher education is obviously another key area for consideration. Until relatively recently, special education was given minimal attention within initial teacher education and tended to be regarded as an optional extra. Teacher education aims to develop reflective, knowledgeable practitioners, and insights gained from the study of special education have an important contribution to make to this process.

The route map

Within this book we have aimed to provide the reader with a route map through the area of special education. This book is not intended to be a comprehensive manual covering all aspects of special education. Rather, the authors aim to provide the reader with foundation knowledge and understanding of the area and a framework for analysing and reflecting on the many critical issues involved in special education in a contemporary Irish context. We also introduce the reader to the basic concepts underpinning special educational provision and practice.

The purpose of our book is encapsulated in the title: *Responding to Special Educational Needs: An Irish Perspective.* This consists of a reflection on the unique cultural dimension in the Irish engagement with the concerns of special education. We will see how the interplay of historical and cultural factors has shaped and continues to shape special education policy and practice. The Irish dimension enables us to reflect on where we have come from, what's happening now and where we are going. We acknowledge the commitment and endeavours of teachers, the genuine concern of parents and the aspirations of children and young people with special educational needs to meet their potential. It is now time to harness the energy, vision and resources to create inclusive learning environments for all our children.

Within each chapter, the reader will be given an opportunity to extend his/her thinking around particular issues through the use of discussion points. From our experience in education, we believe that we are always learning and so we recommend that readers take the opportunity to reflect with their colleagues as we endeavour to develop appropriate responses for children and young people with special educational needs.

This book is divided into four interrelated sections: *setting the scene*, where key milestones in the development of special education will be identified and analysed; *beginning the process*, where crucial issues around how we think about special education and begin an intervention will be examined; in our third section we will focus on the critical issue of *developing classroom strategies*; and in our final section we will examine some ways of *sustaining collaborative approaches*.

We believe that special education is not a separate kind of education. Rather, it is a quality orientation to all education which places the needs of the learner as central to the process. We think of special education as incorporating an 'A-B-C' approach that embraces the linked concepts of Attitudes, Breaking Barriers and Collaboration/Communication as key tasks for the educator.

Figure 1.1: **The ABC approach**

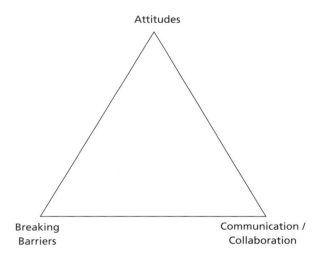

Special education has tended to adopt a 'deficit' model, emphasising the child's limitations and inabilities. This position has been challenged by an alternative model that emphasises the mismatch between the child's learning needs and the provision available. We would strongly argue that special educational needs occupy a place on the continuum of needs which is the domain of all learners. A systemic/social understanding of special educational needs is also vital to a fuller understanding of special education.

Section 1
Setting the Scene

Chapter 2
The Experiences of People with Disabilities: Marginalisation, Recognition and Rights

---

Learning outcomes/objectives

On completion of this chapter, the reader will be able to:
- Identify key turning points for people with disabilities from an historical perspective.
- Understand the impact of negative labelling on the life experiences of people with disabilities.
- Critically discuss the stereotypes of disability as sometimes represented in print media, visual depiction and cinema representations.
- Outline an understanding of the different models of disability and their implications for education.
- Critically examine first-hand accounts of people with disabilities and reflect on the impact of attitudes in an Irish cultural context.

Introduction

'People with disabilities do not want to be pitied nor do they want their disabilities to be dismissed as of little importance. All that is required is a little respect and basic needs and rights. Surely this is not too much to ask?' (Government of Ireland 1996: 4)

Throughout recorded history, people with disabilities have occupied a position on the margins of society. There have been examples of enlightened practice informed by humane motives, but these are far outweighed by the consistent attempts to exclude, control and regulate people with disabilities within society. Disabled people have been seen as 'other' and often as a threat to the well-being of the community.

Within this chapter we explore the experiences of disabled people from historical, social and experiential perspectives. These perspectives will enable us to develop an awareness of the impact of societal attitudes on educational provision for, and the life experiences of, people with disabilities. We will also be able to examine the implications of the traditional historical and social exclusion of people with disabilities for the development of inclusive educational provision.

Historical perspective

Braddock and Parish (2001) provide a comprehensive overview of the historical experiences of people with disabilities. In ancient Greece and Rome, children born with obvious disabilities (primarily physical) were viewed as a sign that the parents had displeased the gods. Infanticide of these children was widely accepted and practised as a sacrificial appeasement of the gods. However, there appeared to be a toleration of disabilities acquired later in life as a result of war or unhealthy living environments. Wealthy people sometimes kept slaves of short stature or slaves with general learning disabilities to entertain their guests.

In medieval times it was believed that many disabling conditions (general learning disabilities, mental illness, epilepsy, deafness) had supernatural or demonological causes. It was thought that epilepsy and mental illness were the result of demonic possession and exorcism was required. However, more positive attitudes also existed, as some towns funded pilgrimages for people with epilepsy or mental illness to travel to obtain cures. In medieval society, poverty and disability were closely related. In a situation of extreme poverty, families faced tremendous difficulties when one member was unable to work due to a disability.

In the early modern period, attempts were made to cure various disabilities. These attempts were generally crude and displayed a very limited understanding of human anatomy. However, this focus on a physical cure for disability indicated a significant move away from the dominant supernatural understanding of the causes of disability. Changes in societal attitudes to poverty had a deep impact on the treatment of people with disabilities. For many, poverty had been viewed as an opportunity to give alms and please God, though increasingly the poor and consequently disabled people were seen as a social menace and begging was outlawed in Paris in 1657. This view was strengthened as responsibility for the poor passed from family to the community, and workhouses were established throughout Europe by the beginning of the nineteenth century. The increasing involvement of the medical profession resulted in the establishment of a range of institutions, including county asylums, for 'idiots, blind and cripples', and residential schools for children and young people with sensory impairments.

In the nineteenth century the institutional segregation of people with mental illness and those with general learning disabilities became more evident. Many of these institutions became overcrowded and rehabilitating people to return to the community became neglected. Abuse of residents was common. Training schools were supposed to enable people with intellectual disabilities to acquire the requisite skills to function effectively in their communities. This ideal was abandoned and residents worked in laundries, workshops and farms to maintain the economic viability of the institution. The categorisation of disabled people and their placement within impairment-specific residential schools had one unexpected outcome – the first self-advocacy organisation of disabled people (British Deaf and Dumb Association) was formed as a protest against the banning of sign language and the continued promotion of oralism in schools for deaf children.

There also appeared to be a revival of 'freak shows' involving people with intellectual/physical disabilities. The strange fascination throughout the ages with 'spectacles of difference' through a focus on 'defective' or 'abnormal' bodies and minds appeared undiminished. These people were classified as 'monsters' and reaffirmed the viewer's own normality as well as evoking an element of fear and trepidation.

The eugenics movement had a powerful impact on societal attitudes towards and treatment of people with disabilities from the end of the nineteenth century until well into the twentieth century. Supporters of the eugenics movement asserted that people with general learning disabilities constituted a social menace and a threat to the purity of the gene pool. Many eminent doctors, psychiatrists, scientists, writers and politicians supported the eugenics movement. It was maintained that a general learning disability was an incurable disease and associated with criminality and immoral behaviour. Society needed to be protected from this danger, and placing people with general learning disabilities in institutions became the favoured solution. In the US, intelligence tests acquired what was later proved to be a spurious scientific legitimacy. These tests were increasingly used to classify children as having general learning disabilities and to place them in segregated special classes. As a result of these tests, immigrants and poor Americans were far more likely to be classified as having general learning disabilities.

The eugenics movement also influenced doctors' refusal to treat infants born with disabilities, and life-saving treatments were routinely withdrawn. Legislation was enacted to prevent people with general learning disabilities from getting married and producing children. Sterilisation of residents of institutions became commonplace in some states in America, in Denmark from 1930 to 1954 and in Sweden during the 1930s and 1940s. Sterilisation was also practised in Nazi Germany on the grounds of 'feeble-mindedness' (general learning disability). It was also in Nazi Germany that approximately 200,000 to 275,000 people with physical/general learning disabilities were killed by the authorities.

By the middle of the twentieth century, significant indicators of change began to emerge. These ground-breaking initiatives were initiated by people with disabilities, their families, friends and supportive professionals. The independent living movement recognised that 'the barriers that confront people with disabilities are less related to individual impairment than to social attitudes, interpretations of disability, architectural barriers, legal barriers and educational barriers' (Braddock and Parish 2001: 48). Many institutions were closed and the emphasis shifted towards supported community living for people with general learning disabilities. The Americans with Disabilities Act (1990) (ADA) marked a significant shift in official thinking, as:

This law recognised that discrimination against people with disabilities in the form of purposeful unequal treatment and historical patterns of segregation and isolation was the major problem facing people with disabilities and not their individual impairments. The ADA also stated that people with disabilities have been relegated to powerless positions based on stereotypical assumptions about their disability (Braddock and Parish 2001: 50).

Naming the world: 'Label jars, not people'

In order to understand our reality, we have to name our world. This is a human activity that has gone on through the ages. The language we use reflects our understanding of the objects and relationships that surround us. This naming process enables us to distinguish between objects, exert a certain amount of control over them and communicate with each other about their significance in our lives. Our own names give us a sense of our identity and our position within our family, the community and the wider society. Labels are also conferred on people both as individuals and within groups. Some of these designations are straightforward and convey factual information, such as man/woman or old/young. Other designations may not be as harmless, as we will see when we examine how minorities tend to be labelled. Labels can be a source of pride or humiliation and can evoke feelings of dominance or dependence. Essentially, the designations assigned to individuals and groups reflect their relative position within society. The names in themselves are not automatically good or bad. Difficulties arise when these names become associated with negative, stereotypical imagery of the individual or group concerned. Swain, French and Cameron (2003: 12) observed that 'labels are usually bestowed by those who have power and authority ("experts") upon those who do not'. In addition, there is a real danger that these powerful experts, 'by defining what is considered aberrant the boundaries of what is deemed acceptable (or normal) are marked out' (p. 12).

Swain and French (2003) assert that the traditional division of people into disabled and non-disabled categories is artificial. Impairment cannot be the basis for this divide, as many non-disabled people may have impairments (problems with sight/hearing) but are not generally considered to be disabled. Neither can the experience of oppression be the defining feature, as many non-disabled people also experience discrimination on the basis of race or poverty, for example. Swain and French (2003) believe that the divide lies in societal perceptions of disability and their impact on the daily lives of disabled people: 'Perceptions and experiences on which they are founded vary considerably, not least as many people become disabled in later life having constructed understandings and lifestyles as non-disabled people. Nevertheless, there is a divide in perceptions which is most clearly related to a divide in experiences, being disabled or non-disabled' (p. 151).

Disability is often represented in terms of personal tragedy, with disabled people (particularly children) reported as 'suffering from' or 'victims of' a particular impairment or enduring medical condition. Disabled people have challenged the assumption that disability automatically equals personal tragedy.

Despite this, the personal tragedy perspective retains a powerful influence, in particular in media representations where disabled people are often presented as bravely overcoming their disability to lead a 'normal' life.

This perspective can ignore or gloss over real barriers to participation within society. As Watson (1998) points out, this can lead to the development of stereotypical beliefs assuming that dependency and helplessness are innate qualities in disabled people. He goes on to state that non-disabled people's interactions with disabled people can be dominated by fear. This fear appears to be based on the fact that this encounter reminds them of their own frailty and vulnerability and as a result becomes a barrier in these types of interactions. Swain and French (2003) observe that this fear could have a rational basis, as non-disabled people believe they are fortunate not to be disabled and also realise that they could conceivably cross the divide into disability at some stage of their lives. To become visually impaired, for example, could represent a personal tragedy for someone 'whose life is based around being sighted, who lacks knowledge of the experiences of people with visual impairments, whose identity is founded on being sighted, and who has been subjected to the personal tragedy model of visual impairment' (p. 154). The notion underlying the tragedy model is the belief that disabled people 'want to be other than as they are, though this would mean a rejection of identity and self' (p. 157). Colin Cameron (1999) succinctly rejects this assumption about disabled people: 'We are who we are as people with impairments, and might actually feel comfortable with our lives if it wasn't for all those interfering busybodies who feel that it is their responsibility to feel sorry for us, or find cures for us, or to manage our lives for us, or to harry us in order to make us something we are not i.e. "normal"' (Tyneside Disability Arts: 3, cited in Swain and French 2003).

In their analysis of the representation of disability in literature and film, Mitchell and Snyder (2001) identified negative stereotypical images. They pointed to some of the most famous figures in literary fiction, including Shakespeare's Richard III (hunchback), Melville's Captain Ahab (one-legged) and Dickens's Tiny Tim (limping waif). Disabled people appeared to be portrayed as a threat to ordinary society or as people whose misfortune should be pitied. Common stereotypes maintained by depictions in the electronic media included: 'Disability is a punishment for evil: disabled people are embittered by their "fate"; disabled people resent the non-disabled and would, if they could, destroy them' (Gartner and Joe 1987: 67).

Disabled people are sometimes viewed as 'brave' or 'amazing' for getting on with their lives. This type of designation, while superficially positive, is rejected by disabled activists as an unrealistic representation of most disabled people's lives and a failure to recognise the disabling barriers that exist in society. People with general learning disabilities are often perceived to be and treated as 'eternal children'. 'He only has the mental age of a child' is still quite a common statement that ignores the person's capacity to develop socially and emotionally and make decisions about his/her life. Children who have Down syndrome, in particular, can be subject to the 'happy, smiling little angel' imagery. These types of designations can severely limit the independence of people with general learning disabilities and their ability to participate in society.

Disabled people have attempted to develop their own self-identity and confront the values underpinning institutional discrimination. Swain and French (2003) observed that Disability Arts has played a key role in this development: 'Through song lyrics, poetry, writing, drama and so on, disabled people have celebrated difference and rejected the ideology of normality in which disabled people are devalued as "abnormal". They are creating images of strength and pride, the antithesis of dependency and helplessness' (p. 159).

Does language disable people?

The prevailing negative imagery surrounding disability also applies to the language used in relation to disabled people. Generally speaking, the words used to describe people with disabilities are almost always either negative or passive. In the past, *The Collins Dictionary* definitions of 'disability', 'disabled' and 'invalid' reinforced this view:

> **Disability:** 'physical incapacity, disqualification, lack of some asset, quality or attribute'.
> **Disabled:** 'unable to function, maimed or crippled, unable to act or move, an invalid'.
> **Invalid:** 'someone suffering from a chronic illness, enfeebled, weak'.

These definitions strengthen the notion that disability means an inability to function normally and that disability can be equated with illness. Negative perceptions of disability are deeply rooted within our culture, as our use of everyday phrases can illustrate. For example, a person who does not listen is 'deaf', a person who is unaware of something important may be ridiculed as 'blind', someone who lacks insight can be described as 'short-sighted', while a person who does not succeed in a task could be termed a 'retard'. In these situations the language used to describe disabled people has become a term of abuse and the 'assumption is that blind and deaf people cannot interact effectively with their surroundings and that people with learning difficulties have no capacity to understand at all' (Swain et al. 2003: 138).

Quite commonly, people are labelled by their impairment ('he's cerebral palsy', 'he's a paraplegic', 'she's an amputee'; even 'he's an epileptic' and 'she's Down syndrome'), as if that totally defined the person. Disabled people are often referred to as 'the disabled' or grouped under specific disability labels. This tends to obscure the reality that on the basis of age, gender, sexuality, ethnicity or class, disabled people are as diverse as the rest of the population. Some of this confusion undoubtedly arose from the historical portrayal of disabled people as faulty able-bodied people.

Disability activists are often accused of conforming to 'political correctness' when they advance this interpretation of common, everyday language. However, the language used about minority groups usually reflects both public attitudes and their relative position within society. This becomes even clearer when we examine the type of language used about disabled people in the past. In official records, terms such as 'idiot', 'cretin', 'moron', 'feeble-minded' and 'imbecile' were used to describe and categorise people who had some kind of general learning disability. Distinctions were made between 'idiots' and 'imbeciles', with 'idiots' displaying a greater deficiency of intellect than their peers who were classified as 'imbeciles'.

Gradually, professionals and later people with disabilities challenged these stereotypical categorisations. Positive naming attempts to use terms that have positive nuances or at least minimises the overtly negative depiction. Swain et al. (2003: 145) cite the example of the United Kingdom Spastics Society, which changed its name since 'spastic', or 'spa', had become a well-known term of abuse (often in playgrounds) and they believed that 'there was no way of "rescuing it" as an acceptable description of people with cerebral palsy'. Further, Swain et al. (2003: 146) observed that positive naming 'suggests changes in terminology which alters perceptions of disabled people by focusing on capacities rather than limitations, and differences rather than deviance'. However, simply changing terminology will not fundamentally alter the devalued status of disabled people within society. A more radical approach is required.

Defining disability: 'Nothing about us without us'

Disability is a complex, multifaceted concept that is very difficult to define. As Altman (2001) points out, disability has been explained from numerous viewpoints, including medical, social, political, economic and administrative. In addition, disability does not remain a fixed, unchanging entity, as no common definition exists across health, education and social welfare. So, for example, a person may be disabled in one situation (receive treatment for a severe impairment) yet be deemed non-disabled in another (not qualify for disability-related benefits). From an administrative standpoint it is essential that the person is defined as either disabled or non-disabled: 'The administrative perspective suggests an emphasis on the individual and the categorisation of the individual as a member or non-member of the disabled class or category' (Altman 2001: 98). In these circumstances a definition of disability is developed that will determine who qualifies for inclusion in particular programmes, for benefits and for protection under anti-discrimination laws: 'For programmatic, administrative purposes, disability is usually defined as situations associated with injury, health, or physical conditions that create specific limitations that have lasted (or are expected to last) for a named period of time' (Altman 2001: 98).

This approach is usually associated with what has become termed the medical model. Braddock and Parish (2001: 51–52) traced the origins of the medical model:

After the seventeenth century, medical science and the rise of custodial institutions undermined the self-determination of people with disabilities during a period of rapid and continuous urbanisation and industrialisation in the West. It did this by over-medicalising what was, in large measure, a social and economic problem, separating many disabled people from their families, communities and society at large. This socially sanctioned segregation reinforced negative societal attitudes toward human difference.

The medical model approach has been hugely influential in shaping the direction of thinking, policy and services for people with disabilities. Williams (2001: 125) comments:

> The medical model that informs traditional approaches to disability takes the presumed biological reality of impairment as its fundamental starting point. This biological reality is taken to be the foundation of all forms of illness and impairment, whether 'mental' or 'physical'. Although ill health may arise from sources in the environment surrounding the individual person, it is the individual body within which illness is situated.

Bio-medicine focuses almost exclusively on the impairment, as disability becomes synonymous with the impairment: 'Impairment *per se* is of central concern – its detection, avoidance, elimination, treatment and classification' (Thomas 2002: 40).

International classifications of disability (usually based on the medical model approach) have been formulated. *The International Classification of Impairments, Disabilities, and Handicaps*, published by the World Health Organization (1980), was one notable example of this approach. The emphasis on restrictions in an individual's abilities as a result of bodily impairments was rejected by the disability movement. However, the recognition that barriers to full participation existed within society was an indication of a subtle shift away from the dominant medical model focus.

Crow (2003: 140) outlines four traditional responses to bodily impairment:

(i)   avoidance/escape: this can include abortion, sterilisation, refusal to treat disabled babies and euthanasia.
(ii) management: difficulties associated with impairment are dealt with though impairment itself does not fundamentally change.
(iii) cure: medical treatment.
(iv) prevention: vaccination, health education and better social environments.

Impairment is almost always interpreted in a negative fashion as tragic and difficult for the person involved. This one-dimensional interpretation takes little account of the wide variety of life experiences of the people concerned.

Rehabilitation programmes for disabled people tended to be informed by this perspective and interventions concentrated on minimising the impact of functional limitations on daily activities. Though widely discredited among disability activists, the medical model retains a powerful hold over institutional responses to people with disabilities.

The charity model response to people with disabilities is closely connected to the medical model. Charities had initially been founded to tackle social problems, though from the beginning the philosophy underpinning their interventions can be questioned. Swain et al. (2003) observed that charitable organisations had been based on the notion that social problems were due to individual inadequacy and so the focus was on changing individuals. After World War Two many charities became service providers for people with disabilities and tended to cater for single impairments and/or medical conditions. More recently, charities have been criticised by disability organisations for their portrayal of disabled people as passive recipients of charity. Charity advertisements have often used undignified images of disabled people, thus reinforcing stereotypical images of disabled people as helpless and dependent.

The social model of disability was based on the view that society is responsible for creating barriers to the full participation of disabled people. This perspective was articulated by the Union of the Physically Impaired against Segregation and the Disability Alliance (UPIAS 1976: 14) in their statement on Fundamental Principles of Disability: 'In our view, it is society which disables physically impaired people. Disability is something imposed on top of our impairment by the way we are unnecessarily isolated and excluded from full participation in society.'

Within the social model a critical distinction is made between the terms 'impairment' and 'disability', as is illustrated in the following from Disabled People's International (adapted by Barnes 1991: 2): 'Impairment is the functional limitation within the individual caused by physical, mental or sensory impairment. Disability is the loss or limitation of opportunities to take part in the normal life of the community on an equal level with others due to physical and social barriers.'

In social model thinking, a person with a physical disability has an objective, visible impairment (cerebral palsy). However, the inaccessibility of transport or buildings, for example, combined with difficulties accessing suitable work severely limits their ability to interact and participate in society. Tregaskis (2004: 11) illustrates this point with the example of a wheelchair user unable to access a building: 'the building's owner could say "What a shame you can't get into the building because you can't walk up the steps".' This explanation appeared plausible within medical model thinking that attributed social exclusion to a person's impairment. However, the social model approach reframed the issue and would say: 'Actually, you can't get into this building because it has been poorly designed.' The social model view, then, is that disability is caused by human factors, like a poorly designed building or an organisational promotions policy that puts disabled employees at a disadvantage compared to their non-disabled colleagues. Thus, disability is not a characteristic of, or the fault of, individual people with impairments, but is instead a term used to describe all the extra difficulties that people with impairments face because society is not organised in ways that take their needs into account (p. 11).

Within the social model approach, the voice of disabled people is recognised and affirmed as central in decision-making processes that affect their lives. It advocates a power shift from service organisations and professional expertise towards the empowerment of people with disabilities and their organisations.

More recently, attention within the disability movement has focused on following the lead of other minority groups who have experienced discrimination and exclusion from society. A rights-based model has begun to emerge as campaigns have been waged to secure legislation that outlaws discrimination and affirms disabled people's entitlement to participate in society on an equal basis alongside their non-disabled peers. As Johnstone (1998: 21) commented: 'A rights-based discourse spreads the dimensions of disablement to include civil, political, economic, social, cultural and environmental obligations.' International charters and declarations such as the recent United Nations Draft Convention on the Rights of Persons with Disabilities (2006) have affirmed the rights of disabled people to full participation in all aspects of societal life. The rights-based model focuses debate on legally enforceable rights and anti-discrimination legislation. The agenda for disabled people has moved on significantly, with the shift in emphasis from 'individual needs' towards 'civil rights'.

Disability: An Irish perspective

Disabled people have tended to exist on the periphery of Irish society. Recently, policy initiatives in health, education and transport combined with legislative change have made disability issues more prominent in Irish society. In addition, the voices of disabled people have begun to make an impact on policy and practice in relation to disability issues. In this section, the limited data on disabled people are examined and the reflections of some Irish people with disabilities are recounted.

Within an Irish context, we do not have detailed information on the lives of people with disabilities, though recent studies by Gannon and Nolan (2004) and Fitzgerald (2004) do reveal some interesting insights into their lives. Gannon and Nolan collated existing data and concluded that people with disabilities were:

- much more likely to have few, if any, educational qualifications.
- at a substantial risk of poverty (dependence on social welfare).
- more socially isolated and have limited social participation.

Almost half of the people with a disability/chronic illness had no formal educational qualification compared to one-fifth of the rest of the population. In addition, twice as many non-disabled adults have third-level qualifications compared to those who have a disability/chronic illness. Also, those who have a disability from birth or acquire one before age twenty-five have a substantially greater probability of having no educational qualifications and less chance of achieving a Leaving Certificate and/or third-level qualification than someone who becomes disabled after age twenty-five. Fitzgerald (2004) explored available data relating to children with disabilities and found the information to be seriously lacking and fragmented. In the absence of a complete record of children with disabilities, there does not appear to be any way of calculating the appropriateness or otherwise of educational provision. Current statistics are based on the resources provided by the system (support teachers, special needs assistants) 'rather than on the child's needs and how these are being met' (p. 34). As education levels have a major influence on employment prospects, income and participation in society, the findings from these studies have major implications for the Irish education system.

Irish attitudes towards disability do not appear to vary enormously from international trends. The National Disability Authority survey (2002) revealed a fairly low level of knowledge about disability and its prevalence. In common with comparable international studies, this study showed that people were more comfortable with physical disability than general learning disabilities or mental health difficulties. These findings are remarkably similar to the nationwide Irish survey reported by McConkey and McCormack in the early 1980s. McConkey and McCormack (1983) reported that the public were very ambivalent in their attitudes to people with general learning disabilities and there was confusion between general learning disabilities and mental illness. Also, the public preferred distant rather than intimate contact with people who have general learning disabilities. The authors attributed these findings to the dearth of contact between people with general learning disabilities and the rest of the community.

The National Disability Authority survey also revealed that there was general acceptance that disabled people should be treated fairly and that they had a right to equal citizenship and full participation in Irish society. There was substantial recognition that disabled people faced significant barriers to access and that they were subject to unfair treatment. A significant minority questioned the integration of children with disabilities in mainstream schools and 13 per cent concluded that 'it depends on the disability' (p. 66). Irish attitudes appear to be underpinned by a considerable amount of goodwill, serious reservations about mental health issues and some questioning of integrated education, though a majority believe that all children should experience diversity.

Toolan (2003: 92) examined how growing up with a physical disability had shaped his identity:

Perhaps it should not, but having a physical impairment in a culture that is (at a minimum) passively uncomfortable with perceived difference, I have grown up constantly seeing my experiences as *having been* different or *going to be* different. … Because of my experience of disability and how society engaged with that experience, I occupied at least two distinct worlds from birth up to my teenage years.

His experience of rehabilitation in hospital had a profound effect:

Spending time in a clinical, institutional space away from family and community was difficult, as was the rehabilitative process I was going through and what it was telling me about myself and my identity. I was spending time in these environments not only engaging in tests to determine why my muscles did not allow me to walk, but also painfully learning to walk at other people's bidding … As a child in these environments, the first question I was asked and learned to ask other children was 'What's wrong with you?' (p. 93)

On returning to home and a rural primary school, he found acceptance, though he noted: 'Nonetheless, I grew to expect from an early age that people would stare at me and talk about me as if I was not there' (p. 95). He concluded that the ways in which we construct our identity as Irish people will have a significant impact on how disabled people are perceived and accepted: 'If our (Irish) identity is to be seen purely in economic terms, or in terms of a narrow definition of what is the norm, then those we perceive as different will be perceived as a threat to that notion of identity' (p. 99).

Disabled people, in Ireland as elsewhere, are seriously under-represented in paid employment and can face discrimination with regard to pay and promotion. The majority of disabled people rely on disability-related benefits, and as a group of disabled people in Donegal commented, the levels of these payments, 'whilst sufficient to keep them alive severely constrained their standard of living and restricted their social and recreational life' (Kitchin et al. 1998: 790). The apparently endless cycle of training schemes that fail to produce viable employment was a constant source of frustration: 'Andrew: It's like they've been forgotten like, this training scheme ends and another one begins. People spend years and never get a job' (p. 794). The trainers on these courses were perceived to lack any disability awareness, 'which manifested itself in patronising and all-knowing attitudes, misconceptions of people's capabilities, and a school-like atmosphere where the disabled person is "talked-down to" rather than engaged' (p. 794). According to this group, employers were unprepared and lacked knowledge:

Sarah: They see the chair, or they see the disability, they don't see the ability … I think also, I think it is a fact, that sometimes disabled people can be seen as an embarrassment. And I've heard so many people say that when you actually go in for the interview and they see you in the chair or you happen to say that you have a disability their faces change. And you … it's almost as if they're writing you off (p. 795).

Once in work, the disabled person faces many challenges when interacting with the non-disabled world. O'Leary (2006: 32) observes that this interaction usually leads to a form of accommodation: 'This accommodation is often unspoken, a silent shift of place and space in the way in which different parties may interact. It is my experience that this "accommodation" will result in a negative shift in nuance, in attitude to the person with a disability.' As a teacher who has a disability, she perceived that she faced a stark choice: 'either allow oneself to be categorised as someone to be "minded" or literally pass oneself as non-disabled' (p. 32). Being 'minded' would inevitably involve a form of marginalisation, as the disabled person would assume a less demanding position and never be considered for promotion and full participation in the policies and practices that shape school life. While there have been improvements in awareness, O'Leary comments that schools generally still view the child with a disability as a problem: 'The focus is on managing the problem, reducing the fallout as much as possible' (pp. 33–34). O'Leary concludes: 'So, am I in the box or outside? Am I on the margins or at the heart of things? The truth is probably that I inhabit both camps as disabled person and as professional, with hopefully the insights to marry the two to the benefit of all my students' (p. 34).

Children and young people with disabilities

Children with disabilities include those who have physical or sensory impairments, those who have a range of identified general learning disabilities and others who have mental health difficulties or hidden/invisible disabilities. Traditionally, children with disabilities were grouped according to a disability category (physical, sensory, general learning disabilities, emotional and behavioural difficulties) and educated separately from their peers. It is now recognised that children with disabilities are a heterogeneous grouping and do not necessarily share similar cultural backgrounds, family values or even similar educational or health needs.

Many factors interact and impact on the life experiences of children with a disability. These factors can include social class variables, prevailing societal attitudes, kind of provision in health, social services and education and the type and extent of disability. Families with adequate incomes can help to bear the financial costs of disability that can determine the level of access to provision and extra support. However, children are often limited more by people's negative/lowered expectations and consequent labelling than by 'intrinsic conditions' (Down syndrome, spina bifida). To a noticeably larger extent than their peers, children with disabilities are subject to paternalistic attitudes and conventions and as a result may experience significant difficulties in having their views noted and acted upon: 'We lack children's accounts of pain, discomfort, dependence on others for feeding, bathing and toileting. We do not know how they feel about the way doctors, social workers, therapists and other children treat them' (Baldwin and Carlisle 1994: 35).

International research studies suggest that generally children with disabilities have fewer friends and socialise less than their peers without disability. They may also experience greater rejection. Negative perceptions of disability within society have probably created barriers to positive interactions between children with and without disability. Gash (1993, 1996) investigated Irish children's representations of their peers who had special educational needs. He reported that girls were more positive about and more sociable towards children with general learning disabilities than boys. Older children appeared to be more socially concerned and more positive about the integration of children with general learning disabilities. Gash et al. (2004), in a cross-cultural study of Spanish and Irish children's attitudes towards their peers who have general learning disabilities, reported that Spanish children were more sociable towards their counterparts who have general learning disabilities than Irish children. The authors suggested that the active promotion of integrated education over a prolonged period of time in Spain compared to Ireland may be the reason for these differences in attitudes.

Watson et al. (1999) reported that interaction between children with and without disability was often stalled by the existence of physical barriers and attitudinal issues. Interactions appeared to be dominated by a discourse of need and care and as a result 'the non-disabled children behaved not as equals, but as guides or helpers' (p. 17). There is a real danger that disabled children may accept and internalise this discourse of dependency, as by adopting this identity they are guaranteed attention and support as non-disabled peers react positively to dependence on them. This risk is heightened as generally disabled children lack positive role models within society. For the young people with disabilities in this study, disability meant 'we all get picked on' and examples were recounted of physical, emotional and verbal bullying that obviously shaped their sense of self-identity. Young people with disabilities realise very quickly that they are meant to be grateful for any service offered, no matter how inadequate or inappropriate, and reasonable in their responses to fit in with societal perceptions. Overprotection by well-meaning adults is often cited as a barrier to social experiences, as some young people reported that teachers 'treated them like "Babies", giving them work which was too easy and not expecting enough of them. This was particularly true for students with speech and language difficulties, or who used wheelchairs' (Wilson and Jade 1999: 5). Some young people with less visible disabilities attempt to escape negative peer attitudes by 'passing for non-disabled' (denying disabled identity), a common tactic among minority ethnic groups such as Travellers.

Increasingly, children and young people with disabilities are being included in Irish mainstream schools, though a consensus has yet to emerge around the most effective ways of ensuring full participation within the mainstream. International and local research provide some insights into the inclusion process and guidelines have been developed around 'best practice' in including children and young people with disabilities in mainstream settings (United Kingdom: Cornwall 1997; Kenward 1997; Ireland: Grogan and Offaly Centre for

Independent Living 2001). Access is a critical issue in the inclusion process, though it is often conceived of in the narrowest sense of physical access. Ensuring access for children and young people with disabilities involves 'getting into the school around the corner', 'getting around in the learning environment' and 'getting on socially and academically' (Kenny et al. 2000). As inclusion has gathered pace, some Irish research studies have explored the perspectives of children and young people with disabilities. These studies have principally involved children and young people with physical and sensory disabilities, as recently these children have appeared more regularly in mainstream settings.

Rooney (2003) examined the experiences of a group of young people who have hearing impairments within a second-level mainstream school. These young people felt most included when 'they were engaged in structured activities within the classroom setting. Outside of this structured setting, the majority of the hearing-impaired pupils perceived their disability as being a hindrance to social interaction with their teenage peers' (p. 161). However, their hearing peers regarded their hearing-impaired counterparts as being 'equal members of their class, capable of participating fully in all activities and being completely accepted as individuals' (p. 162). Teachers were generally perceived to be very helpful in giving extra time, though at the same time many failed to anticipate individual needs and as a result, in explaining his difficulties one young person stated: 'I feel really awkward, so I do, I don't like making myself look different' (p. 164). Teacher expectations were positive: 'I'm no different from other students in my class, so I don't think they expect anything less' (p. 165). Young people with a hearing impairment believed that many barriers remained to full social inclusion. Effective communication skills are essential and these are not always present, as one young person with a hearing impairment recounted: 'They think, well I think they think that … if they talk to me I won't be able to understand them, right? So, when they ask a question, I just guess and say yes or no and they just think that I don't want to continue in the conversation, so that's a problem. I only once said "pardon" and they would go away' (p. 170).

In O'Donnell's (2003) study, children and young people with physical disabilities who had transferred from special schools to mainstream provision recounted their experiences. There were some initial difficulties in adjustment and one young person felt 'weird and different because nobody was in a wheelchair except myself' (p. 236). Seating arrangements could exacerbate this difficulty: 'The worst thing about school was being put up in front of the class on my own because there was no room for my table and wheelchair. I have a bit bigger table because I'm higher, everyone is sitting on little chairs and I'm huge' (p. 240). Teachers were generally positive, encouraging and kind. Opinion among the young people was divided about whether their classmates should be given disability-specific information. One young man was vehemently against the provision of information: 'I feel it's not for other people who do not like me; it's not their business. It's kind of my dark secret so I only tell my best friend that' (p. 242). Name-calling and 'slagging' appeared to be a common experience and resilience was needed to survive: 'Sometimes I'd tell the teacher if it's really bad 'cos they call you a rat if you tell without having a good reason. Well, I've been slagged quite a few times, but I seem to be able to put up with it, I don't know how though' (p. 244). The young people were generally positive about their experiences and valued the opportunity to mix with their able-bodied peers in a mainstream setting: 'Meeting normal kids and having a normal life'; 'Being treated like everyone else'; 'Being near home and nearly normal' (pp. 247–248). Despite teacher kindness, O'Donnell concluded that 'adequate provision was not made for the pupils' specific difficulties, both academically and physically' (p. 250).

In Horgan's (2003) study, a group of young disabled adults (Educable 2000) examined educational provision for young people with physical disabilities in Northern Ireland. Bullying was a major issue in mainstream schools for young people with physical disabilities: 'When I was in mainstream I got bullied and I kept it inside myself and I went and told the headmaster I was getting bullied. He did nothing about it at all. Brushed it under the carpet, like nothing was happening … and then one day I got kicked down the stairs, two flights of stairs because I was different' (p. 109). The lack of subject choice in special schools was of particular concern to the young people: 'My sister is at grammar school now and I can see the choice she gets and I realise what a bad deal I got. We're forced to go on to further education really because the education we got at school wouldn't get us a job' (p. 111). Low school expectations and the assumption that these young people would not be able for exams was challenged:

> It's not that I couldn't do them [exams], they just never gave me a chance to do them and I had seen other people doing exams and I thought, why can't I do them? Every time I asked them, it was like 'because' all the time. When I went to Pathfinders [support scheme in Further Education colleges for disabled students], I put the emphasis on them that I want to do an exam in whatever and they said 'no problem, go for it', and I left there with GCSEs (p. 112).

The young people concluded their review as follows:

> No one expects us to do well in exams and go on and have a career or even a decent job. Changing this means challenging a mindset that sees the disability, not the person, and that fails to recognise that while it might take a young person with a disability longer to achieve their goals, we can still do it (p. 117).

It became very clear in Kenny et al.'s (2000) study that limited physical access had a profound effect on both social and curricular access. Requiring peer support for basic access often distorted social relationships for the young person with a physical disability: 'It was kind of difficult just to get around. And asking for help. I found that difficult. I didn't like asking the same person all the time. Some people would make a fuss over me and others wouldn't think – it was a mixture of reactions' (p. 16). Lack of appropriate technical aids shaped curricular access: 'I did Home Economics for my Junior and Leaving Cert. Myself and my teacher wanted a low accessible kitchen unit for me but they wouldn't give it. (Q: Who?) The architects and the government ... the Principal' (p. 15). Achieving physical access was not easily won, as private needs (going to the toilet) entered the public realm for one young boy with a physical disability in primary school: 'If I wanted to go to the toilet, the cubicles were very small; I had to go to the teachers' room. They knew and I had someone outside the door just in case they'd come. It wasn't too bad' (p. 15). For some, the struggle appeared endless and as with the previous speaker the situation was accepted with a sense of passive resignation: 'But you get used to it after a while' (p. 16).

Lowered teacher expectations also affected opportunities to succeed within mainstream: 'There was an attitude if you have something wrong with you, you don't have to reach the same standards others do' (p. 20). Positive teacher expectations and encouragement had the opposite effect: 'One teacher kept driving me the whole way. Kind of "put it in a context, fair enough you have a disability but throw it away from you and continue on" like. From that day on I've never looked back. It was the best thing ever that, to stand up for ourselves' (p. 21). School responses to an acquired disability (brain tumour), while well intentioned, can highlight a gulf in understanding the real needs of the person involved: 'I was out for most of fifth year and I actually won student of the year, voted by the students. I always thought it was out of pity and they were only trying to be nice. But when you actually think about it, it was kind of ... funny' (p. 35).

Social interaction can be influenced by lack of knowledge and experience and the young person with a disability often has to be proactive: 'When I first went to primary school people were in awe of me, but after – I wouldn't say I fitted in like a jigsaw piece, people got used to me. Young kids didn't know how to go up to me. I'd say "don't be afraid to come over to me or something"' (p. 34). 'A lad in my class ... said "being sick wouldn't have anything to do with your brain" and I said I think it might. He didn't realise what was wrong with me, which is hard to cope with in some ways. I feel I have to put it out in the open when I see people' (p. 34).

Concluding comments

There appears to be a consensus within international and local research that school ethos, organisation and teaching approaches significantly influence the quality of social and academic experiences of children and young people with disabilities. Cornwall (1997: 21) believes that 'choice and opportunity do not exist where the physical, social and learning environments are not *planned to include* pupils and students who are disabled.' Creating schools that welcome diversity remains a challenge when, in general, the young people with a disability are expected to adapt to mainstream without always receiving the understanding and support required.

Discussion points

1   A young man with a physical disability commented: 'It would become normal, just everyday life and people would be able to understand it, "ah sure we don't even know what that is, we just know it's a normal thing [he's] like everyone else." When it comes like that we would get good jobs' (Kenny et al. 2000: 40).
    (a)   Identify the barriers within society and in schools that prevent this vision from becoming a reality.
    (b)   What factors within society and in schools could help to realise this vision?
2   Swain et al. (2003: 12) observed that 'labels are usually bestowed by those who have power and authority ("experts") upon those who do not'.
    (a)   Why do you think that so many labels associated with disability become pejorative?
    (b)   How can schools and teachers help to empower children and young people with disabilities in their school lives?
3   As a teacher, you have just been told that a child/young person with a physical disability who uses a motorised wheelchair is joining your class.
    (a)   What is your immediate reaction?
    (b)   What key issues need to be considered in relation to:
        (i)   classroom organisation
        (ii) social interaction with peers
        (iii) guaranteeing access to the curriculum?

Chapter 3
Historical Emergence: The Irish Experience

Learning outcomes/objectives

On completion of this chapter, the reader will be able to:
- Outline and discuss aspects of Irish cultural attitudes to disability in former times and the effect of 'schooling' on attitudes to learning disability.
- Discuss examples of the evolution from medical interest to efforts at developing educational potential in the Irish experience.
- Identify significant milestones in parental and teacher involvement in special education in Ireland.
- Sketch the emergence of policy development and influences on special education from the 1960s to the 1990s.

Introduction

In terms of a dedicated and established service, special education in Ireland dates only from the 1960s, when a Department of Health Commission was established to examine 'the problem of mental handicap'. The Commission's *Report* (Department of Health 1965) recommended that a system of residential and day special schools should be constructed to cater for about 1 per cent of the school-going population. In other countries at this time, the practice of segregation was being seriously questioned. At the attainment of independence in 1922, education in Ireland was characterised by an overarching concern in the school system for the government's Gaelicisation policy. The education of children with disabilities and learning difficulties held a very low place on the list of political priorities of the new state.

This chapter traces the historical evolution of special education in an Irish cultural context. It explores the attitudinal and societal responses to disability over the ages and identifies the patterns and influences that contributed to the emergence of a system that presents some particular challenges and possibilities for parents, pupils and teachers, especially as it has developed over the past two decades. Special education in Ireland, in a developed sense, has been a child of the changes and influences impacting on our society in the past generation.

Over a broader period of time, however, there have been a number of notable examples of pioneering initiatives by benevolent individuals and organisations, some dating back to the eighteenth century and earlier, that were important milestones on the path of future progress. In more recent times, the part played by parent-led initiatives and by institutions such as the Irish National Teachers' Organisation (INTO) also contributed to significant developments in special education which had, and continue to have, far-reaching effects on the education system in general. A historical perspective helps us to examine the past so as to understand the present better. The following historical timeline will help us to review major developments in special education in Ireland.

Table 3.1: **Historical timeline**

	Ireland	Influences
c. 1200	Brehon Laws	English law
1775	Manson of Belfast	Rousseau/Enlightenment
1816	Claremont Institute	Pestalozzi/Deaf Education
1831	National schools	Industrial Age/basic literacy
1868	Stewart's Institute	Medical philanthropy Education as well as care
1870s	Compulsory schooling	Standards in education
1900	New programme Primary schools	Practical handwork Kindergarten/infant education
1922	Irish independence Small number of special institutions	Gaelicisation programme Charitable/religious Independence in education/care
1947	Recognition of special schools Primary Certificate	1944 Education Act in UK post-WWII development Certification of basic education for all
1952	INTO reaction	Concern for 'failing children'
1955	Patricia Farrell, Declan Costello	Parent demands for special education
1960	St Michael's House	Independent special education services
1962	White Paper: 'Problem of Mental Handicap'	Department of Health
1965	Commission Report policy document	Department of Health
1967	'Free' secondary education	*Investment in Education* report
1970	Special schools New primary school curriculum	Commission report Child-centred education Abolition of Primary Certificate
1973	Remedial teachers	Greater recognition of learning difficulties
1978	Integration	*Warnock Report* UK European Union membership

Table 3.1: Historical timeline (cont'd.)

	Ireland	Influences
1987	EU Ministers' declaration on integration policy	European Union
1993	Special Education Review Committee (SERC) Report	Warnock Report UK and 1981 Education Act UK Parental/teacher demands to resource system
1993	O'Donoghue judgment	Parental concerns/rights
1994	Inclusion	UNESCO Salamanca Statement
1998	Education Act	
2004	Education for Persons with Special Educational Needs (EPSEN) Act	
2005	Disability Act	

Brehon Laws and protection for people with disabilities

One of the most prevailing misconceptions and popular prejudices has been the association of mental or psychiatric illness with conditions of learning disability. Significantly, early Irish society recognised a distinction between insanity and general learning disability. The Brehon Laws, the codes that regulated conduct among the princely tribes of Ireland from the fourth century up to the imposition of English law in the twelfth century, made specific provision for the protection of people with disabilities. The laws categorised the rights of people termed (in the English translation) 'idiots, fools, dotards, persons without sense and madmen'. Behind the quaint terminology is a societal concern for the needs of people born with differing degrees of learning disabilities, people with psychiatric illness and people with senile dementia. A major influence on the classifications seems to have been the extent to which the affected person was deemed capable of work or who had the potential to contribute to society – even if this amounted only to the 'power of amusing'. The story is told that the Irish legendary hero Finn MacCool had a diminutive musician, named Cnú Dereoil, who was said to be the best harper in Ireland, indicating that early Irish society also valued people with physical disability and honoured their achievements and potential (Robins 1986).

The entitlement of people with disabilities to have a place in the local economy and the obligations of society to recognise levels of autonomy and dependence were observed in the Brehon Laws. Where a person was judged to have exploited, neglected or abused a disabled person who had some land or resources or the 'power of amusing', there was a fine imposed on the guilty party of five cows. However, if the offence had been committed on a person whose disabilities were such that he was completely dependent on society, was without resources and had no capacity to amuse, the fine was doubled to ten cows.

In the ancient codes the Irish word for a 'fool' was *drúth*. The fool was accorded a protective position in society, being recognised as *co rath Dé* – 'with the grace of God'. This may be the origin of the more modern Irish phrase *Duine le Dia* (God's person) in reference to people with a congenital learning disability such as Down syndrome. Some ancient Irish texts make reference to three classifications of *drúth*. There were the slow-witted but strong and capable persons called *bóbre* – 'having the behaviour of a cow'. The *caeptha* – a 'person of half-sense' – was someone needing supervision and protection most of the time. The third category, *salach drúth* ('unclean fool'), indicated a level of disability requiring a high level of personal care and dependency. In all cases, the social aspect of disability was recognised.

The 'fool' at school

Later Irish texts refer generally to the male 'fool' as *amadán* and a woman with a learning disability as *óinseach*. These terms began to take on a derogatory connotation only with the advancement of formal institutional schooling.

School was not a pleasant place for a 'fool' in the eighteenth century. William King, later to become the Anglican archbishop of Dublin, wrote of his experience of schooling thus:

> Driven by whippings, I learned to repeat the alphabet by rote but could not distinguish a letter. After half a year, I learned the alphabet, and by enumerating the letters, pronounced words. But when the Westminster Catechism was put into my hands, I did not understand the words, and was disgusted by books ... trying to write I formed exceedingly rude letters; and being often flogged on account of them, I trembled at pens and ink, my ignorant master being more apt to punish than instruct (Corcoran 1928).

King probably had a condition like dyslexia. Even a privileged education, in the days when formal schooling was not available to the greater part of the population, was a source of violence, humiliation and shame for someone with special educational needs. The institution of school was a structure where the power of the master and subjugation of the pupil were the expected norms. The principles that learning was not intended to be a pleasurable activity or that skills and knowledge could not be comfortably obtained were long-established in Western philosophy (Davidson 1900). Great thinkers such as John Locke (1665–1704) considered that the purpose of education was to direct the young person away from their natural propensity to evil. And as for those who were born with disabilities in physical or learning aptitudes, the prospect for progress was regarded as distinctly pessimistic. Physical punishment was an accepted response to children who were unable or incapable of adapting to society's expectations of conformity to school requirements.

David Manson of Belfast: Pioneer of special education in Ireland

In contrast, during the eighteenth century, David Manson of Belfast, Presbyterian, master brewer, inventor and an imaginative, independent schoolmaster, conducted an academy which advertised an inclusive policy that welcomed pupils – boys and girls of both religious traditions – who had an aversion to the harsh regime of traditional schooling, who had what today would be termed emotional/behavioural problems and who presented with severe literacy difficulties. In 1755, David Manson was a pioneer of Irish special education (Griffin 2006).

Choice, not compulsion

In his school, corporal punishment of any kind was expressly forbidden. He developed a method of teaching that was considerably ahead of its time in that it was play-centred; school was meant to be enjoyable. Children were motivated rather than driven, encouraged to advance at their own pace and praised rather than punished. In Manson's method, lessons were to be proposed as an amusement, not as a burden. He coaxed pupils to take part in card games, first of the conventional kind and then adapted to incorporate spelling games and word recognition. In Manson's enlightened psychology he contended that 'the love of liberty is as natural to children as grown adults. The method then to make them easy under a state of discipline is to convince them that they are free; that they act from choice not compulsion' (McCallister 1931).

Manson invented an early form of bicycle, or velocipede, which was used as a reward for pupils who progressed in their lessons. Pupils also had use of a bowling green and other amusements provided by Manson for their recreation hours.

Manson departed from Locke's view that obstinacy always justified the use of punishment. His approach was to treat stubbornness not with a command but by proposing a course of action as a matter of choice or as a particular favour granted to the child, in which case a refusal would not interfere with the teacher's authority. The self-discipline that comes from freedom, choice and activity was articulated by Maria Montessori in more modern times: 'To obtain discipline it is quite useless to count on reprimands or spoken exhortations … discipline is reached always by indirect means. The end is obtained, not by attacking the mistake and fighting it but by developing activity in spontaneous work' (Montessori 1964, cited in Wentworth and Lubienski 1999).

The choice for the pupil was either to seek learning assistance from a partner in the class or to join the 'Trifling Club'. This was a kind of standing 'purgatory' where the idle, mischievous or neglectful pupil was given 'time out' to reflect on their reputation and to demonstrate a specimen of good progress or behaviour by the end of the day.

Cooperative learning

Manson's achievements with his challenging pupils were not as a manager of discipline, but as a teacher who encouraged learning. Children who were familiar with the indignity of reading difficulties and had resentful memories of harsh regimes in their earlier experiences of schooling were encouraged by being able to choose their own lessons, set their own objectives and avail of good-humoured incentives to keep them motivated. Manson's system took account of individual differences in ability. A system of paired pupil partners working together to prepare reading lessons was encouraged and reading aloud was a privilege to be earned. Prompting, instead of being forbidden, was made part of the system and ritualised with the appointment of pupil monitors for spelling out and announcing the meaning of words when errors or hesitations occurred in the reading aloud lesson.

Manson intuitively understood the child's need to belong to a group, to have a sense of achievement and satisfaction in his/her work, to have some hope in a future, to receive affirmation and praise and to have some fun. Teachers who provide engaging opportunities for collaborative learning and who prioritise developing a classroom culture where success and self-esteem take precedence over information acquisition discover that the delineation between 'work' and 'play' becomes less sharply defined.

From medical interest to educational potential

Most of the early interest in the education of disabled people emerged from medical science. Itard's study of the 'Wild Boy of Aveyron' in the late eighteenth century – an abandoned child left in the woods in southern France, possibly autistic, who had no language or social skills – and Seguin's early nineteenth-century development of instructional materials opened up an awareness of the possibilities of educating children with sensory and intellectual disabilities. The move from a dedicated medical model based on care, categorisation, treatment and possible 'cure' to an emerging social and educational model which recognised human strengths and potential with an aim towards independence and autonomy began in the nineteenth century and was significantly pioneered in Ireland.

Claremont Institute, Glasnevin

Dr Charles Orpen, a native of Cork, inspired by the work of Johann Heinrich Pestalozzi, whose institute he had visited in Switzerland in 1815, became involved in the education of a deaf boy, Thomas Collins, in the Foundling Hospital of the Dublin House of Industry where Orpen was the Medical Officer. Charles Orpen described Thomas Collins as the most wretched and pitiful of the orphans he had encountered there. Together with his wife, Orpen adopted the young deaf and mute boy. So impressive was the progress made with his pupil that Orpen set about establishing the first school for the deaf in Ireland in 1816. The National Institution for the Education of the Deaf and Dumb at Claremont in Glasnevin was conducted according to innovative Pestalozzian methods. The importance of sense experience as a doorway to learning was one of the Pestalozzian principles applied in the school. The atmosphere of the school conducted by another Corkman and Quaker, Joseph Humphreys, was one modelled on a family community where children were respected and nourished physically, emotionally, intellectually and spiritually. Pupils were trained for independence and self-support.

Thomas Collins's self-esteem grew proportionate to his skills in reading and writing, so much so that he penned a letter to King George IV of England, who made a royal visit to Dublin in 1821. The letter was proudly reproduced in the annual Reports of the Claremont Institute (Pollard 2006):

> My Dear George
> I hope I will see you when you come and see the deaf and dumb pupils. I am very sorry that you never did come to see them; I never saw you. The boys and girls are very much improving and are very comfortable here. Are you interested in seeing the deaf and dumb?
>
> I am very much pleased in writing a letter to you. I want to get a letter from you. How many brothers and sisters have you? Would you like to see me at Claremont? I could not go to London because there is too much money to pay to the captain of the ship for me. I am an orphan and a very poor boy. God will bless you. Do you know grammar, bible, arithmetic, astronomy, and dictionary? I know them very little ... I am thinking of every thing and to be polite to every one. I have been at school four and a half-years. I am sixteen years of age. I am very delighted that I am improving so much; perhaps I will be an assistant in the deaf and dumb school. There are forty pupils in Claremont. Where were you born? I was born in Dublin ... Would you like to correspond with me? I would be very fond of you ... What profession are you at?
>
> I am your affectionate friend,
> Thomas Collins, Claremont, Glasnevin, near Dublin.

The king, clearly charmed by the letter, delivered by courier a reply and a cheque for ten pounds to Thomas. This was sufficient to purchase an apprenticeship to a printer. In fact, he went to work as a printer to a Pestalozzian teacher and landowner in an experimental school on his estate in Roundwood, Co. Wicklow. The teacher was John Synge (later grandfather of the dramatist J.M. Synge), who was one of the first people to introduce translations of Pestalozzi's writings to the English-speaking world. Thomas Collins printed these works along with instructional materials and charts used in the Roundwood school. He also printed the Claremont Institution Reports and the memoirs of Dr Charles Orpen. Finally, Thomas Collins returned to Claremont to become the first deaf-born teacher of deaf children in the school (LeFanu 1860).

The Statistical Society and Stewart's Institute (1869)

The first official demand for special provision for people with general learning disabilities in Ireland was made by Sir William Wilde (father of Oscar Wilde) in 1851 (Byrne 1980). Wilde was the Medical Commissioner for the population census conducted in that year. A response from the state was not forthcoming then, nor when the same appeal was made in the census report a decade later. The challenge was taken up by a philanthropic and reforming society called the Statistical and Social Inquiry Society of Ireland. Jonathan Pim, Vice-President of the Society, and later an MP, wrote: 'It is a duty, incumbent on society to educate and instruct the imbecile ... and idiotic; so that as far as it may prove practicable, they may be rendered capable of contributing to their own support' (cited in Byrne 1980: 11).

A pamphlet written in 1865 by Dr George Kidd, physician in the Coombe Hospital, showed a sound awareness of developments in mainland Europe and gave detailed accounts of Seguin's methods of instructing children with general learning disabilities (imbeciles and idiots in the terminology of the time) and proposed how such methods might be applied in a dedicated institution in Ireland. A fundraising campaign was organised and by 1867 the project was given a major boost when Dr Stewart, who owned a private asylum at Lucan outside Dublin, made his premises available as a gift to the committee. From the beginning, Stewart's Institute focused on education and training rather than mere custodial care. Ten years later, the Institute moved to an extended site at Palmerstown, where it still exists today. Stewarts School and Residential Centre remains the oldest functioning centre for people with special educational needs in the state.

Changing attitudes to people with disabilities

Two developments initiated by the British administration in Ireland in the early nineteenth century, while considered at the time socially progressive in their intent, actually contributed to the consolidation of negative social attitudes to people with disabilities. This was in marked contrast to the provisions of the native Brehon Laws of the Middle Ages and the social consciousness which they inspired and reflected.

Asylums and workhouses

The first of these initiatives was to create a culture of institutionalisation relating to disability that would remain a pervasive social response for over 150 years. An unfortunate and inevitable side effect of institutionalisation was the overlapping association in the public and official mind of learning disability and psychiatric illness – and the attendant stigma and shame that became attached to having a disabled family member. The second development was the establishment of a national system of education in 1831 and the building of national schools in every parish in the country. Schooling – made compulsory in the late nineteenth century – brought with it advantages for the able, but also misery, failure and unfair comparison for those with learning disabilities and special educational needs who could not cope with the curricular requirements or the standards demanded by the teacher.

In the 1830s, the building of District Lunatic Asylums in Ireland was a response to the widespread social problem of what was described as 'lunatics at large' – people with psychiatric illness and general learning disabilities abandoned by their families. An English visitor to Ireland in the 1820s reported that one particular 'idiot' had been tolerated on the road from Cork to Carrigoline 'where he was given to pinching unprotected women on the back and arms', very possibly a case of a person with Tourette syndrome. The 1838 Poor Relief Act also led to the construction of 130 workhouses in Ireland, institutions where those deemed dependent on the charity of the state would be housed and fed in return for manual labour. This was not a system based on care, but on the blame and shame associated with having to accept public charity.

The workhouses were also to make provision for the separate containment of 2,300 'idiots, imbeciles and lunatics' (Robins 1986). The workhouses, even when they became designated as 'county homes', took on a supportive role to the lunatic asylums. In the 1860s, up to 10 per cent of residents of the lunatic asylums were listed as 'idiots and imbeciles'. Between the 1850s and the turn of the twentieth century, the number of disabled people housed in the notorious workhouses more than doubled (Census of Ireland 1851, 1901). Given the generic term of 'lunatics', they were neglected and ignored. In a report of 1908, Dr Connolly Norman noted:

> In the workhouse, there is no classification among these people, no attempt at education and little or no effort to improve defective habits ... There is no staff for teaching ... Old and young, low class idiots, high grade imbeciles, chronic dements and cases of senile decay are placed together promiscuously ... The period of life when education might be possible passes away; bad habits are acquired and become ineradicable (Royal Commission 1908).

The institution of school

The introduction of a national system of education in Ireland in 1831 was established not by legislation, but by the commitment of an annual parliamentary grant to be administered by the Commissioners of National Education, based in Dublin. Local schools (almost exclusively church parish schools) that conformed to the Commissioners' rules retained ownership and management rights while agreeing to employ recognised trained teachers – who would then be paid by the state – to teach the prescribed curriculum, to be open to inspection and to avoid denominational religious instruction except during strictly designated times. Originally intended as a system of joint-management between Catholics and Protestants, this idealistic aspiration soon settled into the official acceptance of denominational ownership and management. This was essentially the system that was retained up to the Education Act 1998 and its essence is still observed in the present legislation.

Prior to the establishment of the national schools and to some extent up to the Great Famine of 1847, ordinary Irish people placed great value on being able to choose education for their children from the freelance teachers who were generically known as 'hedge-school masters' (McManus 2002). The reputation of the 'master' went before him and his capability as a versatile and effective teacher was undoubtedly put to the test by a range of learning abilities. The individual nature of the tuition and the independent scope of the teacher may well have provided the support needed to overcome specific learning difficulties in some instances, particularly in reading and writing.

Educational invisibility and state neglect (1922–1952)

At the foundation of the Irish state in 1922, there were only eight institutions, all charitable, private and voluntary, dedicated to serving the needs of people with disabilities and special needs. A special school for blind boys established in 1870 by the Carmelite Brothers in Drumcondra, Dublin, had applied for and received recognition as a national school in 1918. Like the school for 'deaf and dumb' boys at Cabra, Dublin, founded by the Irish Christian Brothers in the nineteenth century, which was also recognised as a national school in 1926, no additional funding or special resources were available from the state. The first special school for children with general learning disabilities to be recognised by the state was St Vincent's Home for Mentally Defective Children in 1947. It was not until 1952, when the schools for the blind were allowed a special pupil-teacher ratio of 1:15 and financial aid towards the purchase of specialised equipment, that state intervention in special education became a reality (Department of Education 1993).

Despite the aspirations to 'cherishing all the children of the nation equally' in the Proclamation of the Republic, the special needs of children with general learning disabilities were not acknowledged in the educational priorities of the new Irish state. As far as school was concerned, the imperatives were to provide basic instruction to a largely rural and religious-minded population, but above all to implement the government's Gaelicisation programme. This required teachers to make the Irish language the sole medium of instruction for all children in their first years at school at four and five years of age. This policy was endorsed by one of the government's leading educational advisors, Fr Timothy Corcoran SJ, Professor of Education at University College Dublin. He argued that he had seen the success of this method used with children of non-English-speaking immigrant families arriving in New York. The situation in Ireland was significantly different. Relatively few children, and indeed few teachers, had access outside of school to a living, communicating culture involving the Irish language. The results were generally unsatisfactory, often creating learning problems for otherwise able children. The 'total immersion' policy for infant classes was afterwards modified, resulting largely from the protests of the Irish National Teachers' Organisation.

A formal state examination, the Primary Certificate, was made compulsory from the 1940s for all primary school children aged twelve years. The plight of children with general learning disabilities who went to school was little more than prolonged punishment. The situation was summed up by the General Secretary of the INTO in 1952 in these angry words: 'One of the greatest crimes of our system is the callous disregard for subnormal and backward children. Many of these are condemned as fools and dunces according to our conventional academic standards. They are the victims of those who define education as a matter of books and words' (Brosnahan 1952).

Dr Louis Clifford: Survey of Learning Disability (1943)

Interestingly, it was by and large the efforts of the medical profession, as distinct from those responsible for education, that impelled change and improved services for marginalised and excluded people with learning disabilities. The report prepared by Dr Louis Clifford in 1943 for the Hospitals' Commission – the statutory body responsible for the disbursement of the Irish Hospital Sweepstake funds (a precursor of the National Lottery) – incorporated what is probably the first attempted census of 'mentally handicapped' people in the new Irish state. Clifford's *Report* (Robbins 1986) was hampered by lack of resources and lack of cooperation by school authorities. It nevertheless gives a picture of the general attitudes that were prevalent in Ireland 60 years ago.

Having a disabled child, according to Clifford, was widely seen by parents of the time as a disgrace and a reflection on the family. The more affluent and socially superior the family, the more the condition was resented and abhorred. Families from lower socio-economic backgrounds were usually more philosophical about their misfortune. In his account, Dr Clifford records that disabled children were sometimes hidden away in top rooms and seldom taken out except at night. Those who were attending school were kept at home on the day of Clifford's visit so that a labelling stigma would not adhere to the family name. Interestingly, Clifford notes that in rural areas parents were sometimes complicit in encouraging intellectual underachievement among able children so that they would remain working on the land. The report also noted that the conflict between the academic demands of school and the hostile attitudes of parents resulted in signs of emotional disturbance in the children. What services of education and care that were available to persons with disability were institutional in nature and remained so until the mid-1960s.

Parent and teacher initiatives in special education: Patricia Farrell, Declan Costello and St Michael's House

Desperation was the catalyst that drove a Westmeath parent of a child with learning disabilities to place a personal notice in *The Irish Times* on 2 June 1955 inviting those suffering similar frustration from the paucity of official interest to contact her. Patricia Farrell could have sent her son to a residential school, but she wanted something better than this. Her notice read:

Association for Parents of Mentally Backward Children.
Lady wishing to form above would like to contact anyone interested. Box
Z5061 Children.

She was inundated with enquiries and offers of support. One of those who
offered support was Declan Costello, who was not only the sibling of an
intellectually disabled child himself, but was an influential young barrister and
politician and the son of the then Taoiseach, John A. Costello. At a very large
meeting held in the historic Round Room of the Mansion House, Dublin, the
Association of Parents and Friends of Mentally Handicapped Children – later
called St Michael's House – was founded. In the face of considerable opposition
and distrust by the powers of Church and state, in 1960 the Association finally
succeeded in opening its own special school in Rathmines, Dublin. It was a
revolutionary achievement, engendered more than 40 years after the birth of the
nation. Not only was a special school founded, funded and managed by parents,
but it was also the first national school recognised by the state which was not
managed by a religious authority. Declan Costello (later to become President of
the High Court) indeed made history by being the first layperson to become the
manager of a state-aided primary school in the Republic.

Nancy Jordan: Montessori and special education

One of the early pioneers in the education of emotionally disturbed children in
Ireland, Nancy Jordan from Bagnelstown, Co. Carlow, was inspired by the
successes of the Montessori movement. Maria Montessori (1870–1952) began
her educational research and developed her philosophy and method from her
initial work as a medical doctor with children with general learning disabilities
in the psychiatric asylums of Rome. It was there that Montessori realised that
all children, whatever their needs and abilities, had a powerful aptitude to
learn if given the right learning environment and a teacher who was
knowledgeable about the unique nature of the child. In 1935, Nancy Jordan
qualified as a teacher in the Montessori Method in London; the course was
conducted by Maria Montessori herself. In Ireland during the years of the
Second World War, Nancy Jordan gained a reputation as a skilled tutor to sick
and hospitalised children who were unable to receive their education through
the normal school system. In 1945 she was invited to join the staff of St Ultan's
Infant Hospital, Charlemont Street, Dublin, where she set up the first
Montessori class in a medical environment. The Child Guidance Clinic
attached to the hospital saw the particular potential in the Montessori Method
for supporting the learning needs of children with behavioural problems. In
1956, Nancy Jordan began the first class for emotionally disturbed children in
the state.

Since the 1930s, an accredited training course for Montessori teachers had
been established in Sion Hill, Blackrock, Dublin. In St Ultan's Hospital School,
Nancy Jordan also conducted demonstrations and seminars for students in

Montessori education who wished to specialise in teaching children with disabilities. She also lectured in the Montessori College in Blackrock. Nancy Jordan was also a pioneer in the education of pre-service training for teachers in special education. In 1961 she became principal of Benincasa Special School for Emotionally Disturbed Children in a house near the Montessori College campus. This was the first special school in Ireland to adopt the Montessori system. The school was recognised as a national school by the state in 1962.

In 1961, a post-graduate Diploma in Special Education course was established in St Patrick's College of Education in Dublin. This course was given the rather exceptional privilege of being able to select students from among working teachers in special education settings who would continue to have their salaries paid while attending the course as well as having their tuition and substitution costs met by the Department of Education. A specialised diploma was also made available to teachers of the deaf and blind. This significant advance marks the beginnings of official policy in relation to meeting special educational needs provision in Ireland. It followed on from the appointment in 1959 of the first departmental inspector with responsibility for all aspects of special education in the country.

Policy development: *Commission on Mental Handicap Report* (1965)

In 1961, Declan Costello, one of the leading political advocates of disability policy development, introduced a Private Member's Bill in the Dáil on general learning disability. It followed on the publication in 1960 of the White Paper *The Problem of the Mentally Handicapped*, which prompted the first government inquiry in this area since the foundation of the state. A Commission was appointed by the Minister for Health which published the results of its deliberations in 1965 (McCormack 2004). *The Report of the Commission of Inquiry on Mental Handicap* effectively became the substance of state policy on special education development for the next three decades. The report recommended that special school provision should be the principal way forward. It proposed to increase threefold the number of places in residential special schools and to create 3,000 places for children in day special schools and in special classes attached to regular schools.

At this time in the United States and in Scandinavia, fundamental rethinking on the institutionalisation of people with disabilities was beginning to be reflected in educational legislation and practice. The 1965 report in Ireland, however, did not question the value of segregated provision. It also recommended the distinct delineation of children with different levels of learning disability – something that would be challenged within a decade. It did, however, see a place for special classes for children with mild general learning disabilities in mainstream schools – though mainly for pragmatic and demographic reasons. Unsurprisingly, the 1965 report accepted the prevailing medical model of service provision, though it did recommend closer cooperation between the health and educational professionals. One significant proposal was the establishment of a Diagnostic, Assessment and Advisory Service that would consist of general teams and school teams, although a school-based service was never established. The report was forward looking in that it recognised the educational potential of children with moderate general learning disability; it did not, however, challenge the prevailing view of the ineducability of those in the severe and profound categories for whom care was considered the only option (McGee 2004).

Educational developments in the 1960s and 1970s

The 1960s witnessed the first signs of economic resurgence since the foundation of the state. The influential report *Investment in Education* (1966) became a blueprint for government policy shifts that would have implications for the next and future generations of children and young people. In 1967, secondary education, previously open only to those with academic merit and with money, became an entitlement for all. The Primary Certificate Examination was also discontinued. Significantly, and controversially, research had shown that the Gaelicisation policies in schools, far from assisting the revival of the Irish language, had apparently contributed to the retardation of reading comprehension levels in the English language (Macnamara 1966). There were implications for secondary schools in particular, with the broader range of abilities becoming more evident in the annual intake. Remedial teachers were appointed at both primary and secondary level to provide focused tuition for individuals and small groups who were exhibiting literacy and numeracy difficulties.

A major review of the primary school curriculum, which had been considered too narrow and subject centred, was undertaken in the late 1960s and was introduced into schools in 1971. The New Curriculum (*Curaclam na mBunscoile* 1971) emphasised individual differences, advocated child-centred, activity-based teaching approaches and introduced opportunities for collaborative learning. Unfortunately, the level of in-service training for teachers was wholly inadequate for making the kind of widespread changes that were envisaged in the system. The Department of Education did, however, support the initiatives of the Irish National Teachers' Organisation to provide short courses and seminars; the establishment of Teachers' Centres, largely in the major urban centres, in the early 1970s provided an important infrastructure for teacher-led in-service. The Irish Association of Teachers in Special Education (founded in 1969) was an example of the voluntary effort that emerged to provide the professional support engendered by teachers for teachers that ultimately contributed (and continues to contribute) to the enhancement of the learning and the lives of children with special educational needs.

Obstacles to progress and provision

By the mid-1970s a network of over 100 special schools and a growing number of special classes (mainly for children with mild general learning disabilities) in ordinary schools had emerged. It is worth restating the fact that because of the unique development of state involvement in education in Ireland, these services were all instances of voluntary effort, initiated and managed by religious, parental or in some cases enlightened entrepreneurial initiative. The Department of Education, apart from the establishment of Vocational Schools in the 1930s and the foundation of a small number of Community and Comprehensive secondary schools in the 1960s and 1970s, did not own schools and consequently had limited power and control over them. While considerable progress had been made towards facilitating the provision for children with special educational needs, less than half of those needing special education had recourse to such services (McGee 2004).

A further barrier in the way of progress was the limited availability of the assessment procedures by which it was necessary to gain access to special education services in the first instance. Waiting periods for assessment frequently amounted to years. When finally offered to children with special educational needs, placements were frequently too late to be of real value. Responsibility for assessment was in the hands of the Department of Health; there was no generally available educational psychological service. The central problem was that no agency or individual appeared to have a statutory requirement to provide these services as a right. Added to these difficulties was the centralised nature of Irish education. Unlike other countries, there were no regional educational authorities (apart from the Vocational Educational Committees at post-primary level) to respond to local needs.

Irish reactions to the UK Warnock Report

By the end of the 1970s it was increasingly clear that no serious progress could be made concerning special educational services development without the introduction of legislation. In Britain, the *Report of the Committee of Enquiry into the Education of Handicapped Children and Young People*, published in 1978 and commonly known as the Warnock Report, made a range of far-reaching proposals to government which substantially became codified in the UK Education Act of 1981.

Ireland, along with Britain and Denmark, had become a member of the European Community in 1973. Right across Europe during the 1970s, the educational rights of children with disabilities were being enshrined into law. In 1975, Italy took the bold decision of closing down most of its special schools and set about a policy of supporting the integration of children with special educational needs into ordinary classes in ordinary schools. Resources for any innovation in Ireland were extremely scarce, but a Department of Education circular issued in 1977 proposed that children with a mild general learning disability could be accommodated in special classes in ordinary schools. It was the first official statement to support what the Warnock Report called 'locational integration'.

In 1980 the government issued a White Paper on Educational Development which confirmed that integration was to become official policy in that it would be the first option to be considered in the education of children with disabilities. Official statements tended to be a mixture of aspiration and caution, as reflected in the 1987 declaration to the meeting of European Ministers of Education by the then Irish Minister, Mary O'Rourke:

> It is the policy of the government to support actively the trend towards integration both at school level and in society generally. On the other hand it is felt that any sudden dismantling of segregated educational provision would not be in the best interests of the disabled. There are certain demographic and geographic features of our country which render the provision of high quality services for some categories of the disabled in any setting other than in special schools both impractical and unrealistic ... It is also felt that the pace of the move towards integration must, for practical reasons, be in harmony with the public demand for it.

A more decisive forward move in policy development, however, was the publication of *The Education and Training of Severely and Profoundly Mentally Handicapped Children in Ireland* in 1983. An exercise in collaboration between the government Departments of Education, Health and Social Welfare, the report acknowledged for the first time in Ireland, as the Warnock Report had done in Britain, that no child was ineducable. A limited pilot project involving teachers was introduced but was never expanded. Ironically, within ten years the Department of Education found itself in court, being sued on an argument that it had already conceded (Hughes 2000).

Special Education Review Committee Report and beyond

The 1980s in Ireland was a period of emigration, frustration and economic restraint. Official figures projected (inaccurately, as it emerged) a general drop in school enrolment and subsequently less demand for teachers. One of the major teacher-training colleges was closed down when state funding was withdrawn. Funding for special educational needs resources was minimal and schools were often disinclined to initiate a referral process for a pupil with a learning disability, as the outcome of the assessment might lead to the child's placement elsewhere (McGee 2004).

European and international policy had increasing influence on Irish education in the 1990s. The 1989 UN Convention on the Rights of the Child explicitly incorporated the rights of children with disabilities to an appropriate high-quality education suited to their learning needs. It was signed by Ireland in 1992. The EU Council of Ministers' Charter, adopted by Ireland in 1990, had already committed the government to a future policy that reflected the philosophies of integration adopted by the member states. However, parents and teachers were increasingly frustrated by the gap between political rhetoric and the reality where action and resources were few or unforthcoming. A long-standing complaint was the existence of impossibly long waiting periods for assessment of special educational needs. In 1990, a pilot educational psychological service for schools was initiated, offering some hope for future expansion.

The most significant development of the early 1990s was the decision in 1991 to establish the Special Education Review Committee (SERC), whose brief was to examine how the existing system could be resourced in order that the policy of integration could be effectively implemented. The report published in 1993 was the most significant and comprehensive policy document in special education that the state had ever produced (Spelman and Griffin 1994) and has provided a blueprint for the development of special education that continues to influence policy decisions up to the present day.

The 1990s must be highlighted in any historical overview for the emergence of two powerful influences on the future direction of special education in Ireland: successful parental appeals to the courts and the introduction of educational legislation. In the same year that the SERC report was published, the landmark High Court judgment in the O'Donoghue case underlined the state's responsibility to provide appropriate educational opportunities for all children, whatever their disabilities or learning needs – as of right. It expedited the introduction of legislation in 1998 when Ireland's first comprehensive Education Act made specific provision in the law for all children, 'including those with disabilities or other special educational needs', and the milestone announcement by the Minister for Education in October 1998 of the guarantee of 'automatic entitlement' of provision by right of any child who has special educational needs.

Concluding comments

It is clear that our thinking about people with disabilities and the provision of special education has moved through a number of critical phases. We can trace early community support followed by institutionalisation and segregation as society became more organised. Today we have moved towards the concept of community responsibility and support. However, it is also evident that a number of radical educationalists from previous times are still relevant to our thinking today.

Discussion points

1 During the 1980s and 1990s, children attending day special schools were often transported home in buses labelled 'ambulance'.
   (a) Does this still happen?
   (b) What was the rationale for this practice?
   (c) What alternatives might be possible and what kind of arrangements would be required in order to meet the rights of pupils/students and to take into consideration the concerns of the service providers?

2   In the eighteenth century, Manson of Belfast developed a method of schooling that involved a commitment to 'enjoyment' on the part of teachers and students.

   (a)   Is this a realistic possibility in the era of the twenty-first century, when there are so many challenges?

   (b)   What kinds of approaches, policies and practices would be necessary to make this practical and appropriate for pupils/students and teachers in the present age?

   (c)   Would such an approach be desirable or possible?

3   Prior to 1967, the major concern of teachers in the primary school system was that a sufficient number of pupils in their school/class would succeed in passing the Primary Certificate Examination.

   (a)   Have primary schools been liberated from the tyranny of examinations?

   (b)   Do pupils with special educational needs have the opportunities to have their learning achievements appropriately certified and recognised at post-primary level alongside their peers?

4   (a)   What were the particular skills and competences in the Montessori Method that made teachers with this qualification valuable to special education settings in Ireland since the 1960s?

   (b)   What contributions could such a method make to the policy of educational inclusion in the present day?

Chapter 4
Developing Policy and Provision in Special Education

Learning outcomes/objectives

On completion of this chapter, the reader will be able to:

- Identify and critically examine the policy shifts in the health sector towards people with disabilities in Ireland in the 1980s.
- Analyse the policy progression as outlined in the key reports, judicial decisions and legislative developments in Ireland from the SERC Report (1993) to the Sinnott judgment of 2000.
- Evaluate the impact of the Education Act 1998 and the Education for Persons with Disability Act (EPSEN) 2004 on special education policy and provision.
- Critically consider the systemic resourcing and restructuring of special education services in Ireland and the establishment of the National Council for Special Education (NCSE).

Introduction

In this chapter we will examine the radical shift in special education policy that occurred throughout the 1990s and into the present century. As Hill (2005: 4) observed, 'the policy process is essentially a complex and multi-layered one.' Special education policy evolved rapidly from a primary focus on educational provision for distinct categories of disabled children towards a more inclusive view of special education principally delivered within mainstream settings. This significant policy evolution occurred through the interplay of a variety of factors at national and international levels.

Internationally, the rights-based principles underlying policy statements from the United Nations, European Community, UNESCO and the OECD had resulted in a fundamental re-examination of educational provision for children with special educational needs. There was an increasing recognition that these children and their peers without special educational needs would benefit from being educated together and learning to live together.

Nationally, the last decade of the twentieth century witnessed the unfolding of major educational initiatives that shaped the organisation and delivery of educational provision. This involved significant changes in system administration, school management and curriculum. Special educational provision was documented and critiqued through government-sponsored reports that resulted in major changes in policy and provision. Parental litigation challenging inadequate educational provision for their children who had special educational needs also had a significant impact in promoting change in special education policy and practice. Developments in social policy with regard to disability issues and the rights of children also accelerated changes in perspectives on special educational provision.

Internationally, policy development in special education and health-related service delivery for people with disabilities has been profoundly influenced by supra-national bodies such as the United Nations. The United Nations Declaration on the Rights of Disabled Persons (1975), for example, and the subsequent UN-sponsored International Year of the Disabled in 1981 signalled the beginning of a public policy debate around the rights of people with disabilities to equitable access to and participation in mainstream societal activities. Within the European Community, funding programmes for training and employment schemes have been based on the principle of ensuring equitable access for all disadvantaged minorities, including those with disabilities.

National policy: Initiatives in the health sector

Within Ireland, public policy in relation to people with disabilities remained relatively unchanged until the 1980s. Until then, the Department of Health was principally responsible for the medical treatment, care, education, training and even the employment of people with disabilities. There was a gradual realisation, informed by international developments, that the marginalised position within society of people with disabilities required urgent action on many fronts. Doyle (2003: 26) observed: 'In the last decade, public policy has tried to address the twin issues of equality and universal access through anti-discrimination legislation, with right of redress, coupled with a mainstream approach to service delivery.' As will be evident in the discussion below, Ireland has attempted to follow this path through enacting enabling legislation and the gradual mainstreaming of provision in both education and health services.

In consultation with organisations representing disabled people, the Department of Health developed a number of significant policy initiatives that influenced the direction of educational provision for people with disabilities. These included the *Green Paper on Services for Disabled People* (1984) and *Needs and Abilities: A Policy for the Intellectually Disabled* (1991). The Green Paper opened with a government commitment to developing 'services and facilities which will enable disabled people to achieve full participation and equality in our society' (p. 9). It goes on to state that the Department of Education has been 'intensifying efforts to enable disabled children to receive their education in the least restrictive environment' (p. 45). The Green Paper recounted the recognition of the increasing demands for integrated education for children with disabilities alongside their peers in their local community, as outlined in the *White Paper on Educational Development* (1980). Various recommendations for increased resources in relation to psychological and care needs in particular were advanced in the Green Paper, though there did not appear to be a coherent vision of what integrated education would actually involve.

It is evident that despite the reference to education in the least restrictive environment, parallel systems of special and general education would remain for the foreseeable future. There appeared to be resistance to safeguarding the rights of disabled people to equitable services through legislation as enacted in other countries. The Green Paper reinforced charitable responses to disability issues: 'The most important thing which any disadvantaged minority needs is good-will and understanding' (p. 112).

In 1991 the Department of Health published *Needs and Abilities: A Policy for the Intellectually Disabled*, in which mainstream provision through the Department of Education, among others, was strongly recommended. The Review Group welcomed 'the fact that increasing numbers of pupils with general learning difficulties are now being provided with educational opportunities in their local environment' (p. 15). As Doyle (2003: 15) comments: 'The new direction signalled in this report sought to transfer responsibility for key elements of disability service provision away from the health sector and towards mainstream public service providers.'

The trend towards mainstreaming public services was maintained and enhanced as we now look at developments in education policy in the 1990s.

National policy: Developments in education

Special education policy development within Ireland during the 1990s was principally informed by government-sponsored initiatives (usually based on collaboration with the education partners) in both general and special education combined with very effective parental litigation campaigning for appropriate education for their disabled children. Enabling legislation was the end result. Developments in general education also influenced the direction of special education policy and provision.

In order to provide a coherent account of these significant developments, the following approach has been adopted. First, government-sponsored reports concerning special education will be explored (*Report of the Special Education Review Committee*, 1993; *Report of the Commission on the Status of People with Disabilities*, 1996). This is followed by an examination of parental litigation (O'Donoghue case, 1993; Sinnott case, 2000). Then, policy documents that affect special educational provision will be described (*The National Education Convention Report*, 1994; *Government White Paper on Education: Charting Our Education Future*, 1995). Legislation governing the system of special educational provision will be analysed (the Education Act 1998; the Education (Welfare) Act 2000; the Equal Status Act 2000; the Education for Persons with Special Educational Needs Act 2004; the Disability Act 2005). Major government task force reports on autism and dyslexia will also be discussed along with recent NCSE (National Council for Special Education) research reports focusing on autism and sensory disabilities. Finally, we will provide an overview of systemic supports available to schools and pupils/students with special educational needs.

Significant policy developments are outlined in Table 4.1.

Table 4.1: **Significant policy developments**

Government reports	• *Green Paper on Services for Disabled People* (1984) • *Needs and Abilities: A Policy for the Intellectually Disabled* (1991) • *Report of the Special Education Review Committee* (1993) • *Report of the Commission on the Status of People with Disabilities* (1996) • *The Report of the Task Force on Autism* (2001) • *Report of the Task Force on Dyslexia* (2002)
NCSE research reports	• *International Review of the Literature of Evidence of Best Practice Provision in the Education of Persons with Autistic Spectrum Disorders,* Parsons et al. (2009) • *Evidence of Best Practice Models and Outcomes in the Education of Deaf and Hard-of-Hearing Children: An International Review,* Marschark and Spencer (2009a) • *International Review of the Literature of Evidence of Best Practice Models and Outcomes in the Education of Blind and Visually Impaired Children,* Douglas et al. (2009)
Litigation	• The O'Donoghue case (1993) • The Sinnott case (2000)
Policy documents	• The National Education Convention (1994) • *Government White Paper on Education: Charting Our Education Future* (1995)
Legislation	• The Education Act 1998 • The Education (Welfare) Act 2000 • The Equal Status Act 2000 • The Education for Persons with Special Educational Needs Act 2004 • The Disability Act 2005

Reviewing special education, recommending changes

Over the years, special education and general education, while connected, had developed separately and appeared to run along parallel lines. Special education had little presence in general education decision making and policy development, and as a result often appeared to be fragmented and lacking coordination. This marginalised position within the education forum reflected the largely peripheral position children and people with disabilities occupied within Irish society. However, two significant reports (*Special Education Review Committee*, 1993; *A Strategy for Equality: Report of the Commission on the Status of People with Disabilities*, 1996) transformed this situation.

Special Education Review Committee (1993): Recommending resources for an under-resourced system

In response to growing concerns about the implications of integration, both nationally and internationally, the Department of Education and Science (DES) established the Special Education Review Committee (SERC) in 1991 to examine existing special education provision and make recommendations for the future. In particular, the committee was asked to focus on procedures for identifying children with special needs, determine the appropriate extent of educational integration in mainstream schools for these children, suggest the in-school support services required to deliver suitable educational provision and recommend the types of linkages that should be established between the Department of Education and other relevant government departments.

From the outset, it was acknowledged that the term 'special educational needs' was problematic, as it covered a broad range of educational difficulties ranging from those children who experience relatively mild learning difficulties requiring limited intervention to those who experience severe and multiple disabilities that involve multi-disciplinary approaches.

The report adopted a relatively broad definition of special educational needs that resembled the definition advanced by the influential Warnock Committee (1978), though as we will see later, there were important divergences. Pupils with 'special educational needs' included all 'those whose disabilities and/or circumstances prevent or hinder them from benefiting adequately from the education which is normally provided for pupils of the same age, or for whom the education which can generally be provided in the ordinary classroom is not sufficiently challenging'. (p. 18). This definition, while relatively encompassing, especially in the recognition of the needs of exceptionally able (gifted) children, focused on within-child deficits, though the influence of socio-economic issues is acknowledged. The report provided a relatively straightforward factual definition of special education as 'any educational provision which is designed to cater for pupils with special educational needs, and is additional to or different from the provision which is generally made in ordinary classes for pupils of the same age' (p. 18). Educational integration constituted a major topic of discussion and was defined as 'the participation of pupils with disabilities in school activities with other pupils, to the maximum extent which is consistent with the broader overall interests of both the pupils with disabilities and the other pupils in the class/group' (pp. 18–19). This approach, while broadly supportive of social integration, allows room for the exclusion of children with disabilities if their inclusion in classroom activities disadvantages their peers.

The SERC report suggested seven principles to underpin the development of comprehensive special education provision. Broadly speaking, these principles affirmed the right of children who have special educational needs to an appropriate education, emphasised that provision should be determined by the child's individual needs and parents should be involved in the decision-making process. It was envisaged that a continuum of services would be developed to include educational provision in both ordinary and special schools, though it is clear that the committee believed that as far as possible special educational provision should take place in the ordinary school.

While acknowledging that 'the nature of the additional educational services that a pupil may require is often not adequately established by identifying that pupil's primary disability or special circumstances' (p. 20), the committee opted to retain a categorical approach to educational provision, principally, it appears, for administrative and organisational reasons. This represented a major divergence from the Warnock Report (DES, England and Wales 1978), which abolished the traditional categories of disability and established the term 'special educational need'.

The report documented serious shortfalls in provision, inadequate curricular provision, constraints on integration in schools and the lack of specialist training for teachers. Serious concerns were expressed about the paucity of pre-school provision in the context of the urgent necessity for early intervention for children who experience special educational needs. The lack of comprehensive support teacher provision was also highlighted. It was evident that the existing structure of special educational provision required a total overhaul and the Special Education Review Committee believed that the report could provide the impetus to move special education from an optional extra towards the centre stage of educational debate. Substantial additional resources were recommended to support the continuum of educational provision envisaged in the report. It was strongly argued that enabling legislation was required to uphold the rights of children with special educational needs and their parents to appropriate educational provision.

The SERC report concluded that adopting an ideological position in relation to the contentious issue of educational integration would be unhelpful and remained equivocal by stating that 'we favour as much integration as is appropriate and feasible with as little segregation as is necessary' (p. 22). Increased integration for many categories of pupils, in particular those with mild general learning disabilities and those who have physical or sensory disabilities, was viewed as a natural outcome of existing trends. Structural links between ordinary and special schools were recommended to ensure that specialist expertise in the special school sector could be shared with mainstream counterparts. Creating a support infrastructure for schools through the creation of a comprehensive School Psychological Service was considered essential. It was also envisaged that the role of the support teacher required modification to enable collaboration with the classroom teacher and reduce the dominant practice of withdrawing pupils from class for support. The report found that ordinary and special education operated in virtual mutual isolation and noted that this system 'inhibits the realisation of one of the main goals of education for such students (students with special needs), namely that they should be capable of living, socialising and working in their communities' (pp. 63–64).

Key recommendations aimed at improving educational provision included:

- Access for parents to an early education expert.
- More classes for children with special educational needs between the ages of three and four years and supports for pre-schools that enrol those children.
- Resource and visiting teacher supports.
- Increased training and skills in special education for teachers.
- Appropriate curriculum guidelines.

However, despite the in-depth analysis of existing provision and detailed recommendations for future services, there were some significant shortcomings. Disability groups pointed out that the SERC membership did not contain people with disabilities and as a result reflected the dominant viewpoints of service providers. In addition, the parental role remained relatively underdeveloped within the framework for provision outlined in the report. Parents of children with autism, for example, viewed the report with considerable unease. While the report contained recommendations for increased support for children with autism, they continued to be treated within a frame of emotional and behavioural disturbance, a designation challenged by parents and an issue that resulted in a massive increase in litigation throughout the 1990s to secure appropriate provision.

The report represented the first comprehensive review of special educational provision and was a credible attempt to improve system capacity in relation to special educational provision. Given the variable nature of provision highlighted in the report, it is hardly surprising that the main focus was on securing additional resources rather than closely examining and critiquing the mindsets underlying the existing categorical approaches to provision. The report charted a significant move away from a system overly reliant on goodwill and charitable impulses.

The Department of Education and Science established an internal working party to implement the proposals contained in the *Report of the Special Education Review Committee*. It is fair to say that the report became the cornerstone of DES policy in relation to special educational provision. Many developments can be traced from this source, including the policy inputs to the White Paper, an expanded National Educational Psychological Service (NEPS), curricular developments through the National Council for Curriculum and Assessment (NCCA), increased in-career opportunities for special education teachers and improved funding for schools to cater for children who have special educational needs.

A Strategy for Equality: Report of the Commission on the Status of People with Disabilities (1996): Challenging an inequitable system

The commission report highlighted many of the barriers that prevent the full participation of people with disabilities within Irish society:

> People with disabilities are the neglected citizens of Ireland. On the eve of the 21st century, many of them suffer intolerable conditions because of outdated social and economic policies and unthinking public attitudes ... Whether their

status is looked at in terms of economics, information, education, mobility, or housing they are seen to be treated as second-class citizens (p. 5).

In addition, the commission rejected the dominant model of disability, adopted a social model and advocated responses from a civil rights perspective, recognising that 'equality is a key principle of the human rights approach' (p. 8). Lack of access to and participation and success in appropriate education programmes represented a major barrier: 'There was serious concern too about education: a failure to provide comprehensive education for people with disabilities results in their being denied access to employment and training opportunities comparable to those available to people without disabilities' (p. 6).

It was asserted that children with disabilities have an inalienable right to an appropriate education in the 'least restrictive environment'. There is a clear presumption that the vast majority of children with disabilities will be educated alongside their peers in mainstream schools, though this is qualified by the following statement: 'except where it is clear that the child involved will not benefit through being placed in a mainstream environment, or that other children would be unduly and unfairly disadvantaged' (p. 33). The responsibility of all schools to include children with disabilities was reiterated: 'Each school plan must strive to make schools inclusive institutions. To facilitate inclusive education, due recognition must be given to the rights and needs of teachers for resources, initial education, and continuing professional development' (p. 34).

Further, it was recommended that an inclusive Education Act should be enacted to support inclusive provision while providing improved levels of funding for specialist schools. The commission report was clearly influenced by enabling legislation such as the American Individuals with Disabilities Act (IDEA), originally enacted in 1975 and regularly updated since, wherein 'appropriate education' is defined as responsive to individual educational needs as outlined in an Individual Education Programme (IEP).

At a systems level, the commission highlighted the lack of coordination between the Departments of Education, Health and Justice and urged greater collaboration, with the Department of Education taking the lead in facilitating the delivery of high-quality educational services to children with disabilities. The commission identified the lack of support services (psychologists, therapists, specialist teachers) as central to preventing equal participation in education.

In a sense, the commission report reiterated many of the inadequacies outlined in the Special Education Review Committee report. However – and more fundamentally – the commission report based its recommendations within the frame of a human rights perspective rooted in a social model of disability. Serious gaps within provision were further highlighted by a series of high-profile court cases initiated by parents challenging the appropriateness of existing provision for children with autism and/or severe/profound general learning disabilities.

O'Donoghue case (1993) and Sinnott case (2000): Campaigning for fundamental rights

During the 1990s a series of court cases against the state were initiated by parents attempting to obtain improved educational provision for their children who had autism and/or severe/profound general learning disabilities. As Whyte (2002) observed, 'litigation strategy was consciously pursued in an attempt to compel what was perceived as an indifferent political system to devote more resources to these particular marginalised groups' (p. 177). Parents felt that they had few options left except litigation, and two cases in particular (O'Donoghue 1993; Sinnott 2000) resulted in significant changes in educational provision for these groups of children.

Traditionally the Department of Health was responsible for the education of children with severe/profound general learning disabilities, which, hardly surprisingly, resulted in the dominant view that education for these children principally consisted of meeting their medical/care needs. The struggle that ensued was essentially between two conflicting views of what was an appropriate education for these children. Put simply, the state adopted a medical model approach and parents pursued a human rights stance based on a social model of disability.

In the O'Donoghue case, the state argued that 'the applicant, by reason of being profoundly mentally and physically disabled, was ineducable and that all that could be done for him to make his life more tolerable was to attempt to train him in the basics of bodily function and movement' (Whyte 2002: 200). Further, the state maintained that the constitutional entitlement to 'free primary education' referred to traditional primary schooling and did not include the type of education/training appropriate for children with severe/profound general learning disabilities. International evidence suggested that this position was untenable. In recent decades many countries have adopted educational programmes that signal a clear shift away from medical care towards multi-disciplinary teams offering a more holistic education for these children. Justice O'Hanlon concurred with this view and asserted that Paul O'Donoghue was educable and that the state was obliged to provide 'free primary education for this group of children in as full and positive a manner as it has done for all other children in the community' (*O'Donoghue v. Minister for Health and ors.* (1996) 2 IR 20, pp. 65–66).

The O'Donoghue case was obviously significant in establishing the rights of children with severe/profound general learning disabilities to an appropriate education based primarily on educational needs rather than medical/care needs, as traditionally delivered. Whyte (2002: 203) concluded that this judgment required the state to develop measures that 'include a modification of the primary school curriculum to accommodate children with disabilities who are not adequately catered for under current policy and the provision of special support services.' Vastly increased resources for the education of these children constituted an immediate outcome. The state set up approximately ninety classes with six pupils in each to cater for this group of children and employed extra teachers and special needs assistants.

In the Sinnott case (2000), Justice Barr concluded that Jamie Sinnott had received 'not more than about two years of meaningful education or training provided by the State, despite incessant efforts by his mother to secure appropriate arrangements for him' (Whyte 2000: 205). Further, Justice Barr maintained that the state was obliged to provide lifelong education for people with severe/profound general learning disabilities. This provision was successfully challenged by the state and as a result the state's obligation to provide a primary education for people with severe/profound general learning disabilities ends at age eighteen.

Whyte (2005: 357) concluded that this litigation strategy brought about tangible changes in educational policy and demonstrated 'the potential of public interest litigation ... to convert a hostile or indifferent political system to the cause for reform.'

Examining and evaluating: Planning for the future

The National Education Convention (1994) addressed special education within the framework of equality issues, and treatment of this issue was evidently influenced by the considerations of the Special Education Review Committee. Debate within the convention focused on the integration of pupils with special educational needs into mainstream schools. Participants agreed that policy should be governed by the basic principle that every child is educable. In order to facilitate parental choice there needed to be a continuum of provision ranging from integration into mainstream schools to special schools. However, in the move towards integration there was a palpable fear that unsupported integration could emerge as the norm unless positive attitudes were combined with a government commitment to increased resourcing: 'Real integration involves identification of the child's needs, an appropriate curriculum, resources such as support staff, and in-service education for all involved teachers' (p. 123) and 'positive attitudes are essential to a successful policy of integration and to the removal of stereotypes and fear' (p. 124).

The *Government White Paper on Education* (1995: 7) adopted a philosophical framework that included a principled commitment 'to promote equality of access, participation and benefit for all in accordance with their needs and abilities.' Children and young people with disabilities were entitled to benefit from educational opportunities alongside their peers: 'All students, regardless of their personal circumstances, have a right of access to and participation in the education system, according to their potential and ability' (p. 24). Promoting this type of equality will involve 'allocating resources to those in greatest need, providing appropriate support systems, and changing the tangible and intangible qualities of the system itself to cater for the diverse educational needs and interests of the population' (p. 7). The White Paper's stated objective was to 'ensure a continuum of provision for special educational needs, ranging from occasional help within the ordinary school to full-time education in a special school or unit, with students being enabled to move as necessary and practicable from one type of provision to another' (p. 24). In essence, the recommendations of the Special Education Review Committee were endorsed and incorporated into the White Paper.

Legislation: Enabling significant change

Traditionally, people with disabilities tended to be separated from the mainstream of society and this situation was often underpinned by legislation. However, more recently, many countries have enacted anti-discrimination legislation aimed at asserting and protecting the rights of people with disabilities. As Glendenning (1999: 135) points out: 'While equality and participation lie at the core of law reform in this sphere, education holds the key to empowerment as it alone has the potential to unlock the door to equality and participation.'

Many countries have developed comprehensive legislation to ensure that children with disabilities receive appropriate education. The 1975 Education for All Handicapped Children Act (USA) guaranteed all children with a disability, no matter how severe or profound, a right to a free and appropriate public education. The recommendations of the ground-breaking Warnock Report (UK) in 1978 were incorporated into future legislation governing special educational provision. This type of legislation simultaneously reflected the reality of increased mainstreaming of children with disabilities and encouraged this process.

In the absence of enabling legislation, Ireland had failed to match international developments in the education of children with severe/profound disabilities and those who experienced autism. As Glendenning (1999: 146) has pointed out: 'In the absence of a statutory framework to meet the needs of children with behavioural problems and/or learning disabilities, who attend mainstream schools, has placed them at a huge disadvantage.' Since the 1980s the courts have played a prominent role in establishing educational rights for children with disabilities.

Devising legislation in social policy is complex and difficult and 'this is particularly true of Irish education with its diffuse nature, denominational character and tradition of negotiated consensus' (Glendenning 1999: 163). Remarkably, Irish education was almost totally unregulated by legislation until 1998 with the enactment of the Education Act, which has been followed in quick succession by the Education (Welfare) Act 2000, Education for Persons with Special Educational Needs Act 2004 and the Disability Act 2005. Also, the Equal Status Act 2000 has implications for ensuring equitable access to and delivery of special educational provision.

The Education Act 1998 provides a statutory basis for policy and practice in relation to all education provision. Throughout the Act, every reference to people availing of education is followed by the phrase 'including [those] who have a disability or who have other special educational needs'. For example, within Section 7 the first function of the Minister is 'to ensure ... that there is made available to each person resident in the State, including a person with a disability or who has other special educational needs, support services and a level and quality of education appropriate to meeting the needs and abilities of that person.' Further, the Act defined 'special educational needs' as 'the educational needs of students who have a disability and the educational needs of exceptionally able students' (s. 2(1)), though a primarily medical definition of disability was adopted, for example:

(a) the total or partial loss of a person's bodily or mental functions, including the loss of a part of a person's body, or
(b) the presence in the body of organisms causing or likely to cause, chronic disease or illness ...

This almost exclusively medical definition located the source of educational difficulties within the child who has a special educational need and ignored critical environmental and contextual issues. Current special educational discourse recognises that inflexible school structures, inadequate specialised training for teachers and inappropriate curricula can all contribute to learning failure.

In addition, the Education Act required school admission policies to respect the principles of equality and parental choice, and according to Meaney et al. (2005: 16) this represented the 'first legislative step towards inclusive education for persons with special educational needs'. The Act also aimed to improve the educational environment for children experiencing difficulties in learning by promoting 'best practice in teaching methods with regard to the diverse needs of students and the development of the skills and competencies of teachers.'

Responsibility for access to schools and reasonable accommodation in terms of technical aids/equipment for students with disabilities was assigned to the Department of Education and Science. Under Section 29 of the Act, parents have the right to appeal certain school board decisions in relation to permanent exclusion, suspension and refusal to enrol a child to the secretary general of the Department of Education and Science. This section could have particular relevance to children who have emotional and behavioural difficulties and can be more vulnerable to school exclusion. The National Council for Curriculum and Assessment is required to advise the minister on the 'appropriate methods for the assessment of the effectiveness of the education provided in schools, with particular regard to mechanisms whereby students who have problems achieving their potential may be identified as early as practicable' (s. 41(1)). The inspectorate has an important role in evaluating the effectiveness of education programmes for students with special educational needs and in supporting schools through advice on policies and strategies for the education of these children.

The Education (Welfare) Act 2000 provides for the entitlement of every child to a certain minimum education and focuses on developing strategies to encourage attendance in schools and implement measures to prevent non-attendance. Children with special educational needs are included within the remit of the National Educational Welfare Board established under this legislation.

The Equal Status Act 2000 prohibits discrimination in the provision of goods and services, accommodation and education on nine grounds, including disabilities. Schools are governed by this Act as regards enrolment and access to programmes. Under the Equal Status Act a school is required to provide reasonable accommodation, including special treatment, facilities or adjustments, to meet the needs of the child with a disability if without this accommodation the child would find it unduly difficult to participate in school. In recent years, the Equality Authority has taken a number of cases on the disability ground in relation to accessing schools and particular subject areas (Lodge and Lynch 2004).

The Education for Persons with Special Educational Needs (EPSEN) Act 2004 marks a significant milestone in education legislation provision for pupils with special educational needs. The central purpose of the Act is to ensure the provision of inclusive education unless there are specific reasons why a specialised placement is required for the child. It also:

- outlines procedures for assessment of special needs and for ensuring provision of appropriate intervention, services and reviews
- establishes the National Council for Special Education
- gives parents a key role in decision making
- establishes an appeals board to which decisions relating to the education of people with special educational needs can be appealed.

Inclusion represents a core value in the Act and in the preamble to the Act it is stated explicitly that school provision should be informed by rights and equality principles:

> to provide that the education ... shall, wherever possible, take place in an inclusive environment with those who do not have such needs, to provide that people with special educational needs shall have the same right to avail of, and benefit from, appropriate education as do their peers who do not have such needs.

The ultimate aim of inclusive education is to facilitate full participation in adult life: 'to assist children with special educational needs to leave school with the skills necessary to participate, to the level of their capacity, in an inclusive way in the social and economic activities of society and to live independent and fulfilled lives.' Parental involvement is also central to developing inclusive school provision 'to provide for greater involvement of parents ... in the education of their children'.

Defining and responding to special educational needs

The definition of disability adopted in the EPSEN Act 2004 contrasts markedly with the definition used in the Education Act 1998. The medicalised definition in the 1998 Act is replaced with one that does not focus exclusively on within-child deficits and recognises that difficulties in learning are relative rather than all-embracing. In the Dáil debates (28 November 2003) the Minister for Education and Science asserted that this new definition 'is a good one because it concentrates on the effects of disability rather than the cause. This is more appropriate in an educational setting.' As a result, the definition adopted in the 2004 Act reads as follows: 'a restriction in the capacity of the person to participate in and benefit from education on account of an enduring physical, sensory, mental health or learning disability or any other condition, which results in a person learning differently from a person without that condition.'

Section 3 of the Act sets out the conditions under which identification and assessment should occur; this is envisaged as a staged process. In the first stage the principal must, in consultation with the parents, take such measures as are practicable to meet the child's educational needs. Where such measures are seen as not benefiting the child, the principal, in consultation with the parents, may call for an assessment; this must be commenced within one month of the request and completed within a three-month period. Within one month of receipt of assessment (if it is successful), the principal is obliged to put an education plan in place. The principal convenes a team, which may include the school, parents and appropriate health and educational professionals, and draws up this education plan to fit the needs of the child.

New structures and fresh approaches: The National Council for Special Education

Prior to the establishment of the National Council for Special Education, the Department of Education and Science (DES) was trying to administer provision for special educational needs from a centralised structure. With the rapid growth of demand for provision for special educational needs in the late 1990s, this proved to be inadequate and unwieldy and the DES was overwhelmed with applications for support as a result of the automatic response procedure (1998). It had been evident for some time that a more localised, flexible structure was necessary to respond appropriately to the inherent complexities involved in special educational needs provision.

The DES decided to establish an organisation modelled on the semi-autonomous education bodies already in existence, such as the National Council for Curriculum and Assessment, the National Educational Psychological Service and the State Examination Commission. This policy development resulted in the establishment of the National Council for Special Education (NCSE) through the EPSEN Act 2004. The NCSE and the Special Educational Needs Organiser

(SENO) service are intended to ensure that provision is flexible and suited to individual need. The council must operate within the parameters of policy as developed by the minister and the Department of Education and Science. The NCSE has responsibility for many facets of school provision for special educational needs, including the provision of resources and supports to ensure that a continuum of special educational provision is available. In addition, the NCSE must guarantee that the progress of students with special educational needs is regularly monitored and reviewed. The council also has an advisory role to the minister in relation to any matter relating to the education of children and others with special educational needs. Functions also include the conduct of relevant research and the dissemination of information relating to best practice, nationally and internationally.

Guidelines regarding allocation of resources will still be set out by the DES but the NCSE, NEPS, the inspectorate and the education partners will be part of the planning process. Through its Special Education Unit, the DES will be involved in developing policy and evaluation regarding resource allocation, but the unit will not implement policy. The NCSE has developed the Special Education Needs Organiser (SENO) service (80 staff) to provide a localised service that will facilitate the process of identification, assessment and resource provision.

Challenges in implementing the EPSEN Act 2004

The enactment of the EPSEN Act 2004 has radically changed the educational landscape for children with special educational needs. As Meaney et al. (2005: 209) comment, the Act will:

> ... accelerate the changes within the education system from one in which the provision of inclusive education was an emerging feature of schooling to a system in which the provision of inclusive education is mandatory, except where this would not be in the best interests of the child or would be inconsistent with the effective provision of education for children with whom the child is to be educated.

Creating an inclusive school environment, as outlined in the Act, represents a considerable challenge for the whole school community. Meaney et al. (2005: 216) point out that the EPSEN Act 2004 'imposes very specific obligations on principals/teachers in the area of special educational needs'. The Act confers arduous duties on the school principal, who has overall responsibility for establishing a coherent system of special educational provision within the school and ensuring that the child's current special educational needs are effectively addressed. Given the relative lack of experience of many mainstream schools in the area of special educational needs and the recent advent of inclusive practice to Irish schools, it is hardly surprising that many schools feel ill-equipped to cope with this new situation.

Disability Act 2005

The Disability Act 2005 begins by stating that the purpose of the Act is to 'enable provision to be made for the assessment of health and education needs' of people with disabilities. Disability is defined under the Act as 'a substantial restriction in the capacity of the person to carry on a profession, business or occupation in the State or to participate in social or cultural life in the State by reason of an enduring physical, sensory, mental health or intellectual impairment' (s. 2(1)). The terms of the Act support the provision of an education assessment to determine the educational needs of people with disabilities.

Task force reports:
Report of the Task Force on Autism (2001)
Report of the Task Force on Dyslexia (2002)

In the early years of this century, two important task force reports were produced: the *Report of the Task Force on Autism: Educational Provision and Support for Persons with Autistic Spectrum Disorders* in 2001 and the *Report of the Task Force on Dyslexia* in 2002. Both reports represented a concerted effort by the government to draw together expertise in both areas to plan a way forward for children with autistic spectrum disorders and those with dyslexia. Educational provision for both groups of children was the subject of intense debate and not a little controversy, and in the case of children with autistic spectrum disorders, parents had initiated litigation against the state to secure appropriate education for their children. Until 1998, children with autistic spectrum disorders were usually categorised according to an accompanying condition such as general learning disability or often as emotionally/ behaviourally disturbed and as a result were enrolled in special schools dealing with that particular category of children. Since 1998, these children have been recognised as belonging to the distinct category of autism and education is now provided in a series of placements, including mainstream classes, special classes, special schools and special centres for education.

The remit for both task forces was expressed in a similar fashion and involved reviewing the current range of educational provision and the support services available, assessing the adequacy of this provision having regard to the varied needs of these children, examining the appropriateness of integrated or specialised provision and making recommendations to guarantee the provision of a suitable, effective and efficient service for these children.

The task force report on autism acknowledged that there is a wide variation among individuals who have autistic spectrum disorders and the condition is best understood as a continuum from those who have a severe learning disability to those of average or above-average intelligence. However, 'all share the triad of impairments in reciprocal social interaction, communication, and a lack of flexible thinking' (p. 20).

In relation to inclusive practice, there was particular concern about educational provision for children with Asperger syndrome/high-functioning autism (AS/HFA) who are mainly to be found in mainstream classes. These children require additional support to enable them 'to overcome the disadvantages of core social and communication impairments' (p. 123). Furthermore, teachers need to be aware that these children are often the subject of bullying from their peer group, as 'it routinely prevents students with AS/HFA from attending school and remains a significant causal factor in the high drop out rate at second level' (p. 125). A psychiatrist commented that while these children often have the ability to manage the second-level curriculum, they often 'do very badly there because the system there does not suit them and they must run at very high stress levels. Individual schools try to do their best but they do not understand what is involved' (p. 125).

In its review of current educational provision for children with autistic spectrum disorders (ASDs), the task force concluded that 'the capacity of current provision and resources has been, and is, critically unable to meet the needs of all children with ASDs in Ireland, and that extensive strategic and practical changes are necessary to secure a range of provision, to train relevant professionals and to establish appropriate arrangements to guarantee the effective delivery of services' (p. 5). On the basis of this conclusion, the task force made wide-ranging recommendations, including the urgency of early identification accompanied by early intervention; the creation of a continuum of provision; close partnership with parents; a collaborative approach by services; a multi-disciplinary approach to delivery and functioning of services; appropriate training for all professionals involved; and appropriate measures to monitor and evaluate effectiveness of provision.

It is a little too early to judge the overall impact of the task force report on policy and practice, but a recent evaluation report on educational provision for children with ASDs by the DES inspectorate concluded: 'It is apparent from this evaluation ... that considerable progress has been made in establishing a range of services since autism was given recognition as a discrete disability category in 1998' (Inspectorate, DES 2006a: 91). Notwithstanding this positive conclusion, the evaluation report makes a number of pertinent recommendations aimed at improving the range, depth and quality of educational provision. Key recommendations included collaboration between health and education services to ensure early identification and effective intervention; the design and delivery of a broad, relevant curriculum to respond to complex needs; the provision of comprehensive teacher training combining theoretical and practical aspects; and training and support for parents in acquiring essential techniques to respond to their child's needs.

When reviewing current provision, the task force on dyslexia highlighted particular inadequacies, including the lack of reliable data on numbers of pupils with dyslexia, limited information on the effectiveness of support interventions, difficulties accessing appropriate psychological assessments, limited early identification procedures and misunderstandings by schools and teachers about the nature of dyslexia and how it affects the child's learning.

The task force asserted that it is inappropriate to categorise students as the basis for provision and recommended a differentiated response based on the continuum of learning difficulties that arise as a result of dyslexia. The task force produced a comprehensive set of recommendations aimed at improving provision for and understanding of students with dyslexia. Deficiencies at system level are addressed and it is recommended that information and advice should be readily available for parents, the learning support services should be expanded, reasonable accommodations in state examinations should be reviewed and effective monitoring procedures developed to assess the effectiveness of intervention strategies. Many recommendations attempt to remedy the lack of widespread teacher knowledge of the learning difficulties associated with dyslexia and proposed more intensive pre-service and in-service training. Other recommendations aimed to improve school knowledge and capacity to respond effectively to students with dyslexia.

Both reports have made an important contribution to documenting strengths and deficiencies in current provision and providing a route map for policy makers and practitioners in the development of appropriate and effective educational provision for children who have autistic spectrum disorders and those who have dyslexia.

NCSE research reports:
International Review of the Literature of Evidence of Best Practice Provision in the Education of Persons with Autistic Spectrum Disorders, Parsons et al. (2009)

Since the publication of the *Report of the Task Force on Autism* in 2001 there has been an expansion of provision for children and young people on the autism spectrum. As mentioned earlier, the DES Inspectorate report (2006a) concluded that there had been significant progress in establishing appropriate educational provision for children on the autism spectrum. Notwithstanding this positive conclusion, the evaluation report made a number of pertinent recommendations aimed at improving the range, depth and quality of educational provision. Key recommendations included collaboration between health and education services to ensure early identification and effective intervention; the design and delivery of a broad, relevant curriculum to respond to complex needs; the provision of comprehensive teacher training, combining theoretical and practical aspects; training and support.

It is apparent that increased numbers of children on the autism spectrum are attending mainstream provision, with 2,571 in 2008–2009, compared to 1,675 in 2006–2007 (Parsons et al. 2009) and, consequently, that there are expanded numbers of autism-specific classes in mainstream schools (87 classes in 2001 compared to 339 classes in 2008). In addition, autism-specific classes at post-primary level did not exist in 2001, yet there were 36 in 2008. Parsons et al. (2009) reviewed the international evidence on best practice models for children and young people on the autism spectrum. Best practice models tended to focus on early assessment and intervention, appropriate staff training, ensuring that families are centrally involved, and developing effective multi-agency collaboration. Parsons et al. (2009) observed that:

> Given the diversity of needs on the autism spectrum, one type of approach or intervention is unlikely to be effective for all. Consequently, a range of provision should be maintained so there is a better chance of being able to provide appropriately for this diversity of need (p. 5).

Evidence of Best Practice Models and Outcomes in the Education of Deaf and Hard-of-Hearing Children: An International Review, Marschark and Spencer (2009a)

Marschark and Spencer (2009a) reported that there are an estimated 2,000 children of school age in Ireland who are deaf or hard-of-hearing and over three-quarters of these children are in mainstream classrooms with additional support from resource teachers, visiting teachers and special needs assistants. Only children who have serious hearing loss or are deaf are entitled to additional support, though the authors point out that even mild hearing loss can have a detrimental effect on a child's ability to participate appropriately in classroom activities. Children who are deaf or hard-of-hearing perform as capably as their hearing peers on non-verbal measurements of intelligence and cognitive ability, yet their academic achievement often fails to match their hearing peers. The authors recommend that 'the identification of hearing loss and the immediate provision of effective intervention services can raise the general levels of language skills attained by DHH children, as well as later literacy and general academic achievement' (Marschark and Spencer 2009b: 7). Early intervention is crucial and the child's family must be full participants in this process if it is to succeed. Instruction by highly skilled and knowledgeable teachers in 'meaningful and interactive settings leads to better reading and writing skills than the instruction available in ordinary classrooms' (Marschark and Spencer 2009b: 9). The authors point out that despite the common perception that pupils who have hearing loss demonstrate deficits in literacy, in fact these children have difficulties throughout the curriculum. These difficulties:

> ... appear to be related to such factors as underuse of metacognitive strategies (self-directed strategies for learning), decreased visual attention to information in the classroom, lack of language skills for understanding texts and information presented in class, and insufficient experience with problem-solving activities (Marschark and Spencer 2009b: 9).

Research evidence appears to indicate that placement in segregated or inclusive settings appears to have little impact on pupil attainment. Emotional and social development appears more positive for children when there is a critical mass of deaf/hard of hearing children in the ordinary classroom rather than the single child who can end up very isolated and lonely.

Based on international practice, Marschark and Spencer strongly recommend the introduction of Universal Newborn Hearing Screening (UNHS) accompanied by a comprehensive early intervention programme focused on the needs of children and their families. The authors argue that with regard to appropriate educational models:

> Available research clearly points to the need for an array of alternative educational settings, ranging from separate schools or programmes for the deaf to fully inclusive classrooms in which children can obtain all necessary support services while integrated with their hearing peers (2009b: 15).

International Review of the Literature of Evidence of Best Practice Models and Outcomes in the Education of Blind and Visually Impaired Children, Douglas et al. (2009)

Douglas et al. (2009) examined the international literature in relation to best practice concerning the education of children and young people who are blind or visually impaired. The authors examined the implications of this international review for Ireland and provided a series of recommendations relating to a number of areas, including educational services; inter-agency collaboration; educational infrastructure; the role of special schools and specialist centres; identification of visually impaired children.

The authors comment that curricular access needs to be conceptualised as access to core curriculum and access to additional curriculum. Core curriculum consists of the prescribed curriculum, and additional curriculum refers to the need for these children to acquire skills in mobility and independence, social and emotional development, and the use of Information Communication Technology (ICT). Access to the core curriculum can be facilitated by a modified educational provision, and the following issues need to be addressed: assessment of learning needs; the teaching strategies adopted; approaches to formal examinations; approaches in relation to the teaching of literacy (including print and Braille) (p. 151). Inter-agency collaboration is highlighted as a crucial element in effective service delivery for these children and their families. This type of collaboration is particularly beneficial for early intervention, low-vision training and mobility independence training. Curricular access for children with visual impairment requires the availability of additional materials and equipment. The authors contend that 'there is support in the literature for a continued and expanded role for special schools for the visually impaired that would allow them to work in partnership with mainstream schools to facilitate effective inclusion' (p. 155). There appears to be an underestimate of the number of children who have a visual impairment in Ireland compared to international prevalence rates. The authors estimate that there could be up to 2,000 children of school-going age, while only 780 children are currently registered with the visiting teacher service.

Provision

In this final section we will document systemic support structures for the delivery of special education provision. Within-school support services will be addressed in Chapter 14.

The EPSEN Act (2004) has clearly set out the provision required to support children and young people with special educational needs. However, given current economic constraints, aspects of the legislation remain to be implemented, including the critical section on individual education plans.

The establishment of the National Council for Special Education (NCSE) represents a significant modification of the systemic organisation and delivery of special educational provision. The NCSE became operational at the beginning of 2005 and is responsible for the organisation and delivery of special educational provision at both national and local level. It is also expected to conduct relevant research and give expert advice to the Minister for Education and Science on the educational and service needs of children with disabilities and/or special educational needs. Through its country-wide network of Special Education Needs Organisers (SENOs), the NCSE will be responsible for the organisation and delivery of services at local level. This will involve close liaison with local health services to ensure that children can access the relevant support services usually supplied by health providers, e.g. speech therapy, occupational therapy, physiotherapy. They will also be responsible for dealing with applications on behalf of children deemed to have 'low incidence' disabilities (physical disabilities, visual and/or hearing impairment, severe emotional disturbance, moderate to severe/profound general learning disability, autism, specific speech and language disorder, assessed syndromes and multiple disabilities). In order to develop a system for the allocation of special educational resources at primary level, the DES has divided children with special educational needs into 'high incidence' (borderline/mild general learning disability, specific learning disabilities, e.g. dyslexia, funded under the general allocation scheme) and 'low incidence', as described above.

The general allocation scheme

Until 2005, within the primary system, learning support teachers were appointed on the basis of school enrolment levels and resource teacher posts were authorised on the basis of the number of pupils with assessed special educational need. In 2005, the DES introduced the general allocation scheme, which is designed to 'ensure that all schools have enough resource teaching hours to meet the immediate needs of pupils with high incidence special educational needs and those who require learning support. It reflects the fact that most schools would have children with these needs' (DES Circular SP. ED. 02/05: 1).

It is emphasised within Circular 02/05 that the general allocation system 'is intended to make possible the development of truly inclusive schools' (p. 3). Schools will have the requisite resources to respond to what are termed 'high incidence' special educational needs. Three categories of high incidence special educational needs are listed:

1   pupils who are eligible for learning-support teaching ... priority should be given to pupils whose achievement is at or below the 10th percentile on standardised tests of reading or mathematics;

2   pupils with learning difficulties, including pupils with mild speech and language difficulties, pupils with mild social or emotional difficulties and pupils with mild co-ordination or attention control difficulties associated with identified conditions such as dyspraxia, ADD, ADHD;

3   pupils who have special educational needs arising from high incidence disabilities (borderline mild general learning disability, mild general learning disability and specific learning disability) (p. 3).

The level of resources for each school is determined by a number of factors, including gender (more favourable weighting for boys), socio-economic disadvantage and school size (quotas for posts in small schools are lower).

The additional resources guaranteed under this scheme have received a general welcome, though it is too soon to judge its effectiveness in achieving the stated aim of developing inclusive schools. Serious questions remain to be answered around the equity of giving a greater weighting to boys in the allocation of resources and the possible impact of parents challenging the designation of 'high incidence' as the EPSEN Act 2004 becomes fully operational.

Pupils assessed as having 'complex and enduring needs' (now termed 'low incidence') will continue to be allocated resource teaching hours on the basis of psychological assessment reports combined with the SENO's evaluation of the application. The schema of resource hours allocation is outlined in Table 4.2.

The National Council for Special Education's *Annual Report* (2009) provides a detailed breakdown of the successful applications for resource hours in primary and post-primary schools. In the year 2008–2009, 4,427 applications for resource hours were granted in primary schools, and figures for resource allocation among the different categories of disability/special educational needs included children with an emotional and behaviour disturbance (28%); children with specific speech and language impairments (22%); children on the autism spectrum (16%) and children who have physical disabilities (16%). At post-primary level the general allocation model does not operate, so resource hours are granted for children and young people in the high incidence categories (mild general learning disability, specific learning disability, for example) as well as for children and young people in the low incidence categories. In the year 2008–2009, 4,169 applications were granted for resource support, with 60 per cent of additional teaching hours allocated for children and young people in high incidence categories, including borderline mild general learning disability, specific learning disability and mild general learning disability. Children and young people who have either an emotional and behavioural disturbance or a severe emotional and behavioural disturbance were allocated 15 per cent of the additional teaching hours granted to post-primary schools.

Table 4.2: Resource allocation model for 'low incidence' disabilities

Low incidence disabilities	Hours of resource teaching support available to school per week
Physical disability	3
Hearing impairment	4
Visual impairment	3.5
Emotional disturbance	3.5
Severe emotional disturbance	5
Moderate general learning disability	3.5
Severe/profound general learning disability	5
Autism/autistic spectrum disorders	5
Specific speech and language disorder	4
Assessed syndrome* in conjunction with one of the above low incidence disabilities	3 to 5, taking into account the pupil's special educational needs, including level of general learning disability
Multiple disabilities**	5

*e.g. Down syndrome, William's syndrome and Tourette syndrome.
**Two or more of the disabilities listed in this table.
Source: DES Circular 02/05.

The National Educational Psychological Service (NEPS) has a critical role to play, both as a provider of support to schools in relation to special educational provision and as a 'gatekeeper' of resources. NEPS was established as an executive agency of the DES in 1999 and it provides services to primary and post-primary schools as well as educational centres approved by the DES. Initially NEPS prioritised providing support to children with special educational needs. The work of NEPS psychologists has tended to focus on providing a psychological assessment of special educational needs and resources. Teaching hours/special needs assistant support, for example, are allocated to the child on the basis of the diagnosis.

This process of tying resources to assessment has resulted in long waiting lists for assessment and limits on the numbers of assessments per school. As a result of the emphasis on assessment, to date NEPS has not been able to develop a comprehensive psychological support system for schools and individual children with special educational needs, though this has been prioritised as part of the overall expansion of the service.

The Special Education Support Service (SESS) was established in September 2003 by the In-Career Development Unit of the Department of Education and Science with the aim of improving the quality of teaching and learning in relation to the education of children and young people who have special educational needs. The SESS will play a central role in coordinating and developing professional development opportunities and support structures for school personnel working with children and young people with special educational needs in a range of educational environments, including mainstream schools (primary/post-primary), special schools and special classes.

There are three main elements to the work of the SESS: the Local Initiatives Scheme, Strategy for Support Provision and Accredited Long-Term Professional Development. Within the Local Initiatives Scheme, individual schools and teachers can seek support for identified professional needs in relation to special education. The Strategy for Support Provision involved the identification of areas of priority for professional development need within the system, e.g. Autistic Spectrum Disorder, Dyslexia, SEN in post-primary schools and Challenging Behaviour in special schools, and the establishment of expert teams of teachers to provide support to schools. This prioritisation process is ongoing and in 2006 there was a further expansion of this service. Accredited Long-Term Professional Development involves the provision of opportunities for school personnel to participate in a variety of programmes, ranging from induction to more advanced professional development at post-graduate level (www.sess.ie/sess/Main/About.htm).

The Special Education Support Service (SESS) has responded to the need for accessible information for educators in relation to special educational needs by producing a publication entitled *Meeting the Learning and Teaching Needs of Students with Special Educational Needs: Signposts (A Resource Pack for Teachers)* (2008). It is explicitly recognised that: 'The complex and diverse nature of learning precludes the development of definitive reference material to meet the needs of all individual learners' (Foreword); however, it is anticipated that detailed information regarding specific special educational needs/disabilities will be helpful to teachers as they develop their teaching and learning programmes. In addition, the SESS has recognised that differentiating the curriculum for students with special educational needs is a challenging task for teachers and in response has published *Science Differentiation in Action: Practical Strategies for Adapting Learning and Teaching in Science for Students with Diverse Needs and Abilities* (2008). This publication consists of differentiated lesson plans, worksheets and suggested activities to enhance the participation of students with special educational needs within the science class.

The National Behaviour Support Service (NBSS) was established by the Department of Education and Science in 2006 in response to growing concerns about levels of inappropriate student behaviour in schools as articulated in *School Matters: The Report of the Task Force on Student Behaviour in Second Level Schools* (2006). The NBSS aims to enable schools to develop and maintain positive teaching and learning environments: 'through the provision of a systematic continuum of support to school communities, grounded in evidence based practice' (NBSS 2009: 6). More specifically, the NBSS works with partner schools to develop sustainable school-wide models of positive behaviour support. Behavioural concerns are addressed at three distinct though interrelated levels: Level One: whole-school approaches focusing on positive behaviour support; Level Two: targeted interventions with specific classes and small groups; Level Three: intensive behaviour interventions with specific individual students. This model is based on the premise that whole-school approaches will address the social and behaviour needs of 80–90 per cent of the school population, targeted interventions will be required for 5–10 per cent of the student body, while more intensive interventions and programmes will be necessary for 1–5 per cent of students who have serious behaviour difficulties. The NBSS publication *A Model of Support for Behaviour Improvement in Post Primary Schools* (2009) presents the evidence-based rationale for the recommended school approaches to behaviour concerns and documents how this model can operate in post-primary schools. The NBSS is currently working with more than 80 post-primary schools.

The National Council for Curriculum and Assessment (NCCA), the statutory body responsible for advising on curriculum and syllabus requirements, is centrally involved in developing curricular guidelines for teachers working with children and young people who have general learning disabilities (borderline/mild), moderate general learning disabilities and those who have severe/profound general learning disabilities. These guidelines are intended to develop teacher capability in relation to these groups of children and young people and increase opportunities for curricular access.

Other systemic supports include enhanced capitation rates for children with special educational needs and 'start-up' and annual grants for learning support/resource teachers for the purchase of specialised materials. Grants are also provided to individual pupils with a disability for the purchase of computers, word processors, tape recorders, software, braillers and audiology equipment. Accommodations for state certificate examinations are also provided for students with special educational needs who are deemed eligible.

Visiting teacher service

The visiting teacher service was established in the 1970s to support children with hearing impairments attending mainstream schools. A few years later the service was expanded to include support for children with visual impairments in mainstream settings. The increased integration of children with general learning disabilities in mainstream schools resulted in the service being extended to support these children. The visiting teacher service encompasses all levels of education, from pre-school through primary and post-primary up to higher education. Generally, visiting teachers have the dual role of some direct teaching of the pupil combined with an advisory role in relation to class teachers and parents. The Irish National Teachers' Organisation (INTO) Report (2000) concluded that the advisory role of visiting teachers (in relation to class teachers, subject teachers at post-primary, resource teachers and parents) needed to be strengthened.

Concluding comments

It is apparent that special education policy has undergone significant changes throughout the 1990s and the early years of the new century. As a result, increasing numbers of children with special educational needs are educated in mainstream schools. However, while legislation and policy documents make the presumption for inclusion, a number of challenges remain. Extra resources have been provided, but an ongoing commitment will be needed to develop the infrastructure required to deliver inclusive provision. School and teacher knowledge around the education of children and young people with special educational needs requires concrete support and encouragement.

Discussion points

1   Identify critical milestones in the development of special education policy. Assess the relative importance of government initiatives compared to community/parent interventions.
2   It is generally recognised that this is a time of transition in special education policy and practice.
    (a)   What challenges does the National Council for Special Education face in moving towards the development of inclusive learning environments?
    (b)   What crucial policy issues will need to be addressed to ensure effective special education practice?
3   In the past, mainstream and special education tended to operate along parallel lines. Can you suggest some ways in which links between mainstream and special schools can be established and strengthened?

Chapter 5
Moving towards Schools for All

Learning outcomes/objectives

On completion of this chapter, the reader will be able to:
- Identify and discuss the key perspectives in the development of special educational policy.
- Critically discuss the factors and influences in the emergence of international policy towards integration/mainstreaming.
- Explore the elements in the agenda for change, which aims for a policy of inclusion, and the movement towards 'schools for all'.
- Examine the moves in Ireland towards inclusive education and the challenges involved.

Introduction

Inclusion has rapidly gained international prominence in the last decade and appears regularly in policy documents produced by international bodies, governments, disability service organisations and representative groups of disabled people. However, despite this prominence, inclusion remains a contested term and there is no agreed definition of its meaning. This is partly explained by the variety of influences, social, political and economic, that combined to produce the idea of an inclusive society: 'Inclusion, it transpires, represents the confluence of several streams of thought, social and political as well as educational' (Thomas and Vaughan 2004: 1).

It is also explained by the difficulties encountered in translating the inclusive ideal into everyday practice. As Clough and Corbett (2000: 5) assert: 'the notion of an inclusive society is at the same time difficult to contest in moral terms. As a basic tenet of belief, should not everybody have the same rights of access to education? Of course.' Overuse of the term 'inclusion' and inappropriate application to practices that are far from inclusive have certainly compromised the credibility of the term. Further, when practical decisions have to be made regarding resources and supports, other factors, including vested interests, often come to the fore. As a result, inclusion advocates have been particularly concerned to bridge this perceived rhetoric–reality gap in practice. Inclusive education has encountered similar difficulties around definition and the accusation that this agenda has become an inflexible ideology that sounds fine in theory but is extremely difficult to implement in practice. In response, advocates of inclusive education maintain that developing inclusive education systems needs to be viewed as a process (as yet unfinished) rather than an ideology or a particular collection of practices.

Key perspectives

There is general agreement that policy making in the area of special education can be divided into three phases: segregated provision, integration/mainstreaming and inclusion. Segregated provision was developed for various categories of disabled children from the end of the eighteenth century and was generally viewed as a humanitarian response to a particularly marginalised group. However, more recent commentators have adopted a less benign view, and McDonnell (2003a: 33), for example, notes: 'During this period special schooling constituted one element in a more general process involving the regulation and institutionalisation of "anomalous" populations in society.' Within wider society, many interrelated factors began to have an impact on social policy and practice. These included the civil rights movement, the 'normalisation' movement originating in Scandinavia, anti-discrimination legislation and an increase in self-advocacy by disabled people and their organisations.

In their review of the development of special educational provision in the United Kingdom, Clough and Corbett (2000) outlined five key perspectives: the psycho-medical legacy, the sociological response, curricular approaches, school improvement strategies and disability studies critique. They emphasise that 'these perspectives are never wholly exclusive of each other, nor are they strictly chronologically sequential' (p. 8). This approach avoids the danger of over-simplifying historical developments through viewing them as purely linear. As we explore these perspectives, it will become evident that the psycho-medical legacy, for example, has retained a powerful influence in the existing systems of identification and assessment of children who have special educational needs.

Until relatively recently, the psycho-medical perspective has dominated policy and practice in special educational provision. This is hardly surprising, as the medical profession was centrally involved in the initial recognition that children with disabilities were capable of learning and many physicians were at the forefront of establishing educational provision for these children. Not unexpectedly, within this perspective the primary emphasis focused on disability as a problem to be solved. As a result, there was an over-emphasis on 'within-child' deficits that required remediation. The primary purpose of the assessment process became the identification of the individual deficit within the child and the subsequent assignment of the child to a disability-specific school for education. More recently, psychologists have become involved in developing innovative approaches linking assessment with appropriate teaching and learning strategies.

Clough and Corbett (2000: 15) note: 'If the psychomedical perspective saw special educational need as arising from the children's own characteristics, by contrast the sociological response sees them as the outcome of social processes.' The rationale for special education and the professional disciplines involved in the delivery of special educational provision were subjected to a sustained sociological critique. This analysis of special education was located within a broader critique of societal inequality and the role of institutions in reproducing disadvantage. Tomlinson (1982), for example, questioned the presumed benign nature of special schooling informed by concerned and committed professionals. Tomlinson pointed out how special education suited the 'vested interests' of the medical and psychological professionals in maintaining their pre-eminent position within the decision-making mechanisms. Also, it was argued that the existence of separate provision absolved mainstream schools of responsibility for teaching children with special educational needs.

While the sociological analysis tackled the broader issues of inequality and disadvantage at societal level, the curricular approaches attempted to develop appropriate curricula for children who have special educational needs. The recognition that the causes of learning difficulties were not confined to within-child factors facilitated a radical change in thinking around this issue. For many years, children with special educational needs had been expected to adapt to the existing curriculum with resultant failure to achieve rather than have the curriculum adapted to suit their learning needs. Gradually, curricular adaptation initiatives focused on including those with learning difficulties within the framework of a common curriculum and accreditation.

School effectiveness strategies originated within the mainstream sector and the underlying principles were adapted in attempts to create a more inclusive education system. It was realised that inflexible school structures combined with inappropriate teaching methodology could contribute significantly to learning failure. School improvement strategies focused on schools examining their practice systematically through action research and collaborative inquiry. Ainscow (1996: 73) believed that this approach could help to create more inclusive schools:

> It seems possible that as schools move in such directions the changes that occur can also impact on the ways in which teachers perceive pupils in their classes whose progress is a matter of concern … What may happen is that as overall working conditions in a school are improved such children are gradually seen in a more positive light. Rather than simply problems that have to be overcome or, possibly, referred elsewhere for separate attention, such pupils may be perceived as providing feedback on existing classroom arrangements.

The final perspective, the disability studies critique, came from academic disciplines outside education that were particularly concerned with the impact of exclusion and segregation on the lives of disabled people. Oliver (1995) vehemently argued for the deconstruction of the whole special education system, as it has, in his view, patently failed to deliver equitable educational opportunities for children with disabilities and/or special educational needs. He, among others, located the inclusive education discussion within the broader framework of societal inclusion for people from marginalised groups: 'What is needed as far as education is concerned, is a moral commitment to the inclusion of all children into a single education system as part of a wider commitment to the inclusion of all disabled people into society' (p. 75).

Tracing the origins of change

As mentioned earlier, the debate around the appropriateness of separate provision can be traced to a combination of factors. Two movements in particular had a profound influence internationally on the whole system of special education. The struggle for civil rights, particularly in America, and the Scandinavian-influenced normalisation principles had a major impact on human service delivery for people with disabilities. This resulted in a serious questioning of the role of professionals in the conceptualisation and delivery of special educational provision. Another factor included critiques of existing special educational provision.

The civil rights movement provided a powerful stimulus to change as minority ethnic groups challenged the barriers preventing their full participation in society. Other marginalised groups, including those with a disability, copied this example. According to normalisation principles, people with a disability should be enabled to live their lives as close to the cultural norm as possible. However, the specialisation of services developed for people with a disability (medical, educational, social) inevitably resulted in separation from the mainstream of community life. Services needed to be reframed to ensure that people with disabilities could participate to the greatest extent possible in their communities. The practice of separate special schooling came under close scrutiny as it appeared to violate these normalisation principles. It began to be asserted that the child with a disability was entitled to attend school with his/her peers and be educated alongside them.

Goffman (1963) challenged the rationale for separate provision and concluded that institutionalisation served to resolve difficulties for mainstream provision. Dunn (1968) reinforced this view through his analysis of the inadequacies of special educational provision. He argued that for children labelled 'mildly mentally retarded', poverty and social deprivation were the major contributory factors to their learning problems rather than inherent within-child factors. Further, he pointed out that the special programmes had not resulted in a significant increase in the learning opportunities for children with special educational needs. Research studies revealed that children with special educational needs who remained in regular class performed as well as if not better than their counterparts in special provision. Dunn was very concerned about the negative impact of the special needs label on the child's self-esteem and some research had shown that teacher expectations for these pupils were negatively affected by the special needs label. Finally, Dunn believed that mainstream schools were now better equipped to respond appropriately to individual differences. This belief was based on innovative curricular advances and a better-prepared and supported teaching force.

In the US, major legislation was enacted in response to civil rights campaigns, parental concerns about appropriate educational provision for their children and the increasing public disquiet over segregated provision for children with special educational needs. Public Law 94-142 (1975) marked a significant milestone in the move away from segregated provision towards more inclusive settings. This federal law required states to provide free appropriate public education for children and young people with disabilities aged three to twenty-one. The legislation also required that children be placed in the least restrictive environment, meaning the most ordinary setting possible that could provide an appropriate education.

The Warnock Report (DES, England and Wales, 1978) had a similar impact on special educational provision in the United Kingdom. The report recommended ending the practice of identifying the child according to category of disability and automatically providing education in disability-specific schools. It was concluded that this approach was inappropriate for a number of reasons. Labelling children according to disability category often stigmatised these children and was of little practical value in deciding on appropriate educational provision. Further, children with the same disability label often had widely varying educational needs and yet were placed together as a homogeneous group supposedly having a similar educational profile. The report concluded that up to 20 per cent of the school-going population could encounter difficulties in learning at some point in their school careers, though a much smaller number would experience serious, long-lasting difficulties. It was decided to replace the existing multiple categories of disability with the generic term 'special educational need'.

This term applied to any pupil who required additional help that could be either short- or long-term, confined to specific aspects of learning/subject-related or more general across most subjects and aspects of learning. Beveridge (1999: 4) observed that the Warnock Report marked a significant shift away from the traditional psychological-medical frameworks of children's learning difficulties and represented:

> ... an explicit attempt to break with traditional notions of educational difficulty as being primarily rooted and fixed within the individual child. It did not deny that within-child factors can have a significant impact on learning, but the concept of special educational need which was put forward was far more concerned with the interaction between the child and the learning contexts which the child experiences.

Three types of integration were identified by the committee: locational, social and functional. Locational integration represented the lowest level, as children with special educational needs were placed in the school, usually in a special class or unit, though little interaction occurred between these children and their same-age peers in mainstream classes. Social integration focused on providing opportunities for social interaction between children with special educational needs and their peers, usually through shared play/lunch. Functional integration represented the highest level of contact, as the child with special educational needs was included in mainstream class either on a part- or full-time basis.

Despite its claim to have abolished categorisation, it soon became evident that the Warnock Report had provided the basis for a new form of categorisation based on the concept of special educational need. According to Thomas and Vaughan (2004: 120), the endorsement in the report of the three forms of integration outlined above 'permitted and encouraged the continuation of a segregated framework and increased the odds against an effective development of integration'.

Despite these reservations, it is clear that the Warnock Report marked a significant turning point in the thinking around special educational needs and the organisation of the delivery of special educational provision. Substantial improvements in funding were soon evident, enabling legislation was enacted and parents became centrally involved in the decision-making processes around the education of their child. Perhaps most importantly, consideration of special educational needs moved from its traditional peripheral position and increasingly became the concern of the whole educational system.

Integration/mainstreaming: A false dawn?

While integration has been the key concept of an international movement aimed at achieving a fundamental reform of special educational provision, no generally accepted definition of integration has emerged. This is probably due to the fact that the term 'integration' has generally been used 'as a collective noun for all attempts to avoid the segregated and isolated education of students with special needs' (Meijer and Pijl 1994a: 4). Integration involved complex realities, as special educational practice varied widely both between and within countries. Despite this variation, there appeared to be widespread agreement that the integration of pupils with disabilities into the mainstream of education was desirable, and the Organisation for Economic Co-operation and Development (OECD 1994: 3) reported that integration has been 'a goal of education for many countries and is a significant trend in almost all OECD countries.'

Increased acceptance of the value of integrated education has not been achieved without a struggle. Advocates of integration have advanced a variety of arguments to support their case. Probably the most powerful contention has been that at heart, the integration of pupils with disabilities is a moral issue. Enabling these pupils to participate fully in the educational system constitutes a moral choice for society. This moral choice is closely linked to fundamental questions within society, such as how do we create a fairer world and how do we recognise and respond to common human needs? In essence, integration is a process for achieving educational equality for pupils with disabilities and/or special educational needs. This involves increasing their participation in the school community and promoting the acceptance of diversity in wider society. It is anticipated that this will lead to significantly reduced marginalisation for these young people and ensure that they become fully integrated into their community as adults. This form of integration is an essential part of the wider quest to create society where everyone's human rights are respected and their contribution is alued.

The implicit appeal to social justice contained in these values-based guments has been supported by the argument that integrated education can nefit both the children with disabilities and their same-age peers. Research dies have supported this viewpoint. Peck et al. (1990), for example, reported t non-disabled pupils outlined six types of benefits which they had gained n sustained interaction with their disabled peers. These benefits included rovement in self-concept; growth in social competence; increased tolerance ther people; a reduced fear of human difference; development of personal ciples; and interpersonal acceptance and friendships. Positive social and ational outcomes have also occurred for pupils with a general learning ility, usually in the context of structured interventions such as cooperative ing groups, peer tutoring approaches or social skills training programmes. e pupils had acquired increased self-confidence in social interactions with mainstream counterparts and in the process had gained invaluable social that could be used in a variety of community environments.

eijer and Pijl (1994a) identified three broad policy options in integration ices in a number of countries. In countries such as Italy and Sweden, a 'one-' integration policy operated whereby children with special educational were educated in mainstream schools to the greatest possible extent. 'Two-' integration policies were in evidence in the Netherlands, Belgium and any, where the two school systems work independently. The third group of ries, including Denmark, England, Wales and the United States, followed i-track' policies where a flexible system of educational provision was ed and a continuum of services offered to pupils with special educational . It was clear that philosophical approaches to the concept of need often mined the type of educational provision a country offered. The belief that idual pupil deficits lead to special educational needs resulted in an emphasis parate educational provision, whereas flexible and responsive systems of sion appeared to be linked to the belief that needs arise from an interaction dividual and environmental factors.

upporters of integration envisaged that the integration process would lve the move from segregated provision to social and curricular integration pupils with disabilities and/or special educational needs. From his rvation of provision in England and Wales, Hegarty (1993b) concluded that gration spanned a continuum from greater levels to lesser forms of gration: child with special educational needs (a) fully included in class and an e participant in curricular activities; (b) receives specialist support within class; (c) withdrawn from ordinary class for specialist work; (d) part-time in special class and part-time in ordinary class; (e) full-time in special class in mainstream school; (f) part-time in special school and part-time in mainstream school. The first option requires all teachers to be competent in teaching children with special educational needs and represents a considerable challenge to many schools. Hegarty commented that the special class option corresponded to little more than locational integration. It is clear that the continuum of integration arrangements is simply a way of enabling us to understand a very complex reality. The process of integration does not usually progress smoothly across the continuum from segregation to social and then to curricular integration, as the range of variables involved in this transition is too complex. Such variables include a country's special education policy, the administration structure, school organisation and the attitudes of teachers and pupils.

It is generally acknowledged that to ensure the success of integration, highly structured and well-planned initiatives are required. A number of approaches evolved that were designed to facilitate the participation of pupils with various disabilities in the mainstream of school life. These include specific programmes such as 'Special Friends', which aimed to assist peer interaction (Voeltz et al. 1983), and classroom organisation that encourages cooperative learning strategies for all pupils. The Special Friends programme was a systematic, structured peer interaction programme for pupils with and without a general learning disability. The ultimate aim of the programme was to prepare both groups of pupils for the transition to integrated educational provision. Peer interaction took place in leisure time within school, and activities were geared to develop positive, mutually rewarding personal relationships between both groups of pupils. While supporting the social skill development of pupils with a general learning disability, the emphasis within the programme focused on peer exchange in preference to peer instruction.

The traditional emphasis on competition within classrooms was believed to be particularly harmful to the success of those children of lower ability or those who had a general learning disability. The concept of cooperative learning was developed as an alternative. Arranging pupils in groups and instructing them to work together will not automatically create cooperative learning. Johnson and Johnson (2004) maintained that it was necessary to create a positive interdependence among the pupils involved for cooperative learning to succeed. Positive interdependence was reinforced when pupils were taught how to support one another's efforts to learn. Cooperative classroom structures that included pupils with and without a general learning disability improved the social acceptance of pupils with a general learning disability and resulted in more positive interactions among both groups. Peer tutoring has also been beneficial in developing integration programmes. However, the traditional notion of peer tutoring as more able pupils supporting less able pupils in curriculum-related tasks needed to be revised. Pupils with special educational needs must be given opportunities to reciprocate the teaching and social interaction given by their peers in ordinary classes. Otherwise, deficit models of need and dependency will be reinforced.

Hegarty (1993b) reviewed the research literature on integration and identified three broad trends: investigations of efficacy of segregated/integrated provision; features of successful integration programmes; and the centrality of attitudinal factors. Early research, particularly in the US, focused on the efficacy of integrated or segregated provision in the areas of academic and social and emotional development. Given the difficulties in comparing the two types of provision and the variability within both, it is hardly surprising that the results of these studies were generally inconclusive. However, as Hegarty (1993b: 198) points out: 'The case for integration does not depend solely on empirical claims regarding its superior efficacy; there are also substantial moral arguments.' Unless segregated provision is demonstrably superior to integrated provision, it is difficult to justify its existence. The often highly politicised arguments between proponents of integrated and segregated provision dominated the 1980s and the real educational needs of children were sometimes relegated to second place in this extremely charged debate. Hegarty concluded: 'There has to be a presumption in favour of integration and, in the absence of decisive countervailing evidence, it must be regarded as a central principle governing provision' (p. 198).

Successful integration programmes share a number of common features. Ensuring access to the curriculum is critical and involves the differentiation of objectives, of materials and of teaching methodologies. A modified curriculum may be appropriate in certain situations, though care must be exercised that this does not result in lowered expectations for these pupils. Involving the pupil in taking responsibility for their own learning combined with a careful match between learning needs and teaching strategies has proved effective. The importance of ongoing collaboration between classroom teachers, support teachers and parents cannot be overemphasised. Positive teacher attitudes and expectations have been critical factors in successful integration programmes.

However, according to Avramidis and Norwich's (2002) extensive review of teacher attitudes towards integration/inclusion, positive teacher attitudes were not necessarily the norm. Teacher willingness to implement integration programmes were influenced by the nature of the child's disability/educational difficulties. Favourable attitudes were apparent towards those children with mild disabilities or physical/sensory impairments. Teachers appear to be negatively disposed towards those children who have more severe disabilities or those who display behaviour difficulties. These attitudes appear to emanate in the teachers' lack of experience in working with these children and consequent lack of confidence in managing the classroom environment. Teachers also feared being left on their own to deal with this situation, so the quality of support available was considered critical. Positive teacher experiences in implementing integration programmes produced more positive attitudes towards the whole integration process.

Despite the enabling legislation and ground-breaking national and international reports, it was evident by the 1990s that progress towards integration varied widely, both between and within countries. It appeared that bringing about the change from segregated to integrated provision had proved more difficult than the proponents of integration had anticipated. Hegarty (1993b) observed that general support for integration had not led to extensive integration because of the inherent difficulties in changing long-established patterns of provision and inadequate progress in changing provision in mainstream schools. Lewis (1995: 4) commented that the term 'integration' was increasingly used 'in a narrow sense of placement only' and concluded that 'placement in a mainstream school is a necessary, but not sufficient, condition for realising the goals of integration'. It became clear that successful integration would require a radical overhaul of existing provision and a reorientation of teaching, curricula and accreditation to match the learning needs of all children. There was evidence that some groups of children with disabilities (physical/sensory) were making more progress in mainstream than others, including those children with emotional/behavioural difficulties and moderate/severe general learning disabilities. It appeared that mainstream schools were increasingly of the view that there were limits to the types of children that could be successfully integrated. There has been a growing acceptance that 'integration is in the end a matter of school reform. It entails creating schools that respond to students' individual differences within a common framework' (Hegarty 1993b: 199).

Changing the agenda

In the late 1980s and early 1990s there was growing dissatisfaction with what was perceived as inadequate progress in realising the goals of the integration movement. In many cases, it appeared that the children with special educational needs were expected to conform to mainstream expectations and the process was characterised 'as resembling assimilation rather than real integration' (Carpenter and Shevlin 2004: 82). In effect, this assimilation model meant that mainstream settings often remained relatively unchanged and as a result integration efforts focused particularly on those groups of children with disabilities (principally physical/sensory) deemed the least difficult to include. There was a gradual realisation that the integration movement had failed to achieve its aims and mainstream schools could not guarantee equitable access for children with disabilities. A new paradigm was needed.

The inclusion movement originated in Canada and the United States in the mid to late 1980s as there was a concerted effort to develop programmes to include all children with disabilities in mainstream classrooms. Since then the inclusion movement has gained considerable momentum. International bodies such as the United Nations and UNESCO have made a significant contribution to the development of the concept of inclusive education.

Major international documents have both reflected and supported the moves towards inclusive schooling for children with disabilities and/or special educational needs. The United Nations Convention on the Rights of the Child (1989) reinforced the human rights perspective and called for the child to be enabled through education to achieve the 'fullest possible social integration and individual development' (Article 23). In addition, Article 12 is unequivocal in demanding that all agencies that work with children and young people take account of the views and ideas expressed by children in relation to all decisions which have a direct bearing upon their lives. This has particular relevance for children with disabilities and/or special educational needs who in their educational experiences have often been cast in a passive and dependent role. Prior to a special session on the rights of children at the United Nations General Assembly in New York in 2002, an invited group of young people from around the world called for fundamental educational reform that would guarantee equal opportunities and access to quality education that is free and compulsory. Increasingly, including children with disabilities in mainstream schools became an essential element in guaranteeing equality of opportunity for these children. This was reaffirmed in Article 6 of the Standard Rules on the Equalization of Opportunities for Persons with Disabilities, passed by the United Nations in 1993: 'States should recognise the principle of equal primary, secondary and tertiary educational opportunities for children, youth and adults with disabilities. They should ensure that the education of persons with disabilities is an integral part of the education system.'

The Salamanca Statement (1994) produced by United Nations Educational, Scientific and Cultural Organization (UNESCO) reinforced the human rights perspective in relation to education for children with disabilities and/or special educational needs. It was argued that the concept of special needs education needed to be expanded considerably to 'include all children who, for whatever reason, are failing to benefit from school' (p. 15). The notion that learning difficulties could be solely attributed to the child was explicitly rejected:

> It is clear that the origins of their difficulties lie not just in themselves but also in the social environments in which they are living. The task for the future is to identify ways in which the school as part of that social environment can create better learning opportunities for all children and by this means to address the challenge that the most pervasive source of learning difficulties is the school system itself (p. 15).

Support for inclusive schooling was unequivocal and viewed as an essential contribution to the creation of a more socially inclusive society: 'Regular schools with this inclusive orientation are the most effective means of combating discriminatory attitudes, creating welcoming communities, building an inclusive society and achieving education for all' (p. 10). Inclusion should no longer be an option to be dispensed on a 'grace and favour' basis. UNESCO's Salamanca Statement and the subsequent Framework for Action have had a profound influence on policy and practice in many countries. The inclusion agenda became firmly established in international consciousness and debate focused ever more clearly on the question of how to best include children with disabilities and/or special educational needs rather than whether, when or why this should be done.

The Centre for Studies of Inclusive Education (CSIE, 2002) expressed the principles of the inclusion philosophy in the following terms:

- All children have the right to learn and play together;
- Children should not be devalued or discriminated against by being excluded or sent away because of their disability or learning difficulty;
- There are no legitimate reasons to separate children for the duration of their schooling. They belong together rather than need to be protected from one another.

Despite intensive debate around the notion of inclusion, no commonly agreed definition of inclusion has emerged. Definitions have focused on many aspects of the efforts to achieve inclusive schooling, for example, how inclusion differs from its predecessor, integration, and the ways in which inclusive schooling can foster greater personal interaction. Other definitions concentrate on how inclusion involves a transformation of existing mainstream systemic provision and school organisation, curricula and pedagogies. Thomas and O'Hanlon (2004) emphasise that 'inclusive education is really about extending the comprehensive ideal in education. Those who talk about it are therefore less concerned with children's supposed special educational needs … and more concerned with developing an education system in which equity is striven for and diversity welcomed' (series editors' preface).

The move towards inclusive schooling has involved a radical shift in the philosophy underpinning policy and practice and one consequence of this rapid change has been that 'philosophical thought outpaces practice' (Florian et al. 1998: 1). The terms 'integration' and 'inclusion' are often used interchangeably, though there are considerable differences in philosophy and practice between the two concepts. Integration has generally been conceived of as making additional arrangements (teaching/support/assistive technology) for a specific group of pupils labelled as having special educational needs, though there was minimal change to the overall school organisation.

Educational inclusion, on the other hand, involves a radical restructuring of the education system to enable all children to participate and achieve within mainstream settings:

> … educational inclusion, which we see in terms of the presence, participation and achievement of all students in local mainstream schools, rather than simply focusing on any one group of vulnerable learners. This means that we see the task of inclusion as being essentially transformative, requiring better use of available resources to improve policies and practices. It also leads us

to argue that existing arrangements, at all levels of the education system create barriers for learners (Ainscow et al. 2003: 230).

In essence, the movement towards inclusive schooling represents an effort to advance the human rights agenda, identify barriers to inclusion for all marginalised groups and create responsive schools within a more inclusive society. This entails a move away from focusing on children with special educational needs and special education per se towards a focus on more equitable educational provision for all children:

> ... the history of inclusion is the history of these struggles for an educational system which served the interests of communities, and which does not exclude anyone within those communities. It needs to trace its roots within community and comprehensive education as well as within the struggles for rights of women, black people, gay people and disabled people and other groups whose participation is made conditional and vulnerable. The history of inclusion does not take you back to special education (Booth 2000: 64).

Few would disagree with the rights-based philosophy that asserts the entitlement of children with special educational needs to the same educational opportunities as their peers. However, difficulties have arisen in attempting to translate these principles into practice. Existing special education policies are based on a within-child deficit model that emphasises diagnosis, assessment and specialised teaching to meet individual needs. Also, as Florian et al. (1998: 3) observed, 'it is needs-led provision which characterises special needs legislation as well as other policies.' As a result, there are inherent difficulties in developing inclusive schooling when provision is determined on an individual needs basis. Critics of inclusion have challenged the view of inclusion as indisputable moral imperative and argue that 'the rights of the child to have maximum access to mainstream education need to be balanced by their right to an effective education, appropriate to their needs' (Frederickson and Cline 2002: 73).

Supporters of inclusion have sometimes been accused of indulging in high-flown rhetoric that bears little relation to the reality of the classroom. The Index for Inclusion (Booth et al. 2000) was developed in the United Kingdom and represented one attempt to give practical support to schools in the development of inclusive approaches. The index 'is concerned with improving educational attainments through inclusive practice' (p. 7) and involves a process of self-review by the school. Inclusion and exclusion are examined through three linked aspects of school life: creating inclusive cultures, producing inclusive policies and evolving inclusive practices. The index 'focuses on all aspects of school life and is concerned with the participation of all members of a school's communities' (p. 12). Within the index, the concept 'special educational needs' is not used and the term 'barriers to learning and participation' is used instead. The authors believe that the label 'special educational needs' leads to lowered expectations by focusing on the educational difficulties experienced by one group of children and 'may obscure barriers to learning and participation that occur at all levels in the system and those developments in school cultures, policies and practices that will minimise educational difficulties for all students' (p. 13).

In their review of the index from the perspective of early years educators, Clough and Nutbrown (2003: 90) commented that the index enabled schools to evaluate the strengths and shortcomings in their inclusive practice and address 'aspects of gender, class, race, religion, sexuality, social class as much as learning difficulty or disability'.

There appears to be general agreement that quality is the crucial factor in determining the effectiveness of any inclusion programme. In response to this, researchers have attempted to identify the characteristics of successful inclusion programmes. Critical factors include participation of the whole school community in developing shared vision and practice; collaborative teamwork and planned time for teachers to work together; effective child/parental/family involvement; and adaptation of existing curricula and instructional practice (Frederickson and Cline 2002). However, supporters of inclusion face the constantly recurring question of whether inclusion programmes can fully provide for the individual needs of children who have special educational needs. Doubts have been raised about the degree of individualisation and differentiation within inclusion programmes. Promoting inclusion at classroom level has involved a variety of strategies, including cooperative learning, peer tutoring and in-class support from extra adults. However, as Frederickson and Cline (2002: 95) observe:

> ... no single, specific strategy is going to provide 'the' answer. In fact, there is the risk that by concentrating on particular strategies they will become 'bolt-on' additions for the 'special' children. By contrast, in an inclusive school they will be seen as important ways in which access and participation can increasingly be achieved for all children and they will be used in a range of contexts.

Developing inclusive education programmes in our schools involves moving beyond the traditional barriers that prevented the full participation of many children who have been marginalised and at risk of school failure for a variety of reasons, including special educational needs, socio-economic disadvantage or socio-cultural differences. Essentially, as Barton (2000: 53) says, inclusion is 'a political issue because of the way in which it may be connected to wider inequalities in society'. Inclusion involves transforming existing school capacity to respond effectively to diversity and is not simply a reformulation of traditional special education programmes. However, for inclusion to be effective, 'it will be important to monitor individual students' progress on an ongoing basis in order to ensure that they receive their full rights – an education appropriate to their needs as well as an education in an inclusive setting' (Frederickson and Cline 2002: 97).

Ireland

So, where does Ireland sit on the segregation–integration–inclusion continuum? For a number of reasons it is very difficult to give a definitive answer. In terms of recent policy and legislation Ireland has very clearly adopted an inclusive position. However, in practice, special education in Ireland involves a broad continuum of provision, including elements of segregation, integration and inclusion. This is hardly surprising when we consider the context of rapid changes in policy and provision in the recent past. The implications of this policy shift are still being worked out at both school and system level. Undoubtedly, recent policy and legislation (see Chapter 4) will have a significant impact on the thinking about and actual delivery of special educational provision for many years to come.

So what do we know about inclusion within an Irish context? Rose et al. (2010) reviewed Irish research on inclusion in the first decade of the 21st century. The authors identified four key themes in this review: policy, provision, experience and outcomes. Under policy, the authors considered evidence of the development and implementation of policy related to special and inclusive education at both national and local level.

In the past two decades Irish policy and legislation have established the foundation for significant advances in understanding and responding appropriately to special educational needs. As Griffin and Shevlin (2007) pointed out, reports from the Special Education Review Committee (SERC) (1993), the Commission on the Status of People with Disabilities (1996), and the Education Act (1998) paved the way for the substantial Education for Persons with Special Educational Needs (EPSEN) Act 2004 which aims to develop inclusive learning environments. The research commentary on policy has tended to critique the psycho-medical model underpinning these developments (McDonnell 2003b, Kinsella and Senior 2008) and advocated a cultural shift away from the traditional focus on individual deficits towards more fundamental environmental change. MacGiolla Phádraig (2007) suggests that while recent legislation has promoted the concept of inclusive schooling, the reality in schools is somewhat different.

Rose et al. (2010) observe that Irish research has tended to be dominated by debates about the principles of inclusive schooling while there has been a narrow focus on issues concerning provision for children and young people who have special educational needs. Classroom practice has tended to be analysed in relation to classroom support (Logan 2006, O'Neill and Rose 2008); curriculum differentiation (Coffey 2004, Day 2005) (see Chapter 9); and implementation of programmes for pupils with diagnosed needs (Scott 2009, Ware et al. 2005).

There is general agreement that there has been a significant investment in resources for special educational provision, such as increased numbers of support staff. However, Kinsella and Senior (2008) believe that the development of inclusive provision requires further refining, with a focus on the availability of expertise within schools and the growth of integrated service provision at school level. Drudy and Kinsella (2009) argue that inclusion encompasses more than special educational needs and that serious consideration must be given to increasing school capacity to deal with diversity, including children and young people from different ethnic backgrounds.

Developing inclusive provision for a child with an intellectual disability in a multi-grade class of 30 pupils in a rural four-teacher mainstream primary school was examined by Ring and Travers (2005). The authors explored curricular and social access, the child's perception, and the effect of this child's inclusion on his peers. Teachers agreed that, although an individualised programme had been developed, there were great difficulties in including the child in common curricular goals with his peers. They also believed that specialist pedagogy was required and that they lacked the necessary expertise. The child in question appeared reasonably happy in school though the authors observed that he was not fully included socially. The authors recommended that collaboration between classroom and resource teachers needed to be actively facilitated and opportunities provided for professional development to: 'support a whole-school response to inclusion, with an emphasis on inclusive pedagogical practices' (p. 55).

Travers et al.'s (2010) study focused on inclusion provision in relation to students with special educational needs, minority ethnic and minority language students, and students experiencing educational disadvantage. Schools reported significant difficulties in developing inclusive provision for these groups, including assessment issues, in particular: 'the difficulty of making a distinction between a learning and a language difficulty; access to psychological assessment and CPD (Continuing Professional Development) in relation to assessment; the link between assessment and the allocation of resources; and inadequate formative assessment practices in schools' (p. ix). Schools were very concerned about the lack of coordination between services and inadequate supports for transition between different levels of education. In addition, student behaviour difficulties, absenteeism and lack of appropriate supports for these students constituted major barriers to inclusion. At classroom level teachers expressed concerns about their capacity to differentiate the curriculum appropriately to meet the individual needs of students. Lack of time to plan individual programmes was cited as another major barrier to inclusion. There was evidence that the case study schools had adopted very flexible approaches to delivering special educational provision, including intensive within-class support for literacy and numeracy in Junior Infant classes; team teaching shared between a special educational needs team and classroom teachers; the development of a team approach to inclusion involving whole-school approaches.

There has been increased recognition from the DES that post-primary schooling can present considerable challenges for the development of inclusive learning environments, in part because of the focus on the preparation of pupils for state examinations. The DES published *Inclusion of Students with Special Educational Needs: Post-Primary Guidelines* in 2007 which 'advocate a whole-school approach to inclusion and provide practical guidance on roles, responsibilities and collaboration for inclusion as well as best practice strategies at the level of the classroom for individual students' (Winter and O' Raw 2010: 7). Within these guidelines the DES outlined effective strategies to improve the teaching of students in an inclusive school:

- a variety of teaching strategies and approaches
- clear learning objectives outlined at the beginning of the lesson, reference made to them during the lesson, and a review with students of what has been learned at the end of the lesson
- formative assessment strategies for identifying students' progress which are used to inform teaching approaches
- the content of lessons matched to the needs of the students and to their levels of ability
- multi-sensory approaches to learning and teaching
- materials, including concrete materials, appropriate to the needs, ages, interests and aptitudes of students
- deviations from lesson plans when unexpected learning opportunities arise, which do not result in the loss of the lesson's original objectives
- appropriate time allowed for practice, reinforcement and application of new knowledge and skills in practical situations
- students are reinforced and affirmed for knowledge and skills learned
- opportunities are in place throughout the curriculum to enable students to develop language and communication skills (e.g. listening, speaking, reading, writing)
- opportunities are taken throughout the curriculum to develop personal and social skills
- students are encouraged to explore links with other areas of the curriculum
- homework is designed to consolidate and extend, to promote independent learning, to monitor individual students' and class progress, and to evaluate the effectiveness of the teaching and learning (DES 2007: 105)

Irish research on the schooling experiences of pupils with SEN has tended to focus on access issues and parental perspectives.

Parents of children with Down Syndrome in the Shevlin et al. study (2003) perceived that school access for their child was conditional and dependent on the goodwill of the school: 'You were always cap-in-hand, as in "I'm not entitled" or she wasn't entitled to the same treatment and it's the same thing about approaching schools' (p. 7). However, there was evidence that when children were admitted to the school, teachers made considerable efforts to differentiate the curriculum to meet the individual learning needs of the child: 'Initially we had problems getting in there, but once she got in there and once they saw her, they actually started coming up with very brilliant ideas and techniques and everything to work with her on her reading and her maths and her social skills and all sorts of programmes and they actually started to experiment themselves' (p. 7). Flatman-Watson's (2009) study of access issues for children with an intellectual disability and/or developmental disability suggested that parents often encountered serious problems in gaining access for their children to the local school. Schools justified the deferral and/or refusal of entry on the basis of insufficient resources, lack of trained personnel and the belief that the child's perceived 'care' needs or behavioural difficulties could not be accommodated within the school.

To date, the reported experiences of pupils with SEN in Ireland appear to be 'characterised by a lack of understanding of how best to ensure that they gain appropriate access to teaching and learning in schools' (Rose et al. 2010: 366). In the Kenny et al. study (2003a) pupils who had physical or sensory disabilities reported that despite positive aspects to their experiences of schooling they had encountered difficulties with the built environment, curriculum access and social interaction with their peers. There were examples of teacher-adapted activities to ensure curricular access: 'We'd pair up and my partner used to do all the physical work. I just couldn't do it. I couldn't hold a glass of water' (p. 149), while others became passive observers rather than active participants: 'In science, using things on the bench. I just sat down and watched' (p. 149). Rose and Shevlin (2004) reported similar experiences for pupils with special educational needs who, due to lowered teacher expectations, were prevented from achieving appropriate accreditation.

Rose et al. (2010) concluded that there had been little systematic research in Ireland concerning outcomes for children and young people who have special educational needs. Often when outcomes are reported the focus tends to be on social outcomes as described in the Hardiman et al. (2009) study of the social competence of children with moderate intellectual disability aged 4–16 years in both segregated and inclusive settings. The authors argue that the lack of empirical studies on the impact of inclusive provision on pupil outcomes severely limits the development of future inclusion policies. Murphy (2008) commented that schools, in many instances, are uncertain about how to guarantee curricular access and accreditation for pupils with SEN within the prescribed curriculum. One result can be school disaffection on the part of pupils who have SEN and the heightened risk of early school leaving.

Until relatively recently research within the area of special educational needs policy and provision tended to be patchy and quite fragmented. Recently, however, the NCSE has adopted a strategic approach to research in this area and has commissioned a considerable volume of evidence-based research on special educational needs policy and provision within an Irish context. Initially this research has focused on developing a strong international literature base, providing models of good practice and examining the implications for Irish policy and provision in relation to special educational needs. The literature reviews to date have focused on policy and provision in relation to children and young people who are deaf and hard-of-hearing (Marschark and Spencer 2009a); blind or visually impaired (Douglas et al. 2009); on the autistic spectrum (Parsons et al. 2009).

In addition, there has been published research examining inclusion principles and practice (Winter and O'Raw 2010) (discussed in this chapter); identification and assessment of special educational needs (Desforges and Lindsay 2010) (see Chapter 7); the role of special schools and special classes (Ware et al. 2009) (see Chapter 6).

More specifically, the NCSE initiated discussions with its Consultative Forum (a statutory committee established under the Education for Persons with Special Educational Needs (EPSEN) Act 2004 to support and advise the Council) in relation to inclusion policy and practice within Irish education. An international literature review on inclusion policy and practice was developed to support this consultative process (Winter and O'Raw 2010). There was general agreement that in accord with international literature there is no one agreed definition of inclusion. However, the Consultative Forum decided that a combination of definitions contained in the UNESCO (2005) report and the DES (2007) report would be appropriate:

Inclusion is defined as a process of:

- addressing and responding to the diversity of needs of learners through enabling participation in learning, cultures, and communities, and
- removing barriers to education through the accommodation and provision of appropriate structures and arrangements, to enable each learner to achieve the maximum benefit from his/her attendance at school. (Winter and O'Raw 2010: 39)

Concluding comments

In conclusion, it is clear that Ireland is facing a considerable challenge in developing inclusive provision for children with disabilities and/or special educational needs. Some pieces of the complex jigsaw are in place – enabling legislation and substantial increases in resources, and there is evidence that the education system is beginning to develop responses to increased diversity. However, we can conclude that inclusion is an ongoing process aimed at removing barriers and ensuring that those groups at risk of marginalisation become full participants in the education system.

Discussion points

1　'Inclusion is fine in theory but extremely difficult to implement in practice.' Discuss.
2　Creating an inclusive learning environment involves considerable changes in the ways schools and teachers think about and respond to special educational needs.
　(a)　What existing school practices tend to disadvantage pupils with special educational needs?

(b) What types of teaching strategies would help the student with special educational needs to improve?

3 Can full inclusion ever be achieved in a society that has in the past and continues to marginalise particular groups?

4 Academic competition is an increasing feature of our schools and children and young people with special educational needs will probably not fare too well in this context. How can we ensure that they can achieve certification without unduly restricting their curriculum?

Section 2
Beginning the Process

Chapter 6

Addressing Core Issues in Special Education

Learning outcomes/objectives

On completion of this chapter, the reader will be able to:

* Critically discuss the meaning of special education and explore the philosophical and practical implications of adopting a particular understanding of this concept.
* Outline how special schools and special classes form part of the continuum of special educational provision in Ireland.
* Describe how school leadership is an essential element in developing effective special educational provision.
* Describe approaches that support self-esteem building and the promotion of vigilance in combating the failure cycle in schools.
* Identify and describe skills and strategies that value communication, collegiality and collaboration and the fostering of independent learning for all.
* Evaluate the argument that there is a 'special' pedagogy for delivering special educational provision.

Introduction

Within this chapter we will consider core issues in relation to understanding the concept of special educational needs, how this concept has changed over time and which children are included in the legal definition of special educational needs and are entitled to special educational provision. We will also examine how a child's failure to grasp basic concepts can lead to the child becoming embedded in a failure cycle in relation to learning. This chapter will also explore some of the key general areas of relevance for the teacher/educator in considering what it means to become knowledgeable and skilful in special education in Ireland in the twenty-first century. The reader is invited to keep in mind the following central question: in what ways, if any, do the processes of special education differ from the exercise of education in general?

Not very long ago, there would have been little ambiguity about what 'special education' meant. The ordinary person and the educationalist alike would have understood it as a specialist form of teaching aimed at people who could not, by reason of their 'handicaps', be accommodated in the mainstream system. In regular education, pupils and students were expected to progress through a set curriculum of learning within an understood timeframe and without significant deviation from the norm. Difficulties of a short-term and specific nature might be managed by a 'remedial' approach – a temporary instructional lay-by from which one could return to the main flow of educational traffic in due course. For all others, there was 'special education'.

Insights into and clearer understanding of the nature of teaching and learning over the past generation have led many to challenge the conceptual consensus previously accepted on special education. The emergence of an appreciation of disability and 'special needs' as social constructs shaped by societal attitudes has led to a sharper critique of the traditional 'medical model' of disabilities and special needs whereby the problem originated within the child and 'treatment' required a specialist and expert response. In contrast, the social model of disability has brought focus on a more accurate understanding of 'handicap' as a barrier or obstacle placed in the way of a person achieving their maximum potential in learning. The responsibility is on the agents of society – the managers of cities, transport systems, housing, employment and education – to remove or minimise these barriers for all citizens. This broader appreciation, informed in particular by the people directly involved and their immediate advocates, leads us to use the term 'handicap' only in the societal context and not as a descriptor of the nature of a person.

Concepts of special educational need

The concept of 'special educational need' emerged from the Warnock Report (DES, England and Wales 1978) in the United Kingdom and was an attempt to move away from the traditional categories of disability used in special education. The Warnock Report marked a significant turning point in the thinking about special education. Until then, special education tended to be on the periphery of the mainstream education system and was seen as the responsibility of specialist teachers and professionals such as educational psychologists and occupational therapists. The Warnock Report produced a number of conclusions that have affected the development of special education policy and provision, initially in the United Kingdom, and later in Ireland.

The Warnock Report first used the phrase 'special educational need' and stated that anything up to 20 per cent of the school population could experience some type of special educational need at some stage in their school career. Previously it was believed that special education was appropriate for a much smaller proportion of school pupils (2 per cent) generally defined as having some type of disability and provision usually consisted of special schooling or placement in special classes in mainstream schools.

Eleven categories of disability had been defined in the Education Act 1944 (UK), including 'varying degrees of blindness or deafness, physical impairment, speech defects, educational "subnormality" and "maladjustment"' (Beveridge 1999: 2). Educational provision was closely tied to the category of disability and as a result category-specific schools for children were developed, including educationally subnormal ESN (mild), educationally subnormal ESN (moderate), schools for the blind, schools for the deaf and various schools for different types of physical disability.

The Warnock Report criticised this dominant policy of categorisation that determined educational provision and suggested an alternative view. Categorising pupils according to disability was deemed to be educationally inappropriate and often stigmatising. We cannot assume, as the categorisation process does, that all children who have, for example, cerebral palsy have the same educational and learning needs. Also, knowing that a child has Down syndrome will tell us very little about what type of educational interventions are appropriate until we have examined the child's learning strengths and his/her problems in learning in greater depth. In fact, there is a wide variation in the learning needs experienced by children who have the same type of disability.

The Warnock Report adopted a wider perspective and defined special education as consisting of 'any form of additional help, wherever it is provided ... to overcome educational difficulty' (DES, England and Wales 1978: para. 1.10). It was also proposed that there was a continuum of individual learning need among all pupils and that the existing categories of disability should be abolished and replaced with the generic term 'learning difficulties' (special educational needs) to refer to all pupils who for whatever reasons require additional educational support. It was recognised that difficulties in learning are an integral part of school life, as many pupils may struggle at some stage of their school careers. It is only when these difficulties are so severe and insurmountable without substantial extra help that the pupil may be deemed to need special educational provision that is extra to what is on offer in the ordinary classroom.

Three dimensions of special educational need were identified in the Warnock Report: 'special educational needs might be long-lasting or short-term, specific to particular aspects of learning or more general, and will also vary in the degree to which they affect a child's learning' (Beveridge 1999: 3). The degree of learning difficulties could be described as 'mild', 'moderate', 'severe' or 'specific'. 'Special educational need' is a fluid term that clearly implies that any child might experience difficulties in learning in relation to a certain task in particular circumstances rather than saying that there was a defined group of children who had special educational needs.

This view was naturally controversial, as it challenged the thinking underpinning the provision of special education. It represented an attempt to move away from the perception that the causes of any learning difficulty were solely due to within-child factors such as limited cognitive ability, a physical disability or a speech difficulty. The role of within-child factors was acknowledged, though the concept of special educational need focused on the interaction between the child and the learning environment experienced by the child. Thomas and Loxley (2001) observed that attributing difficulties in learning to within-child factors failed to take account of the complex social and cultural factors involved. This insight has had a profound influence on the thinking about how learning difficulties are caused and the role of the learning environment.

Since the publication of the Warnock Report there has been a growing acceptance that difficulties in learning arise from a combination of within-child factors and aspects of the child's learning environment: 'It allows us to view children's needs as a result of a mismatch between the knowledge, skills and experiences they bring to their learning situations and the demands that are made of them' (Beveridge 1999: 4). This is an essentially optimistic view of learning difficulties that enables schools to develop appropriate responses that support children, minimise and perhaps overcome certain problems and even prevent other difficulties from arising. The traditional outlook on learning difficulties left little space for optimism, as learning difficulties were seen as an intrinsic part of the child and as a result the room for progress in learning was believed to be very limited.

These two approaches to understanding learning difficulties are evident in special education policy and provision since the Warnock Report. The traditional perspective has been characterised as the 'individual pupil view' and asserts that learning difficulties are best understood by examining individual differences between children. Solity (1993) believes that this approach is based on untested assumptions: 'it is often assumed that children have had appropriate learning opportunities; that the teaching available has been effective with their peers but not them; and that the discrepancy cannot be attributed to starting school with lower attainments than peers or to widely differing preschool experiences' (cited in Frederickson and Cline 2002: 39).

The alternative view, often referred to as the 'environmental demands' approach, is based on the assumption that 'children's current attainments reflect the nature of previous learning experiences and that children will learn when taught appropriately' (Frederickson and Cline 2002: 40). This approach attributes learning failure to factors such as poor classroom organisation, unproductive teaching strategies and an insufficient match between task demands and learner skills/knowledge.

Frederickson and Cline (2002) maintain that the 'environmental demands' approach does not take account of the variety of individual responses to learning difficulties and teaching interventions. Different children respond to teaching in diverse ways. Some children will display different strengths and discover ways of overcoming the cycle of failure in learning. Others, despite sustained and skilled teacher support, will appear to make little progress. It was understandable that in the wake of the Warnock Report there would be an increased awareness of the importance of the learning environment in understanding the causes of learning difficulties/special educational needs. However, the reasons for learning difficulties are complex and probably lie in a combination of both approaches, and this has been described as an interactional analysis of special educational needs that views 'the level of need as a result of a complex interaction between the child's strengths and weaknesses, the level of support available and the appropriateness of the education being provided' (Frederickson and Cline 2002: 42).

We also need to distinguish between special needs and special educational needs. Sometimes these terms are used interchangeably and this can cause confusion. A child may have special needs, but this does not imply that he/she automatically has special educational needs. For example, a child who has a physical disability may require assistive technology, e.g. ICT software programmes, to enable her/him to gain access to the curriculum, but in no way does this mean that the child requires substantial additional support in comparison to his/her peers and cannot be said to have special educational needs. Rose and Howley (2007) warn of the danger of automatically deciding that because a child has a disability he/she will also automatically have a special educational need. Teachers obviously need to know the educational implications of a particular disability such as cerebral palsy, but they have to be very careful that 'the low expectations which are often fuelled by disabling labels can lead to under-achievement and a denial of entitlement to appropriate learning opportunities' (Rose and Howley 2007). In addition, children from ethnic minority groups where English is a second language may require language support, but this does not necessarily mean that they have special educational needs.

Some commentators have observed that far from abolishing categories, special educational needs has become the new all-embracing category. Others have been concerned to rename and redefine special educational needs in order to capture the essence of the interactive nature of learning difficulties. Hart (1996), for example, replaced 'special educational need' with 'individual educational need' and Booth (1998) preferred to focus on identifying barriers, both individual and environmental, to learning.

Who are the children with special educational needs?

Obtaining precise figures of the numbers of children and young people with disabilities and/or special educational needs within schools has been fraught with difficulty. The NCSE has commissioned a national prevalence study that will provide valuable information for special educational planning and provision (Banks and McCoy 2011, forthcoming). In the NCSE *Implementation Report* (2006) it was estimated that up to 18 per cent of children and young people had a disability and/or special educational need. There is evidence from comprehensive parent and teacher reports in the current Growing up in Ireland longitudinal study that the prevalence of disability/special educational need can range between 20–25 per cent of nine-year-olds in primary schools (Banks and McCoy 2011, forthcoming).

There has been an increased concern to adopt a broader definition of special educational needs to include any child who experiences a learning difficulty of whatever kind during their school career. The traditional narrow definition of special educational need that focused on categories of disability was becoming increasingly untenable as government policy and provision shifted towards developing inclusive learning environments for all children. Greater numbers of children who had traditionally attended special schools or self-contained special classes were attending their local mainstream school. It became clear that schools needed to adapt and restructure existing educational provision to include these children. Schools faced the challenge of developing their capacity to respond appropriately to this increased diversity. This has involved greater attention to developing whole-school responses, differentiating the curriculum and creating support structures to address special educational needs among pupils.

An all-encompassing definition of special educational needs is appropriate at school level to ensure that schools can respond to the range of special educational needs experienced by pupils, no matter how minor and temporary or serious and long-lasting these learning needs may be. The legal definition of special educational needs, however, is used to decide whether particular children are eligible for special education provision and is intended to address the learning needs of children who experience substantially greater levels of special educational need than their peers.

Within an Irish context, the Special Education Review Committee (1993: 18) decided that pupils with 'special educational needs' included all 'those whose disabilities and/or circumstances prevent or hinder them from benefiting adequately from the education which is normally provided for pupils of the same age, or for whom the education which can generally be provided in the ordinary classroom is not sufficiently challenging'. While the focus of this definition equates disability and special educational needs, there is also the recognition that disability is not the sole cause of special educational needs and, in contrast to the United Kingdom, exceptionally able children are included in the definition. In its definition of special educational needs, the most recent legislation in special education, the Education for Persons with Special Educational Needs (EPSEN) Act 2004, recognises that difficulties in learning cannot be solely attributed to within-child factors: 'a restriction in the capacity of the person to participate in and benefit from education on account of an enduring physical, sensory, mental health or learning disability or any other condition, which results in a person learning differently from a person without that condition'.

These definitions make a distinction between children who experience serious difficulties in learning and require substantial additional support and those who have less serious learning difficulties. The first group of children, in contrast to the latter group, will require a series of interventions, including modified teaching approaches, specialist resources and curriculum modification. Children with less serious difficulties can access a lower level of support through a differentiated curriculum and access to learning support. Those children experiencing serious levels of learning difficulty are usually referred to as having an assessed (usually through a psychological assessment) special educational need. We can obtain an overall national perspective of the numbers of children with assessed special educational needs availing of special educational provision in the primary sector.

Children who have mild general learning disabilities have been assessed by a psychologist and recorded an IQ score in the range of 50 to 70, which is considerably below average. The causes of mild general learning disability are not always evident, though there may be brain damage at birth, but for many there is no apparent cause. These children can be educated in mainstream through a combination of resource support, adapted teaching strategies, differentiated curriculum and appropriate examination procedures.

Children with specific learning disabilities (dyslexia) usually attended mainstream in the past and their difficulties in literacy were attributed to a lack of intelligence, lack of concentration or laziness. 'Specific learning disabilities' is a generic term that includes dyslexia (the most common), a difficulty with reading, writing and spelling; dyscalculia, a difficulty with mathematics; dysgraphia, a difficulty with handwriting; and dyspraxia, a difficulty with motor coordination.

A recent Irish publication (Ball et al. 2006) provides a useful guide to provision for children and young people with dyslexia. The authors assert: 'Educationalists now agree that dyslexia is a fact; while there is still some argument about the prevalence of the difficulty, nobody seriously questions its existence' (p. 1). While educational provision for these children and young people has existed since 1975, it is only in the last decade that significant developments have taken place.

Screening procedures in primary schools are identifying these children at a much earlier stage and it is possible to implement intervention programmes to address their difficulties. When assessed by a psychologist, these children are within the average range of intelligence, but their basic reading, writing and mathematical skills are at or on the second percentile (to qualify for special educational provision). In other words, these children are in the lowest 2 per cent in comparison to their peers on tests of reading, writing and mathematical skills.

Over the last 30 years, special classes in mainstream schools have been established for children with assessed special educational needs. Initially these classes catered for children with mild general learning disabilities, but from Tables 6.1 and 6.2 we can see that a large number of special classes have been established for children who have autistic spectrum disorders and others who have specific speech and language disorders.

Autism is an extremely complex condition and it is not proposed to provide an in-depth analysis here (for fuller discussion, see Chapter 12 of this book and the *Report of the Task Force on Autism*, 2001). However, we can note that there is a triad of impairments associated with autism: social interaction – the child has great difficulty in initiating and maintaining contact with others and may exhibit age-related inappropriate responses; language and communication – the child often has a literal understanding of language and has real difficulties with the social aspects of language, such as turn-taking; imaginative thinking/limited behavioural pattern – the child will often engage in repetitive play activities and have a very narrow range of interests (Carey 2005).

Table 6.1: Mainstream primary schools with special classes for particular categories of SEN

Category of SEN	*Number of schools with special classes
Mild General Learning Disabilities	206
Moderate General Learning Disabilities	14
Severe/Profound General Learning Disabilities	6
Multiple Disabilities	4
Specific Speech and Language Disorder	46
Specific Learning Disabilities	11
Autistic Spectrum Disorders – early intervention classes	6
Autistic Spectrum Disorders	66
Asperger Syndrome	4
Attention Deficit Hyperactivity Disorder	1
Emotional Behavioural Disturbance	9
Severe Emotional Behavioural Disturbance	1
Hearing Impairment	8
Physical Disabilities	2
Total	384

Source: Adapted from Ware et al. (2009: 46).
*Based on figures for 2008 school year

Table 6.2: Special classes and pupil numbers in mainstream primary schools

SEN Designation	*Number of classes	*Total number of pupils
Mild General Learning Disabilities	211	1,512
Autistic Spectrum Disorders	77	349
Specific Speech and Language Disorder	54	333
Moderate General Learning Disabilities	15	71
Specific Learning Disabilities	15	119
Hearing Impairment	10	30

Table 6.2: **(Contd.)**

Emotional Behavioural Disturbance	8	39
Severe and Profound General Learning Disabilities	6	29
Multiple Disabilities	3	13
Severe Emotional Behavioural Disturbance	1	4
Visual Impairment	0	-
Total	**[385]	2,499

Source: Adapted from Ware et al. 2009: 144.
*Based on figures for 2008 school year
**as appears in report

Children with specific speech and language disorders have been assessed by a psychologist and a speech therapist, and while their non-verbal skills are within the average range, their verbal skills are below average. The difficulties experienced by these children are not due to any physical, emotional or hearing difficulties. These children can experience difficulties across a range of communication skills, including spoken language, ability to understand and respond to what is said and capacity to commit information to memory. Limited availability of speech therapy within schools can delay the identification of this difficulty and the establishment of an intervention programme.

The DES inspectorate report, *An Evaluation of Special Classes for Pupils with Specific Speech and Language Disorder* (2006b), provided an overview of educational provision. Fifty-four special classes have been established in forty-five primary schools with a reduced pupil teacher ratio of 7:1. These pupils are enrolled in these classes for one to two years and receive a minimum of four hours of speech and language therapy per day. The inspectorate expressed serious concern that only 42 per cent of pupils had been identified before the age of six and strongly recommended the establishment of more effective early identification procedures to enable the development of early intervention programmes. While many teachers in these classes had extensive teaching experience, fewer than half had specific training in the area of specific speech and language disorders. According to interviewees in the report, participation in the special class had 'a positive impact on the pupils' communication skills, social and emotional development, and behaviour. All noticed the growth in children's confidence and self-esteem, how they interacted and mixed well with peers and how they acquired skills in playing together, sharing, chatting together, engaging in formal conversation and taking turns' (p. 75).

For many years, special schools have been the main providers of special education and these schools tended to be organised on a categorical basis. Children usually spent the whole of their school career in a special school spanning both primary and post-primary and sometimes even pre-school provision. As can be seen from Figure 6.1, which provides a profile of special schools by category of disability, the largest number of schools in any category caters for children who have moderate general learning disabilities.

Children with moderate general learning disabilities have been assessed by a psychologist and score approximately within the 35–49 range on an IQ test. These children can experience severe learning needs across many aspects of the curriculum. This does not mean, however, that they cannot learn. They require concerted and coordinated support from teachers, parents and support staff as well as access to appropriate teaching strategies and a suitable curriculum that will prepare them for life in an adult world.

Figure 6.1: **Profile of special schools by category (N = 115)**

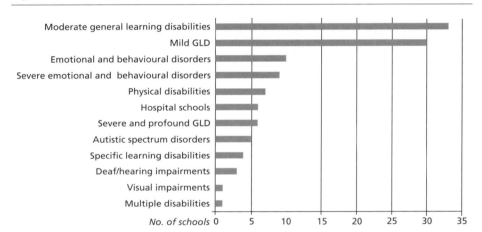

Source: SESS website, Special Schools list. Kenny et al. (2006).

The learning needs of able (often called gifted) pupils were included in the Special Education Review Committee (1993) definition of special educational needs. However, the definition of special educational needs contained in the Education for Persons with Special Educational Needs Act 2004 appears to exclude consideration of able pupils within the remit of the legislation.

The National Council for Curriculum and Assessment has published a set of guidelines for teachers in relation to exceptionally able pupils (2007). The aims of the guidelines are to:

- raise awareness of the needs of exceptionally able students
- support management and teachers to:
  - o audit and review school policy and practice
  - o differentiate the curriculum
  - o develop effective strategies
  - o further develop an inclusive school ethos

- provide models of good practice which support and nurture the development of exceptionally able students (p. 7).

The guidelines highlight that exceptionally able pupils are a very diverse group and while many adapt to their educational and social environment with relatively little effort, others may experience emotional problems and adjustment issues.

Eyre (1997) observed that UK inspectorate reports regularly commented on the lack of challenge and insufficiently high expectations for able pupils in schools. There has been a gradual recognition that traditional definitions of giftedness focused too narrowly on academic achievement and that a multi-dimensional view of giftedness was required. This view would include not only those children and young people with cognitive abilities, but also those with outstanding ability in art, music and sport. Eyre (1997: 7) identified three key components of able pupils who attain outstanding educational achievements:

(i)   innate ability;
(ii) opportunity/support;
(iii) motivation/hard work.

Eyre observed that the greatest obstacle to successful provision for able pupils was inappropriate school and pupil attitudes. When it is 'not cool to be bright', able pupils can underachieve in order to retain credibility with their peer group. It is critical that school policy reflects an understanding of and a commitment to meeting the needs of able pupils. Teachers also require support in developing extension activities as part of a differentiated curriculum.

It should be noted that able pupils can be found among children and young people who have a disability. Eyre gives the example of an eight-year-old with cerebral palsy who is exceptionally able. His speech and co-ordination are both slow and underdeveloped and he uses a computer with an adapted keyboard. However, the materials available through this technology are designed to give basic access. This is totally insufficient to meet his need to express sophisticated ideas. Pupils with disabilities who are exceptionally able often face the difficulty of accessing higher-level tasks that are sufficiently challenging.

Able children can also be located among those children identified as having emotional and behavioural difficulties. Some of the behaviour issues may be due to lack of challenge and consequent boredom and disruption. Positive school attitudes and appropriate curriculum provision can address some of these difficulties. Some children who are exceptionally able may have dyslexia and as a result will require additional support, perhaps technological, to access higher-level and extension tasks.

Eyre commented that effective provision for able children requires 'careful planning, development work and monitoring ... and needs the involvement of a wide variety of staff' (p. vi), a positive school climate and training and support for teachers. While effective provision may be difficult to achieve, Eyre concluded that it is possible within the mainstream school.

Failing to learn and learning to fail

Once it is acknowledged that difficulties in learning are due to complex interacting factors, we can begin to understand how children fail to learn and often, as a result of this experience, learn to fail. When confronted with learning failure, it is often an automatic reaction to focus on what is perceived to be wrong with the child. However, this focus on within-child deficits will at best provide only a partial answer to the task of devising an effective learning environment for the child. Creating an appropriate learning environment will involve consideration of factors outside the child, such as 'quality and type of instruction given, teacher expectations, relevance of work set, classroom environment, interpersonal dynamics within the class social group and rapport with the teacher. These factors are much more amenable to change than are factors within the child or within the family background or culture' (Westwood 1997: 9).

Westwood (1997) describes how experiencing repeated failure to learn can plunge a child into a failure cycle, as illustrated in Figure 6.2.

Failure to learn a basic skill when her/his peers have already mastered it can result in the child lacking confidence in their ability to learn this skill. Consequently, the child may deliberately avoid the task and miss out on opportunities to gain proficiency. Task avoidance can consist of a passive withdrawal by the child or attempts to distract attention by disrupting classroom work. There is also the added risk that the child may become totally disaffected with classroom learning. This child may attribute any successes in learning to factors outside himself/herself, such as luck or teacher help. The child who experiences repeated failure 'can develop the perception that achieving success in learning is completely outside their control no matter what they do' (Frederickson and Cline 2002: 322).

Preventing children from entering the failure cycle in relation to reading forms the focus of the Success for All programme developed in the US by Slavin et al. (1996). Success in the early stages of schooling is usually defined by whether the child has successfully learned to read. Slavin et al. (1996) describe how failure to read can lead to a downward spiral for the child. The child becomes anxious, harbours serious doubts about his or her ability to read and may lack motivation to continue to tackle the task of reading. The Success for All programme is based on the belief that every child can learn: 'We mean this not as wishful thinking or as a rallying cry, but as a practical, attainable reality' (p. 3). Success for All devises intensive early intervention programmes using a range of strategies, approaches and personnel to ensure that children do not enter a failure cycle in relation to reading. The programme has been used extensively and with a significant success rate in schools in socio-economically disadvantaged areas.

Figure 6.2: **Cycle of failure in learning**

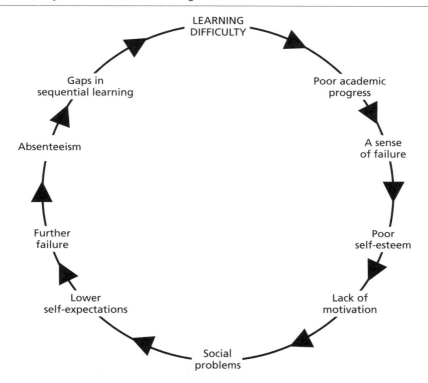

Westwood (1997) pointed out that the only way to break the failure cycle is to structure tasks in a way that enables the child to achieve success. In this way, the child regains the belief in his/her own ability and recognises the improvement that has taken place. Also, the child can begin to attribute his/her success in learning to strategies he/she has developed rather than being overly reliant on outside help or depending on luck.

Two models have emerged that seek to explain why pupils encounter difficulties in learning. The traditional model, often called the deficit model, explains the difficulties in terms of individual pupil deficits. These deficits can be grouped into a number of categories: below-average intelligence; difficulties processing information; problems generalising learning to new situations; struggling to stay on-task; low self-esteem and lack of confidence; and behavioural and emotional reactions to failure. As can be seen from this list, there is the very real risk that the teacher could decide that progress in learning will be almost impossible for this child. However, as Westwood (1997: 11) points out, teacher awareness of these difficulties can inform lesson planning, and further, each of these 'so-called "deficits" has an immediate implication for what we teach and how we teach it'.

Another model takes a more optimistic stance and attributes the difficulties in learning to an inefficient approach to the learning task. Educators have observed that these pupils often have a very ineffective style of learning; weak task-approach skills; employ haphazard strategies; little forward planning; or reflection on own performance. The end result is a high failure rate in tackling learning tasks and low motivation to stay on-task and persist in attempting to learn. Westwood (1997: 12) argues that this perspective strengthens the view that these pupils benefit most 'from explicit teaching of new concepts, skills and strategies'. These students need 'to be placed in well-managed classrooms, with clear, active teaching and where students spend productive time on-task, experiencing successful practice and knowing that they are reaching mastery'.

Involving pupils with special educational needs in their own learning

Involving pupils and students with special educational needs in the planning and monitoring of their own learning represents one positive way teachers can help these children to move out of the failure cycle. As mentioned earlier, the learning profile of pupils and students with special educational needs is often characterised by a high level of dependency and an extensive need for personal support. Children and young people with special educational needs quickly become accustomed to learning failure and can believe that they will never learn, and this process can become embedded very early in the child's school career (Rose and Howley 2007).

The process of teachers engaging in consultation with their pupils about their learning, whether or not they have special educational needs, has proven to be very beneficial for all concerned (Flutter and Rudduck 2004, Rudduck and McIntyre 2007). Potential benefits for pupils from this type of dialogue include:

- an understanding of learning processes
- the acquisition of practical language for discussing learning
- an opportunity to develop higher-order thinking skills
- increased self-confidence (Flutter and Rudduck 2004: 21).

Younger pupils are very anxious not to fall behind their peers in learning, and there is a real risk that children experiencing substantial difficulties in learning will opt out of the challenge and perhaps engage in inappropriate behaviour to avoid being 'found out'. Pupils in the Flutter and Rudduck (2004) study identified the following as critical in helping them to learn:

- Giving pupils enough time to complete tasks
- Enabling pupils to understand the criteria for 'good' work
- How peers/friends can help them to learn
- Helping pupils to become persistent in tackling learning tasks that are difficult
- Building a positive identity for the pupil as a learner (adapted from Flutter and Rudduck 2004: 80).

Rudduck and McIntyre (2007) reported that teachers of lower achieving pupils who generally disengage from learning did not believe that these pupils could contribute anything meaningful about the learning process and observed that it was very difficult:

> ... to disentangle the mutually reinforcing tendencies for the less successful pupils to have less expected of them by their teachers and therefore be less motivated to engage with school learning, less enthusiastic about being able to comment on it and less confident that if they do express a view that anyone will take any notice of what they have to say (p. 159).

Lower achieving pupils tended to acquire a 'learned helplessness' which affected both their ability to persist with learning tasks and their confidence in their own ability to learn effectively. These pupils believed that they had little if any control over their own learning and that any learning that occurred was attributable to teacher support rather than their own effort and ability. However, the teachers in the Rudduck and McIntyre (2007) study were surprised at the level of insight into learning offered by the disengaged pupils. Consultation with these disengaged pupils was essential to trying to change the negative dynamic of teacher–pupil relationships and discover whether: 'the respect, recognition and trust that are fundamental to consultation could help restore their (pupils) belief in schooling' (p. 160).

Jelly et al. (2000) demonstrated that the active involvement of pupils with special educational needs in their own learning programmes had a number of beneficial outcomes. A teacher consulting pupils directly:

> ... begins to empower learners by allowing them to hear themselves talking about their needs. The experience of having their views heard and valued by an adult can provide an enormous boost to the self-esteem of students who believe they have little control over their lives and can make a positive contribution to pupils' capacity to learn effectively (Jelly et al. 2000: 14).

Empowering teachers respected the privacy of pupils and offered help in a sensitive manner, as illustrated in Hornby and Witte's (2008) study:

> There were one or two [teachers] that helped. One teacher I respected was patient with students if there was a problem. He would talk to you in private versus in front [of the class]. There was mutual respect. I instantly knew he could be respected and was trustworthy (p. 105).

Rose and Shevlin (2010: 136) suggest that the following principles can guide the pupil consultation process:
- When pupils evaluate their own performance demonstrate to them that you will act upon their evaluations and take them seriously.
- Be prepared to modify teaching practice in order to take account of pupil evaluations of learning and teaching.

- Revisit pupil evaluations regularly with the pupil and discuss whether they can recognise any changes you may have made as a result of these.
- Involve pupils in planning the implementation of change following evaluations.
- Encourage pupils to discuss their evaluations with their peers and to identify how they may work together to improve their own and each others' performance.

Teachers' cycle of failure

Teachers are just as vulnerable as children to loss of self-esteem. However, because the teacher has been vested with a role of power and responsibility, the effects of self-esteem damage can have a serious impact on the teaching–learning dynamic, with negative implications for a wide range of people, as outlined in Figure 6.3.

Figure 6.3: **Teacher failure cycle**

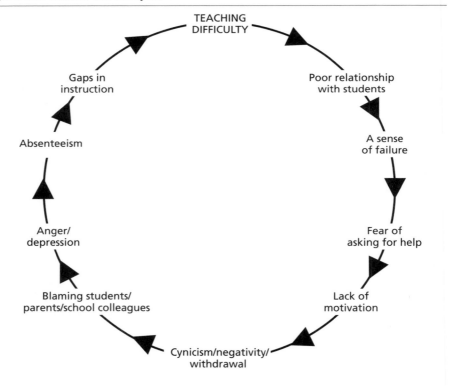

Traditionally, the teacher has been viewed as someone who has commanded authority. Control and discipline, as well as knowledge expertise, have been associated attributes of the successful teacher. The ability to 'keep order' has often been regarded as a pre-eminent aptitude. The world has changed, however, since the 'military model' of school life was an accepted and unquestioned institution of society. While school has also changed, the culture of the autonomous, self-sufficient, all-capable teacher has not yet fully given way to a model of a self-aware, willing-to-learn, collaborative team member who knows that the exacting and complex work of a teacher is not possible without giving and receiving help in relation to one's colleagues.

Loss of self-esteem happens when one feels habitually powerless, when there is an abiding sense of failure, when support is not forthcoming or when it appears that no one values or respects one's efforts. This may sound like the experience of a pupil/student with learning difficulties. It can also be the experience of an unsupported teacher.

The cycle may begin with a sense of failure in respect of not meeting the learning needs of children, being overwhelmed by discipline problems or by sensing a lack of appreciation from colleagues or the principal. In attempting to preserve one's dignity, the teacher withdraws from contact with other colleagues or may project an attitude of negativity, criticism or cynicism in the staff room. The teacher's internal image of himself/herself as a 'failing' teacher tends to be consolidated and reinforced by repeated experiences of further 'failure' in the classroom to maintain discipline or to achieve sufficient success in examination standards. The stress and tension of having to maintain a demeanour of 'confidence' while experiencing the dislike and opposition of students drives the teacher towards further negativity. Social problems may now become more apparent. Stress breaks out in bad-tempered exchanges with colleagues; there are personal problems in home and family life.

Unless the loneliness of the teacher is expressed and recognised as a normal condition of someone attempting to achieve an impossible standard of perfection, further isolation and depression may result. The teacher is effectively now unable to meet the challenges of the classroom. Pupils and students themselves, frequently experiencing low self-esteem and lack of success, cannot find sufficient support from their teacher. Their negative reaction towards their teacher is reinforced by his/her teacher's negative demeanour.

At this point, teacher stress is sufficiently great to require absence from school. Illness and incapacity become additional obstacles for the struggling teacher. Necessary absence has its own stressors: preparing substitute teachers, dealing with parent complaints, contending with compounded learning difficulties and failure among students.

The cycle of distress is now complete and unless it is breached by a positive input in the form of a project or activity enhancing the self-esteem and success of the teacher by some agreed means, the cycle will continue, damaging the prospects of pupils and students, collaborative opportunities with colleagues and gaining the confidence of parents.

'Special' education?

Lewis and Norwich (2005) present a detailed critique on the questions relating to the specialist or generic nature of special education. They conclude: 'Practical pedagogies for those with special educational needs might look different from dominant mainstream pedagogies, but these are differences, we have argued, at the level of concrete programmes, materials and perhaps settings. They are not differences in the principles of curriculum design and pedagogic strategy (Lewis and Norwich 2005: 220).

This position identifies the concept of a 'continua of teaching approaches' from the commonality of general needs to the specific nature of the needs of certain learners. The authors explain:

> In proposing the notion of continua of teaching approaches we are not suggesting that practical instances of teaching at distant points on the continua do not look distinct or different. However, teaching that emphasises high levels of practice to mastery, more examples of a concept, more error-free learning, more bottom-up phonological approaches to literacy, for instance, is not qualitatively different from teaching that involves less emphasis on these approaches (Lewis and Norwich 2005: 6).

This understanding of special education has implications for all levels of professional teacher education. The cultivation of craft knowledge (as distinct from a 'quick-fix' approach) is required, beginning with the 'commonality' position and 'moving through degrees of intensification and deliberation', which might also involve adapting teaching approaches successfully used with one area of special need to apply to another (Lewis and Norwich 2005: 216). Broad and holistic insights from the psychology of learning and child development should be applied to the whole continuum of learning needs. Also, placing the teaching of children with SEN within the wider cultural and social contexts of school underlines the fundamental level of commonality of all learning needs. Most importantly, professional education and training must go beyond a competency model based on practical knowledge and skill to embrace the self-knowledge and reflectivity that supersedes the level of teacher as a technical operative and conduit for the curriculum.

In a perceptive analysis of what is 'special' about special education, Ó Murchú (1996) warns that professionalism can sometimes serve as a label of exclusivity. According to Ó Murchú, the kind of professionalism that disempowers others or creates distances in nourishing relationships is a disservice to the essential role of the teacher. Such a role would recognise professionalism in special education as the domain of those:

- who would be supporters full of hope and optimism;
- who embrace wide horizons;

- who evaluate their own position, their own existing contribution critically and ask to what extent they are empowering people;
- who are processors of goals chosen by the people they serve;
- who would be professional enough to admit that they do not always know the answers;
- who would monitor the standards of quality of service within their own organisations (Ó Murchú 1996: 260).

This values-based position does not identify any explicit quality that would not be entirely relevant to education in the general context.

It is asserted that special education is not a different form of education dispensed in different kinds of schools for pupils who are different by teachers who are different. So what, then, is 'special education' if it is to be seen as the professional responsibility of all teachers? It is argued that, in essence, education is the same for all. As the Latin root word *educare* indicates, it is a 'drawing out' of the potential and possibilities of the learner. What is special about special education is the manner in which the teacher accesses the curriculum for the pupil with special needs by means of appropriate methodology, materials and resources and with an attitude that actualises all this by way of a meaningful and empowering relationship with the learner (Ó Murchú and Shevlin 1995). Neither can it be argued that this explication points to any position that would not be applicable to quality education at any level.

Gaden (1993) takes a less sanguine view of the way education in Ireland has shown signs of this kind of flexibility and openness to embracing diversity: 'Neither in our educational philosophy, nor in our mainstream educational practice, have we understood "education" in a way which is hospitable to people ... [of disability and diversity]. In contemporary schools, such people could not consistently expect to be accorded a respect and standing equal to that of the intellectually able' (Gaden 1993: 66).

In one of the very few such treatments from a philosophical perspective in the context of modern Irish policy and practice, Gaden asserts the moral principle of respect for persons as a benchmark concept for determining how our society responds to special educational needs. This, as Gaden argues, is not as simple as it sounds. In Western society, the attributes of self-conscious rational understanding and the development of the literate intellect are held up as the marks of true humanity. According to philosophers such as Oakshott (1972: 21), 'to be without this understanding is to be, not a human being, but a stranger to the human condition'.

Schooling which sees education implicitly as an intellectual and literary pursuit presents a challenge not just for children and young people with special educational or diverse learning needs and for their teachers, but for all who are concerned about the values inherent in our society at every level.

The role of special schools and special classes

Ensuring the continuum of provision

Traditionally, special schools have played a prominent role in educational provision for pupils with special educational needs in Ireland. Parent groups and voluntary bodies were centrally involved in the development and expansion of special school provision from the 1950s onwards. The special school model of provision was endorsed by the *Report of the Commission of Inquiry on Mental Handicap* (Government of Ireland 1965). By the 1990s, however, this model of provision was increasingly questioned and there were growing demands for more integrated forms of educational provision for pupils with special educational needs who attended special schools. One of the key principles informing the influential *Report of the Special Education Review Committee* (Department of Education 1993) consisted of the provision of a continuum of services for children with SEN to meet a continuum of special educational needs.

The future role of special schools has been questioned within the context of an increased focus on inclusive policy and schooling. McGee (2004) and O'Keefe (2004) both highlight the vulnerability of special schools and special classes within this radically changed situation. McGee believes that special schools form an important part of the continuum of special educational provision though O'Keefe appears less certain that this role is valued and acknowledged within the education system. This uncertainty around the role of special schools was even more pronounced in the Education for Persons with Special Educational Needs (EPSEN) Act 2004, which mandates the creation of inclusive learning environments. The report by Ware et al. (2009) is particularly timely in this regard as it examines the current situation in special schools and classes and makes recommendations for future policy and practice in this area. The authors concluded that special schools form a significant part of the continuum of educational provision for pupils with SEN. There was evidence that special schools were catering for pupils with increasingly complex and severe needs. There appears to be agreement internationally that: 'part of the future role of special schools will be to cater for pupils with severe and complex needs.' (Ware et al. 2009: 7). This view was reinforced in a Department of Education Northern Ireland (DENI 2006) study in which special school personnel expressed serious reservations about the capacity of mainstream schools to meet:

> ... the needs of pupils who experience more severe learning and behavioural difficulties and who require higher degrees of adult support. Mainstream schools will require support to ensure that pupils have appropriate access to the statutory curriculum and that they make suitable progress (p. 10).

It was noted in the Ware et al. (2009) study that the majority of pupils in MGLD (Mild General Learning Disability) schools were of post-primary age and that significant numbers of children were transferring into these schools after primary mainstream schooling. It appeared that many of these children had additional needs (to their MGLD designation), including behavioural difficulties. The authors observed that: 'special schools provide students with access to appropriate curricula with emphasis on the development of life skills. This is facilitated through the informed preparation of IEPs' (p. 7). Within the international literature it is envisaged that special schools could offer valuable support to mainstream schools in responding appropriately to the needs of pupils who have SENs. Existing links between mainstream and special schools in an Irish context, while valued, tend to be informal and ad hoc arrangements. In another study (McCarthy and Kenny 2006), the concept of structured collaboration between mainstream and special schools was recommended as a way forward, as both sectors would gain: 'for mainstream in terms of accessing training and expertise, and for special schools in terms of reducing isolation and extending social opportunities for pupils' (p. 12).

Special classes were perceived by participants in the Ware et al. (2009) study as a significant element in the continuum of educational provision for pupils with special educational needs, with the following advantages:

- Enabling inclusion within the mainstream class
- Provision of a 'sanctuary' for some pupils
- A favourable pupil/teacher ratio
- Ensuring that children can attend schools in their locality
- Facilitate flexibility in the organisation of teaching and curriculum provision (p. 9).

In general, it can be concluded that personnel in special schools/special classes believe that they can contribute to the education of pupils who have special educational needs and they suggest that:

> The concept of inclusion should be broadened, to incorporate the idea of an inclusive system of provision at national and local levels, wherein special schools are an integral part of the spectrum from policy development and planning through to delivery and evaluation (McCarthy and Kenny 2006: 14).

Leadership and special educational needs

School leadership is considered a crucial factor in the establishment of inclusive learning environments. School leaders are expected to give direction to the school community through the development of a vision and sense of shared purpose for the education of children and young people (Leithwood and Reihl 2003). According to Ainscow et al. (2006), inclusive schools are characterised by concerted attempts to encourage presence, participation and achievement in all aspects of school life. The development of inclusive learning environments is an ongoing process and involves increasing the capacity of school leaders and staff to respond effectively to the needs of all learners in the school community (Devecchi and Nevin 2010).

The role of the principal in post-primary schools in the development and implementation of inclusive school policies and practices is clearly outlined in the DES Inspectorate publication *Inclusion of Students with Special Educational Needs: Post-Primary Guidelines* (2007: 64). Undoubtedly, the school principal is a central figure in developing a school culture that welcomes diversity and addresses the needs of children and young people. A principal in the Shevlin and Flynn (2011) study reported that inclusive practice in school was epitomised by respectful relationships between school leaders, teachers and pupils:

> I'd be really proud of the atmosphere in the school – the way in general that students treat teachers and teachers treat students. There's a real element of respect around the school I think and it's often been noted, you know, when people come in … from other schools (Principal, 457, original transcript).

As Winter and O'Raw (2010) observe, policies on admission and exclusion often reveal the underlying school culture and attitudes to children and young people who have special educational needs. Another principal in the Shevlin and Flynn (2011) study conceptualised inclusive schooling as involving open access and welcoming minority groups:

> … when I look in an inclusive school I am thinking of our international pupils and our Traveller pupils so I'm thinking of encompassing the whole lot – that you have open access for all pupils coming into your school so that your enrolment policy is the starting point, they know from your enrolment policy that all children are welcome into your school. Then that there is no exclusion clause really and hopefully that you are able to provide a differentiated teaching programme within your school (Principal, 445, original transcript).

Horne and Timmons (2009) observed that a proactive leadership style was essential in fostering inclusive provision in schools. The direct participation of the principal in supporting inclusive provision was a critical factor in the success of inclusive practice (Winter and Kilpatrick 2001). The case study principal in Shevlin and Flynn's (2011) research reinforced this approach to school leadership:

> … you need the school to be highly organised, people need to be very flexible, you need to create a 'can do' atmosphere and a place where it is accepted that people are allowed to make mistakes … it is highly liberating.

The collaborative approach adopted by this principal involves a reciprocal response from staff:

... when you are doing your job by supporting people – you are also saying to them, quite obviously I can't do any more than I am doing now ... so take some responsibility yourself ... because sometimes it is too easy to hand over a problem to other people.

The case study principal acknowledged that school leadership in the area of special educational needs is challenging and requires a leader who is able to articulate a vision for inclusive schooling, motivate staff to work together to establish inclusive school cultures, and, above all, 'the leader of the school has to have courage to act'.

Concluding comments

Oliver (1995: 75) has asserted that the role of special education in the future will need to fundamentally address the issue of 'empowerment'. When he says 'the failure to empower is not something that will be tolerated in the twenty-first century', it is a challenge for us to reflect in what ways teacher education at pre-service and in-service levels, classroom practice, school management and ongoing policy formation address this core issue.

Burke (1992: 207) reminds us that 'if teachers want to be regarded as professionals ... they will have to be seen to provide a better informed and more professional quality of service to the public.' In Ireland, despite difficulties and inadequacies in the resourcing of education, at both primary and post-primary levels, there is a widespread willingness of teachers to do their best for their children. Teachers, too, need ongoing encouragement and empowerment to do their work of empowerment. Quality of service is in effect synonymous with the empowerment of children and young people with special educational needs. It embraces an attitude of collaboration, openness to change and methodological flexibility. It is a professional stance that ultimately returns us to the core issues and basic values of education for all.

Discussion points

1   The concept of 'special educational need' has been characterised as another form of categorisation.
    (a)   Is this fair?
    (b)   Can you suggest some ways of overcoming the risk that identification of difficulties inevitably leads to categorisation?
2   Teacher identification of special educational needs usually involved the deficit model, though more recently the inefficient learner model has emerged. Explore the implications of both models for the development of appropriate teaching strategies.
3   Can you suggest teaching and learning strategies that will help the pupil to escape the failure cycle? Give a concrete example from your classroom (primary) or subject (secondary).

4 (a) It has often been argued that children and young people with special educational needs automatically require specialist teaching approaches. In your opinion, how valid is this argument?
   (b) Outline the similarities and differences between general and specialist teaching strategies in relation to addressing an area of the curriculum.

Chapter 7

Identification and Assessment of Special Educational Needs

Learning outcomes/objectives

On completion of this chapter, the reader will be able to:

- Critically discuss what is meant by identification and assessment of children with special educational needs from a teacher/school educational perspective.
- Examine the implications of diagnosis and labelling on children and families and to reflect on the purpose of assessment.
- Explore the elements of curriculum-based assessment and the opportunity it offers to empower teachers to develop 'assessment for learning'.
- Identify and understand the operation of the three-stage assessment process for children with special educational needs relative to the EPSEN Act 2004.

Introduction

The process of identifying and assessing special education needs is complex and multi-layered. There has been and continues to be debate around what constitutes appropriate identification and assessment procedures for children who have special educational needs. This debate has been informed and influenced by a similar discussion in the wider education community about appropriate forms of assessment for all children. The National Council for Curriculum and Assessment (2006) defined assessment in education as:

> ... gathering, interpreting and using information about the processes of learning. It takes different forms and can be used in a variety of ways, such as to test and certify achievement (e.g. Junior and Leaving Certificate), to determine the appropriate route for students to take through a differentiated curriculum or to identify specific areas of difficulty (or strength) for a given student.

Teachers use varied assessment methods to collect information about a child's learning, including asking questions, setting and giving feedback on homework assignments and giving tests on units of work. However, teachers have tended to view assessment in terms of assessment of learning which happens after the learning is completed, grades are assigned and individual performance is compared to others. In contrast, the recent emergence of assessment for learning has focused attention on how assessment can promote learning. Assessment for learning regards assessment as essential to the learning process. Information on the quality of learning is shared with the learner, progress is measured in terms of the individual's learning targets and this forms the basis for planning the next stage of learning.

Within the context of special educational needs, the topic of assessment is also associated with the psychological assessment linked to the diagnosis of special educational need and subsequent special educational provision. Within this section we will explore how our understanding of the identification and assessment process has evolved. Identification of a learning difficulty is followed by an assessment process that possibly includes a psychological assessment but definitely includes proactive assessment for learning approaches using a number of strategies. No longer is assessment regarded as a once-off event that listed the deficits in learning within the child. Rather, the assessment process involves focusing on the learning environment, the development of individual education planning and generating strategies for more effective teaching and learning.

Identification and assessment process

Traditionally, identification of a difficulty in learning led to a psychological assessment to determine the cause and extent of the difficulty. Assessment came to be viewed almost exclusively in terms of a psychological assessment that diagnosed the difficulty within the child and assigned the child to a specific category of disability, with subsequent educational provision usually within special settings. This view has been challenged and a more holistic approach has emerged that assigns psychological assessment a place within a broader context of a range of assessment procedures. The identification and assessment process needs to be firmly rooted in a learning context which emphasises the development of appropriate interventions and regular monitoring and review of their effectiveness. This point is demonstrated in Figure 7.1.

Figure 7.1: **The identification and assessment process**

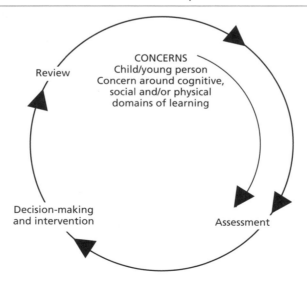

The assessment process has major implications for the pupil involved and his/her family and has the potential to affect not only the educational future of the pupil, but also his/her life opportunities. Diagnosis of a special educational need and subsequent placement in a special programme has wide-ranging and possibly long-lasting ramifications for the pupil and his/her family. It cannot be presumed that everyone will view the assessment process as benign and that its sole purpose is to help the pupil overcome his/her learning difficulties. This can explain some of the tensions and conflicts around the assessment process, as parents/caregivers may fear that their child is being singled out from the peer group and labelled as a failure. As a result, this process must be handled sensitively and the legitimate concerns and fears of pupils and their families must be given due consideration.

Identification of special educational needs

It was gradually realised that the majority of children with special educational needs had learning difficulties not directly attributable to a specific impairment, e.g. Down syndrome. It was only possible to assign a label of special educational needs in a small percentage of cases to children who had specific impairments. As a result, the identification process consisted of teacher judgment that pupils were faring significantly more poorly than their peers in terms of academic progress and/or appropriate behaviour in the classroom.

Identifying special educational needs is a process fraught with potential difficulties. It appears that identification systems vary from country to country and as a result a variety of criteria are used to determine special educational need. A child could be defined as having a special educational need in one jurisdiction but not in another. Children with comparable learning difficulties could be placed in ordinary classrooms or special settings depending on location and the identification system being used. Inherent difficulties in the process need to be acknowledged and catered for in any system employed. Difficulties can include the danger of under-identification and/or over-identification of the extent of learning need.

Schools also need to be aware of possible outcomes of the identification process, including the risks of labelling and lowered expectations for the pupils involved: 'The risks of labelling and creating negative expectations implicit in all such systems need to be balanced by a clear picture on the part of the school of the purposes to be served in identifying special educational needs' (Gross 2002: 52). Labels can misinform, as in the past it was commonly accepted that if children belonged to a particular category of disability they automatically had the same learning needs. Particular labels, e.g. behavioural difficulties, have the potential to dominate teacher views about the child and shape the interaction and the learning environment. Generally more boys than girls are identified as having social, emotional and behavioural difficulties. This raises questions about cultural expectations around gender and about the appropriateness of schools' responses to boys. In addition, schools need to recognise that pupil underachievement can be the result of a number of causal factors, including socio-economic disadvantage.

Standardised tests focus on basic skills in reading, spelling and mathematics and it is clear that the assessment of reading attainment plays a critical role in the identification of special educational needs. This emphasis on reading attainment often results in little attention being given to mathematical or problem-solving difficulties. For teachers, reading difficulties appeared to be automatically equated with special educational needs. While the child's difficulties may be confined to reading, there is the very real danger that the identification of reading difficulties can lead to lowered expectations for the child in other areas of learning.

Beveridge (1999) highlights the importance of identifying a child's strengths across the curriculum and enabling the child to experience success in learning. Otherwise there is the risk that 'anxiety or expectation of failure may often lead to a loss of motivation and self-esteem which can only compound the experience of learning difficulty. For this reason, it is not surprising that poor educational attainment is frequently associated with emotional or behavioural difficulties' (p. 52). Emotional and behavioural difficulties are not the inevitable outcome of learning difficulties and it occurs less often where schools provide a supportive environment and the child with learning difficulties has opportunities to succeed and is valued.

Teachers are generally very discriminating when identifying children with possible special educational needs, however, as revealed in Moses (1982, cited in Gross 2002: 53): 'that when making judgements about whether a particular child has special needs, teachers are heavily influenced by whether the child shows a particular behaviour pattern – low work rate, fidgeting and restlessness – which they associate with the slow learning child'.

Teachers need to be aware of indicators of possible difficulties in learning. However, it cannot be overemphasised that the teacher must be careful in using the many checklists of indicators that have been developed. There will usually be a combination of interrelated factors involved in any learning difficulty experienced by the pupil. Also, some indicators of possible difficulty could apply to a number of causal factors. The key to successful identification is detailed teacher observation, not making assumptions and developing supportive relationships with the pupils involved.

The *Special Educational Needs Code of Practice* (DfES 2001) in England and Wales grouped indicators of possible learning difficulty under four headings: communication and interaction; cognition and learning; behavioural, emotional and social development; and sensory and/or physical needs.

The communication and interaction section included:
- Difficulties with handwriting.
- Poorly developed reading skills.
- Oral skills sometimes better than written skills.
- Weak vocabulary skills.

- Regularly using single words rather than sentences when speaking.
  Indicators within cognition and learning involved:
- Discrepancy between reading level and age.
- Limited attention span.
- Avoidance of 'academic' tasks.
- Saying they have finished a piece of work (especially written work) very quickly but actually having done very little of what was required.
- Persistent off-task behaviours.
  Difficulties in behavioural, emotional and social development consisted of:
- Socially isolated.
- Generally mixing with children a lot younger or older than themselves.
- Temper tantrums.
- Off-task classroom behaviour, e.g. out of seat, distracting others.
- Interfering with what other pupils are doing on the playground.
- Having a poor self-image and regularly focusing on not being able to do things.
- Demanding of teacher's time compared to others in class.
- Generally uncooperative with teacher and peer group.
  Sensory and/or physical needs could be manifested in:
- Medical conditions.
- Inability to complete tasks in allocated time.
- Unclear speech.
- Poor fine/gross motor skills.
  Sensory difficulties, that is, minor visual or hearing impairments, can cause serious difficulties if unrecognised, and a more detailed observational checklist has been developed by Gross (2002: 54) to alert teachers to possible difficulties in these areas. Minor visual difficulties could be indicated by the pupil:
- Finding it hard to copy from books or the board.
- Often losing place or skipping lines, letters or words while reading.
- Taking longer than other children to complete reading assignments.
- Having difficulties with handwriting – unusually large, small or poorly formed letters, poor spacing and inability to stay on the line.
  Minor hearing loss could be a factor when the pupil:
- May not respond when spoken to, asks for things to be repeated or gives answers that seem unrelated to the question.
- Tends to ignore, mistake or forget instructions.
- Speaks unusually loudly or indistinctly, with parts of words missing.
- Has difficulty acquiring phonic skills for reading and spelling.
  As is clear from these examples of possible indicators, there is the distinct possibility that these are all indicators of another form of difficulty in learning, e.g. dyslexia. The teacher's task is to never assume and through detailed observation gather all the available evidence. An insightful psychological assessment can offer some explanations for the difficulties in learning and suggest appropriate interventions.

Types of assessment

A variety of assessment processes have been developed to respond to the prevalence of learning difficulties among the school-going population. Assessment as an overarching concept can be been defined as:

> ... the process of systematically gathering information about pupils' learning and cognition from a number of sources, using a variety of techniques and tools. This information can be used to develop an individual profile on the pupil, and should relate to the instructional environment and/or a particular subject. Diagnostic assessment provides specific information on the reasons why a pupil may be experiencing difficulty with a particular skill, concept or subject. The key purpose of an assessment for pupils with SEN is to ensure that they are provided with the most effective programming possible for accessing learning. (Adapted from *Education for All*, available on www.edu.gov.on.ca.)

Within this broad definition, more specific assessments exist, including educational assessments, psycho-educational assessments and health assessments. Educational assessment comprises the collection of information about the pupil's academic functioning using a number of formal instruments and informal observation. This type of assessment is usually carried out by both classroom and support teachers with assistance from additional specialists as required. Psycho-educational assessment involves an educational psychologist who conducts a series of tests to determine a pupil's pattern of cognitive processes and academic functioning. The outcome of this type of assessment may be a particular diagnosis, such as learning or developmental disability. Health professionals (speech and language therapists, occupational therapists, physiotherapists) are involved in the health assessment process. This type of assessment usually focuses on ascertaining the pupil's functioning in specific areas, e.g. physical/motor skills, and provides some suggested interventions and strategies to address the needs of the pupil.

Needs are generally assessed at three key stages: birth, pre-school and the early years of primary education. Different needs are identified at the various stages, so physical disabilities are recognised early in the child's life, whereas autistic spectrum disorders tend to be acknowledged later, and difficulties acquiring literacy skills even later.

What is assessment for?

Tilstone et al. (2000) advance the view that some of the learning difficulties experienced by children can be attributed to school factors such as the type of curriculum available combined with the approaches to teaching and learning commonly practised within the school. However, within a school that attempts to respond appropriately to the diversity of needs among its pupils, these school-related difficulties would be minimised. Within this context, 'assessment is not about identifying special educational needs. It is a process through which teachers (and others who work in schools) can identify individual pupil levels of development, their strengths and needs, their interests, their favoured learning style, their response to teaching styles, their optimum learning environment and the support they need in order to be able to learn most effectively' (p. 28).

Psychological assessment

Elliott (2000) outlines how a psychological assessment that focuses on the cognitive characteristics of the child who is experiencing a particular difficulty in school-based learning can be very effective in understanding the nature of the difficulty. The difficulty can be attributed to a number of factors, including language-based problems and/or limitations of the working memory. He suggests that children who struggle to understand what is being asked of them may have a language-based problem where the vocabulary and syntax used are beyond the child's comprehension. Alternatively, the child's ability to hold instructions in their minds while undertaking another task may be limited by their restricted working memory.

In addition, children may experience difficulties in applying learning in new situations, or 'an attempt to move from concrete examples to the more abstract formulation of general rules or principles leaves many floundering. Possibly the nature of the problem is grasped but the child is uncertain of how to begin to generate possible strategies for problem resolution' (Elliott 2000: 59). The child may also encounter difficulties in selecting appropriate strategies to resolve problems, and when an appropriate strategy is found, the child may not have a secure method of committing this knowledge to his/her long-term memory. In addition, 'he or she may demonstrate an inflexibility of response and an unwillingness to try alternative means of problem resolution and a tendency to be impulsive or impatient may exacerbate his or her limited powers of attention and concentration' (Elliott 2000: 59).

Other factors (non-intellectual) may have an influence on the child's motivation and task perseverance: 'experience of repeated failure, for example, may result in limited expectations for future success with concomitant anxiety, withdrawal, avoidance and passivity' (Elliott 2000: 59). This analysis of the reasons for the pupil's difficulties can suggest appropriate interventions to support learning.

Psychological assessment has been criticised for an over-reliance on the use of Intelligence Quotient (IQ) tests. These tests of general intellectual ability are based on measurement of areas such as vocabulary, memory, verbal reasoning, spatial ability and numerical aptitude. These tests produce an IQ score that compares the child's performance with others in that population. However, research has indicated that these types of tests can be culturally and socially biased and produce negative results for children from minority ethnic groups. These types of tests rarely offer any help in identifying how the child actually learns. In a broader sense, many norm-referenced standardised tests 'establish current levels of performance but usually tell us little about the processes that underlie that competence' (Frederickson and Cline 2002: 136).

In contrast to the traditional static tests that identified mainly what the pupil could not do, recently emerging forms of dynamic assessment emphasise strengths as well as weaknesses in learning: ' "Cannot do" is of little importance. "Can do" and "almost can do" are' (Tilstone et al. 2000). Elliott (2000: 61) states that dynamic assessment is increasingly used by educational psychologists and concludes that 'one might expect that a measure (dynamic assessment) that directly assesses the process of learning, by means of adult–child scaffolded interaction, and examines the child's potential to learn (given appropriate intervention) might be valuable in helping us understand the nature of a child's difficulties and to devise ways of overcoming them.'

Holistic assessment

In Frederickson and Cline's (2002) overview of four influential approaches to assessment, there is clear evidence of a significant move away from an exclusive focus on the learner towards an understanding of how difficulties in learning can be influenced by a variety of factors, including teaching styles and the learning environment.

- Focus on the learner.
- Focus on the teaching programme.
- Focus on the 'zone of potential development'.
- Focus on the learning environment.

Focus on the learner

The traditional approach to assessment, often termed the 'deficit model', almost exclusively focused on the within-child learning difficulties experienced by the child in question. The assumption underlying this approach was that the source of the difficulty was located in the child's disability, which resulted in limited learning ability compared to his/her peers. Thus, the purpose of the assessment was to identify the disability and compare the child's performance with the norms established for his/her peer group. The within-child factors identified as responsible for the learning difficulty were regarded as relatively permanent characteristics fairly resistant to change. Other factors, such as teaching approaches and/or the learning environment, were deemed to be relatively unimportant compared to the pattern of strengths and weaknesses revealed by the educational assessment.

Focus on the teaching programme

The focus on the teaching programme (commonly known as curriculum-based assessment) emerged from the movement towards inclusive education in mainstream schools. This approach to assessment specifies that there is a mismatch between the current learning needs of the child and the curriculum offered in the classroom. The child's existing skills and knowledge become the starting point and the teacher is expected to adapt the curriculum to correspond more closely to the child's learning needs. Curriculum-based assessment involves the analysis of the school curriculum into tasks that 'can be expressed in the form of behavioural objectives; these tasks can be arranged into pedagogically viable sequences; by checking frequently on a child's attainments within one of these sequences teaching can be matched closely to the learning stage that the child has reached' (Frederickson and Cline 2002: 135). Through this teacher-led intervention, the child can both acquire and maintain new skills over the long term and be able to generalise these new skills to different situations.

Focus on the 'zone of potential development'
This approach is based on the work of Vygotsky, a Russian developmental psychologist who formulated the concept of the 'zone of potential development'. Vygotsky suggests that the 'zone of potential development' consists of the difference between the level children can achieve through independent learning and the level they can attain with support. This implies that 'if teaching takes place within the zone between independent and supported achievement, success should be assured' (Tilstone et al. 2000: 32). Within this approach the focus of assessment is on the child's performance and the support needed to achieve it. What kind of help actually supports the child's learning? What capabilities within the child need to be fostered? The answers to these questions provide some indication of the type of teaching that will help children attain their potential.

Focus on the learning environment
This approach moves the focus onto the child's learning environment and asks whether the child's difficulties are to some extent exacerbated by an unsupportive learning environment. The learning environment in the school consists of a variety of interrelated variables, including the physical setting of the classroom, how the classroom is organised and managed by the teacher and the quantity and quality of the instruction given by the teacher. Children with learning difficulties may be treated differently from their peers by their teacher, with a lower academic output expected and an emphasis on socialisation skills over academic skills.

The combination of the above approaches (focus on teaching, potential development and learning environment) has been characterised as 'assessment for learning'. The over-emphasis on within-child factors within assessment has been balanced by placing teaching and learning processes at the centre of assessment. Tilstone et al. (2000: 33) observe that 'teachers' observations are at the centre of the assessment process that is aimed at preventing the difficulties from interfering with learning. We are not arguing that learning difficulties do not exist but that if assessment really does identify fundamentals about needs, then teaching and learning can be tailored to these needs and children can learn at their own pace and level.'

Implications for teachers and the learning process

An understanding of assessment has emerged that focuses on learning processes and outcomes, and this has significant implications for teachers in devising strategies to address the learning needs in his/her classroom. Gross (2002) suggests that this ongoing classroom-based assessment process involves a series of interrelated teacher inputs:

- Classroom observation.
- Pupil–teacher discussion.
- Miscue analysis.
- Using small steps to identify gaps in prior knowledge or understanding.
- Consulting parents/caregivers.
    The outcome of this approach to assessment is illustrated in Figure 7.2.

Figure 7.2: **Establishing interventions at home and school**

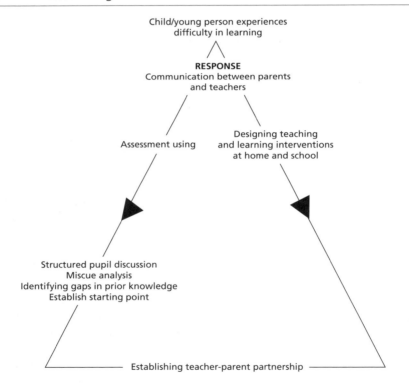

Source: Adapted from Gross (2002: 65).

From basic classroom observation it can safely be concluded that 'within any class group there is considerable variation between pupils in their style and rate of learning, and in their educational attainments' (Beveridge 1999: 80). This statement applies to any class grouping, not just pupils with special educational needs. Once we recognise this fact, individual classroom-based assessment must become the starting point for identifying the types of support pupils with special educational needs require in order to achieve progress in learning.

The first stage involves identifying the strengths in learning that the pupil possesses and enabling him/her to tackle the difficulties by building on these strengths. Once it is accepted that special educational needs are interactive in nature, then it is essential that the teacher collects information on how the pupil's strengths and weaknesses in learning interact with the learning expected in the classroom environment. In this approach to assessment, teachers generally use a combination of direct observation and discussion with the pupil concerned. Direct observation will often focus on the child's ability to self-manage their learning – organising their own materials, keeping on-task and knowing when it is appropriate to seek help. As Beveridge (1999: 82) notes, in order to ensure the child's progress in learning, the teacher will be involved in 'close monitoring of their level of grasp of skills, knowledge and concepts required by specific curricular tasks'. Teachers need to focus in particular on how the child connects with the task set and not just the end product.

Structured pupil–teacher discussion is fundamental to the identification and assessment process (Code of Practice, DfES (UK) 2001) and this approach enables teachers to gather evidence that will help to:

- Determine priorities and starting points for learning.
- Form hypotheses about factors in the interaction between pupil and learning environment which assist or hinder progress.
- Identify the sorts of flexible adaptation that might best help the pupil to achieve success.

Teachers are primarily concerned with the pupil's grasp of the task (has the pupil understood the task given?) and the strategies he/she employs in attempting to complete it successfully. Through structured discussion, the teacher can discover how the pupil feels about himself/herself as a learner and any misunderstandings about what is expected in terms of academic work, classroom routines or appropriate behaviour. Encouraging this type of active involvement in their own learning challenges the view that these pupils are passive and unable to make much contribution to the learning process. While undoubtedly time consuming, this approach is essential to provide a solid foundation for planning teaching for pupils with special educational needs.

Miscue analysis consists of an examination of common errors made by the child in learning. This can be used to understand the pupil's strategies for learning in relation to reading, handwriting, spelling and maths. Gross (2002: 60) uses a spelling example to illustrate how miscue analysis can shape the teaching programme: 'different spelling miscues indicate different teaching strategies – "sotr" for "story", for example, indicating a need for help in developing auditory strategies, while "store" might lead to teaching the final –y pattern in a word family like "story", "baby" and "lady".'

Using small steps to identify gaps in prior knowledge or understanding involves a fine-grained analysis of the barriers a pupil faces in completing a given task. Gross (2002) believes that this fundamental tool of diagnostic assessment is not always used by teachers to ascertain the actual difficulty experienced by the pupil. She provides an example of a teacher who believes that the child lacks ideas for story writing only to discover after a thorough analysis of task demands that 'it is ordering ideas that is the real problem, and that the child cannot yet cope with the very fundamental step of sequencing a set of pictures into chronological order' (p. 61).

Establishing a partnership with parents/caregivers enables teachers to gain a unique insight into understanding the needs of the children involved. Knowledge of the child's interests, learning experiences and social interactions at home can add considerably to the assessment process and help to foster a joint approach (home–school) to responding to the child's learning needs.

The identification and assessment system employed by the school must be regularly reviewed to ensure that the outcomes of the process support more appropriate educational provision for the pupils involved. Gross (2002: 53) suggests that some outcomes might include:

- Ensuring the effective deployment of resources, both from within the school and from external support agencies.
- Ensuring continuity of response when the child moves from one class or school to another.
- Ensuring that parents or carers are involved very early on in discussions about the best way to support the child.
- Initiating further, more detailed assessment of the child's needs.
- Providing the school with information about areas where the curriculum or teaching approaches may be creating difficulties for pupils.

The end result of the proactive assessment processes described is the development of an action plan that devises strategies to deal with the identified difficulties and reviews the effectiveness of these strategies at regular intervals. The focus is less on the child and more on the context and seeks to answer the question 'What will support this child's learning?' rather than the more common 'What is wrong with the child?' Assessment for learning, therefore, is about 'differentiation: assessing, through trial and error, which particular adaptations to tasks, inputs, teaching and learning styles or pupil response will best ensure curriculum access' (Gross 2002: 64).

Assessment in an Irish context

Developing appropriate assessment processes for pupils and students with special educational needs is obviously of critical importance. This fact is acknowledged and reinforced by recent Irish education legislation. The Education Act 1998, for example, obliges all schools to identify and make provision for pupils with special educational needs. In addition, schools are required to have a published school policy that addresses the admission of pupils with special educational needs and their participation within the school.

The Education for Persons with Special Educational Needs (EPSEN) Act 2004 goes a step further and attempts to provide the legal mechanisms to ensure that special needs education takes place in an inclusive environment and that pupils with special educational needs acquire the skills needed to participate fully in society. The development of an appropriate assessment process is regarded as a crucial element in the creation of inclusive environments for pupils with special educational needs.

Under the EPSEN Act 2004, a child who is regarded as having a special educational need is entitled to an assessment. The assessment process begins when either the child's parent and/or school principal believe that 'the student is not benefiting from the education programme provided in the school to children who do not have special educational needs to the extent that would be expected of that student' (s. 3.1).

Strict timelines are stipulated for the initiation and completion of the assessment and the formulation of an education plan to meet the needs of the child. Assessment consists of a dual process: 'evaluation and statement of the nature of the child's disability (including in respect of matters that affect the child overall as an individual)' and 'an evaluation and statement of the services which the child will need so as to be able to participate in and benefit from education and, generally, to develop his or her potential' (s. 4.6).

The DES Circular 02/05 outlined a three-stage model of identification and assessment of special educational needs. This circular has been supplemented by a series of publications from the National Educational Psychological Service (NEPS), designed to support this process in schools. Initial work focused on primary schools – *Special Educational Needs: A Continuum of Support (Guidelines for Teachers)* (2007a); *Special Educational Needs: A Continuum of Support (Resource Pack for Teachers)* (2007b) – and the following publications supported the assessment process at post-primary level – *A Continuum of Support for Post-Primary Schools: Guidelines for Teachers* (2010a); *A Continuum of Support for Post-Primary Schools: Resource Pack for Teachers* (2010b).

At primary level the NEPS guidelines provide both a rationale for and an outline of how the three-stage model of identification and assessment should work in practice. The NEPS characterise the process as '… a graduated problem solving model of assessment and intervention in schools comprised of three distinct school based processes' (2007: 2): Stage One – Classroom Support; Stage Two – School Support; Stage Three – School Support Plus. This model of assessment and intervention is 'underpinned by the recognition that special educational needs occur along a continuum from mild to severe and from transient to long term' (p. 2).

Stage One (Classroom Support) can be initiated by the teacher and/or the parents/caregivers and encompasses initial concerns about the progress of a pupil across academic, physical, social, behavioural or emotional domains. At this stage the classroom teacher focuses on identifying and responding to the special educational needs of individual pupils who appear to have significantly greater difficulties in learning than their peers. The classroom teacher may also gather evidence for the difficulties experienced by the child from screening measures (for children in Senior Infants and First Class) and standardised, norm-referenced tests and behavioural checklists (for older children), where necessary.

Figure 7.3: **The three-stage assessment process**

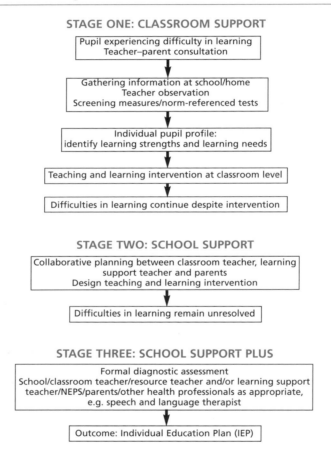

Before initiating the Classroom Support process it is recommended that the teacher address the following questions in relation to the child's performance:

- Do the pupil's skills and behaviour fall within the range considered typical for his/her age group?
- To what extent do any gaps in skills and behaviour affect the pupil's learning and socialisation?
- How is the pupil responding to simple interventions (adjustments to teaching style, differentiation) already in place? (NEPS 2007: 12)

Based on this evidence the teacher may decide that simple adjustments in teaching style or classroom organisation will suffice. However, where more distinct individual learning needs emerge then the Classroom Support process is initiated. The intervention, at this stage, will usually consist of a simple plan devised by the teacher in consultation with the parents/caregivers to provide extra help in addressing the pupil's difficulties within the classroom setting. This plan might include:

- specific classroom/yard management strategies to be used
- use of individualised teaching methodologies and/or curriculum delivery
- a focus on the individual needs of the pupil within whole-class interventions, e.g. Circle Time or small group activities (p. 14).

The Classroom Support process is reviewed at an agreed date to ascertain whether sufficient progress has been made or if further support and intervention is required.

Some children – a minority – will enter school having been assessed at pre-school level as having a physical, sensory or intellectual difficulty that may constitute a special educational need. It would be more appropriate that these children, in consultation with their families, begin with a School Support or School Support Plus Plan in order to address their learning needs.

The School Support process involves a more concentrated intervention focusing on the information gathered from the Classroom Support process. This process is usually coordinated by the support teacher(s) alongside the classroom teacher. The support teacher will usually conduct further diagnostic assessment to try to ascertain the nature of the learning need. As a result of this assessment it may be decided that the pupil would benefit from supplemental teaching from the support teacher, and an intervention plan will be devised in partnership with the classroom teacher and the family. It is recommended that the School Support Plan could include an account of the pupil's learning/social, emotional and behavioural strengths and difficulties; learning targets; classroom and school support for the pupil to achieve targets; staff responsibility for each aspect of the plan; parental involvement. This plan will be regularly reviewed and the pupil's progress monitored, and if serious concerns remain about progress then Stage Three (School Support Plus) of the assessment process can be initiated.

This final stage (School Support Plus) is only initiated when the school-based interventions have been unsuccessful and a more detailed, intensive assessment is required to determine the nature and extent of the learning need. This assessment will be intrusive and affect the individual pupil and his/her family. As a result, the NEPS guidelines recommend that this stage be initiated with caution and the following questions need to be addressed in advance of further assessment:

Is there evidence to suggest that the pupil:

- has needs which are causing significant barriers to learning and/or impeding the development of social relationships?

- is not making adequate progress despite the planned support already provided? (p. 32).

At this point, with parental consent, the school can seek a consultation with and if necessary a professional assessment from a relevant specialist. Depending on the nature of the learning need evident in the pupil, an educational psychologist, a clinical psychologist, a speech and language therapist or a medical professional could be involved in the assessment process. As a result of this assessment a detailed individual education plan will be devised involving all the participants in the process: the parents, the classroom teacher, the pupil, the learning support and/or resource teacher and the relevant specialist. A more detailed analysis of individual educational planning will be provided in Chapter 8.

The NEPS publication *A Continuum of Support for Post-Primary Schools: Guidelines for Teachers* (2010a) develops the support process initiated in primary school. These guidelines focus on supporting schools as they attempt to include all students in appropriate learning processes. The continuum of support comprises three distinct school based processes:

> **Support for All** is a process of prevention, effective mainstream teaching and early identification. These systems are available to **all** students and effectively meet the needs of most students.
>
> **School Support (for Some)** is an assessment and intervention process which is directed to **some** students, or groups of students who require some additional input.
>
> **School Support Plus (for a Few)** is generally characterised by more intensive and individualised supports. This level of intervention is for students with complex and/or enduring needs and relatively **few** students will need this level of support (p. 4).

The guidelines explicitly recognise that the post-primary context is radically different from that at primary level, and the increased complexity of post-primary schools presents distinct challenges for both students and teachers. The Continuum of Support is based on these key principles:
- Effective learning for all
- A preventative, early intervention approach
- A consultative and collaborative solution orientated framework
- A focus on systemic factors – instructional and environmental
- Timely and effective interventions for those with additional needs (p. 7).

Support for All constitutes the first stage in the continuum of support and is based on whole-school approaches to addressing special educational needs. This will typically involve whole-school screening procedures that identify learning and/or behaviour needs of 'at risk' students. It is anticipated that this phase of the intervention should meet the needs of 80–90 per cent of the school population.

School Support (for Some Students) is focused on the needs of 10–20 per cent of students who experience some difficulties in learning and require extra support which could be either short- or long-term. Recommended approaches include:

- A process of consultation and planned intervention
- Group and/or individual plans and interventions
- Subject goals
- Accommodations to support learning and social interaction (p. 8).

School Support Plus (for a Few Students) will typically address the needs of 2–5 per cent of the school population who experience significant difficulties in learning and/or behaviour and who may require systematic individualised interventions including:

- Individual Educational Plans (including behavioural plans)
- Involvement of additional professional input, such as from psychologists/ speech and language therapists, etc.
- Specialist interventions (p. 8).

Desforges and Lindsay (2010) have completed a comprehensive review of the Irish system of SEN assessment and subsequent allocation of resources. The current system (for low incidence disabilities, in particular) entails a diagnosis of disability and/or special educational need with provision dependent on the category of disability/SEN assigned. Florian et al. (2006) comment that children placed in the same disability category may have very different learning needs, and that there is a risk that assigning a particular label/category to a child can lead to stereotypes and consequent lowered expectations for these children. Furthermore, Winter et al. (2006) observe that assessment may become an end in itself in the pursuit of extra resources rather than a key element in a process that supports the child's learning needs. Desforges and Lindsay (2010) recommend that an assessment system should be based on an interactionist/ecological model that:

> … acknowledges that the needs of any child may be considered as comprising (i) those common to all children, (ii) those common to children who share a disability or condition, and (iii) those unique to each child … It also acknowledges a degree of overlapping needs, as well as important variations among children within attributed categories, such as disability types, that reflect individual factors (p. 5).

The National Council for Curriculum and Assessment coordinated an assessment for learning approach in Junior Cycle with ten post-primary schools and an interim report has been compiled (2005). The project aimed to 'provide support for teachers in formative assessment and for schools and teachers in reporting to parents on students' progress' (p. 2). Teachers reported that the most useful approaches in assessment for learning included comment-only marking and sharing the learning intention with the students. One teacher commented: 'Assessment is becoming more a process involved in student learning rather than teacher driven – more democratic, transparent and worthwhile. When students know what is expected they are more confident and able. Criteria are like props and scaffolds to "hang the learning on" and, as a result, help to eliminate confusion and lack of clarity for the student' (p. 7).

Teachers observed that this approach had a positive impact on student learning: 'The students are now involved in their own homework. They feel more autonomous with their increased decision-making power and have responded very positively overall' (p. 8). Teachers believed that assessment for learning was very beneficial for students who experienced some difficulties in learning: 'I found it worthwhile for the weaker students especially. In some cases I think it caused the weaker student to relax' (p. 8). Teachers also reported that this approach had a very positive impact on their teaching methodology:

- 'I am more focused on breaking material down into sizeable pieces to digest as a unit within a class, rather than rolling from one page to the next, each class having its own objective.'
- 'I have got to know the individual needs of my students more quickly than I would have previously.'
- 'It has given me strategies that allow for differentiation in teaching without damaging the self-esteem of the less able student' (p. 11).

Assessment for learning has enormous potential to develop teacher reflection on teaching and learning styles and can contribute to effective differentiation that enables the child and young person with special educational needs to participate actively in classroom activities.

Concluding comments

Davis and Florian (2004) capture the notion that the move towards inclusive practice has profoundly affected thinking around assessment processes:

> There is an increasing acceptance within the literature of the need to locate the education of children with SEN within inclusive policy and practice, with emphasis on improving the whole learning environment and the combination of teaching and learning processes applicable to all children; an approach that should serve to prevent some children from needing to be identified as having special educational needs (p. 6).

Within this assessment framework, the development of an individual education plan becomes both a natural and logical outcome.

Discussion points

1 The vast majority of children and young people with special educational needs are identified in school. Examine the identification and assessment policy and practice in a school and identify the key stages in the process.

2   What role do teacher attitudes and expectations play in the identification process?
3   How should parents and the child be informed of the difficulties in learning?
4   Compose a brief case study of a child with special educational needs, describing how the child/teacher and school move through the three-stage assessment process.

Chapter 8
Individual Education Planning

Learning outcomes/objectives

On completion of this chapter, the reader will be able to:

- Explain the nature and function of an Individual Education Plan (IEP) and for whom such planning is intended.
- Draw on Beveridge's (1999) interrelated model of curriculum design and teaching strategies to inform and assist appropriate individual educational planning.
- Develop an IEP with reference to the guidelines issued by the NCSE (2006).
- Consider appropriate approaches to evaluating interventions and outcomes as specified in an IEP and detail ways and means of recording, assessing and reviewing progress.

Introduction

Ireland has come relatively late to developing Individual Education Plans (IEPs) for pupils with assessed special educational needs in comparison with international experience in this area. That is not to say that all Irish schools were unaware of the process, and in fact many special schools have had individual education planning at the core of their responses to pupils with special educational needs for many years. However, with the combination of increased mainstreaming of children with special educational needs and the mandating of individual education planning through legislation (though this section of the EPSEN (2004) Act has yet to be implemented), this issue has assumed great significance for all schools.

In this next section we will look at who the IEP is targeted at, what it aims to achieve, how the plan can facilitate curricular access and finally we will explore the critical issues involved in the design and implementation of a plan.

Who are Individual Education Plans designed for?

Within an Irish context, IEPs are intended to address the specific learning needs of children who have been assessed as having special educational needs. We revisit the definition of special educational needs contained in the EPSEN Act 2004:

> 'special educational needs' means, in relation to a person, a restriction in the capacity of the person to participate in and benefit from education on account of an enduring physical, sensory, mental health or learning disability, or any other condition which results in a person learning differently from a

person without the condition, and cognate words shall be construed accordingly (s. 1).

From this definition, it would appear that IEPs are aimed at providing for children who have clearly defined and assessed conditions, e.g. physical/sensory disability, general learning disability, autism, etc., though at this stage the extent of who the definition covers has not been firmly established. It is clear, however, that a collaborative approach involving home, school and support services is required to respond effectively to the child's significant learning needs.

What is an Individual Education Plan?

There is general agreement that individual education planning is a central strategy in addressing the learning needs of pupils with special educational needs. Individual education planning focuses on prioritising a set of learning targets and suggesting ways these can be met within a defined timescale. It is also generally accepted that the IEP is 'additional and extra' to the differentiated curriculum already on offer within the classroom. It is clear that the IEP should draw on and build on the differentiated curriculum, though some authors have questioned whether a differentiated curriculum is widely used in ordinary classrooms. The plan is not intended to replace the existing curriculum, but to clearly identify the source of the learning difficulties and design appropriate interventions to address the learning needs.

Within an Irish context, as mentioned earlier, individual education planning has received added impetus as schools address the challenge of responding to more diverse learners, and this type of planning for pupils with special educational needs is not only expected but actually authorised by legislation (EPSEN 2004). In response to this situation, the National Council for Special Education (NCSE) has issued *Guidelines on the Individual Education Plan Process* (2006). Within these guidelines, individual education planning is described as 'a system of identifying where the student is, where he/she is going, how he/she will get there, and how to tell if the journey is successful' (NCSE 2006: 1). More specifically, an IEP consists of a written document designed for a named student, specifying 'the learning goals that are to be achieved by the student over a set period of time and the teaching strategies, resources and supports necessary to achieve these goals' (NCSE 2006: 4).

Thus, an IEP is both a product and a process, which is comprehensively outlined in the guidelines as follows:

> The Individual Education Plan is developed through a collaborative process involving the school, parents, the student (where appropriate) and other relevant personnel or agencies. It refers to the adapted or modified aspects of the educational programme and focuses on priority learning needs, although the student may have other learning needs that will not require the same intensive degree of planning and monitoring. Not every aspect of the

curriculum and school life needs to be modified for every student with special educational needs – only those areas of identified need arising from assessment should be covered. The amount of adaptation and support will vary according to the individual learning needs of each student. Some students with more complex needs may require significant educational modifications (p. 4).

From this, we can conclude that children with special educational needs are engaged with the same curriculum as their peers, though their access route to aspects of the curriculum will differ.

Accessing the curriculum and individual education planning

It is important to emphasise that the individual educational planning process is firmly embedded in the existing curriculum and does not involve devising a different curriculum for the pupil with special educational needs. The aim is to enable the pupil to gain access to a broad and balanced curriculum. In the past, there was a tendency to water down the curriculum based on the belief that these pupils would be unable to cope with the learning tasks involved. This approach was influenced by the view that special educational needs were largely due to within-child factors and that by targeting and working on the specific deficit in learning, the child could be enabled to rejoin the mainstream curriculum. In practice it rarely worked this way. Generally, a restricted curriculum based on fostering literacy and numeracy skills was offered to these pupils and as a result they could become bored and frustrated with the lack of challenge. Once it became established that pupils with special educational needs were entitled to access and experience a broad, balanced curriculum, there was an onus on schools to revise their practice and find ways to facilitate this access.

Beveridge (1999) outlines three interrelated approaches that have influenced curricular design and teaching strategies in special education: the behavioural objectives approach, the extended objectives approach and the ecological perspective.

The behavioural objectives approach to curriculum development focuses on a close examination of the skills required to perform particular tasks and the sequence in which these skills could be gained. Tasks are broken down into the steps needed for successful completion by the learner. Behavioural objectives are devised so the child can demonstrate what he/she has learned. These objectives are usually expressed in terms that are easily verifiable – 'the pupil will read sixty words from the first 100 word list' within a specified time period and with set criteria for success. Beveridge (1999: 67) comments: 'The approach relies heavily on the view that, by comparison with others, children with learning difficulties need more structured and detailed planning of curricular opportunities that are made available to them, and benefit from clearly expressed and finely graded steps in their learning.' This approach has resulted in more accurate and focused curriculum design and has had significant success in teaching basic skills such as literacy and numeracy to pupils with special educational needs.

The extended objectives approach builds on the thorough analysis of curricular tasks in the previous approach, but focuses on 'the processes by which they [pupils] are to be actively involved in extending their knowledge, skills and understanding. This implies that curriculum planning must focus on the strategies that teachers use to promote learning, as well as on the content of what they teach' (Beveridge 1999: 69). This involves a consideration of the social, emotional and cognitive processes involved in learning. These processes are addressed to some extent in the 'process model' developed by Stenhouse (1975). This model emphasises that learning activities should be of inherent value to pupils and should be structured to ensure that they experience success in learning.

The ecological perspective focuses on the learning environment experienced by pupils with special educational needs. The quality of the relationships in the learning contexts of home, school and community is of critical importance in ensuring progress in learning. Various factors need to be considered in this situation, including school organisation for special educational needs, pupil groupings for class placement and for learning activities within class and the quality of relationships between staff and pupils and school and home.

It is reasonable to conclude that all three approaches have something valuable to offer in developing a curricular model that is responsive to the specific learning needs of pupils with special educational needs. Each of these approaches emphasise a critical aspect of appropriate curricular design for pupils with special educational needs, for example, specifically defined learning outcomes; the social, emotional and cognitive processes in learning; and the relationships within the learning environment. A balanced, responsive curriculum should address all these aspects, as it is improbable that any one approach will be sufficient to meet all the needs of pupils with special educational needs.

Developing an Individual Education Plan

The principles underpinning individual education planning are outlined in the *Guidelines on the Individual Education Plan Process* (2006: 5). The IEP is intended to be a practical working document that should be available to and easily understood by everyone directly involved with the child. The context for the plan includes home, school and classroom management and organisation. The guidelines state that effective IEPs are characterised by being:

- Individualised and child-centred.
- Inclusive.
- Holistic.
- Collaborative.
- Accessible.

The contents of the IEP are clearly specified in Section 9 of the Education for Persons with Special Educational Needs Act (EPSEN) 2004:

- the nature and degree of the child's abilities, skills and talents;
- the nature and degree of the child's special educational needs and how those needs affect his or her educational development;
- the present educational performance of the child;
- the special educational needs of the child;
- the special education and related support services to be provided to the child to enable the child to benefit from education and to participate in the life of the school;
- where appropriate, the special education and related services to be provided to the child to enable the child to effectively make the transition from pre-school education to primary school education;
- where appropriate, the special education and related services to be provided to the child to enable the child to effectively make the transition from primary school education to post-primary school education; and
- the goals which the child is to achieve over a period not exceeding 12 months (s. 9.2).

The individual education planning process is intended to encompass identification of learning needs, supports required (personnel, adaptations to curriculum, teaching strategies), facilitation at key transition points and the setting of learning targets within a specified timeframe. It might be useful to consider the process within the framework devised by Tilstone et al. (2000: 17):
- Strengths and needs.
- Setting learning priorities.
- Teaching methods and strategies.
- Keeping track of progress and evaluating interventions.

The *Guidelines on the Individual Education Plan Process* (2006) provide a very useful overview of the process involving the writing, implementation and review of the IEP, as reproduced in Figure 8.1.

Strengths and needs

The strengths and needs of children with special educational needs are identified during the information-gathering phase of the individual education planning process. This stage involves the collation of all relevant information about the child from a variety of perspectives, including home, school, community and the professionals in contact with the child. Many aspects of the child's functioning will be considered, including:
- Cognitive ability.
- Language and communication.
- Motor skills.
- Personal and social skills.
- Attitude and motivation.
- Literacy/numeracy.

- Approaches to learning.
- Ability to access the curriculum.

Figure 8.1: **Writing, implementing and reviewing the Individual Education Plan**

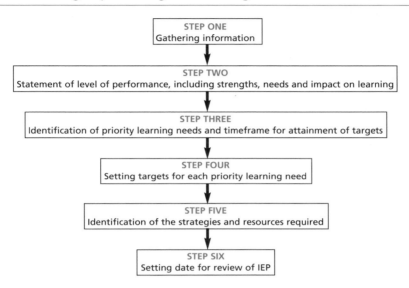

Source: *Guidelines on the Individual Education Plan Process* (NCSE 2006: 30).

It can be all too easy to list the difficulties the pupil is experiencing, so it is important that a conscious effort is made to identify things that the he or she *can* do. Many schools have actively involved pupils in this process by designing pupil-friendly feedback on their strengths and needs in relation to learning. One example of this approach from a special school working with children who have autistic spectrum disorders (ASD) in Ireland is contained in a report on IEPs by McCausland (2005: 76). For example, the pupils identify areas of competence and areas of difficulty in curricular subjects and related tasks:

I am good at:
Telling stories / colouring / writing my name / counting
Being a helper / cutting / reading a story / knowing my telephone number

They are then encouraged to describe strategies and supports that help them to learn:

It helps me when I: (circle as many as you want)
Use a calculator
Use a math chart
Have a homework sheet

Have extra time to complete my work
Have choices for test question
Have a shorter spelling list
Use a dictionary
Have highlighted directions
Have things read to me

I like when my teacher:
Helps me count
Helps me write my letters
Lets me use things to count
Tells me directions again
Helps me sound out words
Helps me on the computer

Involving pupils in identifying their strengths introduces a positive note to the process and makes improved learning outcomes more realistic and achievable.

Setting learning priorities

Setting learning priorities is closely linked to the identification and assessment process and is usually based on a consideration of the following factors:
- The child's current level of performance.
- The child's specific strengths and needs.
- The child's rate of progress.
- The urgency of the child's needs in specific areas of learning.
- The relevance of the learning needs prioritised.
- The child's motivation and interest (NCSE 2006: 33).

Setting learning priorities presents a great challenge to teachers, parents and the pupil, as the identification and assessment process can indicate a number of areas of learning difficulty experienced by the child. It is all too easy to be overwhelmed by the seemingly intractable nature of the identified difficulties in learning. Teachers are often anxious about engaging in this process, as they are unsure where to begin. They often ask themselves what will make a real difference to pupil learning given the range of difficulties.

The *Guidelines on the Individual Education Plan Process* (NCSE 2006: 33) set out the parameters for setting priority needs in order to avoid any confusion around what should be identified as a priority:

Priority learning needs are those needs that have been prioritised for intervention from a range of needs derived from the child's current level of performance. Priority learning needs form the basis for the development of learning targets and represent the anticipated attainment for a child over a pre-determined period of not more than 12 months. Priority learning needs are identified only for those areas where the child is experiencing difficulty.

The process needs to be broken down into manageable steps. For example, it can be useful to think about the factors that affect all aspects of the child's learning and those that affect particular areas. as illustrated by Tilstone et al. (2000: 19), who characterise learning priorities as:

1   those that are broad in scope, covering important aspects of learning that can be developed across the curriculum (e.g. increasing attention or working cooperatively);
2   those that are much more specific (e.g. within subject learning goals or skills needed in unsupervised settings such as the playground).

Generally it is recommended by experienced practitioners and official government guidelines that IEPs should focus on a limited number (three/four) of short-term targets connected to key skills in communication, literacy, numeracy, behaviour and social skills. The SMART acronym has been developed to capture the essence of individual education planning: **S**pecific, **M**anageable, **A**chievable, **R**elevant and **T**imed. This approach focuses on the ways in which the targets selected can realistically be attained within a particular timeframe. Targets need to be expressed positively and written in terms of specific learning outcomes for the pupil, e.g. 'Sean will be able to raise his hand when he wishes to speak and be able to repeat another pupil's spoken contribution in class.' This represents more effective target setting than saying, 'Sean will learn to behave better in class and pay more attention.'

Targets that unmistakably identify the required behaviour make it easier to establish whether the target has been achieved. The number and type of learning targets will vary according to the individual characteristics of each child and the severity of their learning need. Obviously it will be counterproductive to expect a child to master more complex skills when less complex skills remain to be acquired. The language used in expressing targets needs to be precise and unambiguous, e.g. to write or draw, to name (orally or in writing), to select, to identify, to make, to describe.

The *Guidelines on the Individual Education Plan Process* (NCSE 2006) provide an illustration of how priority learning needs can be identified. Oisin, a sixth class pupil, has been assessed as having learning difficulties associated with dyslexia and Attention Deficit Hyperactivity Disorder (ADHD), and as a result his literacy skills are seriously delayed.

His strengths have been identified as:
• Good general intelligence
• Likes computers
• Good at drawing
• Can comprehend information presented orally, when he attends
• Very good at sport; plays in local soccer club.

Oisin's needs have been recognised as:

- To increase reading accuracy and fluency
- To improve written expression
- To recognise medial sounds in individual words
- To settle to tasks and complete seat work independently
- To think before he acts, especially in the yard.

His priority learning needs are expressed as follows:

- To improve his literacy skills and to be able to read stories and to communicate ideas in writing, so that he has the skills to cope with secondary school
- To be able to sit and listen to instruction and to manage his own behaviour (reduce impulsivity).

The learning targets developed for and with Oisin follow logically from the identified priority learning needs:

- Read 60 words from the first 100 word list
- To recognise, read and write words with medial short vowels
- To make personal spelling dictionary and use it for daily writing
- To develop reading fluency by reading and re levels 6&7 of the Oxford Reading Tree
- To be able to type his own sentences and short passages
- To be able to sit and listen to group instructions
- Oisin to successfully play/cooperate with others during yard time (NCSE 2006: 79–80).

From this example it is evident that Oisin has strengths in motor coordination, artistic expression, oral skills and technological awareness and proficiency – all strengths that can be built on to achieve his learning targets. The targets chosen have immediate and medium-term relevance, as Oisin needs to be prepared for the critical transition from primary to post-primary education.

Luke, a fourteen-year-old in second year in a post-primary school, is the focus of another individual education planning example in the *Guidelines on the Individual Education Plan Process*. Luke has been assessed as having Asperger syndrome (on the continuum of autistic spectrum disorder) and dyslexia. As a result, he has clearly visible difficulties in social communication, which affects his ability to communicate with his peers. Due to his difficulties, he finds all academic subjects very challenging and this is combined with difficulties organising books and materials that substantially reduces time spent on-task in lessons.

To address these difficulties, the following priority learning needs were devised:

- Social Communication skills – listening skills & taking turns in conversations with adults and peers
- Keeping to class rules – putting up hand and requesting help
- Self-management/organisational skills – organising books and equipment for lessons

- Reading skills – accuracy and fluency, word identification skill, access to texts (NCSE 2006: 91).

Learning targets were developed in self-management skills, keeping to class rules, social communication skills, literacy and curricular access in history. For example, to ensure access to the history lesson, Luke would be expected to:
- Select and write at least six key terms related to each topic taught in history class.
  The strategies, materials and resources to help in this task included:
- Highlight term in text.
- Record terms and meanings in illustrated dictionary.
- Complete multiple choice and cloze exercises.
  Luke would also be expected to:
- Record (on a mind map) at least six key ideas and supporting details related to the topics taught in his history class.
  The strategy adopted to complete this task consisted of:
- Construct mind maps during and after reading in collaboration with teachers and peers.
  As can be seen from this example, a range of priority learning needs were identified and very precise learning targets developed. Many approaches were used to support Luke's learning, including visual cues, opportunities for reinforcement of learning and collaboration with peers.
  It is generally accepted that active pupil involvement is critical to the successful setting and realisation of targets. The original Code of Practice (1994) in the United Kingdom promoted the concept of active participation by pupils with special educational needs in their learning programmes. Schools were asked to consider how they:

- Involve pupils in decision-making processes;
- Determine the pupil's level of participation, taking into account approaches to assessment and intervention which are suitable for his or her age, ability and past experiences;
- Record pupils' views in identifying their difficulties, setting goals, agreeing a development strategy, monitoring and reviewing progress;
- Involve pupils in implementing education plans (DfE 1994: para. 2.37).

In his study of target setting by pupils with severe learning difficulties, Fletcher (2001: 25) concluded that 'often it is the pupils themselves who can help identify the steps they need in their own learning', and encouraging active pupil participation 'made a considerable impact on the curriculum and implications for planning and teaching'. Pupils were aware of how their involvement in this process was contributing to their greater independence in learning:

- 'We look through our folders, choose what we've found difficult and then

think it over with a member of staff. A lot of people need a lot of help, I need it too.'
- 'It's important so when you leave school you know what you want to do and what you don't' (p. 27).

Hayes (2004) describes a visual annual review of learning involving a child with moderate general learning disabilities who has limited communication skills. Preparation before, during and after the visual annual review meeting are essential components of the process. The review is represented with four named quadrants on a large sheet of paper; the named quadrants consist of school, home, outside agencies (called other people) and next steps. Within each quadrant, the pupil is asked to say what they are good at or enjoy and what they find difficult or dislike. At the conclusion of the process, the pupil was very happy with the outcome, felt she had been listened to and enjoyed showing her mother work she had completed. Hayes (2004: 179) concludes that this approach 'can be powerful in facilitating meaningful participation by young people and adults alike, and in assisting the setting of targets that are grounded in young people's experience and comprehended by them'.

Robert, an eleven-year-old who had transferred from primary to a special school, is described in Jelly et al.'s (2000) study. He has a mild form of cerebral palsy and appeared to have very low self-esteem and lacked confidence. Within the special school, Robert was given opportunities to develop his self-confidence through counselling and assertiveness training. The counsellor recognised how Robert had changed as his voice was acknowledged and affirmed: 'He's come on so much. His self-esteem has grown. Whereas when he started counselling he would not maintain eye contact and would sit hunched up, he now looks at you and sits in a relaxed manner. He would often perceive comments from others as criticism, which doesn't happen any more, and most importantly he will now attempt things he would not have done before' (p. 44). It is anticipated that this type of active pupil involvement will encourage pupil ownership of the process and increase his/her motivation to achieve the learning targets.

The following questions are useful in reviewing the whole target-setting process:
- Do the targets set actually tackle the identified concerns and priorities?
- Do they clearly identify what is 'additional and extra'?
- Do they offer meaningful challenges for the pupil?
- Do they ensure the participation of the child in classroom activities?
- Do they spell out what needs to be taught?
- Does everyone involved understand them?
- To what extent has the development of targets included all concerned, e.g. pupil, parent and special needs assistant? (Adapted from Tod et al. 1998: 44.)

Having examined the process involved in setting priority targets, we now briefly examine the teaching methods and strategies required.

Teaching methods and strategies

The identification of learning priorities is followed at the next stage by a consideration of how we design appropriate teaching strategies to enable the pupil to achieve his/her learning targets. Both ordinary and specialist teaching approaches can be used in addressing priority learning needs. Tilstone et al. (2000) point out that it may be suitable to apply ordinary methods in a more concentrated way by allowing more time and practice, e.g. literacy. However, specialist teaching approaches based on research evidence may be required to respond effectively to more complex priority needs, e.g. autism. To return to Oisin's situation, outlined in the previous section, the following teaching strategies were recommended:

- Precision teaching methods, sight words on flashcards and reinforcement at home
- Phonemic awareness training and phonological awareness training
- Introduction to word-processing skills; typing
- Reward chart to monitor in-task behaviour and playground
- Peers to use 'reminder of kindness' to help Oisin to look at teacher when teacher is speaking (NCSE 2006: 80).

Some specialist knowledge would be required to implement phonemic awareness training and phonological awareness training, though the other strategies would be routinely used in the primary classroom. It can also be noted that the peer group was enlisted to support one of Oisin's priority learning targets.

The following teaching strategies were recommended to address Luke's priority learning needs (see previous section):

- Shorter instructions; where possible illustrate with pictures/diagrams.
- Audio-tape selections from texts, highlight key words, ideas.
- Reduce written work.
- Assess through oral responses, multiple choice and cloze exercises.

These suggested teaching strategies would undoubtedly help any pupil experiencing a level of learning difficulty in a subject area and could not be considered particularly specialist. However, some difficulties could arise in attempting to implement this programme across all subject areas with the large number of teachers involved.

Keeping track of progress and evaluating interventions

While the collaborative process involved in constructing the IEP is exacting and time consuming, it is important to remember that implementing and reviewing the effectiveness of the plan will require a similar type of commitment. It is made clear in the *Guidelines on the Individual Education Plan Process* that a whole-school approach is required for the implementation and review of the plan. All staff (teaching, support, ancillary) could have a role to play and it is important that these roles are clearly defined and understood. Ongoing review of learning targets and teaching strategies will be needed, though 'good practice' in teaching would indicate that the teacher is involved, usually on an informal basis, in a continuous review of practice. In addition to this ongoing appraisal of the plan, a formal review must take place within the timeframe specified, and according to the EPSEN Act, the plan must be reviewed not less than once a year. The purpose of the formal review is to ascertain the child's progress and the effectiveness of the interventions provided. The *Guidelines on the Individual Education Plan Process* suggest that at this point the following questions would be appropriate:

- Has the child reached the targets? Made progress towards the targets?

If the child has not reached the targets set then we need to ask:

- Do the target(s) need to be divided into smaller steps?
- Do the teaching strategies need to be altered?
- Should the student continue with the same target(s) for another specified period?
- Does the target need to be changed altogether? (NCSE 2006: 40.)

The review can be the springboard for further planning, action (interventions) followed by another review of effectiveness.

Issues

While we have outlined 'good practice' approaches to the development and implementation of IEPs, it is only fair to acknowledge that a number of difficulties with the process have been identified from international experience:
- Time and administrative demands placed on schools.
- Enormous amount of paperwork.
- Lack of active involvement by pupils and parents in the process.
  Sopko (2003, cited in McCausland 2005) observes that the development of IEPs took place against a backdrop of the existing barriers to curriculum access, including lack of time, need for teacher training and different views on who could be included and the challenges in meeting the needs of every student.
  Nugent (2002), in a study of individual education planning in an Irish special school, addresses some of these issues. Teachers in her study reported that IEPs were helpful in planning their work and the identification of 'attainable goals' focused their teaching. These positive views can be attributed, partly at least, to the training and support these teachers received.
  McCausland (2005: 53) identifies three key factors in the preparation of teachers for involvement in individual education planning: 'firstly, a good general awareness of disability and special needs; secondly, the specific knowledge and teaching skills required to support children with special needs within their classroom; and finally, a level of information about the IEP process in order to allow them to fulfil their central roles in that process.'

Concluding comments

The difficulties experienced internationally can point us in the right direction with regard to effective individual education planning. Schools and teachers will have to review and adapt their practices in relation to encouraging the active involvement of pupils and parents in the process. Resources and ongoing support will be required to ensure that teachers receive appropriate training and develop the skills to engage in truly collaborative planning.

Discussion points

1 Developing an effective IEP involves the active participation of everyone concerned with the child who has special educational needs.
   (a) What difficulties could emerge as the IEP is developed?
   (b) What strategies could be adopted to ensure that parents do not feel sidelined?
   (c) How would you ensure that the pupil/student with special educational needs is an active participant in the process?
2 Can you think of ways to avoid the possibility that identified learning targets:
   (a) Will be set artificially low to ensure success for the child with special educational needs?
   (b) Essentially become the curriculum for the child with special educational needs?

Section 3
Developing Classroom Strategies

Chapter 9

Accessing the Curriculum: Models of Differentiation

Learning outcomes/objectives

On completion of this chapter, the reader will be able to:
- Outline policy development in Ireland towards curriculum access for all.
- Critically define the concept of differentiation.
- Develop a model for differentiation.
- Outline the components of curricular differentiation.
- Identify and critically analyse examples of curricular differentiation at primary and secondary school level.
- Consider how differentiation can be applied to assessment.

Introduction

> If you'd said to me a few years ago that I'd ever be teaching *Romeo and Juliet* or *Julius Caesar* to my kids, I'd have laughed. I mean, for English we'd mainly been worrying about whether they could fill in an application form or read the destination board on a bus. But now that I'm doing Shakespeare, I wouldn't stop. It's shown what the kids can do if you give them a chance. And there's so much in it for them – not just the language and the heritage stuff, but real, relevant ideas (Byers and Rose 1996: 101).

Providing access to the curriculum for children with special educational needs forms one of the major aims of special educational provision. Traditionally, curricula for children with special educational needs focused on a narrow range of basic skills. While not denying that the acquisition of these basic skills is essential, there is an acknowledgement that the provision of a wider range of opportunities is required for these children to achieve their potential. In this chapter we will examine what this type of curriculum access involves and how the curriculum in mainstream schools can be adapted to ensure that children with special educational needs can experience a broad, balanced curriculum.

Accessing a broad curriculum for all

Curriculum is defined by the government White Paper *Charting Our Education Future* (1995: 18) as involving 'the content, structure and processes of teaching and learning, which the school provides in accordance with its educational objectives and values'. This obviously includes the knowledge and skills attained by the student or child and how these learning experiences are structured by the teacher. The curriculum in Irish schools includes subject knowledge, methodologies employed, rationale for the subjects taught and the learning outcomes for the pupil.

However, as mentioned earlier, pupils with special educational needs generally experience a very restricted curriculum in comparison to their peers. Often there is an increased focus as pupils get older on functional life skills designed to promote autonomy in the adult world. While these skills are undoubtedly necessary, there is a growing recognition that these pupils should experience a broader, more diverse curriculum in common with their peers. Educators are increasingly concerned to ensure that the curriculum offered is not a watered down version or a poor relation of the existing curriculum.

Many of these concerns were prompted by the highlighting of deficiencies in curricular provision for pupils with special educational needs contained in the *Report of the Special Education Review Committee* (1993: 62): 'The main short-comings remaining in the provision of special curricular guidelines, therefore, are in relation to pupils with special educational needs in post-primary schools, with mild mental handicap (general learning disability) in special and ordinary schools.' The committee recommended that the National Council for Curriculum and Assessment (NCCA) should become involved in developing curriculum development projects for pupils with special educational needs and examine the curricular structure at post-primary level in relation to pupils with special educational needs.

Policy developments in Ireland

In response to this recommendation, the NCCA produced a discussion paper, *Special Educational Needs: Curriculum Iss*ues (1999), which outlined key concerns in relation to achieving curricular access for pupils with special educational needs. The aims of education for pupils with special educational needs were described in the following way:

- enabling the student to live a full life and to realise his or her potential as a unique individual through access to an appropriate broad and balanced curriculum.
- enabling the student to function as independently as possible in society through the provision of such educational supports as are necessary to realise that potential (pp. 15–16).

The discussion paper continues by stressing that in developing access to a broad and balanced curriculum, the content and methodologies employed 'should minimise rather than emphasise difference while at the same time facilitating integration in mainstream education where this is appropriate' (p. 25). It is also acknowledged that both the *Primary School Curriculum* (DES 1999) and the Junior Certificate curriculum at post-primary level recognise that pupils 'learn in different ways and at differing rates. This entails the use of a variety of teaching approaches and methodologies, differentiation in the choice and organisation of content, and the development of the student's ability to learn independently' (p. 37).

The recognition that children learn in different ways and at differing rates is encapsulated as a critical feature of the *Primary School Curriculum* (1999: 10): 'It accords equal importance to what the child learns and to the process by which he or she learns it. One of its essential features is a recognition of the principle that there are different kinds of learning and that individual children learn in different ways.'

Coffey (2004: 94) observed that the primary school curriculum encourages curricular modification to enable pupils with special educational needs to have meaningful participation, as it 'espouses the principles of outcomes-based education, respect for difference, constructivist learning, thematic learning, authentic assessment and co-operative learning, all of which acknowledge different learning rates, styles and levels'.

As an initial step in developing guidelines for curricular provision, the NCCA produced the *Draft Guidelines for Teachers of Students with General Learning Disabilities* (2002), which included draft curriculum guidelines for teachers of students with severe/profound general learning disabilities, students with moderate general learning disabilities and students with mild general learning disabilities. Students with mild general learning disabilities comprise the largest group who have special educational needs. The guidelines aim to 'provide educational experiences for these students that will be meaningful, manageable and relevant, and will enable them to access all areas of the mainstream curriculum through strategies of teaching and learning characterised by high levels of differentiation' (p. 11).

In 2007, after a consultation process the NCCA produced the revised *Guidelines for Teachers of Students with General Learning Disabilities*. These guidelines aim to support teachers in developing student-centred collaborative approaches, assist in individual education planning, demonstrate how learning can be differentiated and provide examples of effective teaching strategies. The guidelines offer support to teachers in differentiating the curriculum at primary level and Junior Cycle in post-primary. Currently, the NCCA is developing a Junior Cycle Framework for students with general learning disabilities who do not appear to be benefiting from participation within the Junior Certificate programme, despite intensive levels of support (NCCA 2009).

Challenges in translating policy into practice

These guidelines are extremely useful and informative in providing practical support to teachers as they face the challenge of translating the principle of access into practice (these guidelines will be discussed in greater depth in Chapter 12).

Coffey's (2004) case study on facilitating access to the curriculum for pupils with special educational needs in a primary school illustrates the challenges faced by schools. Large class size, teaching multiple classes and time constraints were identified as major barriers to facilitating curricular access.

Curricular inclusion appeared to be most evident in junior-level primary schools, as the emphasis on activity-based learning encouraged meaningful participation by pupils with special educational needs. At senior primary level, teaching approaches appeared to rely heavily on whole-class teaching, textbook learning and pencil and paper activities as teachers felt they were under pressure to cover more complex subject content. Not surprisingly, these approaches were singularly unsuccessful in facilitating curricular access for pupils with special educational needs. This case study highlights the extent of the challenge schools face in developing appropriate curricular responses for pupils with special educational needs.

Differentiation has been identified as a key feature of enabling students with special educational needs to access a broad and balanced curriculum. In the next section we examine the concept of differentiation and what differentiation of the curriculum entails in practice in the classroom.

Differentiation

Differentiation has become one of the 'buzz words' associated with education over the past two decades. There is a danger, then, that the concept may be devalued or even dismissed as being yet another term in the lexicon of political correctness relating to special educational needs. Contributing to this attitude is the fact that there is frequently a lack of clarity and detail about what constitutes differentiation in practice.

Most teachers will accept that differentiation involves attempting to cater for the individual needs of the student/pupil while teaching in an ordinary classroom. The challenge in making this happen in reality, given such factors as large class numbers, broad ability ranges among learners, limited resources and curricular and examination pressures, tend to relegate the notion of differentiation to an almost unattainable ideal. Yet the application of the principles and practice of differentiation is fundamental to the skills of successful high-value teaching and learning at any level.

This section will examine ways of making differentiation meaningful and manageable for the teacher who is concerned about meeting the learning needs of a wide variety of learners.

Concepts of differentiation

Adapting teaching and learning materials to account for individual differences in learning styles and learning ability has been the traditional understanding of the meaning of differentiation.

It can be argued that this definition, derived from a psychological model of assessing individual and special needs, may be too narrowly focused and may result in little more than the 'often dull and inevitable worksheet' with minor variations for lower-ability learners (Corbett 2001: 47). This approach can lead to a reinforcement of the deficit model of special education where problems with learning are seen as 'internal' to the student or child.

In Ireland, the NCCA has defined differentiation as applying to all learners and adopts a comprehensive definition which emphasises the whole-school and resources context. Crucially, it also identifies the primary underlying aim of differentiation as 'success in learning':

> Differentiation is how a teacher varies content, activities, methodology and resources when taking into account the range of abilities, interests, needs and experiences of students. The purpose of differentiation is to promote students' success in learning. It deals with each student as an individual but is not merely an individualised learning programme that is administered out of context. It values both the teacher and the student (NCCA 2002: 27).

To make these aspirations a reality requires the development of clear school-based policies on dealing with individual differences, straightforward strategies for spelling out staff support implications and the availability and timetabling of additional resources and technologies.

There are dangers in adopting differentiation if it leads only to another means of labelling and segregation. No young person likes to be identified as someone who is unable for the 'real' work of school. Differentiation requires an attitudinal shift from the traditional mode of 'imparting information and transmitting knowledge' to seeing the teacher as 'a supporter of students' learning'. This may involve moving through the different stages of differentiation from the 'worksheet and individual programmes deficit mode' through 'respect for individual learning styles' by means of providing different levels of tasks, then progressing onwards towards 'a wide range of pedagogies' that 'value differences' (Corbett 2001: 48).

Differentiation: Principles of teaching and learning

O'Brien and Guiney (2001) attempt to demystify differentiation by relating it to the way teachers internalise their understanding of what constitutes teaching and learning. Teachers who successfully engage in differentiation identify with a range of important professional and personal skills. Teachers' views of what constitutes learning also have a strong bearing on their understanding and application of differentiation.

Teaching: Professional skills:
- An organised classroom provides an environment for good teaching.
- Ability to understand pupils' 'informal' communication systems, such as body language.

- Creating opportunities whereby students can use intuition and be given responsibility.
- An ability to develop targets and to use objectives-based planning.
- An ability to provide pupils with investigative skills.
- Continually and consistently mediating information in ways that are meaningful to learners.

Teaching: Personal qualities:
- Empathy with both the difficulties and needs of pupils and students.
- Flexibility and adaptability.
- An interest in professional development.
- A sense of humour.
- An inquisitive nature.

A reflection on what constitutes successful learning is seen as a useful starting point for a teacher who is to consider what kinds of experiences, achievements, resources and outcomes will need to be differentiated for learners.

Learning: What is involved?
- Acquiring new skills.
- Changing behaviour.
- Satisfaction and pride in what you have done.
- Slowly making sense of something.
- Demonstrating knowledge and understanding by transference and generalising learning into other areas.
- Independence and autonomy.
- Understanding information previously unknown. (Adapted from O'Brien and Guiney 2001: 7–9.)

Differentiation is not about making adjustments for some learners with special educational needs. It is an understanding of the process of teaching and learning that seeks to be inclusive and to honour the following all-embracing principles (O'Brien and Guiney 2001: 11–13):
- All children have a right to high-quality education.
- Every child can learn.
- Every teacher is also a learner.
- Learning is a social and active process and involves mutual relationships.
- Progress for all learners will be expected, recognised and rewarded.
- All people and systems can change for the better.

Models of differentiation

A model of differentiation initially proposed by Visser (1993) and expanded on by O'Brien and Guiney (2001: 15) identifies three levels of learning needs:
- Common needs.
- Distinct needs.
- Individual needs.

It is sometimes referred to as the 'concentric model of differentiation' whereby the central sphere of common needs is surrounded by related and surrounding zones of distinct and individual needs, as illustrated in Figure 9.1.

The commonality of all pupils is the starting point for differentiation in this model. The teacher who accepts this approach will accept levels of difficulty in learning as an aspect of normal diversity in any group of learners rather than a deficit imposed on the community. This model asserts that all learners have some learning needs that are common:

- A sense of belonging.
- A respect for individual experience and opinion.
- Communication needs.
- A need to feel a sense of achievement.
- A need to have effort recognised and affirmed.

Figure 9.1: **Concentric model of differentiation**

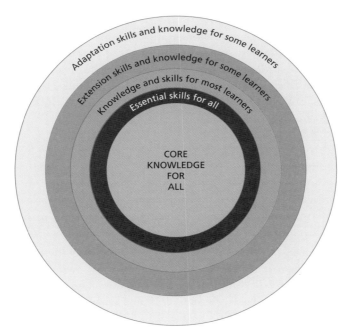

Source: Adapted from Visser (1993) and O'Brien and Guiney (2001: 15).

Distinct learning needs can be associated with groups of learners who as groups may have some specific needs in common. These distinct needs might include:

- Gender.
- Cultural background.
- Family.

- Health.
- Access needs due to disability.
- Religious background.

Individual needs cannot be easily listed in that these learning needs, by their nature, are unique and apply to personal attributes and characteristics that are separate and discrete and require recognition. The following case study presents an example of how a school attempted to meet a young person's common, distinct and individual learning needs.

Case Study 9.1: Meeting common, distinct and individual needs

Kevi is fifteen years old and is in first year in his local post-primary school. He is a little older than his peers as he has had extra time in pre-school and primary school in order to address his learning needs. Kevi has Down syndrome and his parents have always strived to ensure that Kevi attends a school that welcomes diversity. His local post-primary school has a reputation for responding positively to diversity. In planning to meet Kevi's needs, the school recognises that Kevi's need in common with all his classmates is to feel that he belongs and that his social and friendship needs are provided for. In common with all first year students, Kevi has been allocated a student mentor from the Transition Year programme who is responsible for helping him to become familiar with his new surroundings, routines and facilities. He also makes friends outside his own class group.

Kevi's distinct learning needs include having social opportunities to engage in competitive games with other boys. He is enjoying learning the skills of badminton and bowling. However, like some other students who have some health-related conditions, Kevi does not engage in extended strenuous physical sports. He needs to have a rest period, usually in the early afternoon. Kevi has distinct learning needs relating to his level of cognitive development, which is at approximately half of his chronological age. Teachers are aware of general strategies for creating concrete learning opportunities and supportive peer tutoring for students who have general learning disabilities.

Kevi's individual needs include improving his comprehension of reading material of which he has technical mastery. In each of the subject areas that Kevi studies, he is instructed to formulate a written question relating to the material that he has just read. This learning outcome has been identified in his Individual Educational Plan and teachers and special needs assistants are made aware of this.

Curriculum differentiation

Differentiation was first outlined in terms of provision for children and young people with giftedness and exceptional ability in the writings of Maker (1982).

The principles of curriculum differentiation can be adapted for children and young people of any level of ability. The model proposed by Maker suggests that the curriculum needs to be differentiated in terms of:

- Learning environment.
- Content modification.
- Process modification.
- Product modification.

Farmer (1996) elaborates on and discusses the approaches that can be developed under these headings.

Learning environment

The aim here is to bring about a learning environment that encourages young people to engage their abilities as much as possible, including taking risks and building knowledge and skills in what they perceive as a safe, supportive and flexible environment. The learning environment consists of the emotional climate and communication opportunities provided by the teacher as well as the physical arrangements, practical materials and experiences provided to enhance learning. The learning environment needs to be:

- **Learner-centred:** Focusing on the student's interests, input and ideas rather than solely centred on the teacher.
- **Encouraging independence:** Encouraging pupil/student initiative and personal responsibility.
- **Open:** Where possible, permitting new people, materials, ideas and things to contribute to the curriculum and to facilitate interdisciplinary and cross-curricular connections.
- **Accepting:** Encouraging acceptance of others' ideas and opinions before evaluating or judging them.
- **Complex:** Providing a rich variety of resources, media, ideas, methods and tasks so as to embrace all learning styles.
- **Active:** Where possible, encourage movement in and out of groups, desk settings, classrooms and schools.

Content modification

The aim is to extend the boundaries of what is to be learned and use the student's abilities to build a richer, more diverse and efficiently organised knowledge base. This approach can be facilitated by encouraging:

- **Abstractness:** Shifting content from facts, definitions and descriptions to concepts, relationships to key concepts, and generalisations.
- **Complexity:** Shifting content to interrelationships and connectedness rather than considering concepts separately.
- **Variety:** Expanding content beyond textbook material presented in the lesson.
- **Study of people:** Including the study of individuals or peoples and how they have reacted to various opportunities and problems related to the subject matter.

- **Study of methods of inquiry:** Introduce some procedures used by relevant experts and professionals working in this field.

Process modification
The aim here is to promote creativity and, where appropriate, higher-level cognitive skills and to encourage productive use and management of the knowledge the students have mastered. This can be facilitated by encouraging:
- **Higher levels of thinking:** Involving cognitive challenge, moving from answers to 'what' questions to 'how' questions and to 'why' questions.
- **Creative thinking:** Involving imagination, intuitive approaches and brainstorming techniques.
- **Open-endedness:** Encouraging risk-taking and the response that is right for the student by stressing there is not only one right answer.
- **Group interaction:** With highly able and motivated students sparking each other in the task, with this sometimes being on a competitive and sometimes on a cooperative basis (depending on the task and its objectives).
- **Variable pacing:** Allowing students to move through lower-order thinking more rapidly but allowing more time for students to respond fully on higher-order thinking tasks.
- **Variety of learning processes:** Accommodating different students' learning styles, e.g. providing visual material, audio material and opportunity for concrete activities.
- **Reflecting and reporting:** Encouraging students to be aware of and able to articulate their reasoning or conclusion to a problem or question.
- **Freedom of choice:** Involving students in evaluation of choices of topics, methods, products and environments.

Product modification
The aim here is to facilitate opportunities for students to produce a product that reflects their potential. This can be encouraged by incorporating:
- **Real problems:** Real and relevant to the student and the activity.
- **Real audiences:** Utilising an 'audience' that is appropriate for the product, which could include another student or group of students, e.g. a quiz or worksheet, a teacher (not necessarily the class teacher), an assembly, a community or specific interest group.
- **Real deadlines:** Encouraging time management skills and realistic planning, e.g. taped broadcast for community radio programme.
- **Transformations:** Involving new and original manipulation of information rather than regurgitation, e.g. a visual storyboard of an historical event.
- **Appropriate evaluation:** With the product and the process of its development being both self-evaluated and evaluated by the product's audience using previously established 'real world' criteria that are appropriate for such products.

Supporting 'learning things differently'

Westwood (2003: 202) defines differentiation as 'learning things differently according to observed differences among learners'. All effective teaching requires a degree of differentiation, but it is particularly important in supporting students with general learning disabilities. The Special Education Support Service (SESS) notes that differentiation can occur by the teacher taking into consideration these elements:

- **Level and pace:** Students work on a similar topic, at a level and pace appropriate to their ability, e.g. Topic – Money: some students work on coin recognition, others on shopping/change activity, etc.
- **Interest:** Students select a topic of interest to themselves, learning can be enhanced, e.g. Topic – Bar Charts: groups/students select from favourite singer, TV programme, football team.
- **Access and response:** Students respond in different ways to the material presented to them, e.g. Topic – Bar Charts: some draw, some use ICT, some use different formats for presenting data.
- **Structure:** Students guided step-by-step or in whole blocks of integrated curricular content, e.g. Topic – Regrouping in Subtraction: some practice skill independently, others monitored/supported.
- **Sequence:** Different students access different parts of a subject at different times, e.g. Subject – LCA Leisure and Recreation: modular course, students select the elements they wish.
- **Teaching style:** Teacher varies approach/methodology in the classroom, e.g. 'chalk and talk', using ICT or video, research using the internet, class discussion, small group work.
- **Time:** Teacher adapts use of time with class to meet the needs of all children, e.g. Topic – Bar Charts: some students work independently, others closely monitored by teacher/SNA.
- **Classroom structure:** Teacher structures groups in class to maximise learning, e.g. some students work in pairs, others in groups, others individually, each with a purpose and role.

Differentiation: 'Watering down' the curriculum?

Some approaches to curriculum differentiation emphasise an attempt to match the level of curriculum content to the differing capabilities of the learner (Carpenter et al. 1996). Again, it must be highlighted that there is always a danger here that the differentiation process might be viewed as a technique for continually 'watering down' the curriculum. According to McNamara and Moreton (1997), differentiation should be less about altering the level or type of work set by the teacher and more a means of providing alternative paths and additional supports to enable all students to study the same curriculum content and to achieve satisfactory outcomes. Westwood (2003: 208) argues that watering down the curriculum may have a detrimental effect in widening the gap between students who have learning difficulties and other students and perhaps even perpetuating inequalities. Providing alternative routes and scaffolding support systems for students will require commitment and coordinated strategies applied throughout the school.

General examples in differentiating resources

For pupils and students with general learning disabilities who may experience challenges in receptive and expressive communication, the following strategies, identified by Westwood (2003) and others, may be more generally helpful and less difficult to apply:

- Consciously simplify language, use short sentences and uncomplicated terminology.
- Anticipate new or difficult vocabulary and explain terms before students meet them in texts.
- Provide clear illustrations and diagrams.
- Remove unnecessary detail from worksheets.
- Use cues or prompts where responses are required from students, e.g. provide initial letter of the answer, or show dashes to show number of letters in a word or words in an answer.
- Highlight important terms or information, e.g. use underlining or capitals.
- Use bullet points and lists instead of paragraphs.
- Use the active rather than the passive voice in written text to assist comprehension, e.g. use 'The man won the race' rather than 'The race was won by the man.'

In the following case study we explore how information communication technology (ICT) can be used as part of a differentiation strategy to help a young person with special educational needs access the curriculum.

Case Study 9.2: Using information communication technology (ICT) as a resource for enabling curriculum access in a post-primary school

In this example of differentiation, a teacher describes how conscious attempts were made to raise the self-esteem of a child with special educational needs. This involved identifying and utilising the child's strengths in a curricular topic.

Ellie's English class is engaged in a writing task based on the final scene of *Romeo and Juliet*. It is a mixed-ability class of Second Year students, most of whom are handwriting their work. There are some desktop computers in the room with two students at each.

Ellie is using a small portable computer with WordBar word bank software. She types in most of the work from the keyboard but sometimes inserts words or phrases by selecting them from the on-screen grids with a stylus.

Ellie reads well and enjoys literature but she has higher functioning autism, commonly known as Asperger syndrome, and sometimes she encounters difficulties with communication and ordinary classroom interactions. She responds well to ICT and is more comfortable writing with a keyboard than a pencil. It seems to help her focus, and because she also has co-ordination difficulties (dyspraxia), it reduces the physical effort of letter formation. She likes to know in advance what structure the lesson will take. The teacher often provides her with copies of her word-processed lesson notes.

The teacher finds ICT very helpful in providing for differentiation and she uses word processing or presentation software to produce teaching materials that are clear and readable and easily adaptable. Ellie uses a word bank facility to support her writing. It runs alongside her normal word processor. Key words appear on screen in linked grids and because the teacher finds the programme useful for several children in this class, she loads the grids onto the desktop computers as well.

She encourages the students to work both on and away from the computer. They make print-outs of their drafts, then go back to their desks and review them there. They can read them through, discuss them with their friends, scribble insertions on them, cross bits out and even chop the paper up to rearrange the text. Then they go back to the computer to make alterations without having to start all over again.

This particular programme helps Ellie by providing a clear structure and a means of inserting whole words and phrases into her writing. Other students are also helped by the sentence starters and key vocabulary. Ellie's Special Needs Assistant is very interested in ICT and has been given training in the use of key hardware and software to help produce grids from vocabulary lists that the teacher provides. The teacher saves the grids and her notes so that she can use them again with other groups and share them with colleagues.

Source: Adapted from www. becta.org.uk/teachers, accessed 2 October 2006.

Case Study 9.3: Establishing interest, providing language support and encouraging achievement in a primary school

When Jamie was assessed last year at the end of fifth class I think all of us who had taught him felt some guilt. Not so much for his lack of attainment; we all knew about that, to some degree, and could put it down to poor attendance and to inattentiveness when he was present.

What got me and, I think, my colleagues, were the signs of indications of his very low self-esteem. He is a very talented athlete and I had always tried to build on that, but the psychologist's report made it plain that he still saw himself as a failure at school and a disappointment to his teachers and family. We saw that Jamie had been one of those children who dealt with his learning difficulties by keeping his head down and avoiding notice while more troublesome peers got more attention and whatever help was going.

I decided to focus first on reading and, although the indications had been that he would never manage a phonological approach to reading, I believe that the use of the Lexia program has brought real improvement. Much more significantly, however, I found that he had an interest in electricity and I set him up with a free programme which I had downloaded from the internet which he could use to set up virtual circuit boards with switches, bulbs, motors, buzzers, etc. Pretty soon the boy who had spent his school life silently avoiding any contact with classroom activity was asking permission to bring friends into the resource classroom to show what he was doing.

On the day of the Christmas holidays we had a small party in the room for all the 'resource kids' and they were given a range of games and toys to play with. Jamie only wanted to go to the computer with a friend to continue a project he had been working on.

At the end of that day, I happened to be in his classroom when he was leaving. He went out then stuck his head back in and shouted 'Happy Christmas, everybody!' There would have been nothing remarkable about this from another child, but the class teacher and I just looked at each other. We both knew that there was no way that last year's Jamie would have done the like in a century of Christmases.

Jamie's progress in academic areas continues to be slow but definite. I am convinced that the change in his self-image has everything to do with his progress in other areas.

Source: Adapted from www. socsci.ulster.ac/uk/education/scte/sen, accessed 2 October 2006.

Differentiation in assessment

Perhaps one of the most difficult areas that teachers and schools encounter in relation to differentiation is that of assessment. Westwood (2003) warns against any simplistic treatment of this complex consideration. Some of the questions which confront us in reflecting on issues around student assessment relate to the problem of 'fairness'. These and other questions are worthy of careful and critical deliberation:

- Can one justify the judgment of the standard of work produced by a student with mild general learning disabilities or a student who has a sensory impairment against the standard applied to the student of good or average ability in the class?
- How can one justify giving 'good' grades to students who are lower achievers on the basis that they have made a 'good effort'?
- If measured against standard criteria, is it not discouraging and demotivating

to give low-achieving students in an inclusive class an 'unsatisfactory' or 'fail' grade?

Modifications in assessment procedures might include some of the following options:

- Shortening the assignment.
- Allowing more time to complete the task.
- Permitting the assignment task to be submitted in a different medium, e.g. audio recording or photo journal.
- Dictation of the assignment to a scribe.

Wood (1998) suggests some methods of modifying grading that take learning difficulties into account. These include:

- Using 'satisfactory/unsatisfactory' as the criteria for grading a piece of work.
- Providing a descriptive report rather than a grade. This is based on an evaluation of the outcomes achieved by the student.
- Providing grades for achievement and for effort.

Marking written work

Marking written work is another vital aspect of assessment. As teachers, we need to be clear about why we are marking this work and how the marking process can help or hinder the progress of the pupil in learning. It can be too easy to assume that marking the pupil's work will automatically lead to recognition by the pupil of what he or she needs to do in order to improve. Before we set an assignment/test, are we clear about the criteria for marking and are the pupils aware of what is required? The terms 'marking' and 'correcting' are often used interchangeably, yet they refer to quite distinct teacher activities. Marking involves assigning a grade that indicates where the work stands in comparison to his/her previous work and to his/her peer group. Correcting, on the other hand, is concerned with improving the text by pointing out mistakes. Often, there is little consistency in the correcting policy employed by teachers in a school, leaving pupils to figure it out for themselves.

Often pupils' written work is regarded as a product rather than as an integral element in the thinking and learning process. In effect, the teacher has two choices in deciding what stance to adopt when assessing an assignment: 'whether the aim is to check for understanding/knowledge from the written work, as in examinations, tests, finished essays', or 'whether the aim is to achieve understanding/learning through writing as in drafting, note-taking and making, problem solving, thinking in writing' (Garnett 1992: 8).

The teacher can adopt the stance most appropriate to the purpose of the assignment. When the assignment is a test, then it is quite appropriate that the teacher acts as examiner and grades the work accordingly. However, when the aim is to increase understanding, then the teacher can adopt a number of stances, including responsive reader (guiding the pupil), editor (helping the pupil to improve the text and clarify any ambiguities) or proofreader (correcting mistakes and helping pupil not to repeat these mistakes).

Garnett (1992) points out that teachers need to be aware of hidden factors in marking. Teachers' expectations of pupil attainment can be influenced by their previous experience of a pupil's work. Marking is influenced by spelling more than any other factor. Other factors can include handwriting style and legibility, writing speed, grammar and syntax, sequencing, correct/appropriate information and logical development of thought and ideas.

Garnett (1992) developed an 'Items for Learning' framework for marking written work (see Table 9.1).

This framework was based on a belief that pupils had a right to expect a learning outcome from their written work. This learning outcome needs to be clear and conveyed to pupils as the assignment is being set. Pupils 'like to have opportunity to practise new learning, to reflect on their achievement even when it is limited. This may be more true and important for those who have had many experiences of failure than for those who have not but I am not so sure it isn't so for all' (Garnett 1992: 14).

Table 9.1: **Items for learning**

Name: _____   Class: _____

Date of lesson	Assignment description	Item for learning (stated as an objective/ learning target)	Learned by (date when confidence with item is evident)

Source: Garnett (1992: 17).

In the 'Items for Learning' framework, rather than correct every mistake, the teacher identified a small number of items requiring attention. These items formed the basis of the Items for Learning task for the pupil as he/she attempted to address these mistakes in the next written exercise. Garnett (1992: 15) outlined the following factors as critical to the 'Items for Learning' framework:

- all children make mistakes in their writing, many of which they just need to remember not to make again
- but many mistakes indicate that more learning of the skill or concept is needed
- few children manage to deal with all their mistakes in one go so correcting them all is a waste of time

- some cannot cope with more than one mistake at a time but others can deal with up to five
- a written record of this learning allows the child to see how well s/he is doing
- this gives satisfaction and incentive to achieve more.

Often children who have experienced regular failure in learning will need reassurance that the items for learning are an indication of more learning required rather than yet another failure. This approach gives practical support to improve writing skills and enables parents to see how the marking is part of a process aimed at enhancing pupil learning.

Concluding comments

Perhaps the baseline question 'Does this approach facilitate learning?' is the ultimate benchmark for judgment. Differentiation is not an easy practice to maintain and sustain. Apart from the conviction and commitment required to establish differentiation, it requires significant planning time to make it functional and meaningful. Availability of a wide range of material resources is a clear prerequisite. Most of all, however, to make differentiation an honest effort towards inclusive learning, there can be no getting around the responsibility of management and leadership in the school to nurture a climate of unambiguous support and collegiality for all involved.

Discussion points

1 Choose a task you would plan for a group of pupils.
   (a) What skills, knowledge and concepts are required to successfully complete the task?
   (b) How would you teach the requisite skills, knowledge and concepts?
   (c) Identify potential areas of difficulties pupils might experience and plan how these difficulties could be addressed.
2 Teachers might say that large class sizes, time pressures and preparing students for examinations make any meaningful attempt at differentiation almost impossible. How would you respond to this observation?
3 Teachers may be genuinely concerned about giving students in the same class differing levels of work in case certain students are identified as less able than others. How would you address these concerns?
4 Parents of other children who do not have special educational needs may express the view that their child is being neglected as the teacher has to spend so much time supporting children with special educational needs. How might the school/teacher address this sensitive issue?
5 It can be difficult to find topics and design activities that are inclusive of all children, whatever their ability level. What criteria would be appropriate in deciding on suitable topics and activities that enabled all children to participate?

Chapter 10

Examining Difficulties in Literacy and Numeracy

Learning outcomes/objectives

On completion of this chapter, the reader will be able to:
- Discuss a definition of literacy and numeracy that identifies areas of potential difficulty and challenge for children and young people in school.
- Outline the language arts hierarchy and identify appropriate methods of teaching and learning that reinforce each stage in the receptive/expressive process.
- Evaluate the language experience approach as a way of supporting children with reading/writing difficulties.
- Examine approaches to mathematics teaching that attempt to balance learning needs in mathematics calculation and mathematics reasoning.

Literacy difficulties: Introduction

Recent national and international assessments of Irish pupils in literacy and numeracy assessments have caused serious concerns for policymakers and educators. The PISA 2009 report (Perkins et al. 2010) appeared to indicate that the literacy knowledge and skills of Irish 15-year-olds had seriously declined since 2000. The national assessment of mathematics and English reading (Eivers et al. 2010) had also raised issues in relation to pupil proficiency in these curricular areas. Policymakers have been aware for some time of worrying trends in relation to pupil proficiency in literacy and numeracy, and a draft national plan to improve literacy and numeracy in schools was published in 2010.

Failing to develop adequate literacy and numeracy skills has serious personal consequences for the children and young people concerned and has a negative impact within the wider society. Research has demonstrated that (DES 2010) developing literacy and numeracy skills confers social, economic and health benefits on both the individual and society. It is also evident that children who do not acquire adequate literacy skills: '... are more likely to leave school early, be unemployed or in low skilled jobs, to have poorer emotional and physical health ...' (DES 2010: 9). The draft national plan emphasises the urgency of ensuring that: 'every child leaving our school system is numerate and is able to speak, read, write and spell at a level that enables them to participate fully in education and in Irish life and society'(DES 2010: 9).

The Programme for International Student Assessment (PISA) consists of an international assessment of the knowledge and skills of 15-year-olds in reading, mathematics and science. This international assessment has been organised on a three-year cycle since 2000. In 2009, reading constituted the main focus for assessment. Ireland ranked twenty-first among 65 participating countries in 2009 and had declined substantially from 2000 when ranked fifth compared to seventeenth among the 39 countries who had participated in both the 2000 and 2009 assessments (Perkins et al. 2010). Of equal concern was the fact that one in six Irish students achieved below the minimum level considered necessary to function effectively in future education and adult life. Ireland's score on mathematics proficiency was considerably below the OECD average and Ireland ranked thirty-second out of 65 participating countries.

The *2009 National Assessments of Mathematics and English Reading* (Eivers et al. 2010) ascertains current reading and mathematics standards for children in second and sixth classes in primary schools. In general, children at both grades found Retrieve items in reading easiest, while Infer items (Second Class) and Interpret and Integrate items (Sixth Class) proved to be most difficult. In mathematics, items assessing Measures, and Apply & Problem-Solve caused most difficulties at both grade levels. This assessment also examined the pupil characteristics related to achievement and discovered that higher performance was associated with those children with high attendance rates, positive self-ratings, positive mathematics self-concept (for mathematics) and enjoyment of reading (for reading). Pupils who receive support in mathematics and/or reading performed poorly on both assessments, while those receiving language support performed poorly on reading and were slightly below average on mathematics. Lower pupil attainment was also related to a number of factors, including being part of a family with low socio-economic status, parental unemployment, belonging to the Traveller community, speaking a first language other than English or Irish and living in a one-parent household.

The draft national plan on literacy and numeracy aims to achieve a number of targets to improve pupil performance in these critical areas, including:

- improve the oral-language competence of children in early childhood care and education (ECCE) settings, using baseline data from assessments to inform the planning of learning goals
- ensure that each school sets and monitors progress in achieving demanding but realistic targets for the improvement of literacy and numeracy skills of its students
- increase the percentage of primary children performing at Level 3 and Level 4 (the highest levels) in the national assessments of mathematics and English reading by at least 5 per cent at both second class and sixth class by 2020
- reduce the percentage of children performing at or below Level 1 (minimum) in the national assessmenst of mathematics and English reading by at least 5 per cent at both second class and sixth class by 2020
- increase the percentage of students achieving the equivalent of Grade C or

above in the Mathematics Ordinary Level examination at the end of junior cycle (i.e. Junior Certificate examination or its equivalent) from 77 per cent to 85 per cent by 2020

* increase the percentage of students taking the Higher Level mathematics examination at the end of junior cycle (i.e. Junior Certificate examination or its equivalent) to 60 per cent by 2020
* increase the percentage of students taking the Higher Level mathematics examination in Leaving Certificate to 30 per cent by 2020. (DES 2010: 12).

Defining literacy

Literacy is more than the ability to read and write: it is also about 'constructing meaning' from the various modes of communication valued by society. Literacy is described as the 'ability to understand and use those written language forms required by society and valued by the individual. Young readers can construct meaning from a variety of texts. They read to learn, to participate in communities of readers and for enjoyment' (Campbell et al. 2001: 3).

Current definitions show that literacy:

* Involves different abilities – reading, writing, oral language, viewing.
* Being literate involves constructing meaning, reflection and expressing thought.

These abilities can be applied in different contexts, subject areas or in different communities.

Understanding literacy difficulties

Levels of literacy difficulties may range from mild to severe and may result from specific or general learning disabilities. A knowledge of the general framework for an understanding of language and literacy development will be fundamental to the application of appropriate assessment methods and teaching approaches.

The role of language in the development of thinking skills and concept formation has been explored and examined by authorities such as Piaget (1952) and Vygotsky (1962). Words become symbols for objects, categories of objects and ideas. Language embodies the building blocks of learning, assisting the child to express past experience, future aspirations and, through imagination, allows the child to articulate things unseen and actions not yet lived out. It is the tool that permits the learner to retain, recall, record and communicate information and to shape and control the environment. The progressive mastery of language and literacy gives the learner a vital sense of empowerment in meeting the challenges of living. The young person who may be disabled in language acquisition needs to be given access to this affirming knowledge by whatever means possible.

A vivid illustration of the dependency of thought on language is contained in the account of how Helen Keller, a deaf and blind seven-year-old child, was led to discover the excitement of language and literacy as 'meaning making' through the efforts of her enlightened teacher, Anne Sullivan:

I made Helen hold her mug under the spout while I pumped. As the cold water gushed forth, filling the mug, I spelled 'w-a-t-e-r' in Helen's free hand. The word coming so close upon the sensation of cold water rushing over her hand seemed to startle her. She dropped the mug and stood as one transfixed. A new light came into her face. She spelled 'water' several times. Then she dropped to the ground and asked for its name and pointed to the pump and the trellis and suddenly turning around she asked for my name (Keller 1961: 273).

Over a century ago, Helen Keller, at the age of 24, graduated from Radcliffe College in the US, the first deaf and blind person to attain such an achievement. She later went on to become a world-famous writer and activist for the rights of people with disabilities.

Language arts hierarchy

It is important for every teacher to appreciate the balance, weight and progression that needs to be accorded to the different levels of the language arts hierarchy. This is especially true for meeting the needs of children with literacy difficulties and challenges. The inter-relatedness of these elements can also be exploited to support strategies for 'meaning making' in reading and writing.

Language arts incorporate the areas of learning in the curriculum that involve listening, oral language expression, reading and written expression, including spelling. It may also be appropriate to consider gesturing, body language and other forms of non-verbal communication, e.g. sign language, to this list.

Figure 10.1: **Language arts hierarchy**

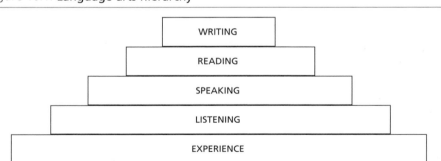

Source: Adapted from Lerner (1981: 254).

The illustration of the language arts hierarchy is symbolised by a flight of stairs on which the child proceeds slowly upwards. In real life, stairs are either possibilities or perils to the child learning how to master the environment. A too rapid acceleration up the steps may result in confusion and disorientation with the strong possibility of a fall and a consequent fear of further failure. Translated into the world of teaching, children who are impelled by competitive anxiety to read and write before they have spent sufficient time in safely mastering earlier stages of literacy development are more prone to experience problems and setbacks at later levels of progression when the acquisition of reading and writing require the assimilation of skills absorbed at the foundation phases.

Receptive and expressive skills

Across cultures, the human race has followed the hierarchy of stages which are represented in ascending order as:

- Listening.
- Speaking.
- Writing.
- Reading.

In historical terms, human society evolved to a sophisticated level with developed communication skills of listening and speaking, providing early civilizations with a rich oral culture that did not develop until much later into modes of recording and reading. Oral language skills of listening and speaking, being developed first, are referred to as primary language skills; writing and reading are secondary language skills. Spoken language is a symbol of a thought, an idea. The written word is a symbol of a symbol – the spoken word. For most people, the importance of the spoken word cannot be overestimated. Two of the four elements of the language arts hierarchy – listening and reading – can be categorised as receptive skills. Speaking and writing are designated expressive skills.

A major implication for the teacher is the understanding that the quality and quantity of receptive skills will have a major impact on the effective acquisition of expressive skills. It is important, therefore, that children of every level of ability have sufficient experience in the receptive modes of language acquisition before output exercises are required. The receptive mode will include listening and reading; both require sensory stimulation – one to the ear, one to the eye. Both will need a memory bank of vocabulary to relate to the words being heard or read. Both modes will require a grasp of the various linguistic systems of the language, including syntax and semantics. Both will require an attentive attitude and the application of specific thinking skills for the comprehension of the ideas in the narrative being listened to or decoded in reading.

Experience

All the skills of language and literacy require a fundamental level of experience in order to interpret and 'make sense' of the symbolic modes. For the child who is progressing along the milestones of development at an ordinary pace, experience will entail encountering and interpreting receptive and expressive language in a variety of social surroundings, usually in an automatic and unaided way. The child with developmental delay or with sensory or motor disability may need more focused assistance and more deliberate and structured arrangements so that a full range of sensory experiences can be encountered, assimilated and recalled. An appreciation of the importance of consolidating and extending the timeframe for sensory experience for children with learning disabilities needs to be part of the professional repertoire of skills drawn on by the effective teacher. Time spent enriching and extending the environment of children who might not automatically seek out or absorb experience of the wider world is attention given to laying the foundations for future progress.

A word might be said about first-hand and second-hand experience. Visual and audio stimuli, however vivid and dramatic, when experienced by means of television or other electronic media, are always second-hand encounters. However, when carefully and judiciously used, they can be important supplementary aids to experience. They are most powerful in introducing or recalling first-hand experiences such as a visit to the zoo, a street scene, a family occasion, shopping or transport, but they cannot be a substitute for first-hand experience. Television is a passive medium and requires careful control by the teacher so that it complements rather than replaces experience.

Listening

Listening is an underdeveloped skill for many children. In the past, traditional modes of instruction implied that children could automatically adopt a listening mode. The fact is that many children do not acquire functional skills in listening by themselves and need to have these skills identified and deliberately taught. Some children have a learning difficulty that arises out of an inability to comprehend spoken language. The child with a receptive language difficulty may try to avoid language activities, may demonstrate an unwillingness to listen and may find verbal exchanges unpleasant and unwelcome.

Listening and hearing are not the same thing. Hearing requires functioning auditory capability. For instance, it is possible to hear a foreign language being spoken but still experience a barrier in listening to what is being communicated. In contrast to the physiological process of hearing, listening requires the following range of sub-skills:

- Evaluation.
- Selection.
- Comprehension.
- Organising ideas.
- Acceptance or rejection.
- Internalising ideas.
- Appreciation.
- Relating to previous understandings.

Relationship between listening and reading

While there are similarities in the receptive modes of listening and reading, there are also notable differences. With the exception of recorded audio material, the listener usually has just one transient opportunity to receive and interpret the spoken voice. The reader has more control over the received data and can retrace words and sentences or regulate the speed of interpreting the written symbols according to the requirements of the exercise or the difficulty of the contents. The listener's rate of receptivity, however, is determined by the speed and clarity of the speaker. On the other hand, the listener has the advantage of deriving additional information from tone of voice, gesture, emphasis, appearance and proximity of the speaker.

The opportunities for preparing appropriate pathways for the maximum mastery of the skills of reading are to be found in the quality of the previous mastery of listening skills.

This will be particularly important for the child for whom literacy will present extra challenges. The relationship between the receptive skills is illustrated in Table 10.1.

Table 10.1: **Receptive skills**

Receptive skills	Listening	Reading
Sensory stimulation	Hearing	Seeing
Decoding skills	Auditory perception Recognition of words and sounds heard	Visual perception Recognition of words in print
Comprehension	Listening	Reading

Teaching listening

Listening skills need specific, direct teaching strategies. These skills can be categorised into levels that require progressively more complex outcomes and abilities. These include:

1 Auditory perception of non-language sounds.
2 Discrimination of isolated single language sounds.
3 Building a listening vocabulary.
4 Understanding linguistic elements.
5 Auditory memory.
6 Listening comprehension.

It is worth noting that some students who are exhibiting learning difficulties at second-level schooling may have deficits in a number of these areas. Strategies appropriate to students' age and level of experience, as well as inclusive exercises useful for reinforcing the skills of all students, will need to be developed or adapted.

Strategies for teaching listening skills

1 Auditory perception of non-language sounds

Recorded sounds of noises in the environment (door closing, car starting, footsteps on gravel, vacuum cleaner, etc.). These can be illustrated on a worksheet and numbered in sequence by listeners. Individual cards illustrating sounds can be arranged in sequence.

2 Discrimination of isolated single language sounds
Use real objects or pictures of an object to elicit initial consonant sounds from child. Pictures of initial consonant sounds may be pasted together in the pages of a scrapbook.

Younger children:
- Sound boxes (shoeboxes labelled with initial consonant or vowel sound) can be used for gathering pictures or actual objects that begin with the initial sound.

Older children/students:
- Listen to a series of multi-syllabic words, e.g. 'illustrated', 'unfortunately', 'energy', and list the number of syllables in correct sequence.

3 Building a listening vocabulary
A good receptive vocabulary requires knowledge not only of names of objects, but of actions, qualities, attributes and abstract concepts.

Younger children:
- Words that describe the attributes of objects and actions can be taught by providing concrete objects and pictures that illustrate contrasting sets of experiences, e.g. little/large; hot/cold; rough/smooth; early/late; public/private.

Older children/students:
- Categorisation and concept development – the concept of an object, e.g. chair, can be enlarged and illustrated by listing all the different kinds of chair, e.g. deck chair, dentist's chair, throne, banquette, stool, toilet seat.

4 Understanding linguistic elements
Words need to be understood in the context of their linguistic units and not just as single words. Children with linguistic difficulties may have a tendency to use one-word utterances.

Practice in understanding sentences will be particularly useful for children with receptive language difficulty.

Younger children:
- Riddles: On a worksheet there are a series of numbered pictures and related words. The teacher asks the child to listen to the riddle and to tick or circle the correct picture, e.g. 'Something to keep your neck warm when it is cold' (scarf).

Older children/students:

- Directions: Directional instructions require sequential comprehension and spatial orientation. Give older children practice by gradually increasing the number of sequential activities and by introducing specific directional vocabulary (left, under, diagonally). Students may be given drawing exercises using squared paper and responding to spoken instructions. Working in pairs may help avoid confusion and frustration and help in completing the challenge successfully.

5 Auditory memory

Auditory memory refers to the ability to store in the memory from spoken instruction and to accurately recall the information when required. Children with general learning disabilities may exhibit considerable trouble in retaining and recalling more than one item of information at a time. Some exercises can help reinforce and improve the child's auditory memory skills.

Younger children:

- Listening for details: Read a story to the child and ask questions that are detailed in nature but require only a true/false response.

Older children/students:

- Mnemonics or memory cues: Sequences and lists such as the signs of the zodiac, relating birthday months to classmates' names, capital cities of Europe, etc., can be taught by visual association or rhyming devices. Ask students to devise ways of memorising lists and to describe their methods.

6 Listening comprehension

Exercising comprehension in the process of hearing involves a combination of listening skills and thinking skills.

Younger children:

- Getting the main idea: Read a short and unfamiliar story to children and ask them to select the main idea from three choices. Ask children to choose an appropriate title for the story, incorporating the main idea.

Older children/students:

- Critical listening: Listen to recordings of radio advertisements and identify the techniques the advertiser is using to get the listener to buy the product. Record a short story and stop the sequence at a point that requires the listener to make inferences and draw conclusions about what is going to happen next.

Speaking

Teaching has traditionally been focused on the written forms of communication – reading and writing – despite the recognition of the primacy of listening and speaking in developing literacy competence. More recent curricular revisions, particularly at primary level, have recognised and emphasised the importance of creating oral language opportunities in every lesson. For the child who has deficiencies in verbal expression, structured and systematic practice in a way that guarantees success and supports effort is a necessary requirement for ongoing progress.

Strategies for teaching speaking skills

1 **Telephone speaking skills:** Teacher models procedure for clarity in speaking and good etiquette when answering a phone.
2 **Puppetry:** Children who are reluctant to speak out in class may be encouraged to help a glove puppet to speak.
3 **Interviewing:** Children can plan a series of questions to ask each other in the class or to interview a visitor. The interview may be audio recorded if this adds to the positive reinforcement of the pupil.
4 **Show and tell:** Children are encouraged to bring an interesting object into class and talk about it. The class can then be invited to ask the child questions about the item.
5 **Discussion of attributes of an object:** Children can be encouraged to take any object and describe its various attributes: colour, shape, size, tactile quality, weight, material, natural or artificial, function and origin.
6 **Questioning skills:** A chart is posted in the classroom giving the key question words: what, where, when, why, who, whose, which and how. Children are invited to use the full range when asking questions. (Even older children have difficulty using 'which' and 'whose'.)

Among its other benefits, circle time offers real opportunities for developing speaking and listening skills in an inclusive setting. It is a flexible and adaptable methodology that creates a new environment for learning and alters the dynamic of the traditional classroom. The teacher participates on the same level as the pupils. There are devices and techniques within circle time that permit turn-taking, topic maintenance and non-threatening opportunities for verbal exchange and communication (Mosley and Tew 1999, Masley 2005). This approach has also had effective practical application in secondary schools.

Reading

Perhaps there is no skill more powerful than the skill of reading for affirming the child's capability as a learner. The child's struggle with learning difficulties in developing and advancing reading skills is frequently fraught with failure and loss of self-esteem. The teacher who places the process of learning to read in the context of meaning-making and communication will seek to develop ways of motivating and maintaining the pupil's confidence.

The National Reading Initiative was an action plan promoted by the Irish government for the year 2000. Its aim was to improve the level of reading among the population by increasing public awareness of the importance of reading and by improving the quality of the teaching of reading. The continuing urgency of addressing literacy in a societal context is underlined by the finding in recent research by the DES (2005b) that 11 per cent of Irish homes have fewer than ten books.

A videotape and booklet commissioned by the National Reading Initiative in 2001 was aimed at supporting teachers in implementing the then recently revised primary school curriculum with special reference to the teaching of reading.

The conditions under which children will learn to read best was outlined in the material distributed to all schools. McPhillips (2003: 90) summarised these conditions in noting that the climate for optimising the mastery of reading skills will incorporate opportunities in which:

- The child is exposed to all kinds of books: picture books, fiction and non-fiction.
- All senses are involved in an integrated way: listening, speaking, reading and writing.
- Oral language development is encouraged by listening to rhymes, songs, listening to each other talking about books, sharing and enjoying books.
- The classroom becomes a print-rich environment with labels, signs, captions and real writing on display.
- Writing is linked with reading. With guidance from the teacher, children can create their own book(s) using words they know. This makes the experience real – real writing and real reading in which the children become engaged as readers and writers.
- There is partnership with parents. Regular communication with parents regarding the rationale of reading instruction in the school and the involvement of parents in supporting the reading process is a vital part of this three-way partnership of Teacher–[School]–Parents–Pupils.

Children and young people who experience learning difficulties will have an even greater need for these supports. A structured approach will also be necessary and attention given to specific skills and strategies for meeting the challenges of reading and reinforcing success.

Research literature on the teaching of reading frequently highlights the relative merits of a 'skills-based approach' and a 'meaning-making' approach. The first method emphasises phonetic decoding strategies. The other system uses whole-word techniques and focuses on thinking skills in a literature-based context. For most children, both methods have their merits:

> The research ... gives ample evidence that we do indeed know a great deal about beginning reading. Yet divisiveness over code-emphasis (analytical approaches) versus meaning-emphasis (experience-based approaches) rages on. Isn't it time to stop bickering about which is more important? Isn't it time that we recognize that written text has both form and function? To read, children must learn to deal with both, and we must help them' (Stahl et al. 1990: 123).

In relation to the additional learning needs of children with literacy difficulties, Pressley (1994: 211) notes: 'Experiencing more explicit instruction of reading skills and strategies in no way precludes the authentic reading and writing experiences emphasized in whole-language. Rather, explicit instruction enables at-risk students to participate more fully in such literacy experiences.'

Strategies for teaching reading

Analytical approach
The process of learning to read involves a steady progression of skills. The teacher of children with literacy difficulties or general learning disabilities will need to be aware of these stages and to modify, adapt and give particular emphasis to them where appropriate.

Developmental approaches to the teaching of reading

1 Logographic stage:
- Whole-word recognition.
- Building up a sight vocabulary.
- Visual memory.
- Look-and-say strategies.
- Immersion in a print-rich environment.

2 Alphabetic stage:
- Letter and sound correspondence.
- Phonic decoding skills.
- Word-attack skills.

3 Orthographic stage:
- Automatic recognition of words.
- Using contextual cues for comprehension (Frith 1985).

At the alphabetic stage, a structured programme of phonological awareness will be an essential strategy for the teacher, who will need to give continued support and reinforcement to the child's efforts. The child will need to demonstrate mastery not only of the names of the alphabet letters, but the sounds they represent. Teaching phonological awareness will also include:
- Breaking up sentences into separate words.
- Breaking words into syllables.
- Counting syllables.
- Making rhyming words.
- Nursery rhymes and rhymed stories.
- Segmenting words into onset and rime to make word families (s-and; h-and; st-and).
- Clapping games for syllabification.
- Add a sound: Children say their name or a word without the initial sound (-atasha; -ark).

- Take away a sound: Say a pair of words and add a sound to the second word (girl/girls; mile/smile) (McPhillips 2003: 102).

At the orthographic stage, where word recognition skills are developing more automatically, it will be necessary for the teacher to focus more on comprehension strategies. These will include:

- Cloze procedure; finding a missing word in a passage by judging the context.
- Sequencing ideas in the text.
- Locating the main idea in a paragraph.
- Predicting ends of sentences and passages.
- Using dictionaries.
- Overviewing material before it is read.
- Scanning text for essential information.
- Using SQ3R Comprehension Strategy: Survey, Question, Read, Recall and Review.
- Generating questions about the material by thinking aloud.

Westwood (2003: 113) states that 'strategic training to develop effective reading comprehension is one of the most promising areas of instructional intervention.'

Meaning-emphasis approach

Whole-language meaning-emphasis approaches to teaching reading hold that the true nature and purpose of reading is meaning-making. It is argued that a focus on the technical component skills of learning to read, if relied on exclusively, may fail to achieve this goal for the child. The whole-language approach draws on the belief that children acquire reading skills in a similar way that they learn to use speaking for communication. Strategies which are based on this approach include:

- Reading stories to children every day.
- Having 'real' literature available for children to read.
- Discussing and reflecting on stories.
- Encouraging silent reading.
- Integrating language and literacy activities across the curriculum.

Whole-language instruction in isolation may not suit the learning characteristics of every child (Westwood 2003: 103).

This may be a challenge for the child or student with special educational needs in an inclusive setting. However, when combined with systematic, direct and intensive instruction in phonological skill-building, the experience of meaning-making methods will enhance confidence and help motivation.

Multi-sensory approaches towards mastery in reading

Fernald

This method, developed in the 1940s, combines a multi-sensory approach to reading that simultaneously involves four sensory avenues: visual, auditory, kinaesthetic and tactile (VAKT). The words learned are selected from stories the child has dictated to the teacher.

The teacher writes the word to be learned in crayon on paper. The child traces the word with his or her fingers. As the child traces it, the teacher says the word so the child hears it. This process is repeated until the child can write the word correctly without looking at the sample. When the task is completed, the word is placed in a file box for the child to retrieve and eventually accumulate to make a story using the words (Fernald 1943; Westwood 2003: 144).

Montessori

The Montessori Method emphasises a structured multi-sensory preparation for reading/writing which has also been successfully used to support children with learning difficulties in inclusive settings. Children internalise sounds as they trace the shapes of sandpaper letters. When children have mastered the phonetic sounds, they are ready to begin word building with the moveable alphabet. They begin by building two- or three-letter phonetic words (those in which all the letters make their most common sound, like 'dog', 'pig', 'ram', 'bat', etc.). In order to allow the children to work independently, they are given small phonetic objects which represent the words they are to build. Later, pictures of phonetic words can be introduced for variety and additional practice in word building/writing.

Writing

The written form of language is the highest and most complex form of communication. While it comes last on the hierarchy of language skills, it is also correct to note that the skills of reading and writing are most often learned simultaneously with reciprocal overlapping of competences. The Montessori approach recognises that writing is a skill that children are active in before they learn to read. Young children do not see a distinction between 'drawing' and 'writing' and their early drawings and shape-making develop gradually to represent significant symbolic shapes – initially, the letters of their own name.

Writing incorporates the three components of:

- Handwriting.
- Spelling.
- Written expression.

Learning to write is not just a mechanical operation involving the coordination of eye movements and fine-motor finger muscle control. It is also a thinking process. Learning to write requires perception and accurate recall of symbolic patterns not immediately present to the senses. Writing from memory is a complex activity.

Some of the underlying challenges that may interfere with a child's handwriting performance may include:

- Poor motor skills.
- Behavioural difficulties.
- Faulty visual perception of letters and words.

- Difficulty in retaining visual impressions.
- Visual-motor cross-modal difficulties.
- Left-handedness.

Left-handedness

Left-handedness is a normal manifestation of difference and the child who develops a strong preference for the left hand should be facilitated without fuss. To support more comfortable cursive writing for the left-hand user, the top of the paper should be slanted north-east, opposite to the slant used by right-handed children. The pencil should be long, gripped low about 3 cm from the tip with the other end of the pencil pointing to the left shoulder. The position of the hand should be curved, with the weight resting on the outside of the little finger. Hooking the hand should be avoided.

Dysgraphia

Children who display severe problems in handwriting or who write very slowly may find a word processor a more effective means of communication. The use of IT to assist children with handwriting difficulties has proved very effective and the use of equipment such as adapted keyboards and speech-recognition software can provide liberating doorways to reinforcement and success that might not be possible in the struggle with handwriting.

Strategies for teaching handwriting:
- Chalkboard activities.
- Sand tray and finger-painting.
- Practising sitting posture.
- Paper angle for writing.
- Holding the pencil.
- Stencils and templates.
- Tracing.
- Drawing between the lines.
- Headlined paper.

Spelling

Even for children or students who do not have special educational needs, spelling is a difficult task to master. Research conducted in Ireland (Culligan 1997) indicated that more than 50 per cent of the children surveyed were experiencing spelling difficulties. This study also drew attention to the correlation between poor linguistic ability and poor spelling ability.

A child may be able to read a word correctly but not be able to spell it. Recognising a word in print is a decoding exercise in which there are many contextual cues to aid the reader. Reproducing a word through spelling is an encoding task and the opportunity to draw on peripheral cues is greatly reduced.

As in the teaching of reading, a whole-language orientation to spelling places emphasis on instruction for meaning-making. In other words, children should be helped to spell the words they need to use only when they need them to write. Here, word-frequency lists are given prominence rather than random lists of words for spelling tests. In the whole-language approach, when a child requests the spelling of a certain word, the teacher takes the opportunity to teach some phonic or word-attack principles (Westwood 2003: 167). However, this approach to spelling will be inadequate for the child with learning difficulties, who will require more deliberate and structured instruction. Used in isolation, this method may also result in limited understanding of how words are constructed and patterns that many words share.

As in reading, it is important that teachers are aware of the developmental stages in acquiring spelling so that a correct assessment and diagnosis of difficulties may be obtained.

Stages of development in spelling:
1 **Prephonetic:** This is the play stage in writing where capital letters and drawings are interspersed.
2 **Phonetic:** At this stage the child's spelling is dependent on letter-sound correspondence acquired through incidental learning. Children invent spelling based on auditory perception of words. Many poor spellers never progress beyond this phase.
3 **Transitional:** The child has moved to more visual strategies and is aware of words within words and common letter sequences.
4 **Independent:** At this stage the learner uses visual imagery very effectively when writing or checking words. Proofreading, self-help and self-correcting strategies are utilised.

In an expert analysis of the challenge of learning to spell, Culligan (1997) points to an over-reliance on aural-based attempts and attributes this to flawed practices adopted at the earliest stages of the development of spelling: 'Continued reliance on sound as an approach to learning or teaching spelling is detrimental, and unquestionably will not benefit the under-achiever.' Visual and kinaesthetic techniques are recommended so that the child looks meaningfully at words and moves away from the style of trying to spell words letter by letter.

Strategies for teaching spelling:
1 **Visual perception exercises:** Flash cards, overhead projector slides for speed in visual recognition.
2 **Look-say-cover-write-check:**
• Child looks carefully at the word on the list.
• Says the word clearly. How many syllables? Finger-tracing may help some children.
• Cover the word so it cannot be seen.

- Write the word from memory, pronouncing it while writing.
- Check written version with the original. If incorrect, repeat the steps.

Written expression

The ability to compose written ideas in a narrative requires many foundational prerequisite skills, including facility in oral language, reading ability, sufficient skill at spelling, legible handwriting and knowledge of the conventions of written usage. Even with this range of competences, the child or young person must have something meaningful to write about and a convincing purpose for wanting to do so.

For children or young people with literacy difficulties, it is essential that rich input experiences such as field trips, visitors, storytelling and discussions become motivators for written expression. It is difficult to write if there is nothing to write about. There will also be little incentive to engage in written expression if the teacher's response is one of excessive correction. Sensitivity to the communicative intent in the exercise must be the first consideration.

Strategies for teaching written expression

- **Letter writing:** These can be actual letters of thanks to a classroom visitor, a letter to an author or a request for information.
- **Play dialogue:** A conversation in direct speech can be written on a prepared script sheet by a pair of students. A scenario should be briefly outlined with details of characters. This can be 'acted' out.
- **Class magazine:** In this project, all children/students play a part with an appropriate written contribution. These may include illustrations with labels, letters, reports of sporting events, jokes, puzzles or fiction. The magazine is word-processed and printed for class distribution.

Language experience approach

The language experience approach (LEA) is a method that combines all of the language arts and maximises the meaning-making experience of learning literacy. It is in essence a dictated-story method with a strong personal connection to and ownership of the literacy materials. The approach can be summed up as follows:
- What I know about, I can talk about.
- What I say can be written down.
- I can read what I have written/dictated.

Beginning readers and children with literacy difficulties are helped to write something that is relevant and personally meaningful to them and augment the information with photographs or illustrations. With assistance, they can read back what they have dictated and enjoy sharing it with others. There are two major strengths in this strategy. Firstly, the child's own interests become the material for literacy improvement. Secondly, the teacher is able to work effectively within the child's current level of competence. This method also permits the learner to create his/her own reading materials. Attention may be given to layout, illustration, printing and binding of the finished book. Alternatively, a loose-leaf binder can be utilised so that pages can be updated or added. Westwood (2003: 106) presents a seven-step approach to implementing the language experience approach and cites Stauffer (1980) as one of the best sources of detailed information on this method.

Numeracy difficulties: Introduction

The subject of learning difficulties in numeracy has received a lot less attention than other areas of special educational need. Yet for many children with learning disabilities, numeracy may be the specific area of difficulty, both in primary and in secondary schools. A learning disability in the area of arithmetical comprehension is often referred to as dyscalculia. For many other children and young people, a permeating 'maths phobia' results in a sense of alienation from the subject matter. Mathematics remains an almost impenetrable foreign language. It is not unusual to hear otherwise able students say 'I cannot do maths.'

Defining numeracy

Ireland has no explicit official definition of numeracy, despite its widespread use in reports and educational documents (O'Donoghue 2002). The first usage of this term dates back almost 50 years to the publication in England of the Crowther Report (1959). Crowther defined numeracy as almost the mirror image of literacy. Just as literacy is more than the mere technical mastery of reading, numeracy needs to be seen 'more in terms of sense making, application and decision making' (O'Donoghue 2002: 49).

The 1995 IALS Survey, which ranked 25 per cent of the Irish population at the lowest level of literacy competence, also measured 'quantitative literacy'. This was defined as 'the knowledge and skills required to apply arithmetic to numbers incorporated in printed materials' such as timetables, medical prescription information and domestic or food products. In the 2000 PISA Study, Ireland ranked fifteenth from twenty-seven countries in mathematical literacy, which was defined as 'an individual's capacity to identify and understand the role mathematics plays in the world, to make well-founded mathematical judgments and to engage in mathematics, in ways that meet the needs of that individual's current and future life as a constructive, concerned and reflective citizen'.

Learning difficulties in numeracy

Westwood (2003) notes that while approximately 6 per cent of students may have significant difficulties in learning basic mathematical concepts and skills, a much larger percentage present as low achievers in mathematics and exhibit signs of 'maths phobia'. While a small number of students may have a specific learning difficulty related to mathematics (dyscalculia), most will have the source of their difficulties rooted in a range of obstacles, including:

- Insufficient or inappropriate instruction.
- Pacing of instruction not matching students' assimilation skills.
- Insufficient structuring of discovery or experiential learning.
- Problems with teachers' use of mathematical language.
- Abstract symbols introduced too early and concrete materials and experiences withdrawn too soon.
- Students with reading problems have only numerical computation to fall back on and problems are compounded.
- Place value concepts introduced before sufficient understanding of number relationships have been assimilated.

Students with general learning disabilities essentially need to be taught maths concepts that promote understanding prior to the memorisation of isolated facts. A most effective method is to follow the sequence:

- Concrete.
- Representational.
- Abstract.

Only when the learner has mastered the concept at a concrete, manipulative level can knowledge be transferred to a representational medium or illustration. At the representational level, pictures of objects, tallies or graph images serve as bridges between concrete and abstract instruction. When the learner can demonstrate understanding at the representational level, it is only then appropriate to introduce abstract symbols and to focus on memorisation and fluency-building techniques such as tables and formulae.

Students with special educational needs benefit from instruction that is highly structured and organised step-by-step by the teacher. Strategies for solving maths problems are not easily or efficiently adopted. Students with learning difficulties in numeracy must be taught specific strategies that are easily accessible and reliably helpful. Sometimes mnemonic devices may help students who have memory deficits and difficulties recalling lengthy processes needed to solve maths problems. One such device is the RRCC strategy described in Hayes (2003: 50):

- R – Read the problem; say it to yourself.
- R – Read it again.
- C – Check you have the numbers right.
- C – Check you have the question right.

Principles of mathematics teaching

Teaching strategies in numeracy can be divided into mathematics calculation and mathematics reasoning. The first emphasises computation and working out accurate answers to problems by means of predetermined methods and formulae. The second focuses on thinking skills related to mathematics and explores creativity and flexibility in addressing a problem or situation. Both approaches are complementary and need to be given balanced attention.

The principles of mathematics teaching will apply to all learners but are especially essential for meeting the needs of children with difficulties or disabilities in numeracy. They are:

- Progression from concrete to representational to abstract.
- Practice and overlearning.
- Generalisation.

Bereiter (1968) stresses that these principles have to be understood and consistently applied at every level:

- Emphasis in arithmetic should be finding out an answer to a specific question rather than a calculation to be completed.
- Whatever is learned should be generalised to many different kinds of experiences and situations.
- Beginning mathematics should be made coherent and interconnected instead of a series of unrelated topics and tricks.
- Time has to be given for sufficient practice so that concepts are assimilated and overlearned.
- Confidence building has to be a main aim in instruction; mistakes and errors are allowable and welcomed.

McPhillips (2003: 145) has identified the following priority areas for children with learning difficulties in mathematics:

- Basic number skills.
- Problem-solving skills.
- Mathematical language.
- Estimation skills.
- Discussion skills in maths.
- Practical activities.

Teaching strategies for mathematics calculation

Mathematical skills are typically taught in sequence, but the pace of progression through this sequence will depend on the level of ability and the developmental stage of the child.

- **Sets and matching:** Concept of the 'same' and grouping of objects.
- **Relationship concepts:** Comparing and relating objects.
- **Measuring and pairing:** Estimating, fitting objects, one-to-one correspondence.
- **Counting:** Matching numerals to objects.
- **Sequential values:** Arranging like objects in order by quantitative differences.
- **Relationships of parts to whole and parts to each other:** Experimenting with self-correcting materials to discover numerical relationships.
- **Operations:** Manipulation of number facts without reference to concrete objects – number facts up to ten.

- **Decimal system:** Learning the system of numeration and notation beyond ten, to the base ten.

Activities for teaching mathematics calculation

The following list should be considered illustrative rather than comprehensive. Importance must be placed on the interrelatedness of number concepts, their practical application in concrete terms and their relevance and transferability to life situations.

- **Number line:** Stretched around the walls of the classroom, the number line gives a permanent representation and reminder of the place of numbers relative to each other. Addition and subtraction can be demonstrated by counting forwards and back.
- **Balance:** The two-pan balance demonstrates the concept of equals (=) at the fulcrum. The quantities in each pan must balance, but their composition can vary (5 + 3 = 4 + 4 or 8 = 9 − 1). This can first be demonstrated with counters and represented by drawings.
- **Measuring:** Pouring sand, water or beans from a container of one size to a different container helps the child develop concepts of measurement. Estimating quantities, use of measuring cups and use of fractions can be emphasised in such activities.
- **Base-ten abacus box:** This can be a three-compartmented box or represented by a board with three sections. Up to nine counters may be placed in each compartment. With the tenth counter, all are taken out and one inserted in the box to the left.
- **Zero:** The concept of zero/naught is related to there being 'nothing in the box' of the abacus.
- **100 square:** x = 'rows of'. The instruction 3 x 4 asks the pupil to assemble three rows of four counters. These can be represented by drawings on a squared page. The cumulative number (12) can be inserted in the frame of a prepared 100 square where top horizontal and left vertical are numbered from 1 to 10.

Strategies for mathematics reasoning

Pupils and students with learning difficulty frequently experience confusion when faced with a maths problem. Very often there is difficulty comprehending the meaning of specific terminology. There may be uncertainty about which operation or process to use. The teacher's task will be to teach the student strategies for approaching problem-solving without a feeling of panic or helplessness. A useful checklist for self-monitoring and self-correcting is given by Westwood (2003: 199):

- **Identify the problem:** 'What needs to be worked out?'
- **Select or create a strategy:** 'How will I try to do this?'

- **Visualisation:** 'Can I picture the problem in my mind?'
- **Self-monitoring:** 'Is this working out OK?'
- **Evaluation:** 'How will I check if my solution is correct?'
- **Self-correction:** 'I need to correct this error and try again.'

Activities for mathematics reasoning

The focus in the mathematics reasoning approach is to help the learner see that there is a problem to be solved rather than merely attempting a rote solution. Exercises in mathematics reasoning will involve helping the pupil/student to see that there are real-life applications to the calculations they have learned.

- **Shop:** Have pupils compose shopping lists and calculate shopping bills. Writing out cheques involves writing money amounts in words. Each purchase requires a written receipt.
- **Time:** Analogue a.m./p.m. time and 24-hour digital clock. Public transport timetables. How long does a journey take?
- **Measurement:** Calculating area. How can we find the area of the classroom? Air is measured in cubic metres. What is the capacity of the classroom? How can it be calculated?
- **Tangram:** The seven-piece Chinese puzzle fits together to make a square. The relationships between the geometrical shapes make many other fascinating possibilities.

According to Enright and Choate (1997: 280): 'Problem solving is the primary function of mathematics education. Students must learn how and when to use the computational and fact skills they develop or these skills will be of no use at all. Solving problems involves the use of reading, computation and a host of other skills specific to the process.'

Concluding comments

Enabling the acquisition of literacy and numeracy skills is a high priority for all schools and it is vital that children and young people with special educational needs acquire these skills at an early stage of their school careers. Teacher awareness of the particular difficulties these children may experience is an important step in helping them to experience success and gain confidence in connecting the skills of literacy and numeracy to learn more about the world.

Discussion points

1 For most children, reading is a sign of achievement, affirmation of their emerging ability and a cause for celebrating empowerment and self-esteem. Parents, too, are sensitive to the social dimension of reading achievement. What can teachers do to inform and reassure parents about the importance of understanding the wider aspects of reading attainment so that children who are experiencing difficulties or delay will not be marginalised or

stigmatised and so that they can experience success at their own pace and level of development?

2   Investigate the PASSPORT Programme produced by the Curriculum Development Unit, Mary Immaculate College of Education, Limerick, a graded approach to Shared Reading for students who have a mild to moderate general learning disability in both primary and post-primary schools. What is Shared Reading and what are the components of the approach presented in this programme? (See www.cdu.mic.ul.ie/pdf/passport.pdf.)

3   What are the obstacles that create barriers to children developing confident oral language skills? In particular, what are the difficulties that may arise as a result of school practices and policies and some instructional methods?

4   'Maths phobia', or a fear of failure at maths, can be an overpowering reality for many children and young people who are convinced that they are 'just not any good at maths'. Sometimes this conviction is ratified and reinforced by parents. Should teachers accept this as a limitation in the student's learning ability or consider it as an instructional challenge to turn around this way of thinking?

Chapter 11
Understanding and Approaching Behaviour Difficulties

Learning outcomes/objectives

On completion of this chapter, the reader will be able to:
- Identify the characteristics of schools that successfully attempt to address the problem of challenging behaviour.
- Summarise the insights derived from the psychology of Alfred Adler and William Glasser in approaching behaviour difficulties.
- Outline Rudolf Dreikur's four goals of misbehaviour and describe strategies and approaches appropriate for managing and redirecting these goals.
- Describe the positive discipline orientation in a whole-school approach, which appreciates the difference between the 'learning zone' and the 'battle zone'.

Introduction

Corporal punishment existed as a normal response to challenging behaviours in Irish schools until it was made illegal in the 1980s. The abolition of corporal punishment reflected the changing views of society towards children – placing children's individual needs central to the educational process. It is little over a generation since coercion and compliance were the expected norms of classroom culture; for a large number of parents and teachers, these are still abiding memories of school.

Times have changed. Over the past two decades, issues of classroom discipline and the pervasive presence of behavioural difficulties have preoccupied more and more teachers in their daily work. In second-level schools in particular, pupils who display challenging behaviour present problems that frequently create negative attitudes among staff to implementing inclusive policies. Over 70 per cent of teachers in second-level schools report that they have taught classes in the current school year in which students are engaged in continuous disruptive behaviour. The same survey reported that over 95 per cent of teachers attribute emotional and behavioural difficulties as being the main causes of negative student behaviour, while 80 per cent also regarded learning disabilities as major contributory factors in this regard (ASTI 2005: 7).

In special educational settings in Ireland, recent research has indicated that as many as 31 per cent of pupils are presenting with behaviour problems, ranging from physical aggression to non-compliance with instructional requests (Kelly et al. 2004). Many teachers have received little or no professional training in the management of challenging behaviour as part of the continuum of special educational needs presented by all pupils and students.

The *Report of the Task Force on Student Behaviour in Second Level Schools* (Martin 2006) noted that where these problems were being addressed successfully, the schools were characterised by:

> ... an ethos that is pastoral and where the culture is one of listening and communicating. There are good structures in place and a range of policies is implemented fairly and consistently. There is quality leadership throughout the school. Students are empowered and exercise a strong voice in relevant issues that pertain to the healthy status of the school ... Curricular provision is suited to the learning needs and competencies of the students. Teaching methodologies are varied and involve students in an active participative way (Martin 2006: 9).

Further support for schools in developing appropriate responses to behaviour difficulties has included the publication of guidelines to support the development of school-level codes of behaviour: *Developing a Code of Behaviour: Guidelines for Schools* (National Educational Welfare Board 2008) and guidelines to support primary schools: *Behavioural, Emotional and Social Difficulties: A Continuum of Support (Guidelines for Teachers)* (NEPS 2010c).

The National Educational Welfare Board perceived that supporting the development of school codes of behaviour constituted an important strand within their official remit to support school attendance and participation:

> The code of behaviour helps the school community to promote the school ethos, relationships, policies, procedures and practices that encourage good behaviour and prevent unacceptable behaviour. The code of behaviour helps teachers, other members of staff, students and parents to work together for a happy, effective and safe school ... It helps to foster an orderly, harmonious school where high standards of behaviour are expected and supported ... (p. 2).

Within the guidelines it is recommended that school-level codes of behaviour should aim to achieve the following goals:
- creating a climate that encourages and reinforces good behaviour
- creating a positive and safe environment for teaching and learning
- encouraging students to take personal responsibility for their learning and their behaviour
- helping young people to mature into responsible participating citizens
- building positive relationships of mutual respect and mutual support among students, staff and parents

- ensuring that the school's high expectations for the behaviour of all the members of the school community are widely known and understood (p. 22).

The basic principles underpinning an effective school code of behaviour are outlined and include:

Providing clarity
around school expectations for creating a harmonious teaching and learning environment and how disruptive behaviour will be approached within this context

Affirming that everyone's behaviour matters
emphasising that the behaviour of teachers and parents will influence the behaviour of pupils

Focusing on promoting good behaviour

Recognising that relationships are crucial
and that the code aims to foster respect and trust among the school community

Focusing on personal responsibility

Ensuring fairness and equity

Promoting equality

Recognising educational vulnerability
of pupils who have behaviour difficulties and providing positive support for these pupils

Attending to the welfare of students
and affirming their right to participate in, and benefit from, education

Attending to the welfare of staff
and promoting a positive and safe working environment for all staff (adapted pp. 22–23).

Within the NEPS guidelines on supporting primary schools in addressing behavioural difficulties the following working definition of behavioural, emotional and social difficulties is provided:

> … the term refers to difficulties which a pupil or a young person is experiencing which act as a barrier to their personal, social, cognitive and emotional development. These difficulties may be communicated through internalising and/or externalising behaviours. Relationships with self, others and community may be affected and the difficulties may interfere with the pupil's own personal and educational development or that of others. The contexts within which difficulties occur must always be considered, and may include the classroom, school, family, community and cultural settings.

Behavioural, emotional and social difficulties may be usefully thought of as behaviour occurring along a continuum from developmentally appropriate (e.g. normal testing of boundaries) and milder, more transient difficulties to difficulties which are significant and/or persistent, and which may warrant clinical referral and intervention. NEPS considers that diagnosed mental illness/clinical disorders are included in the term, but only a small minority of pupils on this continuum would have a clinical diagnosis (2010c: 4).

This definition recognises that behavioural difficulties occur along a continuum from relatively mild misbehaviour to, in a minority of cases, extreme behaviour that warrants clinical intervention. The guidelines emphasise that addressing behaviour issues appropriately and effectively will involve a whole-school approach that highlights the critical role of school leaders in promoting inclusive values and a supportive school culture (p. 16); demonstrates in everyday routines to pupils that they matter (p. 22); fosters a positive social environment in the classroom (p. 22); recognises that teacher attitudes and behaviour have a significant impact on pupil behaviour (p. 27); and enables pupils to develop the skills to engage with learning (p. 35).

This chapter will provide an overview of modern insights from counselling psychology, human resources management and good educational practice. It presents enlightened approaches that have pointed the way to many Irish schools and teachers to discovering solutions that have been helpful, effective and long-lasting. Specific approaches and practices will be identified for use with younger pupils in primary schools and also for students in secondary education. There are, of course, no simple or easy solutions; behaviour difficulties are both individualistic and complex and require both personalised and collaborative responses.

Understanding behaviour difficulties: Behaviour and primary needs

For a very long time, the rewarding and punishing of children seems to have been the only concept of motivation in Irish schools. Understandably, many teachers in training seminars and courses ask for tried-and-tested techniques that will result in getting children and young people to do as they are told. A crucial, but startlingly simple, realisation has to be accepted at the outset: children will only do something when they want to (O'Flynn and Kennedy 2000).

What motivates children to do anything? An answer to this question can be taken from the psychology of William Glasser (b. 1925); the American psychologist whose reality therapy has provided useful insights into understanding behaviour. Glasser rejects the classical stimulus-response behaviourist theories which have dominated educational thinking during the past century. Glasser does not accept that human behaviour is primarily motivated by external reward and fear of punishment (Glasser 1969). Essentially, Glasser argues that when the basic needs of food, warmth, shelter and safety have been attained, human behaviour is motivated by a desire to satisfy one of the primary needs to:

- Experience freedom.
- Have fun.

- Have a sense of empowerment.
- Have a sense of belonging; to feel loved.

It is not an easy task to change the behaviour of children and young people whose experiences have not sufficiently corresponded to these life-enhancing principles. Teachers who have used Glasser's insights in their classroom interactions and teaching methods have, however, reported significant and sustained improvements in behaviour where other approaches have failed or even exacerbated problems (O'Flynn and Kennedy 2000). When children are offered choices instead of directives, the activity or behaviour is dignified by the exercise of freedom. When the opportunity for some fun is appropriately infused into a classroom environment or a teaching style, the climate becomes more conducive to learning. When learners experience a sense of success, their need to feel empowered becomes fulfilled. When a child is satisfied that he or she can 'do it by myself', the sense of confidence accumulates in a way that encourages further achievements. When one is given structured opportunities for challenge and ultimate success at any age, the result is deeply rewarding. When young people are spoken to with respect, as opposed to being ordered, and when courtesy is modelled by the teacher (particularly when this is not automatically observed by the pupil or student), potential conflict can be defused. Teachers who work to make young people feel they are valued as people of importance find that the belonging needs of their pupils become more fulfilled and misbehaviour is minimised.

Principles of understanding behaviour difficulties

The opposite is also true. Children and young people who constantly experience failure, disempowerment and lack of status become infused with an inner sense of distance and unhappiness and eventually lose all sense of motivation. Some will withdraw into an inner despair where they stop trying. Others will adopt 'acting out' misbehaviour to mask the pain of failure and the constant assault on their sense of self-worth.

There are two significant principles that are important in understanding the nature of behaviour difficulties:

- Behaviour difficulty is always an attempt to communicate something.
- Anger and aggression exhibited by pupils with emotional and behavioural difficulties derive from inner hurt and pain (McNamara and Moreton 1995).

The pain experienced by children and young people with behaviour difficulties may be as a result of upbringing experiences or may arise from causes originating in school. This is most often an unrecognised hurt and is manifested by an anger that is urgent and undirected. Teachers' own feelings are affected by the feelings and consequent behaviours of these children and young people. The feelings engendered in teachers are frequently combinations of concern, frustration, annoyance and anger. An angry response from the teacher will not work, as the origins of the child's anger is pain. The problem may be temporarily suppressed by an angry reaction from the teacher, but the behaviour is also thereby fuelled for future explosion.

Goals of misbehaviour

The work of Rudolf Dreikurs (1897–1972), an Austrian-born American psychologist, has provided helpful insights into the nature of the hidden and subconscious communication attempts behind behaviour difficulties for many teachers and parents. Dreikurs was a disciple and colleague of Alfred Adler (1870–1937), who argued that young people are primarily motivated by a natural drive towards attaining a realisation of autonomy, independence and 'superiority' over a world of imposed external adult control. According to this perspective, behaviour difficulties in school originate in the expression by young people of a sense of inferiority and helplessness.

Dreikurs invites teachers to ask the question: what kind of unfulfilled need is being communicated by this young person's behaviour? The child has a pre-eminent urge to 'belong' – to find a sense of comfort and contentment within his place in the world among his peers. So what kind of mistaken goal is being pursued by the young person in order to attain this sense of 'belonging'? Dreikurs identifies four goals of misbehaviour:

- Attention.
- Power.
- Revenge.
- Withdrawal.

Attention seeking

Attention seeking is perhaps one of the most readily recognised modes of pupil misbehaviour. The usually dominant and authoritative position of the teacher in traditional classrooms can invite competition between children for recognition and notice. Behaviour can range from the child who continually asks irrelevant questions or makes comments during direct teaching sessions to irritating non-verbal behaviour during quiet work periods, such as tilting back on one's chair, making humming noises or animal sounds or rhythmically tapping objects on the desk or table. The origin of this kind of behaviour is a mistaken belief that reassurance about one's existence and importance in the world can only be obtained by eliciting the teacher's direct attention and maintaining that attention on a continual basis. The natural response of the teacher is one of irritation and annoyance. The automatic response is almost certainly to reprimand the pupil, to focus directly on the misbehaving pupil and to continue to follow up persistent attention-seeking incidents with admonishing interventions. The result is that the goal to obtain and maintain the attention of the teacher has been achieved. The teacher's response has in fact had the result of reinforcing the child's behaviour and belief in the effectiveness of their actions. The child has learned how to guarantee a continual and highly satisfying level of attention from a significant authority figure through misbehaviour. Ironically, the teacher has cooperated in this process.

What can be done to change the child's behaviour? The first thing is to recognise that the need for attention is a normal and, indeed, essential human need. Without it we would have no reassurance that our existence had any worth or value in the world. It is only the element of constant attention seeking that is unacceptable. Efforts have to be made to nurture essential attention needs while discouraging persistent attention-grabbing behaviour.

It is not easy to ignore irritating attention-seeking behaviour – and in some circumstances it may not be appropriate or wise to do so. However, there are approaches that can minimise this behaviour while reorienting children's natural need to be recognised. Some broad strategies for giving appropriate attention to children and young people are suggested. There are clearly different approaches more suitable for primary-age and secondary-school pupils.

Providing for attention/recognition needs in the primary school
- **Roll-call recognition:** Use calling the roll/register as an opportunity to say a positive, relevant or light-hearted word to every pupil at least once each day.
- **Symbolic belonging:** Create silhouette cut-outs for the heads of each child and display them high above notice boards on the classroom walls. Allow pupils to choose, if possible, the position where their cut-outs are to be placed. Clearly print the child's first name underneath each shadow picture. Always refer positively to children's images. Ask the class 'who is fourth on the right from James', etc.
- **Positive report home:** Over a period of time, send a brief note/letter to every child's home expressing the teacher's satisfaction with the child's progress and mentioning one specific positive quality or achievement.
- **Utilise circle time:** Circle time, if necessary in a space other than the classroom, can provide each child with a protected, controlled, regulated opportunity to speak, to be listened to and recognised (Mosley and Tew, 1999).

Providing for attention/recognition needs in the secondary school
- **Thanks:** After a student makes a contribution in class, say 'thank you' followed by the speaker's first name.
- **Apology:** Apologise immediately when something unacceptable is inadvertently said or done by you – or if the perception of a student is that you have acted unfairly or embarrassed a student by a remark or action.
- **Assistance:** Ask students for help in setting up or accessing IT equipment (even if you know how to do it) or in assembling or arranging demonstration materials or apparatus.
- **Celebrate achievement:** Utilise student/class/school magazines, school web page or media outlets to celebrate effort and achievement, individual differences and varied contributions.

- **Request advice:** Ask for students' advice or opinions on how to deal with troublesome situations. It may be possible to describe a scenario similar in certain respects to one which is directly relevant to student behaviour, e.g. dealing with put-down remarks.

Managing attention-seeking behaviour

Rather than draw attention to attention-seeking behaviour, it may be more effective to identify appropriate and desired behaviour – in other words, 'catch them doing it right'. With primary-age children, thanking them for observing the rule, e.g. hands up for attention, is far more effective than admonishing them for shouting out in class. Wolfgang (2001: 120) says 'the student who seeks attention should not receive it when he acts out. To give attention to the student for inappropriate behavior would be playing into the student's plan and would not help the student learn how to behave productively in the group.'

Strategy: Proximity and reinforcement

One way of providing attention and recognition to people is to give them proximity, i.e. standing or sitting near them, an act that is a natural action towards people we like. Proximity can also be used to focus or modify a person's behaviour. If a child or young person is trying to attract the teacher's attention by an inappropriate action, proximity control may be a more useful strategy than a verbal injunction. The teacher walks slowly in the direction of the offending pupil(s) but does not make eye contact or any other signs of recognition. Standing near the offending pupil or group but facing the rest of the class, the teacher affirms and verbally praises the desired behaviour observed by the rest of the class, e.g. 'Thank you all for working on your own and not distracting anyone else. I appreciate that.' The teacher should avoid any temptation to recognise the offender by a sarcastic or ironic comment. Any reference to the offending behaviour will have the outcome of reinforcing and consolidating its effectiveness.

Strategy: Quiet proximity

A variation on this strategy is required when an actual verbal intervention is necessary. In this situation, the teacher approaches the offending student/pupil and makes eye contact. The teacher bends close to the offender and in a low voice, almost a whisper, says the pupil's name and requests positively that the desired behaviour will be observed, e.g. 'James, will you please help me by working on your own for the next fifteen minutes. If you need help, just raise your hand.'

There are situations when these strategies will not be effective. It may be necessary to 'confront' the student with his/her behaviour in a safe situation and at an appropriate and private moment. If this can be done in a one-to-one counselling context, the student/pupil may be asked in an enquiring manner if his/her behaviour is 'because you feel you are not being given enough attention' by the teacher. The tone of this enquiry has to be neutral and non-accusational.

The implication has to be that the young person is entitled to sufficient and appropriate attention. The intention of this exercise is not to make the student feel guilty, embarrassed or defensive. It is to create a sense of reflectivity; to make the pupil/student aware that the teacher is conscious of his/her needs and to indicate that those attention needs can be facilitated and fulfilled by more appropriate classroom behaviour.

Wolfgang (2001) suggests some further approaches to dealing with incidents of attention-seeking in the classroom:

- Do the unexpected (turn off/on the lights, play a musical sound, talk to the wall).
- Distract the student (ask a direct question, ask a favour, change the activity).
- Notice appropriate behaviour (thank students, write well-behaved students' names on the chalkboard).
- Move the student (change the student's seat, send the student to the 'thinking chair').

It is important to note that any teacher action should be appropriate to one's personality style, the developmental level of the children and with the purpose of defusing rather than emphasising unwanted behaviour.

Power seeking

When a child discovers that he or she cannot be made to do something, it is a very significant revelation. Only the superior size and strength of the adult makes compliance inevitable in the face of a conflict. And this is a victory for the child – they have 'made' the adult use force to achieve their ends. It is a fundamental truth – people only do something when they want to do it. Yet the world of the child or young person is one where there are many restrictions. Issues of care and protection, order and regulation require that many constraints are necessary and normal. Perceived by the child, and often persisting into adolescence, the world is one where it seems adults dominate and rule with authority and assurance. The young person needs to test and challenge this condition in order to attain a sense of belonging in the world.

Very possibly, the child who exhibits defiance and non-cooperation has experienced the attempts of the teacher to forcibly stop his or her demands for attention. As a result, the young person has become determined to defeat the teacher and gains immense satisfaction from refusing to do what the teacher asks. The child feels that to submit to a demand from the teacher would be a capitulation to a superior power, which would result in a loss of personal value and worth. The need to preserve a sense of worth may lead the child or young person to engage in terrifying efforts to demonstrate their own power (Dreikurs 1990: 61).

Managing power and control issues

It is a natural and desirable thing to want to be in control and in charge of one's actions – to have a sense of autonomy, power and freedom. The child or young person whose behaviour attempts to draw the teacher into a power struggle is, according to Adlerian psychology, motivated by feelings of inferiority and has a compelling need to assert his or her 'striving for superiority' in the adult world. The kinds of behaviour associated with this 'power' mode are an extension of the earlier attention-seeking attempts, but with a more determined goal. The child or student may engage in some repetitive and irritating behaviour (off-task activity or distracting a nearby classmate). When asked to stop, he or she becomes defiant and escalates his or her negative behaviour and challenges the teacher. The teacher will feel annoyed and affronted by the student's actions. Furthermore, there will be a feeling on the teacher's part that their authority has been put to the test and the desire to confront this misbehaviour may be overwhelming. This is precisely the kind of response that the child or young person desires. Once it has been entered into, and having been drawn into battle, the teacher cannot win. Wolfgang (2001: 121) states:

> A student who wishes to possess power should not be able to engage the teacher in a struggle. The teacher who falls for this 'bait' and gets pulled into the battle is merely continuing the excitement and challenge for the student. The student becomes increasingly bolder and pleased with trying to test the teacher. The teacher should attempt to remove the issue of power altogether and force the student to look for some other goal for behaving.

The child or young person who is defiant, sullen and uncooperative has a pervasive feeling of disempowerment and helplessness. Its origins may be complex and multiple. He or she needs to have increased opportunities of experiencing capability and independence. The following strategies may be helpful.

Providing for empowerment needs in the primary school

- **Choice:** Logical consequences should offer the child a clear and logical choice of behaviour and results. The child must perceive that he or she has a choice and accept the relationship of this choice to what followed (Dreikurs and Grey 1968: 82). It is structured and arranged by the adult and must be experienced by the child as logical in nature (Dreikurs and Cassel 1972: 62).
- **Thinking time:** Instead of confronting the child, offer time to consider the request. Say: 'I'll let you think about it for a while and ask you in fifteen minutes.' Some teachers use a 'thinking chair' in the classroom for this purpose. This should be in a position that is not prominent and not seen as a punishment. The 'thinking chair' may be used for uninterrupted quiet time by anyone – even the teacher!
- **Offer responsibility:** The child or young person who has presented with obstinate or resistant behaviour may not immediately seem to be the teacher's choice for someone to undertake some trusted activity (such as organising the class lending library or keeping the computer printer stocked with paper).

This offer of responsibility may be the opposite of what is expected, yet something most needed by the child.

- **Peer tutoring:** Unlikely as it may seem, this child or young person may be the right person to help another pupil with a specific learning task such as spelling, number facts or reading skills. The energy otherwise used in defiance can be rechannelled into a determination to succeed and to help others succeed.

Providing for empowerment needs in the secondary school

- **Involvement:** Plan a chart of the course with students and explain how much work will be achieved by Christmas or the summer term. Involve students in planning and incorporate their expectations and goals.
- **Positive reframing of student opposition:** Teachers can look for positive traits in student oppositional behaviour. Students who 'answer back' may be perceived as cheeky but are also displaying courage in asserting their opinion. Students who argue with the teacher might be accused of arrogance, but from another point of view may be exercising a developing sense of justice and independence of thought. Reframing behaviour and reinterpreting it in terms of empowerment needs may help teachers to react more constructively.
- **Non-verbal communication:** A power clash may be avoided or defused if the teacher chooses to avoid a public verbal reprimand and can instead use a discreet non-verbal signal or gesture to get a student back on-task or to request attention (O'Flynn and Kennedy 2000: 72).
- **Review opportunities:** Giving students periodical possibilities of commenting on lessons may be opening the teacher to vulnerability. An evaluation sheet (such as that illustrated in McNamara and Moreton 1997: 47), if carefully constructed and managed, may empower students to define their problems and to put responsibility on them for seeking clarification and further help. Questions such as: 'What was good about this lesson?', 'What was bad about this lesson?', 'What did I do well?', 'What do I need to get better at?' or 'How do I feel about myself after this lesson and why?' may assist in this self-empowerment process for students.

An important distinction between the child who wishes to obtain attention goals and the child who is focused on power and control is usually manifested in the behaviour of the child on being corrected. The child who is intent on getting attention is likely to stop the behaviour, at least temporarily, when approached by the teacher. The pupil who responds by intensifying unwanted behaviour is in effect trying to show the teacher that he or she cannot be cowed into submission. At all costs, the teacher must read these signs and strategically refuse to be drawn into a power battle.

Revenge

If honest, every teacher will admit that there are some children whom it is very difficult to like. That is, there are some young people who project a demeanour of negativity and social unattractiveness that almost demands a reaction of dislike. Teachers invest enormous resources of restraint and professionalism in order to cope with these children. This young person sometimes appears to be smouldering with an inner anger; sometimes the child's tendencies are not so obvious and there is a quiet subtlety or deviousness about their negative behaviour.

This third mistaken goal, revenge, arises from the intensification of the power contest between the young person and the significant adult (Dreikurs 1990: 62). The child is battle-weary from the continuing struggle to assert his or her position of power; a great deal of energy is consumed in maintaining the conflict and dealing with the dislike and anger that the power-seeking obstinate behaviour tends to provoke. The child becomes discouraged and increasingly anxious about upholding his or her status and feeling of importance in the world. Anger is a way of dealing with fear, and this young person is very angry. Anger bubbles up from the feeling of dislike that the child seems to evoke in others. Becoming convinced that he or she is dislikeable and being increasingly frustrated at the sense of powerlessness that surrounds the child like a fog, a more desperate tactic is employed. The child's goal becomes retaliation and revenge. For this child or young person, the world is a hard and cruel place and there is too much hurt and rejection to bear. The strategy is to hurt before you are hurt.

The behaviour of this child may be physical and overtly aggressive to other children or it may be a hidden and insidious bullying that is difficult to detect. This kind of behaviour may include tearing up other children's work or purposely 'losing' classmates' books or material behind a radiator or cupboard. It may involve repetitive and hurtful name-calling or rumour-spreading or it may manifest itself in unprovoked physical assault.

This also may be the child or student who is noticed as being needy by the teacher and who responds by offering extra help, encouragement and support. For a time, it seems that progress is being made. The pupil seems responsive and the teacher feels gratified and optimistic. Then one day, suddenly, unaccountably, the student or child, with what seems like a cruel awareness, rejects the teacher's efforts and dismisses what seemed like a growing trust and cooperation. The teacher's reaction is one of disappointment, hurt and anger. The feeling is like a betrayal and there is a reflexive urge to deal harshly with the young person who has belittled the care and attention that has been lavished on him or her.

In these circumstances, there is a strong temptation for the teacher to use her or his superior verbal ability by making a sarcastic remark ('It's what I expected!'). There may be a tendency to act unfairly towards the child or by 'freezing out' or ignoring the student in class exchanges. The end result is to reinforce and reaffirm the student's deep sense of his or her unworthiness. The only way that this student or child can attain social status is to be consistently disliked.

To be of help to revenge-seekers, the teacher must avoid retaliation at all costs. As difficult as it may seem, the teacher needs to meet the sullen and uncaring demeanour of the revenge-seeking student by remaining calm and showing professional goodwill. Be prepared for the unexpected: if the war of revenge continues despite your attempts to defuse it, the revenge-seeker may come to feel completely defeated and may give up all attempts to become a contributing member. They may even turn their feelings inwards by displaying manipulation as their next weapon of choice.

Managing revenge and anger

The most important and fundamental reaction of the teacher to the revenge-seeking child or student is to make a clear distinction between the behaviour and the person. While vengeful and hurtful behaviour is not acceptable, the child is welcomed and accepted in the school and classroom. This is not an easy policy to uphold. The children and young people who are engaged in revenge activity are those most likely to qualify for serious sanctions and even suspension from school.

Strategies for dealing with anger/revenge misbehaviour in the primary school

- **Assertive, not angry:** It is appropriate to speak assertively to this child, but not with a tone of anger or menace. Make eye contact, say the child's name and in a firm but unemotional tone say: 'That behaviour is not acceptable here' or 'When you come in to class, I'd like you to leave that behaviour outside the door – but you are welcome here.'
- **Naming feelings:** Encourage the child to express hurt and anger without being hurtful. Help the child to describe and name the feeling he or she has during an angry or hurtful incident. Instructional materials such as *A House Full of Feelings and Emotions* (Laevers et al. 2005) may be useful in helping children to perceive a range of feelings within themselves and others and to give those feelings a name.
- **Creative therapy:** Children who are unwilling or unable to talk about their negative feelings may obtain an opportunity for safe expression in some artistic activity that will help channel aggression into creativity. Working with clay or dough involves having to pound and knead the material, while drawing and painting may allow a child to make images or colours relating to his or her feelings. Good judgment is required, however, before giving a child with angry feelings access to paintbrushes and water where there are other children present.
- **Positive reframing:** The child with even the most difficult behaviour has some positive qualities. It may be prowess on the sports field, a sense of humour, a talent at singing or a good vocabulary. The teacher should seek to identify these qualities and make an effort to remind the child that these are things people notice and admire. When a child is cheeky or argumentative, it may also be the case that he is assertive and that he is courageous in seeking out his own answers. Positive reframing attempts to interpret misbehaviour in terms of the child's needs to belong and to be valued.

Strategies for dealing with anger/revenge misbehaviour in the secondary school

- **Use 'I' messages:** When it is necessary to assert a position on behaviour, the teacher should avoid using the word 'you', as this can be perceived as accusing and personal and thus reinforcing vengeful behaviour. If the teacher uses 'I', it is possible to describe the effect of the behaviour on the work and responsibility of the teacher. This strategy takes some skill and prior reflection to master. For example, instead of saying to an offending student, 'You are constantly cheeky and bad mannered in class', the teacher might say, 'I want to treat all students with respect and I can't accept comments in class that are disrespectful.' The student in anger mode may well retort, 'I don't care.' The response from the teacher, factually and without an angry tone, is, 'But I care – about you and about everyone else here.'

- **Active listening:** A student who has an outburst of verbal anger expects to be met with an angry reaction in return. If it is possible at the time, and there is an opportunity to converse privately, ask the student to describe what is upsetting him or her. When the student speaks, make no comment except to repeat back exactly what the student says. This process reassures the student that what has been expressed has been heard and understood. It is the first step in finding a way to resolve the problem: 'Intelligent and empathic listening by teachers humanises their interactions with students. It enables the students to become aware of "what is going on for them" and what options are open to them' (O'Flynn and Kennedy 2000: 101).

- **Constructive confrontation:** According to O'Flynn and Kennedy (2000: 89), constructive confrontation is a method whereby the teacher can manage a situation of behaviour conflict without having to revert to authoritarian or coercive means. In essence, it involves a teacher 'stating the facts' about an incident of misbehaviour instead of making a judgmental comment. For example, to say, 'Mary, you're late!' is strictly judgmental. Objective evidence might, for instance, find that Mary's watch is running slow and she understood she was on time. It would be more factual to state, 'Mary, it is now 9:05 a.m. by the clock and you are just coming in.' To say 'That's a cheeky remark' is clearly judgmental. It would be more factual to say, 'Mary, just now I heard you say … and I don't like it. It sounds disrespectful.'

- **We have a problem:** Rather than imposing an immediate sanction on the offending student, which can stoke up resentment and non-cooperation, the teacher makes a clear assertive statement: 'We have a problem here and we need to find a solution that we all can agree on.' This statement is followed by silence on the teacher's part. The student may take this as a chance to express angry feelings. The teacher should not respond but stay focused on the common goal of finding a solution to this shared problem.

Withdrawal

The child or student who has adopted this mode of behaviour has decided to adopt a position of assumed disability and helplessness. Unlike the behaviours exhibited in the previous three categories, this child's misbehaviour is neither overt nor confrontational. The student feels worthless and without academic, physical, emotional or social abilities. This student does not interfere with the teacher's teaching or with other students' learning. He or she makes minimal or no effort in any aspect of schoolwork.

The teacher's reaction is to gradually give up on this student by decreasing expectations. With so many other students seeking attention or making demands on the teacher's time and energy, this young person is likely to be ignored, forgotten or treated with indifference. The teacher is likely to feel 'Why should I make the effort if you don't?'

In fact, this young person has become deeply discouraged and defeated. Over time, he or she has tried other strategies for recognition and empowerment, but these have been unsuccessful. The sole purpose of this student's behaviour is to avoid further hurt, humiliation or frustration. The goal of this child's misbehaviour is to convince the teacher that he or she wishes to be left alone and not have to deal with demands or expectations.

Managing withdrawal and inadequacy

The child who has developed strategies of withdrawal and lack of interest provokes a feeling of despair on the part of the teacher, for it seems that nothing can alter the child's resolve to be disengaged with and uninvolved in classroom activities. Sometimes it may even appear that the child is trying to provoke the teacher through passivity and indifference. It may also take the form of the child making negative comments about him or herself ('I'm stupid', 'I can't do it'). The child or young person may have perfectionist traits and will give up because he or she feels that they can never reach a level of achievement or success that will merit praise. Their response is to hide in a turtle-like shell and to seek invisibility. Attention makes this child withdraw even further and lack of attention reinforces the child's feelings of worthlessness. This mode of misbehaviour is difficult to deal with, all the more so because of its covert nature.

Providing for withdrawal/inadequacy needs in the primary school

- **Encouragement rather than praise:** Refrain from making remarks that comment on the quality of the end product or on the person him/herself ('Good boy', 'That's great!', 'You're excellent when you want to be', etc.). These comments, while well-meant, will be rejected by the child, who knows that they are either untrue or exaggerated. Instead, say something encouraging about the child's effort or attempt ('I like what you're doing', 'It's hard but I can see you are really doing your best', 'You're improving all the time', etc.).
- **Non-verbal affirmation:** This child is quite likely to reject even carefully worded encouragement if it is made in a public way. A quiet word – or better still, a non-verbal signal like a thumbs-up sign, a nod or a smile – may be more effective.

- **Guarantee success:** Present the child with tasks or activities that guarantee success. If necessary, break a task down into small steps, each having a clear demonstration of independent achievement. Never do the task for the child.
- **Positive self-talk:** Model for the child ways of internalising expressions of encouragement, e.g. 'This is hard but I'll make an effort', 'I'll try for five minutes before I give up', 'I'll think about this for a bit', etc.

Strategies for withdrawal/inadequacy needs in the secondary school

- **Validation:** Wherever possible, and where it does not attract undue attention from other students or appear patronising, the teacher could invite this student's opinions, views or assistance, preferably in a one-to-one situation. If there is no response, carry on as normal but try again.
- **Giving hope:** Help the student attain hope for him/herself by sharing with the class anecdotes of people who have successfully struggled with a sense of despair. The teacher should be watchful not to 'preach' or overdo this exercise.
- **Learning from mistakes:** Teachers can create a climate in their class where it is acceptable, and even desirable, to make mistakes. A student who answers a question incorrectly can be encouraged by a well-chosen response from the teacher ('I'm glad you made that mistake, Jane, because it's a very common mistake and you've reminded me to point out ...' or 'You're quite close and that was well attempted. That's a useful mistake for learning', etc.).
- **Boost morale:** Preface questions to withdrawn students with a positive comment and with reference to the student's strengths, e.g. 'This is a hard question, Tom, but as you know a fair bit about ...' or 'You're good at art, Jane, you might know the name of that technique when paintings are put in plaster.' By prefacing questions like these, the teacher helps students to feel good about themselves and not to feel too discouraged if they cannot give the correct answer (O'Flynn and Kennedy 2000: 70).

Self-esteem

In most cases, challenging behaviour is a manifestation of low self-esteem. The teacher needs to hold in mind the hidden communication efforts behind the young person's misbehaviour and to ensure that all action towards students and pupils are of a nature that raises self-esteem. Challenging behaviour provokes an emotional response from the teacher and it requires a great deal of professionalism to employ strategies and responses that are not emotionally reactive in return. The teacher must avoid retaliating with sarcasm, cynicism, ridicule, 'put-downs', taunting, negative labelling and 'freezing out' students. Garner (1998) also cites curriculum pressures and performance results as contributing to an unwillingness in some teachers to 'favour an emphasis on emotional well-being and on awareness of "self" that some schools consider indicative of a liberal, mollycoddling attitude to pupils with problems' (Garner 1998: 31).

Humphreys (1993) notes that young people with low self-esteem need to experience certain 'messages' from the teacher more frequently than other students. These messages include (Humphreys 1993: 111):

- Your behaviour is an attempt to communicate important human needs;
- You belong;
- You can make sense and order of your world;
- You are capable in what you do and you please me;
- You are one of a kind and special;
- You have a right to your own unique growing.

Conveying these messages to children and young people who are compliant and responsive is rarely a problem. But challenging behaviour is just that: a 'challenge' to teachers and schools to find positive, hopeful and inclusive ways of responding to what are in effect special educational needs.

Positive discipline and whole-school approach

It is important to emphasise that an individual teacher or staff member should not be expected to deal with the complexities of managing challenging behaviour on their own. Neither should the child or young person be expected to learn to change their behaviour on their own. School managers have a professional responsibility to support staff and pupils who are involved in these situations. O'Brien (1998) emphasises the vital role the whole-school approach plays in developing a 'collective school consciousness' in support of the management of challenging behaviour: 'When pedagogical attitude is based on sensitive, flexible and needs-driven strategies and enhanced by positive, respective and responsive relationships, any intervention – be it based on prevention or resolution – will be more likely to succeed.'

'Positive discipline' is a term that refers to the behaviour of all parties: teachers, staff and pupils (O'Hara et al. 2000). It requires an orientation to what O'Brien (1998) calls a 'learning zone' rather than to a 'battle zone'. In the 'battle zone', the child is the problem and behaviour modification through punishment and reward may be the weapons used. But in the 'learning zone' it is the behaviour that is the problem. Teachers oriented to the 'learning zone' approach will use strategies that will respect the person but positively confront the unacceptable behaviour of the child or student.

For example, a child who is shouting in the classroom would be approached by the teacher who understands positive discipline by an intervention in this sequence:

- Describe the desired behaviour in positive terms.
- Model the desired behaviour.
- Invite a response of the appropriate behaviour.
  Teacher says: 'I want you to speak quietly please, Adam. Listen to me (pause). I'm not shouting. Please talk like I am.' (O'Brien 1998: 23).

Making rules

A whole-school approach to making rules, if rooted in the positive discipline approach, has a greater likelihood of being effective and helpful. Sometimes young children break rules because neither the rule nor its purpose is understood. Older children and students may resent rules because they are imposed by an outside 'power' and see their purpose as one of control. When young people are involved in the process of rule formation – an approach advocated in positive discipline – there is a higher level of awareness, understanding and observance (McNamara and Moreton 1995: 52–64).

When asked to draw up relevant school rules, children are at first likely to express them in negative form ('No leaning back on chairs') and to enumerate far too many. This useful first stage of the process can then move on to helping children express rules in positive terms ('Sit on a chair with its four legs on the ground') and to explore the reasons why such rules are necessary through discussion. The next stage is to combine all the rules on one long list and to have children rate the five most important. Each rule should be practical, reasonable and demonstrable. Individually or in groups, children can model the correct behaviour. Finally, the agreed rules are posted on the classroom wall or pasted into the back of a copybook, or if appropriate affixed to the child's desk. Rules should be:

- Positively stated.
- Few in number.
- Demonstrable.
- Reasonable.
- Capable of being carried out.

A whole-school approach to rule formulation takes time, but the process in itself is a learning experience (Rogers 1994).

Attention Deficit Hyperactive Disorder (ADHD)

An approach to challenging behaviour that recognises that most of the sources of misbehaviour are located outside the child and in the emotional, physical or social environment is a wise one, leading to the application of appropriate attitudes and strategies. Nevertheless, it is also right to recognise that some causes of challenging behaviour have their sources in neurological and medical conditions. One such condition that has become more evident in schools in the past decade is that of Attention Deficit Hyperactivity Disorder (ADHD); see Chapter 12, p. 232. Estimated prevalence rates for ADHD vary enormously, with some research indicating up to 12 per cent of male children and others with much lower estimates (Serfontein 1990). This condition is evidenced in behaviour such as constant fidgeting, regular inattention, hyperactivity, excessive motor activity, restlessness, easily distracted behaviour, clumsiness, inflexibility, low tolerance of frustration and acting before thinking.

Children who have been formally diagnosed with ADHD require structure and predictability in the learning environment and in the teaching style. A predictable environment which can guarantee success has been shown to be effective for children and students with ADHD (Alban-Metcalf and Alban-Metcalf 2001). Westwood (2003) specifies the following additional suggestions, which could be taken into account when attempting to meet the learning needs of children and students with this condition:

- Providing strong visual input.
- Using computer-aided technology.
- Direct teaching of organisational skills.
- Praising on-task activities and giving positive descriptive feedback.

Close cooperative effort between family members and health and educational professionals presents the best way towards effective intervention. From a teacher's point of view, the question posed must be similar to that applied to any child with challenging behaviour – in what way may the teacher maximize the learning opportunity for this child as much as for any other child?

Concluding comments

Children and young people who have social, emotional and behavioural difficulties often pose the greatest challenge to teachers' perceptions of themselves as competent, caring professionals. As teachers, we need supportive colleagues and a school approach that attempts to incorporate an understanding of why this behaviour happens into its policies and procedures.

Discussion points

1   Read the following case study and answer the questions that follow.

> Eoin, a second class pupil (eight-year-old), was prone to severe outbursts of temper and would throw his books and equipment onto the ground. There was no obvious trigger for this behaviour and his parents assured Moira, the teacher, that this type of behaviour did not happen at home. Eoin is a very able pupil who tended to try to answer every teacher question, much to the annoyance of his peers. Moira decided to address the temper outbursts and Eoin's dominance of teacher–pupil interactions. A two-stage strategy was adopted: work with Eoin to identify trigger points for the temper outbursts and develop turn-taking skills.
>
> Eoin said that he felt himself getting very hot and his face appeared to be burning just before a temper outburst. Moira asked Eoin to signal to her when he felt this happening and it was agreed that he would immediately go to a time-out chair near the door of the classroom. In the first few days, Eoin used the time-out chair three or four times per day. However, by the end of the week he was using the time-out mechanism very infrequently and temper outbursts happened very rarely.

In relation to turn-taking, a class rule was established so that no one could make a second contribution until everyone in the class had made at least one contribution. Eoin took a little time to adapt to this rule. One day he had his hand up for a second time and was waving very enthusiastically when for no apparent reason he took his hand down again. When asked later by Moira why he had done this, Eoin replied that he wanted to save his second contribution as he might think of something even better to say.

These strategies were applied consistently over a few months and Eoin's behaviour had become more appropriate and his peer group were more accepting of him. On reflection, Moira realised that prior to the intervention she had never felt able to praise Eoin, even when he had given exceptional answers in class.

(a) What other approaches might Moira have adopted?
(b) Why do you think these approaches were successful?
(c) Why is it so important to involve the pupil directly in any intervention?

2 Identify some problem behaviour that is causing you concern in your classroom. As objectively as possible, outline the main features of the behaviour and the context: What appears to trigger the behaviour? How do you react when the behaviour occurs? How do the other children react? Does the initial behaviour escalate? Based on this analysis, design an intervention to address the needs of the child who is displaying problem behaviour.

3 Some teachers believe that behaviour modification programmes involving rewards are essentially rewarding children for behaving as they should have in the first place. What is your reaction to this view?

4 Many pupils with behaviour difficulties appear to have low self-esteem. Outline teaching strategies that will probably be most effective/least effective in encouraging pupils' sense of self-worth.

Chapter 12
Strategies for Specific Special Educational Needs

Learning outcomes/objectives

On completion of this chapter, the reader will be able to:

- Itemise general strategies to incorporate varied learning styles and to maximise organisational skills and communication for understanding in the classroom.
- Identify the elements in the triad of impairments that are associated with autistic spectrum disorders and discuss strategies of structured teaching suitable for learners with autistic spectrum disorders.
- Express an understanding of the characteristics of the pupil/student with dyslexia and outline suitable strategies for maximising learning.
- Explore general methods and strategies appropriate for teaching pupils/students with mild, moderate and severe/profound general learning disability.
- Explore the implications of creating strategies for learners with Attention Deficit Hyperactivity Disorder-related conditions in school.

Introduction

This chapter looks at issues relating to teaching and learning with suggestions for some 'specialist' strategies useful for pupils with particular kinds of special educational needs. As we have already attempted to underline, there is a danger in uncritically adopting a medical model of special educational needs that tends to categorise conditions, approach the matter as if the 'problem' is always within the child and seek an 'expert' outside solution. However, there is also a real danger in neglecting the reality that some pupils and students will have particular conditions that are significantly different from the majority of learners and will present special challenges for teaching approaches, curriculum adaptation and school management policies.

A number of skilled approaches that have been successfully used to promote teaching and learning for pupils and students with particular special educational needs will be examined and explored. However, it is not intended to attempt a summary exploration of the wide range of sensory, physical, cognitive, emotional, behavioural, environmental, cultural and health-related circumstances that incorporate the spectrum of special educational needs. The following conditions are included for discussion in this chapter:

- Autistic spectrum disorder.
- Dyslexia.
- General learning disabilities.
- Attention Deficit Hyperactive Disorder (ADHD).

Heightened awareness of autistic spectrum disorders in school communities and in society generally in recent times requires that all teachers need to have basic understanding and foundational skills in this area. Dyslexia necessitates a skilful readiness on the part of the teacher to help with the challenges some learners encounter in deciphering and expressing the written word. General learning disabilities constitute the largest group of people with special educational needs in the school system and represent the need for the teacher to master meaningful and effective adaptations to traditional teaching styles. Attention Deficit Hyperactivity Disorder is arguably one of the most labelled explanations for challenging behaviour and has received a great deal of publicity.

These examples of special educational needs might be viewed as unwelcome challenges for inflexible school systems, or where there are inadequate levels of support provision or unexamined and ineffective teaching approaches. However, viewed within the context of the positive challenge of a reflective and inclusive process, many of the strategies that can be applied to give certain pupils or students with special educational needs more access to successful learning can also be implemented to the benefit of the needs of a wider range of learners, including many who do not have special educational needs (Rose and Howley 2007).

General strategies

Learning styles
An appreciation of the varied dominant learning modalities of pupils and students (Gardner 1983, 1999) has prompted many teachers to adopt a teaching style that incorporates a range of visual, auditory and kinaesthetic elements. This approach is most effective when activities and exercises in the classroom are planned towards learners' strengths. However, caution must be exercised that children or students do not limit their learning only to their preferred modality. It is important that opportunities are also provided so that learners who are aware of their strengths can also attempt and experience success in the ways of learning with which they have to struggle. Writers such as Shawe and Hawes (1998) urge teachers to make learning strategies that are linked to specific learning styles explicit in their teaching so that learners become increasingly conscious, encouraged and challenged by a range of tasks.

Organisational skills
Skills that will help children and young people to develop self-help abilities will promote the self-confidence that goes with increased independence and maximise opportunities for success. These skills are essential for children with special educational needs but are also necessary for all children. Here are

some suggested ways that teachers can use at either primary or post-primary level:

- Provide learners with a list of learning outcomes, i.e. the activities, abilities and understandings that are expected of them after a period of teaching ('At the end of this lesson/period you will be able to …').
- At the beginning of each lesson period, state the knowledge content or the skill to be learned during that session. If pupils can see the overall plan of the lesson, they are reassured and are more likely to participate actively and contribute constructively.
- Give guidance to learners on dividing the allotted time for an activity usefully and constructively.
- Provide learners with self-assessment skills (What did I find difficult? What do I need more help with?) so that they can match their learning efforts to the predicted learning outcomes.

Communication for understanding
Other general strategies that are relevant for the learning potential of a wide range of pupils or students, including those with special educational needs, are described by Malone and Smith (1996: 19):

- Monitor textbook and printed material to ensure that it does not exceed pupils'/students' language understanding.
- Help the process of understanding by repeating information or instructions in a simplified way.
- Back up verbal information or instructions by written materials, drawings and diagrams.
- Allow pupils/students plenty of time to think before responding to questions.
- Check pupils'/students' understanding by allowing them to restate the information or instructions in their own words.

Specific strategies for children and young people with special educational needs
It is not our intention to provide an overview of various categories of special educational needs and to sketch out suitable teaching strategies. Categorical approaches inevitably tend to suggest a deficit model of disability and to imply 'corrective' or 'remedial' interventions for problem children. Approaches that emphasise access to quality learning opportunities and appropriate assessment methods to meet the continuum of learning abilities are more likely to incorporate inclusive possibilities.

Autistic spectrum disorders

Understanding autistic spectrum disorders (ASD)
Pupils and students with ASD may experience the dynamics of teaching and learning quite differently to other learners. The core areas of challenge will be

manifested in what has been described in the literature as the 'triad of impairments' (Wing and Gould 1979; Department of Education (NI)/ Department of Education and Science/Irish Society for Autism 2004):

- Social interaction.
- Social communication.
- Social imagination.

The condition of ASD is characterised as a 'spectrum', illustrating that there is a wide range of possible impairment in the above areas of experience, ranging from mild to severe. It also underlines the fact that no two people with the diagnosed condition of ASD are alike.

The child or young person with 'higher functioning autism' (HFA) is most often referred to as having Asperger syndrome (AS), named after the Austrian paediatrician who first described the condition in the 1940s. This child or student is likely to have above-average intellectual ability, manifested most often in advanced verbal, writing or mathematical skills. In contrast, the same person may experience great difficulty in managing the social interactions and routines that are commonly taken for granted.

What makes this condition so unusual are the obstacles to processing and interpreting social experience by reason of an impairment in what is known as 'theory of mind'. From a very early age, children learn to read and interpret the non-language social cues (smiling, voice tone, eye contact, gesture) that help us to make rapid judgments on how we are being received or responded to by others. This requires a constant act of the imagination and for most children becomes a highly developed and automatic skill in deducing social meaning.

It is in this area that the greatest challenge presents itself to young people who have ASD. Interactions that involve humour and irony, verbal jokes or similes and metaphors may be quite troublesome for people with ASD. Much humour and joking involves a degree of deception which is interpreted and recognised by the other party. The young person with ASD may be puzzled and regard the playfulness involved in creating deceptions as pointless. Sometimes this gives the person with ASD a rather over-serious and standoff-ish demeanour, which can be interpreted as indifference. Much of this results from anxiety about the fast-moving verbal banter and non-verbal exchanges that others take for granted. The young person with ASD is sometimes frozen with fear that they will do or say something wrong. Comfort is taken in predictable and stereotypical routines and there may be a feeling of panic or distress if there are sudden alterations in timetables or in regular practices or when there are unexpected changes in personnel (such as when a teacher is absent). It is important to remember, however, that all these reactions and behaviours are on a continuum and many people who do not have ASD also experience shyness, anti-social moments, social embarrassment and a desire for safe and solitary routines from time to time, simply because these experiences are part of the broad range of the human condition.

It is argued by Frith (1989) and others that the different cognitive processes in people with ASD also lead to different ways of perceiving experience. There is difficulty in integrating details in order to compose a 'whole picture' as well as problems in discriminating between important or relevant details and irrelevant details. Powell (2000) underlines the difficulties that pupils with ASD will have in interpreting and extracting meaning. When we consider that most traditional teaching strategies rely strongly on verbal exchanges and receptive understanding based on deduction and induction, there will be significant barriers here in meaning-making for the student with ASD.

Twachtmann-Cullen (2004) enumerates some key areas that need to be addressed by schools and teachers in order to meet the specific life skills needs of young people with AS/HFA. These are described as:

- Perspective taking.
- Socio-communicative understanding and expression.
- Reading/language comprehension.
- Executive dysfunction (problems in organisational skills/planning).
- Problem solving.

Techniques used in Social Stories (Grey 2006), where real-life situations experienced by the child are used to develop narratives, have been found to be useful in creating perspective-making possibilities. Here the teacher uses the story in conversation with the child to elicit specific social cues, anticipated actions and contextual information to explain the reasons why certain things are happening. This exercise promotes cognitive analysis of social situations rather than attempted intuition.

A multi-disciplinary collaboration involving speech-language therapy, psychological support and home-school linkage programmes is implied in maximising these educational aims. While provision has improved in Ireland in support of inclusion, there are still great delays in obtaining these essential services. Unfortunately, schools, teachers and parents often have to improvise resources with limited and sometimes unsatisfactory means. This is not to endorse or condone such a state of affairs, but to affirm dedicated and adaptive efforts in attempting to meet the challenge.

Strategies for learners with ASD

People with ASD are thought to perform better when the dominant teaching/learning style is in the visual mode (O'Riordan et al. 2001). People with ASD themselves have verified this view. Grandin (1995: 19) remarks: 'I think in pictures. Words are like a second language to me ... When somebody speaks to me, his words are instantly translated into pictures.' Many pupils and students who do not have ASD but who have a dominant visual learning style will also benefit from an approach that takes this strength into account. Visual strategies will include:

- Using PowerPoint presentations.
- Linking concepts, definitions and key information with visual images, such as a diagram of a bed illustrating the letters 'b' and 'd'.

- Using jigsaw diagrams to show how different concepts are connected.
- Showing relevant video material with accompanying worksheet with visual cues where students identify and record key concepts or important information.
- Using 'storyboard' illustrations to assist in sequencing ideas for writing.

Using structured teaching

A structured approach to teaching that has been developed around the specific needs of young people with ASD can also have valuable applications for the needs of a range of learners in an inclusive setting. Many learners will benefit from a more structured approach which offers greater opportunity for regular success. Structured teaching is a dimension of the very successful method developed at the University of North Carolina in the 1970s for young people with ASD, known as Treatment and Education for Autistic and related Communication handicapped Children (generally known by its acronym, TEACCH). Structured teaching is described in Rose and Howley (2007: 40) as containing four key elements:

- Physical structure.
- Visual schedules.
- Work organisational systems.
- Visual instruction methods.

Howley (2006) outlines the principles of structured teaching in the following terms:

- Assessment of individual needs – the assessment requires an 'in-depth knowledge and understanding of the unique characteristics of each individual', including assessment of strengths and weaknesses, likes/dislikes, motivational factors and visual cognition.
- Development of individualised structure, comprising all four elements of the approach according to assessed individual needs and taking into account idiosyncratic learning profiles.
- An emphasis on developing independence, self-esteem and effective behaviour management strategies, including self-management.
- Enhanced meaning within the learning context.

Aspects of structured teaching that can be usefully applied to an inclusive setting while meeting the specific needs of pupils or students with ASD could include:

- Using symbols and icons to enhance timetable/schedule information.
- Labelled trays for pupils to place finished or unfinished work on.
- Provision of clearly labelled baskets of materials and resources for specific tasks, e.g. writing, maths, artwork, geography.
- Visual reminders or instructions taped to each group table.
- Visual cue cards or posters for directional words.
- Illustrated dictionary of important terms.

The *Report of the Task Force on Autism* (2001), which is the most comprehensive examination of ASD in an Irish context, agrees with the statement of Strain *et al.* (1998), which cautions that 'the diagnosis of autism does not and should not lead to a specific set of educational strategies' that can be applied without reference to the individual young person's unique needs and strengths. An approach that relies exclusively on one method, such as TEACCH, may not, for example, be appropriate for the child with ASD who needs freedom to select more challenging pathways to success and who can, with support, follow the curriculum at primary or secondary school.

In the following case study we will examine how a young man who has Asperger syndrome was supported in his learning and behaviour.

Case Study 12.1: Empowering a young man who has Asperger syndrome

Thomas is a Year 8 student (twelve-year-old) in a post-primary mainstream school in England. He has Asperger syndrome, which was diagnosed prior to transition. Transfer to post-primary school was especially difficult for him because of the changes to the structure of his day. Currently, a team of Learning Support Assistants are working across several different subject areas to provide in-class support. A designated Learning Support Assistant is assigned to him, working on social skills and one-to-one withdrawal sessions twice a week.

My mum and dad help me with my education. Dad is an engineer and is very good for technical and factual information. They want me to have a good education – doesn't every parent want that? I don't think I should be treated any different because I have Asperger syndrome.

At my school I would definitely get help with work such as planning and good content. My teachers want the best for me and they encourage me. Sometimes when I misbehave they offer me help but I back away. If my parents aren't happy with anything at school they get it sorted. I have a special Learning Support Assistant (LSA) who helps me a lot. She's very patient; I like her. When I had difficulty joining in with others in Year 7, she worked with me and taught me how to do it. Now she's confident I can do that well so she's only working with me from time to time and on other areas. She taught me how to understand the ways in which Asperger will affect me in my school life. We made a personal profile on PowerPoint, then she used it to train the teachers and it helped them to understand me. This has made things a lot better. We're going to do this every year so that I can reflect back on how I've changed.

I know I've made good progress because in junior school my support worker was always beside me in class. I love being the same as everyone else now. The LSAs give me more space in this school and the help I get is not forced on me any more. My education has been well planned and I get individual help when I need it. If I didn't have this help I would never ever want to go to school!

> Before I knew I had Asperger my junior schoolteachers thought I was a bad boy. The other children teased and bullied me and it was a horrible time. Now I am more confident because more people understand me. It's definitely getting better because more people take me as I am. That's because they have learned about me and know what to do for the best and probably most important I am in a good school.
>
> 1   What factors have contributed to the successful transition for Thomas to post-primary school?
>
> 2   How has Thomas been enabled to reflect on the impact of Asperger syndrome on his learning and behaviour?
>
> 3   How does the case study illustrate the importance of a whole-school approach to special educational needs?

Source: Adapted from *Encouraging Voices: Respecting the Insights of Young People Who Have Been Marginalised* (Shevlin and Rose 2003).

Dyslexia

Understanding dyslexia

A preference for the usage of 'specific learning disability' over the term 'dyslexia' was indicated in the *Report of the Special Education Review Committee* (SERC) (Department of Education 1993). In the research literature emanating from the US, the equivalent term used is 'learning disability' (LD). SERC (Department of Education 1993: 86) went on to define specific learning disability as 'an impairment in specific aspects of reading, writing and arithmetical notation, the primary cause of which is not attributable to assessed ability being below the average range, to defective sight or hearing, emotional factors, a physical condition, or to any extrinsic adverse circumstances'.

The *Report of the Task Force on Dyslexia* (DES 2002b) chose a much broader definition which emphasises the continuum of learning difficulties, from mild to severe, which arise from dyslexia – a term considered more user friendly and desirable. The necessity of an individualised response and interventions that reflect the principle of continuum of identification provision is also emphasised and detailed in the report (DES 2002b: 70–71).

Westwood (2003: 11) makes the point that when one examines the literature on teaching methodology for children with dyslexia, it becomes evident that there is no unique methodology applicable only to students with dyslexia, but 'a range of valuable teaching strategies that would be helpful to all children'. The need for high-quality, effective instruction will be an equal requirement for all learning needs. The Task Force report (DES 2002b) also notes that many of the characteristics of children and young people who have learning difficulties arising from dyslexia may also be present in children with a range of other learning needs and difficulties. Reid (Lewis and Norwich 2005: 139) quotes the definition of dyslexia by the British Psychological Society (1999), which suggests that 'dyslexia is evident when accurate and fluent word reading and/or spelling develops very incompletely or with great difficulty ... [and] provides the basis for a staged process of assessment through teaching.' This would imply that the kind of teaching strategies suitable for children with dyslexia would be suitable for all children with reading difficulties, whether arising from dyslexia or not.

Indicators for identifying dyslexia

The *Report of the Task Force on Dyslexia* (DES 2002b) outlines the possible indicators that might suggest learning difficulties arising from dyslexia. While it has been generally held that a discrepancy between potential (as measured by full-scale IQ testing) and performance is one of the key features of dyslexia, it is also a fact that a number of studies have failed to find a difference between students assessed as dyslexic and those who have poor achievement in reading, spelling, phonological processing and memory skills but without the discrepancy between potential and performance (Siegel 1992).

Indicators at pre-primary and primary school

Children from ages three to five years and above:
- Later than most children to speak.
- Difficulty pronouncing multi-syllabic words.
- Experiences auditory discrimination problems.
- Has difficulty with rhyming.
- Has difficulties with rhythm.
- Is unable to recall the right word.
- Is slow to add new vocabulary.
- Experiences problems learning alphabet.
- Trouble with left–right orientation.
- Difficulties with sequences, e.g. days of week, months of year or distinguishing colours or shapes.
- Unable to spell or write own name.

Children from five to twelve years:
- Poor word-attack skills.
- Makes constant letter reversals (b/d).
- Constant letter inversions (w/m).
- Makes constant letter transpositions (felt/left).
- Word reversals (pit/tip).
- Word substitutions (house/home).
- Reads slowly with little expression or fluency.
- Relies heavily on memorising without understanding.
- Listening comprehension better than reading comprehension.
- Has difficulty planning or organising.
- Uses awkward pencil grip.
- Has slow and poor-quality handwriting.
- Reading achievement is below expectation.
- Slow at discerning word prefixes, suffixes, root words and other morphemes.
- Spelling inappropriate for age and general ability.

- Avoidance tactics when asked to read aloud or to write.
- Experiences language-related problems in maths.
- Has slow or poor recall of facts.

Strategies for learners with dyslexia at primary level

Recommendations in the *Report of the Task Force on Dyslexia* (DES 2002b) underline the primary role and responsibility of class teachers and subject teachers in addressing the progress and development of pupils and students with learning difficulties arising out of dyslexia. The intervention of the learning support/ resource teacher is seen as an additional and perhaps necessary assistance to the class/subject teacher, but always as a collaborative activity. Some general interventions are summarised here (p. 85):

- Provide individual or small-group teaching as needed.
- Provide opportunities for relearning and over-learning rules and strategies.
- Provide regular constructive feedback to maintain motivational levels and enhance self-esteem.
- Adapt teaching methods to match child's learning style.
- Where possible, use a multi-sensory approach to reading and spelling that involves listening, saying, looking at and writing words in various combinations.
- Evaluate child's understanding of a text by using oral rather than written questions.
- Ensure that learning materials are at the child's reading level and are age appropriate in content.
- Introduce cursive handwriting from as early a stage as possible to aid spelling, speed, neatness and continuity.
- Focus on the nature of the child's writing errors (quality) rather than their frequency (quantity).
- Expect the child's work to be erratic and inconsistent at times.
- Encourage the child to repeat directions for completing a task.
- Avoid asking the child to read aloud in class unless this has been clearly agreed.
- Do not penalise the child for failing to complete tasks within strict time limits.
- Do not ask child to rewrite work because of spelling errors.
- Where appropriate, use non-printed learning materials, including talking books.
- Use of assistive technology, including use of a word-processor with spell-checker or voice recognition software which allows for dictation of text directly to the computer.

In Ireland, the National Centre for Technology in Education (NCTE) has developed a section for special education support on its website, ScoilNet, to include suggestions for hardware and software solutions for learning difficulties arising out of dyslexia.

Strategies for dyslexia at post-primary level
Students with dyslexia at post-primary age are likely to experience challenges in these areas:
- Still reading slowly with many inaccuracies.
- Inadequate store of knowledge due to lack of reading experience.
- Continues to experience serious spelling difficulties.
- Better oral skills than written skills.
- Difficulties planning, sequencing and organising written text.
- Difficulty with written syntax or punctuation.
- Difficulties skimming, scanning or proofreading texts.
- Difficulties taking notes or copying from blackboard or projected information.
- Poor in answering open-ended questions.
- Problems in recalling names of some words or objects.
- Has trouble summarising or outlining.

Turner (2003) provides useful guidelines in teaching English to post-primary students who have dyslexia. The suggested strategies are helpful to some degree for all students and undoubtedly essential for students experiencing literacy difficulties.

In relation to reading, Turner points out that 'for efficiency and effectiveness, reading is adapted according to the need and purpose of the task' (p. 65). The rationale for different types of reading needs to be taught explicitly. For example, detailed reading is required for examination questions and instructions, scanning is appropriate for obtaining facts or specific information and skimming is suitable to get a general overview, whereas a combination of all three approaches is fitting in reading a novel for enjoyment.

Spelling can cause even greater difficulties than reading for students who have dyslexia. Spelling 'involves the total recall of words, which then have to be reproduced accurately from memory. The skills a competent speller requires are good visual recall of words involving accurate mental imagery, good auditory discrimination and an awareness of sound symbol correspondence' (p. 66).

Turner recommends that students with dyslexia should receive explicit teaching about the rationale for spelling words in a particular way in order to make spelling more logical and predictable:

> ... they need to know what consonants and vowels are, and their functions, the use of short vowels and how they affect letters following them, the work of long vowels, the different ways of spelling a sound and the part that syllables play in both reading and writing ... [they] need to have an awareness of alphabetical knowledge, the importance of vowels and their sounds, rhyming ability, phonemic awareness, a knowledge of segmentation, clear articulation, legible cursive script and good visual brain imagery (p. 67).

Of course, these are the very areas that students with dyslexia find most difficult. Strategies suggested include:

- Visual associations for words.
- Mnemonics, particularly if designed by the student.
- Examining the visual structure of words.
- Using a highlighter to identify parts of words that can be accurately spelled.
- 'Look-say-cover-write-check' technique.

The teacher can support the student by using a proactive correcting strategy, such as the 'Items for Learning' approach outlined in Chapter 9. Covering the script in multiple red biro marks indicating spelling errors is less than helpful to this student and will diminish confidence and motivation to write.

Examinations in English will require students to write essays and demonstrate their comprehension and accurate use of language. We cannot assume that students with dyslexia will understand the function of sentences and paragraphs and these concepts will have to be taught explicitly, perhaps by using visual cues:

> It is therefore worthwhile teaching in a structured, cumulative way, building up concepts of words, sentences, paragraphs to illustrate how they interrelate and are dependent on each other. Teachers should also include parts of speech and figures of speech so that students know how to play with words, use words descriptively and are adventurous with their language (p. 69).

Students with dyslexia tend to be very cautious in their use of language, as they fear spelling inaccurately, so sometimes their writing can appear immature and not reflect their ability level. To encourage and support writing from these students, the teacher could mark the assignment for content rather than accuracy.

Ball et al. (2006) and Peer (2003) provide detailed accounts of other types of problems in reading and writing. Some difficulties in reading include:

- Hesitant and laboured reading, if reading out loud.
- Omitting or adding extra words.
- Reading at a reasonable rate but with a low level of comprehension.
- Failure to recognise familiar words.
- Missing a line or reading the same line twice.
- Losing the place or using a finger to keep the place.
- Difficulty in pinpointing the main idea in a passage.
- Having difficulty in the use of dictionaries, directories or encyclopaedias.
  Difficulties relating to written work may include:
- Poor standard of written work compared to oral ability.
- Poor handwriting, with badly formed letters.
- Good handwriting, but production of work extremely slow.
- Badly set-out work with spellings crossed out several times.
- Words spelled differently in one piece of work.
- Has difficulty with punctuation and grammar.

- Confusion of upper and lower case letters.
- Writing a great deal but 'loses the thread'.
- Writing very little but to the point.
- Difficulty taking notes in lessons.
- Organisation of work and personal timetable difficult.

There may also be difficulties related to mathematics learning that the student with dyslexia can encounter:

- Difficulty remembering tables and formulae.
- Finding sequencing difficult.
- Confusing signs such as + and x.
- Thinking at a high level in mathematics but needing a calculator to remember basic facts.
- Misreading questions that include words.
- Confusing directions – left and right.
- Finding mental arithmetic at speed difficult.

As a result of sheer frustration, perceived misunderstanding on the part of teaching staff and sometimes parents, and often exhaustion from the concentration expended in trying to perform adequately in each class, there are sometimes behavioural problems too. It is clearly imperative to find ways of working efficiently with these children in order for everyone to benefit.

The following case study provides an example of how ICT can be used to support a student who has dyslexia in a post-primary school.

Case Study 12.2: Supporting a student who has dyslexia through ICT

Tom, who has dyslexia, has recently transferred from his primary school to a post-primary school. While in sixth class in the primary school, he was provided with a text scanner and software by the DES. He used this extensively to access reading material that far exceeded his reading age, which included textbook materials across a range of subjects. In addition, Tom was provided by the DES with a voice recognition device which allowed him to record his answers to textbook questions and also to record his attempts at creative writing. Some difficulties arose in that the scanning software had problems in reading mathematical symbols. Also, it was necessary for Tom to withdraw from his classroom to do his work because the voice recognition microphone was very sensitive to background noises.

Reviewing Tom's needs when he transferred to post-primary school resulted in a recommendation that he be provided with a laptop computer with portable scanner and a headset that would allow him to work in his own class regardless of the noise level. A software package that allowed him to record specialised information such as science and maths was also provided. The resource teacher in the second-level school helped to support Tom's use of the technology in his independent work.

Source: Adapted from *Report of the Task Force on Dyslexia* (DES 2002b: 90).

General learning disabilities

Prior to the 1990s in Ireland, 'general learning disability' was usually called 'mental handicap'. While the terminology may have changed, it can still be argued (McDonnell 2000) that in Ireland a category-based clinical/pathological approach founded on narrow criteria of intellectual functioning as measured by IQ may still be a barrier to addressing the learning needs of many pupils and students. The three levels of general learning disability (mild, moderate or severe/profound) are used as a basis for resource provision and in formal assessment. In terms of IQ scores, mild general learning disability translates between IQ 70 and 50; moderate refers to IQ scores between 50 and 35; while severe and profound refer to scores below 35 on the IQ scale. It needs to be noted that UK terminology in the literature on general learning disabilities differs from that used in Ireland. In the UK, 'moderate leaning disabilities' is equivalent to the Irish category of 'mild'.

These categories were used by the National Council for Curriculum and Assessment (NCCA 2002) in drawing up curriculum guidelines for the adaptation of programmes at both primary and post-primary levels. However, the guidelines avoid any tendency to deliver prescriptive stipulations, but instead focus on how the general curriculum can be considered in terms of 'access, opportunities and participation'.

Despite the very many possible causes of what is known as 'general learning disabilities', Westwood (2003: 6) notes that 'most teachers, psychologists and researchers have tended to focus almost exclusively on so-called "deficits" or weaknesses within the learner to account for children's problems in coping successfully with the curriculum.' The role of the school, curriculum, teaching methods and materials have been much less examined as sources of the learning difficulties some children have. However, Robertson et al. (1994: 1) have observed that:

> Low attainment is no longer seen as solely rooted in an individual's intellectual characteristics. Many other factors are now accepted as having an important role in influencing attainment. The curriculum itself can contribute, perhaps being pitched at an inappropriate level or paced too quickly. Also, teaching strategies might not be suited to the ways that pupils learn most effectively.

Understanding mild general learning disabilities

Children with mild general learning disabilities have usually been distinguished from their peers with moderate or severe/profound learning disabilities by the fact that their needs were first noticed once they had commenced formal structured schooling which involved exposure to the regular curriculum (Lewis and Norwich 2005: 181). The learning needs of this pupil might be expressed by the following challenges:

- Delayed conceptual development.
- Difficulty in expressing ideas and feelings in words.
- Limited ability to generalise.
- Limited attention span and retention.
- Clumsiness and difficulties with motor skills.
- Underdeveloped sense of spatial awareness.
- Difficulties adapting to new situations.

It is important to emphasise, however, that pupils and students with mild general learning disabilities have the same range of interests and the same need for affirmation and success as their peers who do not have significant difficulties. Involvement in their own learning and the development of skills in evaluating and articulating their own learning needs will be important in building on their strengths and maintaining confidence in their capabilities. Teachers will need to be vigilant that the slower pace of learning for these students will not be interpreted negatively by the learners themselves or by other classmates. Emphasising understanding rather than rapidity will be an important value to be reiterated and modelled in the teaching style adopted.

Strategies for mild general learning disabilities
- Special attention to language and communication in all areas of the curriculum.
- Use of concrete or visual stimulus material.
- Manageable and varied learning tasks based on mainstream curriculum material.
- Opportunities for achievement and success.
- Immediate feedback and opportunities for self-assessment.
- Continuity and progression.
- Appropriate balance between supported independent learning in individual, small group and whole-class settings.

More detailed discussion of teaching and learning strategies, along with examples of curricular adaptations and adjustments at primary and post-primary levels, are given in the *Draft Guidelines* (2002) provided by the NCCA.

Understanding moderate general learning disabilities
Children and young people with moderate general learning disabilities will have very individual needs but will benefit most when their experiences reflect what is available to their peers. While many pupils and students with moderate general learning disabilities have traditionally received their education in special schools, increasing numbers are being included in mainstream primary and post-primary settings. Children and young people with Down syndrome, for instance, are most often functioning at this level, though by no means exclusively so.

Westwood (2003: 25) argues that the main priority in teaching children who have general learning disabilities at this level of functioning is to make the curriculum relevant and reality based. Learning will be at the concrete operational stage in terms of cognitive development, so a practical, hands-on approach must take priority over verbal instruction. A multi-sensory approach has been found to be effective in keeping children on-task for considerable periods of time and has allowed pupils to demonstrate higher levels of understanding than was expected (Rose and Howley 2007). Visual learners, such as those with Down syndrome, may find that picture cues may help them to integrate visual information with spoken language and may be helpful in learning to read.

Strategies for moderate general learning disabilities

The NCCA *Guidelines* (2002) emphasise experiences throughout the range of curriculum available to children and students in terms of the qualities of 'experience, interaction and independence'. For example, the experience of reading for young people with moderate general learning disabilities will be much broader than the interpretation of printed text. It will involve making meaning in the widest sense from signs, symbols and pictograms used in the general environment. It will involve making sense and deriving pleasure from a variety of visual and tactile representations. Exposure to listening to stories that are well told and interpreting pictures and handling books will be essential aspects of a language curriculum.

A 'communication-friendly' classroom environment is recommended and teachers may find these general strategies useful:

* Identify activities that interest and motivate the student.
* Give the student opportunities to interact and look out for situations which will facilitate this.
* Certain types of equipment/toys may encourage communication; a ball, dress-up clothes or puppets might be helpful in encouraging social interaction.
* Be aware of the pace at which students work and provide sensitive support.
* Choice-making should be built into as many activities as possible.
* Provide access to ICT supports where appropriate.

An example of a structured activity is illustrated in the NCCA *Guidelines* (2002: 47):

Learning objectives:
* Student will identify items of clothing by naming, gesture or signing.
* Given a fully clothed doll/teddy, each student will undress the doll/teddy in the correct order, i.e. shoes before socks and trousers.
  Having undressed the doll/teddy, the student, with prompts from the teacher, will list the steps of undressing in the correct order.
* Given an unclothed doll/teddy, the student will dress the doll/teddy in the correct order.
* Having dressed the doll/teddy, the student will list the steps of dressing in the correct order.

This teaching strategy also involves the teacher modelling the LAMH signs (a sign language adapted for use by children and young people who have general learning disabilities) for the items of clothing and thus extending communication possibilities. Using visual cues such as photographs that are pointed to and touched to initiate tasks and turning the picture over as a sign that the task has been completed encourage self-monitoring and independence in learning (Copeland and Hughes 2000).

Porter (2005) makes the point that when new learning is embedded in existing routines and when they have a naturalistic context (as in the above example of dressing/undressing), there is evidence of more lasting effectiveness.

Understanding severe/profound general learning disabilities

It was not until the mid-1980s in Ireland that it was considered that children and young people with this level of learning disability would be capable of benefiting from formal education as distinct from care (Department of Education 1983). In 1986 a pilot scheme was initiated which involved the appointment of 19 teachers to provide for educational intervention in a small range of health/care settings where children with a severe/profound learning disability had been placed. The NCCA *Guidelines* (2002: 1–2) recognise that pupils and students at this level of ability are 'at the foundation stages of learning', but also remind us that 'the student with severe/profound general learning disabilities has the same general needs as that of any other student ... love, security and affection and will be similarly affected by significant life changes.' Access to a broad and balanced curriculum is advocated, whereby the pupil or student can access the full range of learning areas to understand and assimilate his or her environment while availing of enriching opportunities for addressing priority needs. These needs will include:

- Learning at a very early developmental level.
- Basic self-care skills and routines.
- Communication strategies, including non-verbal gestures and signing.
- Emotional and behavioural support in developing social interaction.
- Help in generalising concepts and skills to accommodate a change of context.

Strategies for severe/profound general learning disabilities

Few teaching strategies are promoted exclusively or specifically for the use of children or young people at this level (Ware 2005: 70). Two main approaches to the priority area of communication needs are described, as based on caregiver–infant interaction and interventions using ICT.

Caregiver–infant interaction approach

Interactive environments consist of surroundings in which people encounter the following experiences:

- Receive responses to their actions.
- Get the opportunity to respond to the actions of others.

- Can initiate or take the lead in an interaction.

These experiences model positive caregiver–infant exchanges which, when operated consistently with children or young people with severe/profound learning disability, can produce patterns of more sophisticated communication behaviour.

Communication through ICT

The use of switches as part of a strategy for teaching communication skills is described by Schweigert (1989). The *Draft Guidelines* (2002: 40) suggest that battery-operated toys with switch devices that give sound effects may offer motivational opportunities for younger children at the beginning of this process. More age-appropriate devices for older students might include switches on a television remote control, an electric fan or a food-mixer. There is potential in micro-technology to teach children with severe/profound learning disability to engage in making choices. Choice-making is an important step towards a level of autonomy and in enhancing the quality of life.

The NCCA *Draft Guidelines* (2002: 33) recognise that the element of curiosity which might be a strong motivator for most children may not be as evident in the reactions of children at this level of disability. The *Guidelines* strongly recommend that the curriculum needs to be seen as an 'enabling curriculum', which suggests 'ways of promoting attention and awareness, ways of provoking responses and ideas for structuring situations that challenge the student to initiate activities and communication' (2002: 7).

Attention Deficit Hyperactivity Disorder

Understanding Attention Deficit Hyperactivity Disorder

While some experts have suggested that as many as 12 per cent of children may experience this condition, Westwood (2003: 80) considers that this estimate is likely to be far too high and that the label ADHD is often 'misused and applied to children who are merely bored and restless' or are victims of poor instruction and inadequate class management skills. It would be wrong, however, to imply that ADHD is not a real disability for some children. It may also exist as a co-existent condition with ASD, a specific learning disability like dyspraxia or dyslexia, or cerebral palsy or brain injury. While a psycho-neurological origin is attributed to assessed ADHD by most experts, it is also suggested by some researchers that factors such as parenting style, inadequate home and social environments and possibly dietary patterns may be significant secondary considerations (Lowe and Reynolds 2000).

Barkley (1997) outlines an integrated model that considers the challenges of ADHD as difficulties in the 'executive functions' of the brain that centre around self-regulation skills. These involve impairments in:

- Working memory.
- Internalised speech.

- Motivational appraisal.
- Reconstitution.

Working memory refers to the ability to draw automatically on internalised information for assessing situations and for forward planning. Linked to this is the facility, familiar to most people, of mentally 'talking to themselves'. This internalised speech is used to rehearse activities, to appraise situations and to organise events. The function of motivational appraisal allows us 'to think before we act' and to judge the emotional impact on other people and the likely outcomes of our behaviour. It is the internalised inhibiting factor that helps us to regulate our impulses. Reconstitution involves the process of deconstructing and analysing past behaviours so that we can plan new and appropriate behaviours.

School is a major source of social construction for children; its institutional routines and classroom culture contribute hugely to this process for most children. Conversely, school also presents major stresses for young people who have a predisposition to attention and activity problems.

Strategies for ADHD

An educational rather than a medical model of ADHD attempts to reframe the characteristics associated with children or young people who have attention or hyperactivity problems as a particular cognitive style. In this way, some of the behavioural tendencies connected with ADHD are seen as 'learning styles' that can be exploited rather than suppressed. Research has shown that when teachers develop strategies that incorporate a kinaesthetic or active learning style, levels of attention are increased and impulsive behaviours are decreased (Hinshaw 1994).

When periods of seat-work are punctuated by regular intervals of structured physical activity, incidences of behaviour problems are decreased. Likewise, the need to talk out at inappropriate times, associated with ADHD, may be positively 'reframed' by increasing opportunities for on-task verbal contributions. Zentall (1995) has suggested that seating pupils prone to inattentiveness or hyperactivity in a semi-circle around the teacher or in small groups produces more on-task behaviours and more appropriate verbal participation. A pre-arranged quiet area may also be provided in the classroom (or, if appropriate, outside the classroom) where the student can remove himself/herself when stressful occasions threaten to cause overwhelming or overexciting responses. This kind of self-monitoring can be valuable and can encourage increased responsibility. Purdie et al. (2002) have concluded that the type of educational interventions described above have been more effective in producing cognitive improvements than clinical-based cognitive interventions.

Some general principles for teaching pupils/students with ADHD may be listed as follows.

Inattention:
- Decrease the length of the task.
- Break the task into smaller parts to be completed at different times.

- Use fewer words in explaining tasks.
- Allow work with partners or small groups.
- Alternate high-interest and low-interest tasks.
- Use overhead projector/PowerPoint in direct teaching sessions.
- Allow pupil to sit close to teacher.
- Use games to overlearn rote material.
  Hyperactivity:
- Channel activity into acceptable avenues.
- Encourage directed movement in classrooms that is not disruptive to others.
- Use teaching activities that involve active responding, e.g. working at board, organising, pinning up posters, etc.
- Give activity rewards: clean board, organise bookshelves, arrange chairs, etc.
- Encourage doodling or play with manipulative materials (paperclips, pipe-cleaners, tangrams, etc.) while waiting or listening to instruction.

It is not considered appropriate within the scope or competency of this discussion to comment on the issue of medication for pupils/students with assessed ADHD. From an educational perspective, ADHD challenges teachers to reflect on the assumptions about the demands of schooling. It invites examination of the rigid, inflexible structures and approaches that may be deemed sufficient for those who can readily conform to school culture but which may effectively be contributory barriers or 'handicaps' for some learners. These problems are not easily addressed. The constraints of examinations and the requirements to pace teaching to meet curriculum considerations are obstacles that cannot be minimised. Nevertheless, ADHD, perhaps more than other conditions of special educational needs, challenges schools to critically examine whether pupils are required to adapt themselves to what may be an unsuitable learning environment or whether schools are honestly taking on the responsibility to explore creative and adaptive practices to create an inclusive and welcoming community of learners.

Concluding comments

It is important to recall again that children and young people with special educational needs and disabilities have more in common with their peers who do not have such learning difficulties than is often appreciated.

All young people have common needs to experience sufficient success and to have tasks that challenge them but are not insurmountable. All learners need to have their difficulties identified and their efforts and successes recognised. There are many strategies that when applied judiciously to a range of differing learning needs can have similar successful outcomes. Similarly, strategies found to be effective for specific learning needs can have useful applications for other learners that may not have the same assessed disability or condition. Knowledge and understanding about categories of disability and special educational needs is an important part of the teacher's professional repertoire. More essential still is the conviction that the child is not a 'label', but a learner. The teacher's task is fundamentally to empower and support learning.

Discussion points

1   Parents and advocates of children with ASD have been vocal in recent years in demanding appropriate educational provision for those who have been neglected or overlooked for too long. Parental demands have been successful in requiring the state to support specialised schools and services for children with autism.

(a)   Find out what you can about Applied Behaviour Analysis (ABA) and why it is considered by some parents to provide the kind of intervention which is most suited to the specific needs of their children.

(b)   A review of services for pupils and students with ASD was published by the Inspectorate, DES, in 2006. What did it have to say about the ABA approach as conducted in some Irish schools?

2   Wyn McCormack, in her book *Lost for Words*, acknowledges that 'subject teachers, who must meet the demands of the state exam system, realistically may find it difficult to give enough individual attention to one particular student who experiences learning difficulties. On the other hand, a teacher who has an understanding of dyslexia and adapts teaching strategies as much as possible will do much for such students' (2002: 126). What kind of strategies could a subject teacher adopt that would be helpful and manageable?

3   The child with general learning disabilities may experience particular difficulty in generalising or transferring knowledge from one situation to another. Identify one concept or learning outcome appropriate for new learning for a child with GLD in the mild/moderate or severe/profound range of ability and consider how experience in transfer of knowledge could be demonstrated and reinforced.

4   (a)   Discuss why it is considered by some experts that ADHD tends to be 'over-diagnosed'.

(b)   What are the possible implications of labelling a child who has been assessed with ADHD?

(c)   Teachers are not qualified to comment on the medication of a pupil with assessed or suspected ADHD. How should a teacher handle the matter if a parent asks a teacher's opinion on the use of drug therapy for their child with attention or hyperactivity problems?

Section 4
Sustaining Collaborative Approaches

Chapter 13

Developing Collaborative Relationships with Parents and Families

Learning outcomes/objectives

On completion of this chapter, the reader will be able to:
- Outline the legislative requirements for parental collaboration in educational settings.
- Identify and discuss Hornby's seven stages of parental adaptation to child disability.
- Reflect on first-hand accounts of family experiences of professional involvement in the initial stages of contact and in the assessment of SEN.
- Examine parents' experiences of home–school relationships.
- Identify the principles of effective collaboration and partnership.
- Consider guidelines for the beginning teacher in communicating with parents of children with SEN.

Introduction

> We all have unwritten lists; we all make presumptions about what the future will hold. Without realising it, I had had a clear assumption of how my child would turn out. Much has come true – she eats ice-cream, likes face-paint, chats endlessly, gossips with her girlfriends and says that when she grows up, she wants to be a witch. But it never occurred to me that alongside these delights, she would never climb trees, never run a race, never walk to the shops. These items on my Life List, so deeply assumed that I had never written them down, were suddenly erased (Birkett 2000: 122).

It is generally accepted that developing collaborative relationships with parents and families represents good practice for all schools and for all children. However, it can be argued that this type of collaboration is even more essential in relation to pupils with special educational needs and their families. Recent Irish legislation (Education for Persons with Special Educational Needs (EPSEN) Act 2004) stipulates certain minimum requirements for the involvement of parents in the identification and assessment of their child's learning difficulties and the drafting of a subsequent Individual Education Plan. Although there are legislative safeguards, this does not necessarily mean that the school–parent relationship will be a collaborative experience. There is a danger that while the 'letter of the law' may be followed, the real purpose of collaboration will be lost and forgotten in the anxiety to ensure compliance with the law.

Some children will come to school with an assessed special educational need, though for a sizeable number of children their learning difficulties only fully emerge in the context of formal schooling. As a result, parents, children, teachers and the school community face a number of challenges to ensure that collaborative relationships develop which support the education of children with special educational needs.

In this chapter we will focus on the concept of parental involvement and how collaborative relationships can be fostered with schools.

Legislation

Over the past decade there has been a noticeable shift in Irish education policy and legislation towards formally recognising the central role of parents of children and young people with special educational needs in the decision-making processes that affect their children. The Education Act 1998 guaranteed that the constitutional rights of children with disabilities and/or special educational needs to education would be protected, though the usual caveat of having regard to available resources is included: 'to provide that, as far as is practicable and having due regard to the resources available, there is made available to people resident in the State a level and quality of education appropriate to meeting the needs and abilities of those people' (Part 2, Section 6b). Parents also have the right to appeal decisions by schools that refuse to enrol their children, and this process has been used by some parents of children with special educational needs who could not gain access to their local school.

Parents are centrally involved in the assessment process as outlined in the EPSEN Act 2004. They can begin the assessment process (with the agreement of the school principal) by expressing concern about the progress of their child; they are entitled to be consulted about an Individual Education Plan (IEP) and their active involvement (if they so wish) must be facilitated by the school. In addition, parents must receive a copy of the IEP, be advised of any major changes to it and receive a report when the plan is reviewed. Parents also have the right to appeal any decision by the school and/or the National Council for Special Education to an Appeals Board. These safeguards are an attempt by the government to give parents practical rights as they negotiate for an appropriate education for their child. Carey (2005) has expressed concerns that the apparently compulsory mediation process to deal with disputes restricts the rights of parents to pursue court cases in relation to securing appropriate education for their child.

Parental attitudes to special educational provision

The National Council for Special Education commissioned a national survey of parental attitudes to and experiences of local and national special education services (Armstrong and Kane 2010). Over a thousand parents of children and young people who have special educational needs participated in the survey. The majority of parents (87%) believed that their child was in the appropriate school due to teachers who understood their child's specific needs and planned their lessons accordingly. While the majority of parents found placement in school for their child relatively straightforward, a substantial minority (20%) had encountered serious difficulties. There was general satisfaction with the assessment process (78%) though concerns were expressed about the length of time involved. Parents were considerably less satisfied with the process for the allocation of resources and cited difficulties getting their child's special educational need recognised and assessed. Parents were generally satisfied with the learning programmes followed by their children though a substantial majority (19%) were dissatisfied, particularly those with children in secondary schools. The authors concluded that the quality of the relationship between parents and the school played a critical role in determining parental attitudes and experiences of special education services. Parents were most satisfied where schools were supportive, facilitated good communication with parents and demonstrated a good understanding of their child's needs. Most frustration was caused by the assessment process and subsequent allocation of resources.

The survey findings from Ireland are generally corroborated by the Lamb Inquiry (Department for Children, Schools and Families 2009) which examined parental confidence with special educational services in the United Kingdom. Lamb comments that:

> The assessment process drives much of the controversy and dissatisfaction in the system. Many parents found the statutory process stressful and difficult due to a lack of information, poor support and the negative attitudes they often encountered. Parents need to have confidence that their children's needs are accurately assessed and regularly reviewed as the child changes and develops (p. 4).

The inquiry strongly endorsed the recommendation that a stronger voice for parents in shaping special educational provision should be facilitated and encouraged. It was pointed out that: 'in the most successful schools the effective engagement of parents has had a profound impact on children's progress and the confidence between the school and parent' (p. 3).

How families react to special educational needs

In this section we will begin to explore how parents and families react to, respond to and live with the news that their child has a disability and/or special educational need. As we will see, there is no uniform response and much will depend on family circumstances and the type and nature of the disability and/or special educational need involved. This is why it is very important that teachers and the school community do not make assumptions about parental perspectives based on what may be stereotypical views or incomplete information about particular disabilities and/or special educational needs.

Before formal schooling, a child can have a physical disability, for example, that on entering school becomes a special educational need if the child has associated difficulties in learning. It is equally true that this child may have special access needs and not necessarily a special educational need (see Chapter 6). As a result, we will use the term 'disability and/or special educational needs' when referring to children and young people in this chapter, as we will be reflecting on issues that affect these children and their families from birth onwards.

We also need to be aware that depending on the nature of the disability, the families may have had extensive contact with a variety of professionals – school and teachers may be the latest in a long line of professionals that parents must encounter. Some of the professional encounters may have been beneficial, while others unfortunately less so. As far as possible, we have tried here to convey the variety of parental experiences and reactions in their own words.

Reaction and adaptation to disability

Parents and families with children who have disabilities and/or special educational needs do not form a homogeneous group, and while they may share some characteristics and experiences, they are as diverse and unique as any segment of society. The disability and/or special educational need may have been identified at birth, during early childhood or in school. Family reactions to this news will vary and much will depend on the family circumstances and the nature and type of disability and/or special educational need experienced by the child. However, some reactions appear more regularly: 'For many parents of a child with a disability their responses are related to the loss of what could have been, of what their child might have had if they had not lost some sensory or intellectual, physical, physiological or neurological capacity' (Fraser 2005: 134).

In facing this reality, parents enter uncharted territory: 'Parents who have a child born or diagnosed with an impairment face a completely new world. Each parent has to begin to come to terms with a changed reality for themselves and what they expected for their child. This is often the beginning of a lifelong journey that involves dealing with medical, educational and human service professionals' (Simpson et al. 2005: 199).

Hornby (1994: 37) has identified seven stages (a continuum of reactions) in parental adaptation to disability, though it should be noted that the process described is not the same for all parents and does not automatically follow the seven stages in sequence:

1 Shock (numbness, confusion).
2 Denial (disbelief, protest).
3 Anger (blame, guilt).
4 Sadness (despair, grief).
5 Detachment (empty, life is meaningless).

6 Reorganisation (realism, hope).
7 Adaptation (reconciliation, coming to terms).

For parents, 'the news that a child has, or is at risk from a developmental disability, is often among the most frightening and confusing pieces of information that parents will ever receive' (Beckman and Beckman Boyes 1993: 1).

Parental experiences of disability

In the following excerpts from parental experiences, we begin to explore how the world changed dramatically for them and their families. On being given the initial diagnosis that her child experienced Down syndrome, this mother felt alone and exposed: 'The night she was born they said "your baby has Down syndrome". I said "they're wrong, they're wrong" because I was young and I didn't expect anything to be wrong, but I was very upset ... I was very vulnerable' (Kenny et al. 2003b: 13).

Sometimes the news that your child has a general learning disability can be conveyed in an inappropriate manner: 'There was a lot of difficulty with the medical profession. The consultant said "Your baby is severely handicapped mentally and physically and will never achieve anything!" Very badly put. There is no easy way to tell parents but arrangements should be made to have someone available to talk the implications through' (Mulrooney and Harrold 2004: 46).

Adjustment was extremely difficult for another parent: 'I adjusted with great difficulty. The first few months were a blur of strong emotional responses – grief, resentment, self-pity, anger. The first year was probably the most difficult period – I would not like to experience it again' (Mulrooney and Harrold 2004: 53).

The shock and uncertainty that enter family life is illustrated by the following excerpts, the first from a mother, followed by a father's reaction:

> It is like being hit with an express train. First of all the engine hits you with the news that your baby has serious problems. Perhaps the birth was difficult, and she didn't breathe properly ... But here she is, hanging on to life by a thread, and suddenly life becomes very fearful ... The track on which the train is running is harsh in the extreme. A continuing sequence of your baby's illnesses, hospital readmissions, sleepless nights, exhausting days and questions to which there are no answers: 'Why did this happen?'; 'Will she ever learn to smile ... sit ... play?'; 'What will she be like when she is older?' (Smith 1997: 2–3, cited in Carpenter 2000.)
>
> This must all be a dream – this thought runs through my mind again and again. This cannot happen to us! In this turmoil, I was conscious of the supportive attitude of the hospital staff, that every effort they made was an endeavour to uphold us, to help us to endure the pain and distress that fell upon us as the reality of our baby's disability dawned on us (Herbert and Carpenter 1994: 40).

In an Irish study (Kenny et al. 2003b) a group of parents of children who experienced Down syndrome shared their initial experiences of bewilderment, lack of information and the urgent need for relevant support and appropriate medical responses:

> **Mother:** 'I was very ignorant, I think I couldn't have applied the term to someone with the condition. Even though where I worked we were all airy-fairy running around. We hadn't a titter. Times we'd organise a function, we'd make a few hundred and we'd [pick a] charity. We might give it to St Michael's House ... but I didn't actually know ...'
>
> **Mother:** 'Until I had my child, I never thought about it.'
>
> **Father:** 'Some parents [in the Down Syndrome Association] heard so they made contact, but we didn't contact them back for a few months because we were so devastated and hurt and physically traumatised and we didn't know what to do. We had to go through all that phase of will she live, won't she live ... and we had this very negative image of Down syndrome, adults overweight, teenagers, even with being teachers we had a lot of baggage in our own heads at the time as new parents.'
>
> **Mother:** 'I remember asking [the paediatrician] "how handicapped is he going to be?" And she said "handicapped is handicapped". It was like a slap in the face ... She asked me to strip Jason off. I don't recall her asking me if the students could come in to have a look at him and she started telling them to note this and note that and I just said "I've had enough." You are so vulnerable at that time ... You are just looking for information. He's a child. Handicapped has nothing to do with it ...' (p. 14)

The chronic vulnerability expressed by these parents appears to be a common feature of initial reactions to the birth of a child with a disability as they face uncertain futures and literally do not know what is coming next. For some parents there is a constant struggle:

> As a parent with a child who has multiple disabilities I got absolutely exhausted with all the explaining and the battle to be heard. First it was the doctors, then the paediatricians, followed by the audiologists, physiotherapists, occupational therapists, ophthalmologists, orthopaedic surgeons, speech therapists, psychologists and numerous others who kept telling me what I should do for my child and what was best for her. In the early days I felt pretty confused and overwhelmed (Fraser 2005: 130).

Other parents have to rearrange their lives and often feel that they inhabit parallel worlds:

> The way I see it, we have two lives, the one that's like everyone else's where we eat, sleep and communicate and see friends and go on holiday, and the

other that's tied to this condition with hospital and hospice visits, and lifting, and phoning and waiting for the special this, that and the next thing and waiting for all the professionals … and so on, a real struggle. I suppose what I try to do is ensure that the second world doesn't take over from the first. Sometimes, amazingly, I succeed (Norris and Closs 2003: 27).

Fraser (2005: 135) observed that some of the initial parental feelings of sadness, loss and uncertainty can reappear at other stages in the life cycle of their child:

It's Dave's 19th birthday this month. That for most people is a time of celebration, and so it is for us. However, the celebratory nature is tinged with sadness and grief, because just as people are saddened by the anniversary of a death of a loved one, I am saddened by the anniversary of the birth of our wonderful son, because life gave us part of the son he could have been. I still wonder "what if", and what would he have been like had he been normal.

This point is echoed by a parent in Mulrooney and Harrold's (2004: 50) study:

We cannot put our finger on it but when she made her Holy Communion and then later had her twenty-first party we were quite low. What should have been the happiest occasions of Evelyn's life just seemed to make the difference that much more obvious. It is as if these milestones made it patently clear that Evelyn will never function independently, will never get married, and will always depend on us.

Parental struggle for support services

From the beginning, parents often face a struggle to ensure that their child receives the appropriate interventions and necessary services. A multi-agency working party report, *Together from the Start,* in the United Kingdom, acknowledged that many barriers exist in accessing appropriate services: 'It is not only disabled children's impairments which determine the quality of life but also disabling attitudes and a disabling environment which can result in unequal access to community services and facilities' (DoH/DfES 2003: 6).

Simpson et al. (2005: 200) elaborate further on this perspective: 'Written and anecdotal history includes family descriptions of isolation, lack of information, unequal power relationships, having one's life bureaucratised, being case managed, researched, controlled and marginalised.' Parents are sometimes forced into adopting a variety of strategies to ensure that their child receives appropriate services: 'I had to beg them to help my son. You have to play the part, I wasn't aggressive, if you are aggressive you get nowhere with the LEA (Local Education Authority), nowhere. You have to be subservient and beg for help' (Duncan 2003: 351).

Fear and apprehension can dominate the parental relationship with professionals: 'I am scared every twelve months, because he has a review meeting every twelve months. I have to be careful what I say, or they'll take him out [of the provision]. This is how you have to behave in Wellbury. It's frightening because I know I will have to fight again' (Duncan 2003: 352).

One parent perceived this struggle in the context of a broader attempt to ensure that access to services was an established right for families rather than being offered on a 'grace and favour' basis:

> It's okay if you're middle-class and educated you're able for them but if you're not ... The doctors and the hospitals treated you and your child as victims ... somehow having a child with Down syndrome or with special needs was some kind of a tragedy ... They feel very sorry for you. But I never felt victimised. I always felt it was convenient for them to bracket us in that kind of 'we're very sorry, we'll do the best we can' – but all that kind of thing is merely a substitute for having rights. We were never able to make a demand, we were never able to say – that person is entitled to A, B, C, D and E, and we don't want X, Y and Z, and sorry we don't want X other things either ... Because we didn't have the rights (Kenny et al. 2003b: 16).

This point was reinforced by another parent: 'Many of the pleasures of bringing up children were displaced by an all-consuming struggle to claim and hold their education rights' (Duncan 2003: 353).

Home–school relationships

Over the past couple of decades, home–school relationships have undergone some dramatic changes as parents assume a more prominent role in their child's education. Legislation has strengthened the parental role and schools have additional statutory duties in developing viable home–school relationships. However, it can be argued that parents of children with disabilities and/or special educational needs have encountered barriers to the participation of their child within mainstream schools. This experience, coupled with previous experiences of difficulties accessing appropriate health and/or social services, may well shape initial encounters with schools and teachers. Schools and teachers may also approach the home–school relationship based on preconceived notions or even lack of knowledge about the disability and/or special educational needs experienced by the child. Establishing sound home–school relationships requires sensitivity, flexibility and willingness on the part of the school to understand and recognise what parents and families may be experiencing. This type of relationship is also essential when a child is identified in the school context as having a difficulty in learning that requires further assessment.

It is evident that multi-disciplinary approaches will be required to respond effectively to the varied educational, social, physical, communication and psychological needs of children and young people experiencing difficulties in learning. Though complex, the relationship between home and the varied professionals and services must be collaborative in nature and involves 'an attitude of sharing, teaching and learning across traditional boundaries. It also recognises the essential role of parents in working in a team approach. It recognises the importance of meeting a child's needs in a holistic way whenever this is possible' (Walsh 1997: 97). In this section we will explore the issues that need to be addressed in order to establish positive home–school relationships built on trust and mutual respect.

Norris and Closs (2003) reported on the school experiences of parents of children who had serious medical conditions that resulted in frequent absences from school. Initial encounters with school were overshadowed by over-protectiveness and uncertainty about whether the child should be treated in the same manner as his/her peers. There were certain inhibitions around illness and death that caused difficulties in creating positive relationships. Teachers' ability to empathise with and interact positively with the child was a critical factor in fostering a supportive learning environment. Parents 'appreciated staff who listened to them, understood their worries about health or educational progress were real, and accepted and used the information they gave' (p. 25).

However, 'any mismatch in values and in aims for children's education between school staff and parents could be exacerbated by issues related to the child's condition. Although rarely made explicit, some teachers seemed to expect families' compliance with school values and practices "in exchange" for the extra effort it took to meet children's needs' (p. 26).

In this situation, schools appeared to be adopting a charity model approach, expecting parents to be grateful for the service offered. Educational progress for their child was a major concern for many parents and they believed that 'regardless of their children's ability, educational achievement at their own level was a marker of their children's existence and in some cases it was also perceived as a compensation for their physical limitations' (p. 27).

The parents in this study believed that schools were capable of responding positively to the sometimes complicated needs presented by their children. One parent, whose daughter had died, said the following about her local primary school: 'I have great admiration for this school. They have done everything they possibly could to help us' (p. 28). Norris and Closs concluded that awareness-raising for teachers in relation to illness and death would be useful in identifying teacher fears and preconceptions that could impede the development of positive relationships.

Many parents first encounter the whole concept of special educational need within the school context when their child is identified as experiencing some difficulty in learning. It is evident that there is enormous variation among schools in their capacity to respond proactively to parental concerns. There were distinct differences in the ability of schools to provide relevant information in relation to special educational needs and in their willingness to share information with parents about the child's progress and their readiness to listen to parents about home-based difficulties. Croll (2001) observed that parents had traditionally been seen as part of the problem and contributing to the child's learning difficulties. This approach made any type of equal partnership between teachers and parents very difficult to achieve.

Parental reactions to assessment of special educational need

Norwich et al. (2005) reported that many parents felt ambivalent about the school's initial reaction to their concerns about their child's learning difficulties. They felt they were dismissed as being over-protective or over-anxious parents and so the identification of dyslexia came as an enormous relief. In some way they had felt that they were responsible for their child's learning difficulties and that the school had assigned blame, regarding them as parents who did too little at home to help their child or who spoiled their child.

Similar reactions from parents were evident when their child had been identified with ADHD: 'It came as a huge relief to know that something could be done for their children and they (parents) were not responsible for their (children's) behaviour through poor parenting' (Norris and Lloyd 2000: 127).

However, prior to the identification of ADHD, some parents had been told in no uncertain terms that their lack of parenting skills were primarily to blame for the child's misbehaviour: 'I was firmly informed that there were no badly behaved children, only those who were the product of bad upbringing, especially by single parents. I was devastated' (p. 127).

Difficulties concerning children's behaviour appeared to cause most concern for schools.

Quinn (2001) describes some parental experiences of the identification and assessment process in Northern Ireland and observes that even 'where the parents may have already been aware that the child is experiencing difficulty in comparison to peers during early development, the announcement will still be distressing and leave parents feeling isolated from the process which will evolve to assess the child. Moreover, there is the fear of not knowing where the process will lead, and to what degree the parents will feel even more isolated.'

As the assessment process developed, parents often felt confused in a world of bureaucracy and this stirred up 'worry ... as to what was ahead, where he would go, what would happen to him'. Others felt shocked at the news that their child was a 'bit slow' and described the process as 'scary, but hurtful because it hits you'. Many parents felt powerless and regarded themselves as bystanders in the process involving the educational psychologist: 'what she wanted you do it. It's as if she was taking over the child ... wanted to rush everything. What she says goes! She did not have to do this because this was a handicapped child.'

Many parents were still in the middle of adjusting to the fact that their child had a special educational need requiring this formal assessment process. Parents believed that it was better to accept the professional judgment, as to challenge it would be seen as 'rocking the boat' and could have a detrimental effect on their child's provision. Parents who had negotiated their way through the assessment process commented that it 'looks scary, looks impossible, but is straightforward as long as you have support and a helping hand'. Quinn concluded that essentially two interlinked processes are involved – enabling parents to become informed and knowledgeable and recognising parents as equal partners in the process with a valuable contribution to make.

Russell's (2005) study of parental experiences of transition into primary school for their children with disabilities highlighted how the development of positive outcomes to expectations can facilitate the development of supportive relationships between parents and professionals. This involves the development of shared expectations between the parents and the professionals concerned. However, parental experiences varied between those who felt supported and those who felt they had to battle for what they considered appropriate provision: 'After the meeting at the Early Years Centre I came out sort of feeling let down, upset and an outsider. I felt my daughter's future had been taken out of my hands. It's as though I'm not going to have a say in her education. It's all been mapped out for her without my consent' (p. 122).

For another parent, the positive attitude of her support worker was the key: 'She's the one that said "this is what we'd like Fay to be aiming for." Whereas everybody else says "she needs to be doing this" and "she needs to be doing that" but not actually formalising anything' (p. 122).

Despite repeated requests to be fully involved in and informed about her son's educational plan, another parent reported that 'I have asked all the way along to be involved in every step of it. That hasn't happened. They have held their meetings without me and then they have had a meeting afterwards to tell me what's been discussed and what is to happen' (p. 122).

Often professionals assumed that parents were familiar with the assessment process when in fact this was a completely new and sometimes bewildering experience for most. Regular clarification of the process by the professionals was required. Once in school, parents appeared to receive regular updates on their child's progress, but it became apparent that understanding of this information varied. Some parents 'found it difficult to decipher reports or were confused by incomplete, conflicting and/or inaccurate information concerning assessment procedures and many did not know of the school special education needs co-ordinator (SENCO) or the local Parent Partnership Service who should be available to offer help' (p. 123).

According to the parents, achieving positive outcomes generally was the result of positive attitudes among professionals and practitioners towards disability and working with parents and the willingness of schools to be flexible in accommodating the needs of children with disabilities and their families.

Building collaborative relationships

In order to build collaborative relationships between home and school, certain realities have to be acknowledged. There is usually an unequal power relationship between teachers and parents, and parents are often at a disadvantage in lacking relevant information about the workings of special educational provision, particularly in relation to the identification and assessment process.

Fraser (2005) identifies and outlines the common obstacles to developing collaborative relationships. For some parents who had a negative experience of schooling themselves, schools can represent a hostile environment. They may feel uncertain of basic procedures in locating the relevant professionals and this will increase their anxiety. These issues may appear minor to school personnel but can assume great importance for parents in the context of meetings concerning the development of Individual Education Plans for their children. Another obstacle consists of the teacher assuming the role of expert. This is not to deny the teacher's expertise in special education. However, teachers need to acknowledge the expert knowledge parents have in relation to their child and they will have valuable insights into their child's specific needs. The 'teacher as expert' stance will inhibit parents from sharing information and insights, as it has already been demonstrated who is in charge and who will make the decisions regarding their child. This approach will severely restrict the capacity of a genuine partnership to emerge that can gather the knowledge and resources required to benefit the child to the greatest extent. Teachers also need to be valued within a collaborative relationship. Many teachers regularly push out the boundaries of their jobs to ensure that children with difficulties can participate and achieve within mainstream classrooms. The professional life of teachers is often frenetic, with many competing and sometimes conflicting demands on their time and energy. This reality needs to be recognised and built into the collaborative process involving school and home.

Principles of effective partnership

Pinkus (2005) points out that while the value of developing collaborative relationships between parents and professionals is universally acknowledged, it can be difficult to achieve effective partnerships in practice. Developing positive partnerships requires attention to the following four principles based on a study of parent–professional relationships (Pinkus 2005: 184):

• Consensus about purpose of partnership.
• Clarity – who is in partnership and why.
• Enabling equal power distribution among partners.
• Implementing transparency and accountability mechanisms for monitoring the partnership.

Parents identified the lack of agreement about the purpose of the partnership and confusion about the roles of the partners involved in the process as the main obstacles to working together effectively. It was particularly important from the beginning of the relationship to establish who was responsible for what aspects of the partnership, e.g. setting up meetings/applying for assessments. Parents appeared to be on a continuum of adjustment both in accepting that their child had a special educational need and in developing a relationship with the professionals involved.

Sometimes, especially when a child had complex needs, many professionals were involved in contributing to the child's educational and health provision. However, there appeared to be little clarification of roles or sometimes no evidence of communication between the various professionals involved. One outcome can be delay and lack of agreement about the provision of support to the child, as the mother of one seven-year-old recounted: 'We seem to be doing everything yet nothing seems to be happening. The whole system is just frustrating, just so frustrating' (p. 185). Another parent commented: 'It has only just gone to the panel after all this time. It has taken hours of professionals' advice, and six months he has been out of school' (p. 187).

Unequal power relationships between parents and professionals can be conveyed in how meetings are conducted and how professionals communicate with parents. In the context of a planning meeting, one parent's reaction was: 'There was no point in me being there really, was there? They had already made up their minds about it' (p. 186). Medical professionals were perceived as the most powerful among the professionals and their opinion often determined the type and nature of provision in particular situations: 'You know if we had medical support, medical backing, then that would seal the case. The school won't move forward because they say there is no medical backing. We have all this stuff (school documentation and yet they say it is easy for the LEA (Local Education Authority) to dismiss the information we have got so far because it doesn't come from a doctor' (p. 186).

Some schools found ways of empowering parents by including them when interviewing a special needs assistant for their child: '"You help us choose, you know your son best" … It was amazing. I was very spoilt' (p. 186). Fraser (2005) describes the experience of one mother of a child who had multiple disabilities who served on the board of trustees of her daughter's school. Initially, Mandy (the mother) assumed the role of advocate for children with special educational needs. However, other members of the board gradually began to recognise that they had an important role to play in these discussions: 'Like the other day, we were discussing a whole school trip to the bush and one of the other parents brought up the point of wheelchair access. Another parent made the point that all school trips should have a policy on full inclusion and that the Board should as far as possible endeavour to see that all children can go' (p. 131). Mandy felt affirmed through this recognition and support: 'It was such a breakthrough to hear other voices saying what I usually said. It was such a breakthrough not to be alone' (p. 131).

Parents often felt confused when special education procedures were not transparent, and this was exacerbated by the conflicting roles of the professional (often an educational psychologist) as 'partner' with parents and also the official 'gatekeeper' of resources. In these circumstances, could the parents be certain that the professional was acting in the best interests of their child?

Ensuring that the four principles outlined above are located at the centre of considerations of home–school relationships remains a significant challenge for schools. Recognition of the need for role clarity and an equalisation of power relationships can mark the beginning of more productive parent–professional relationships. Involving parents in their children's learning can make a positive contribution to effective home–school relationships.

Creating responsive parent–teacher relationships

Beveridge (1999) points out that many children with special educational needs will have literacy difficulties and that home–school collaboration in tackling these difficulties through paired reading programmes, for example, has proved very fruitful. Fraser (2005) and Rose and Howley (2007) provide some guidelines for ensuring that parents and teachers can develop responsive relationships that support the child and enable him/her to make progress.

Fraser believes that teachers who value people regardless of their background and seek to actively listen to and involve parents in the decision-making processes understand the meaning of collaboration. This type of responsive teacher does not make assumptions about the child or young person and his/her family based on their social background or previous negative experiences with other members of the family. There is a focus on the positive achievements of the child and this is communicated to the parents. They do not assume that non-appearance by parents automatically means a lack of interest in their child and understand that parents may be apprehensive about approaching the school for many legitimate reasons and may need to be gently coaxed into the collaborative partnership. Parents valued teachers who were sincere and honest, even when this meant admitting a lack of knowledge and uncertainty about how to best help the child who has special educational needs: 'The teacher said to me she was scared about having my daughter in the class but that she was looking forward to it. I appreciated her honesty in saying that, that she was scared, and I could feel she would do her best because she was scared, that she would find out what she can to benefit the classroom and Haley' (p. 146).

Within the classroom, responsive teachers ensure that the child and young person with special educational needs is given opportunities to be the tutor as well as the tutee and to be the helper rather than always the recipient of help. Teacher modelling of inclusive practice in this way can promote a more positive identity for the child with special educational needs among his/her peer group.

Guidelines for beginning teachers

Rose and Howley (2007: 34) provide useful guidelines for beginning teachers in their interaction with parents of children who have special educational needs.

Teacher understanding:
- Be aware of and sensitive to the anxieties which parents or carers may feel about their child and which may affect their response to you as the teacher.
- Ensure privacy and respect for the parents, e.g. arranging a suitable physical environment for meeting.

Communication with parents:
- Avoid using jargon.
- Listen carefully to any anxieties or questions.
- Do not offer hasty responses or ill thought-out solutions.
- Do not be afraid to say if you cannot provide answers; find out from someone else and inform the parents.
- Be honest when asked about pupil progress but use language which expresses your interest in the pupil and demonstrates that you are working to achieve positive outcomes.

Professional behaviour:
- Keep a record of conversations with parents about any concerns for their child.
- Ensure that parents are informed about other professional visits to their child and the purpose of these visits, e.g. the assessment process.
- Consult with learning support/resource staff about any concerns expressed by parents. (Adapted from Rose and Howley 2007: 34.)

Concluding comments

As can be seen, developing collaborative partnerships is a complex, demanding process. Essentially this process entails professionals moving away from the expert model towards a more responsive model where 'teachers are sensitive to parents' perspectives, take them seriously and respectfully, assume that parents are concerned and interested in their children's education; and that non-involvement does not necessarily mean a lack of interest' (Norwich et al. 2005: 163).

Manuel, a parent, encapsulates what this collaborative parent–professional relationship looks and feels like in practice:

> The professionalism on which you stand is not a different road to the one we tread ... It's also the road that's cushioned and softened by the laughter and the smiles of love, and tears for our children. That road is the same road, and, when we relate to each other we have the partnership that dreams are made of. From the educational psychologist who sits with you and tries to translate the vision you have for your child in the way his or her report is written, to the occupational therapist who'll make a separate attachment to your child's wheelchair so the cat can curl up next to your child, to the midwife who finds a lovely position you can feed your child in even though it's completely against her textbook knowledge ... These are professionals who are working in the spirit of the term 'partnership' (Manuel 1996: 3).

Discussion points

1   Schools are encouraged to develop positive relationships with parents and it can be argued that this is even more vital for parents of children with special educational needs.

(a) What is the best way of making contact with parents when the teacher has concerns about the learning needs of the child?

(b) How can teachers/the school allay parental fears about coming to school?

2 What would you consider to be the main obstacles to developing collaborative home–school relationships?

3 What skills do teachers need to establish positive home–school relationships?

4 'As I see it, you have two choices. One is to hide behind your professional position, your desk and professional ethics (i.e. what is right to do in this situation). The other is to come out from behind the desk, stand alongside us, maybe weep with us, but then help us cope with the practical day-by-day situations. Please tell us that you "don't know" if you don't. But please network, be a lateral thinker to help us sort out the situation as best can be done for everyone' (Janet Dixon 1994: 83, cited in Fraser 2005). What are the implications of this approach for teachers in their relationship with parents of children and young people with special educational needs?

Chapter 14

Creating and Developing Partnerships within Schools

Learning outcomes/objectives

On completion of this chapter, the reader will be able to:

- Identify the steps and structures that can significantly enhance the opportunities to respond appropriately to special educational needs as outcomes of whole-school planning.
- Analyse the practices of streaming and mixed-ability grouping as school responses to the challenges of meeting varied learning needs.
- Critically examine the principles underpinning learning support provision in schools and the consultative/collaborative role of the support teacher.
- Discuss the roles of the resource teacher and special needs assistant in the context of whole-school partnership in supporting inclusion.

Introduction

It has become very common to refer to whole-school approaches to special educational needs, though it is much more difficult to translate a whole-school policy into daily accepted practice at all levels in the school community. If they are to be meaningful, whole-school approaches must enable the school community to make a positive, thoughtful response to children with special educational needs. We need to avoid a situation where the individual classroom teacher (with some limited support) must principally rely on his/her store of knowledge, skills and resources to respond appropriately to the pupils with special educational needs and those with low attainment rates. As we explore this issue, it will become apparent that individualised responses are no substitute for a collective, collaborative approach to what are often complex learning needs that will require responses at structural, pedagogic and curricular levels. Within a dynamic whole-school approach, 'responsibility is shared, advice is available, resources are commonly held, lines of responsibility are clearly outlined and systematic procedures are in place for monitoring and recording pupils' progress' (Gross 2002: 18).

Whole-school approaches

Every Irish school is required to have a school policy on responding to special educational needs. Section 9 of the Education Act 1998 states that a school must 'ensure that the educational needs of students, including those with disability or special needs, are identified and provided for'. In addition, boards of management are required to develop a school plan that shall 'state the objectives of the school relating to equality of access to and participation in the school and the measures which the school proposes to take to achieve those objectives, including equality of access to and participation in the school by students with disabilities or who have other special educational needs' (Section 21.2). As a result, provision for special educational needs becomes the responsibility of the whole-school community, and while support personnel have a major function, they perform their roles in consultation and collaboration with everyone involved in the school community. We will now examine the whole-school issues involved in supporting and encouraging pupils who experience difficulties in learning.

The *Learning-Support Guidelines* (DES 2000) and the *Inclusion of Students with Special Educational Needs: Post-Primary Guidelines* (DES 2007) issued by the Department of Education and Science state unequivocally that supporting the learning of individual pupils is a whole-school responsibility. The *Learning-Support Guidelines* (2000: 9) provide guidance on 'the implementation in all schools of policies which emphasise the enhancement of classroom-based learning for all pupils, the prevention of learning difficulties and the provision of early intervention and learning-support programmes'.

This point is reiterated in the *Inclusion of Students with Special Educational Needs: Post-Primary Guidelines* (2007: 40): 'The process of developing school policy and procedures on special educational needs is most effective when the process is undertaken in collaboration with the various partners in the school community – trustees, board of management, teachers, parents and students – and as appropriate, support agencies and services and the local community.'

The whole-school approach is presented very clearly within the context of the creation of an inclusive school as envisaged in the EPSEN Act 2004. The general principles underpinning the whole-school approach as outlined in the *Post-Primary Guidelines* (2007) apply equally to primary schools. Effective planning and development involves creating structures within schools that improve the capacity of schools to respond appropriately to special educational needs. This will involve the development of strategies for early identification and prevention of difficulties in learning; the design of appropriate and inclusive assessment procedures that take account of the special educational needs of these students; the clarification of staff roles and responsibilities; providing practical support for subject-teachers; the establishment of effective communication with parents and outside support agencies and services; and the provision of opportunities for students with special educational needs to access a broad range of activities within the school.

The *Post-Primary Guidelines* acknowledge that post-primary schools face significant challenges in implementing inclusive approaches for students with special educational needs. These factors include 'certain contextual factors, such as the nature and structure of the syllabus, state examinations, the organisation of classes, timetabling and the conflicting priorities arising [which] can constrain the collaborative planning that is essential for successful teaching and learning' (p. 40). However, these difficulties should not be regarded as an excuse to shirk the challenge, and the *Guidelines* go on to state 'it is critical that such challenges are addressed at whole school level and that effective structures for planning, co-operation and consultation for inclusion are established' (p. 40).

All schools, particularly post-primary schools, have a number of options in organising class placement for pupils with special educational needs. At primary level the pupil is usually within the mainstream classroom or in a special class/unit. However, at post-primary level class placement can include mainstream mixed-ability class groups, streamed/banded class groups or designated special classes. Placement in each of these settings has important implications for the pupil.

Mixed-ability settings have the advantage of including the pupil with special educational needs alongside his/her peer group, improving their academic learning, contributing to their personal and social development and explicitly supporting an inclusive approach to special educational needs.

Streaming involves assigning pupils in a particular year to higher- or lower-stream class groupings on the basis of some type of attainment measure. Banding usually consists of grouping classes in a particular year into ability bands (for example, three higher/two lower), and the result is that pupils who have assessed special educational needs or those considered as being low achievers will be placed in the lower band. Often pupils in the lowest stream(s)/band will be offered a reduced curriculum. The risks associated with the streaming/banding approach in relation to pupils with special educational needs are listed in the *Post-Primary Guidelines*:

> The negative effects of streaming include the possibility that students may be segregated from their peers rather than included with them. Those in low streams may make poor academic progress and may feel marginalised and isolated within the school community. The range of subjects available to students in lower streams may be reduced, and this can have long-term implications for them, for example when a student has not studied Irish or a foreign language (p. 51).

Students placed in these types of classes and their parents should be consulted about the long-term effects of such a placement. Schools also need to consider how they will ensure that a broadly based curriculum will be offered and how the individual needs of pupils with a wide range of abilities, e.g. low achievers in literacy with no assessed special educational need and others who have assessed special educational needs, will be met. There is research evidence that indicates that these concerns about streaming/banding practices have validity. Lynch (1999), for example, expressed concerns about the variability in attainment tests used to determine class groupings, the comparative lack of movement between stream(s)/band(s) once established and how teachers can have lowered expectations for pupils in lower stream(s)/band(s).

Support teaching

Support within schools for pupils and students with special educational needs generally consists of supplementary teaching (additional to pupil's regular classroom programme), personal assistance from a special needs assistant, information technology such as adaptive/assistive software and adjustments to examination conditions. Supplementary teaching is provided by learning support and/or resource teachers, either within the pupil's own classroom and/or withdrawal in small groups or on a one-to-one basis. The roles and responsibilities of learning support teachers and resource teachers were originally intended to be quite distinct, though in practice this distinction can be difficult to maintain. Learning support teachers are involved in developing responses to pupils who have serious literacy and/or numeracy difficulties. Resource teachers support those pupils who have assessed special educational needs as a result of some type of disability, e.g. autism, Down syndrome. However, at the early stages of identification and assessment there may be overlap between the two populations, as pupils with different types of learning difficulties will often experience literacy and/or numeracy difficulties. This emphasises the urgency of establishing a whole-school approach to the provision of supplementary teaching so that confusion of roles is avoided and a timely intervention is facilitated.

At classroom level it is emphasised that the primary responsibility for students with special educational needs rests with the individual subject teacher (classroom teacher at primary level). It is explicitly stated that the provision of additional support should not result in the isolation of the student with special educational needs from his/her peer group or the exclusion of these students from meaningful participation in classroom activities. As a result, the exclusive use of the withdrawal model of support teaching may need to be reviewed and strategies for in-class support and team teaching explored. In addition to direct teaching, the learning support teacher and/or resource teacher are involved in supporting classroom/subject teachers by providing appropriate information on the specific learning needs of students with special educational needs and advising teachers on appropriate teaching strategies, materials, assistive technology (helping students to communicate and receive information), augmentative technology (attempts to compensate for severe expressive and/or language communication disorders) and on the use of information technology.

Learning support

Learning support (formerly known as remedial teaching) has been a well-established feature of Irish schools since 1963. The principal aim of remedial education was to 'remediate' the pupil's specific difficulties in literacy and/or numeracy. Everyone is aware of how critical it is that pupils acquire proficiency in literacy and numeracy skills at primary school in order to progress at post-primary level and later in life. This point was emphasised in the *Report on the National Education Convention* (Coolahan 1994: 69), which stated 'a central task of the primary school is to provide pupils with levels of literacy and numeracy that will be adequate for further education and for their development as individuals who are able to function effectively in society.'

The original *Guidelines on Remedial Education* (Department of Education 1988) attempted to initiate a more integrated approach to literacy issues by emphasising a whole-school approach to remedial education, among other things. A team approach was recommended, with the remedial teacher having a more consultative role and the classroom teacher retaining the major responsibility for the progress of the pupil in his/her class. The *Guidelines* also emphasised the importance of adopting a preventative approach by targeting the junior classes for intervention.

The *Report of the Special Education Review Committee* (1993: 76) described pupils in need of remedial teaching in the following way: 'Those pupils in ordinary first level and second level schools who have clearly observable difficulties in acquiring basic skills in literacy and/or numeracy or who have some difficulties of a more general nature.' The report recommended that remedial provision should be extended to offer support to all pupils in primary and post-primary schools who score at or below the tenth percentile on standardised tests of basic literacy or numeracy. Scoring at the tenth percentile means that 90 per cent of this pupil's age cohort scored better on the proficiency test. The relative lack of emphasis on the development of oral language, mathematical skills and social and personal skills was identified as a serious drawback to existing remedial provision.

Since the 1980s there has been considerable development in educational provision, but despite this, 'national and international studies of reading achievement indicate that reading standards at primary level in Ireland have not improved significantly during this time. Moreover, of particular importance is the fact that a significant number of children continue to leave primary education with less than adequate skills in reading and/or numeracy' (*Learning-Support Guidelines*, DES 2000: 7).

A combination of these factors prompted a re-examination of remedial education (Shiel, Morgan with Larney 1998) and the issuing of the *Learning-Support Guidelines* (2000). For example, the 1995 International Adult Literacy Survey (IALS) (documented in Chapter 10) revealed some disturbing trends, as more Irish adults scored at the lowest level of proficiency than any other country except Poland (Morgan et al. 1997). It was estimated from another international reading literacy study in 1991 that between 6.5 to 8.5 per cent of Irish fourteen-year-olds had literacy difficulties that would probably obstruct their educational progress and their life opportunities (Morgan and Martin 1993). More evidence on the extent of literacy difficulties was produced in the

National Survey of Reading (1993). When asked to specify the numbers of their fifth class who would be expected to have literacy difficulties, teachers estimated that 6.4 per cent of pupils would be unable to manage everyday reading demands in society, while 9.8 per cent were expected to encounter considerable difficulties coping with the reading demands at post-primary level. Low achievement was also evident in relation to mathematics, as the results of the Third International Mathematics and Science study (TIMMS) demonstrated (Beaton et al. 1996).

The review of remedial education commissioned by the Department of Education and Science (Shiel et al. 1998) revealed that there was a serious imbalance between the emphasis on literacy support compared to support in mathematics. For example, all schools with a remedial service provided remedial teaching in English, whereas only 41 per cent of these schools gave remedial teaching in mathematics. The authors also point out that while the *Guidelines on Remedial Education* recommend that the pupil should spend between two and three years at a maximum in remedial provision, the average time spent in remedial English was over four years. The withdrawal of the pupil from ordinary class formed the dominant model of remedial provision. This obviously raised issues around liaison between the classroom and remedial teacher to ensure that the pupil was enabled to participate successfully in mainstream classroom activities. It was clear from the Shiel et al. study that the *Guidelines on Remedial Education* needed to be updated and revised.

The principal aim of learning support as described in the *Learning-Support Guidelines* (DES 2000: 15) 'is to optimise the teaching and learning process in order to enable pupils with learning difficulties to achieve adequate levels of proficiency in literacy and numeracy before leaving primary school'. The principles underpinning learning support provision are also succinctly outlined in the same document:

- effective whole-school policies and parental involvement
- prevention of failure
- provision of intensive early provision
- direction of resources towards pupils in greatest need (p. 14).

It is anticipated that schools adopting this approach will focus on early intervention strategies and assist teachers in providing an enhanced form of classroom-based learning aimed at preventing learning failure. In the past, a pupil almost had to fail first before intervention strategies could be designed and implemented. This often resulted in the vicious cycle of learning failure compounded by lowered self-esteem and loss of confidence as a learner. The *Guidelines* also envisage that an individual learning plan will be drawn up for each pupil receiving learning support. This plan will assess learning needs and specify learning targets for the pupil and will be known as the Individual Profile and Learning Programme. While this programme has many common elements, e.g. assessment of learning needs/specification of learning targets, with the Individual Education Plan (outlined in Chapter 8), it is very important to note some crucial differences. The Individual Profile and Learning Programme does not require a formal psychological assessment of special educational need before being initiated and implemented. Also, unlike the IEP, this programme is not mandated under the Education for Persons with Special Educational Needs (EPSEN) Act 2004. Despite its lack of legislative force, the Individual Profile and Learning Programme represents accepted good practice in planning and provision for pupils with literacy and/or numeracy difficulties. The development of effective home–school partnerships is considered crucial to the success of any intervention programmes.

In addition to individual and classroom-based interventions, the *Guidelines* recommend that whole-school programmes should be adopted in English and mathematics. These whole-school programmes could include the design of:

- Consistent approaches to language development and relevant aspects of English and mathematics across class groupings.
- Additional support for pupils experiencing difficulties in language development and early literacy and/or numeracy skills.
- Parent involvement programmes to promote the development of children's oral language skills.
- Paired reading programmes involving adults in the community and peers in school.

The *Guidelines* also specify the various roles and responsibilities associated with learning support. The classroom teacher has a significantly enhanced role, as s/he retains ultimate responsibility for the pupil who is receiving learning support. This approach prevents a tendency evident in the past where responsibility for the pupil's progress rested mainly with the learning support teacher. Undoubtedly the predominant system of withdrawal from the classroom for learning support provision contributed to this perception. The classroom teacher is also expected to fashion a supportive classroom environment in which learning difficulties can be successfully addressed or at least lessened. The *Guidelines* suggest that this outcome can be best accomplished by 'grouping pupils for instruction, providing lower-achieving pupils with strategies for reading and problem solving, adapting learning materials for lower-achieving pupils and liaising closely with their parents' (p. 42). When a pupil is receiving learning support it is crucial that the classroom teacher contribute to the identification of learning targets and the design of the class programme to support the pupil in their attainment of the agreed targets.

In addition to supplementary teaching, there is a clear emphasis in the *Guidelines* on the collaborative and consultative roles of the learning support teacher. The learning support teacher is expected to consult with the principal, classroom teacher, parents and outside agencies in order to develop a coordinated response to the individual needs of pupils. The multi-faceted role of the learning support teacher can be summarised as follows:

- Contribute to school policy development.
- Assist in whole-school early intervention/prevention.
- Advise staff on selection, use and interpretation of standardised tests.
- Consult with class teachers on selection of pupils for diagnostic assessment (McPhillips 2003: 32).

The *Guidelines* anticipate changes in the predominant withdrawal model of provision for supplementary teaching by pointing out the disadvantages of over-reliance on this approach, e.g. prolonged absence from classroom/difficulties in coordinating interventions, and recommending the 'planned implementation of shared teaching approaches, involving the class teacher and the learning-support teacher, in the pupil's regular classroom' (p. 46). Day (2005) reiterates this point with an analysis of the advantages for teachers and pupils of in-class support models. Advantages of team teaching include the acquisition of a wider range of pedagogical skills by the classroom teacher, increased collaborative planning and the opportunity for the pupil to keep pace with classroom work.

Resource teaching

Resource teaching is less well established in schools compared to learning support provision. Resource teaching originated in the establishment of special classes in mainstream schools for children with assessed special educational needs. However, over the past decade there has been an enormous expansion in the numbers of resource teachers with a consequent development of their role in the inclusion of pupils with special educational needs within mainstream schools.

The role of resource teachers has been defined by the Department of Education and Science as follows:

- Assessing and recording child's needs and progress;
- Direct teaching of the children, either in a separate room or within the mainstream class;
- Team-teaching – so long as the children concerned are deriving benefit from it;
- Meeting and advising parents, when necessary, accompanied by the class teacher, as necessary;
- Short meetings with other relevant professionals, in the children's interest – e.g. psychologists, speech and language therapists, visiting teachers, special school or special class teachers (DES 2002a).

Within the context of the whole-school approach to special educational needs, the resource teacher, in collaboration with the learning support teacher, will probably be involved in a range of activities, including:

- whole-school policies on assessment, homework and planning for individual students;

- organisational arrangements for the provision of additional support to students including involvement in in-class support and cooperative teaching;
- in-school consultation and professional support for mainstream colleagues (DES 2007: 77).

Resource teachers work with pupils who have the most severe learning difficulties that have warranted a formal psychological assessment and the design of an Individual Education Plan. Resource teaching allocation to schools depends on the number of children with special education needs and the severity of their learning need. As with learning support, resource provision can be delivered through one-to-one teaching, small group instruction and team teaching approaches. However, in order to make academic progress, these pupils require a qualitatively different level of provision than that offered by the learning support model. Pupils with assessed special educational needs will usually require intensive support from the resource teacher across a range of areas including literacy and the development of life skills, social skills and learning strategies. This support will usually be offered on a long-term basis, perhaps in varying forms for the whole of the pupil's school career.

According to the INTO report *Supporting Special Education in the Mainstream School* (2003), resource teachers expressed a clear preference for withdrawing pupils from class either individually or in groups for support teaching. The resource teachers perceived their role as primarily supporting the pupil with special educational needs rather than supporting the classroom teacher and the parents. This approach is very much at odds with the more favoured collaborative model of supporting teachers in their classrooms.

Special needs assistants

Special needs assistants (SNAs) were initially known as child care assistants and their work, as their title suggested, consisted of looking after the care needs of children who had a disability and/or serious medical condition. The recent expansion in numbers of special needs assistants is due to increased integration of children with disabilities and/or special educational needs into mainstream settings.

Official DES policy as outlined in Circular 07/02 states that 'Special Needs Assistants (SNAs) are recruited specifically to assist in the care of pupils with disabilities in an educational context.' The assistants' duties are 'of a non-teaching nature' and include both child-specific assistance and general assistance with activities in the classroom or school where this relates to the needs of or results in enhanced participation for the child who is their primary responsibility. These duties can include a focus on 'care support', such as assistance with clothing, feeding, toileting and general hygiene, and the health and safety needs of the pupil. Special assistance may be required to enable the pupil to participate in classroom activities, e.g. helping pupils with typing, writing or computers or other use of equipment.

While DES policy in relation to the role of special needs assistants remains firmly focused on providing care assistance, there is evidence that the role of special needs assistants has expanded beyond these traditional boundaries. Under the direction of teachers, special needs assistants are increasingly involved in supporting the learning needs of pupils. This expanded role has been in operation for some time in the UK and US. The titles assigned to special needs assistants in these jurisdictions reflect the educational nature of their work, e.g. United Kingdom: Learning Support Assistants/Teaching Assistants; United States: para-professionals/para-educators.

Lawlor and Cregan's (2003) study of the role of special needs assistants in schools for pupils with mild general learning disability confirmed that their role, in practice, was predominantly concerned with tasks of an educational nature. Teachers believed that they required additional training in order to work collaboratively with special needs assistants in the classroom. Scanlon and McGilloway (2006) report similar findings from their study of professionals working with children with special educational needs and conclude that while the teacher–special needs assistant relationship appeared to be working, substantial support and training were required. They also reported that many pupils with special educational needs could not cope with classroom tasks without the active assistance of the special needs assistant.

One way of developing collaborative relationships between teachers and special needs assistants has been described by Craig (2006). This involved the creation of a school code of practice guiding collaborative partnership in one special school for pupils with mild general learning disability. Within this partnership, the special needs assistant contributes directly to:

- Supporting students' learning, e.g. under teacher guidance supporting the student/s particular needs in the learning tasks set across the curriculum, and providing feedback on pupil performance.
- Supporting the students' personal and social development, e.g. being a good role model and being consistent, maintaining the code of behaviour in the classroom … encouraging social interaction with and among students by showing interest in them at a personal level and by being caring and approachable.
- Supporting the teacher, e.g. participating in the planning process with the class teacher in order to be informed of the needs of the students and the best ways to support them.
- Supporting the school, e.g. understanding the confidential and sensitive nature of the work with the students and their parents and guardians (pp. 77–78).

Special needs assistants are active partners within the process described by Craig and the collaborative relationship is based on mutual respect. There appears to be a valuable opportunity to use this approach as a model for developing sustainable collaborative relationships that benefit everyone involved.

Reflections on support roles in facilitating learning

Educators constantly face the challenge of how to most effectively support the learning of pupils. This challenge comes into sharp focus when pupils with special educational needs are involved. When children are identified as different, 'regardless of whether they have mild or profound levels of special needs, they become problematic to mainstream schools and teachers' (Emanuelson 2001: 135).

The traditional response of focusing support on the individual child has been shown to have limited effectiveness and increasingly support is delivered in the context of improving school capacity to respond to diversity. Emanuelson (2001) has documented the traditional approach (categorical) and the emerging approach (relational) in the following way.

Categorical perspective:
- Special needs signify individual characteristics.
- Requires some special type of provision.
- Superior support provided – directly connected to the diagnosed difficulties.
- Students with difficulties – intrinsic to the student.

Relational perspective:
- Special needs are social constructs.
- Requires integrated/inclusive provision.
- Superior support for including differentiation into teaching and content.
- Students in difficulties – difficulties can be connected to the learning environment. (Adapted from Emanuelson 2001: 135.)

In a review of support provision in a number of countries, Emanuelson (2001: 134) observed that a 'school code' appeared to be operating which 'determines both how special education is understood and how it is practiced'. This 'school code' has a considerable influence on whether the support teacher works from a categorical (reactive managerial) or relational (proactive reform guiding) perspective. Support teachers in this study appear to reflect 'a heavy dominance of categorical perspective understanding and thinking in the majority of schools' (p. 137). Emanuelson points out that support teachers faced the very real risk of being the scapegoat, as they were expected to be primarily responsible for achieving more inclusive provision within their schools. To avoid this outcome, the role of support teachers needs to be more proactive in improving the capacity of the mainstream school to overcome barriers to learning and participation. The emphasis within the support teacher role would shift to the 'review and development of the processes of teaching and learning rather than support for individual pupils. This involved using the "resources" of special education in a direct way to develop pedagogy rather than to spread them ever more thinly across increasing numbers of pupils experiencing difficulties' (Crowther et al. 2001: 96).

Concluding comments

The process of supporting learning has become more sophisticated as we better understand the interactive nature of learning difficulties. The individual model of support, though undoubtedly valuable to the individual pupil, is unable to address the wider issue of how to ensure that schools are capable of responding appropriately to diversity. However, it appears that, not just within an Irish context, serious obstacles remain in the development of proactive, whole-school responses where pupils with special educational needs are the responsibility of the whole school rather than support staff. In practice, the success or otherwise of creating inclusive schools will depend to a large extent on how successful we are in designing appropriate support structures within schools and in developing a knowledgeable staff who are capable of supporting learning within their own classroom and engaging in collaborative relationships with support staff.

Discussion points

1   Supporting the learning needs of pupils with special educational needs involves a high level of collaboration between classroom teachers, support teachers and special needs assistants.
    (a)   What interpersonal skills do teachers need in order to collaborate effectively?
    (b)   What constraints exist in developing an effective support network around the child?
2   Withdrawal from class remains the dominant mode for delivery of additional support within mainstream schools. This will obviously affect the child's contact with the regular curriculum. What can be done to minimise this difficulty?
3   The resource teacher offers to work with you in a team-teaching approach in your classroom.
    (a)   How would you react to this suggestion?
    (b)   What issues would need to be considered?
4   The special needs assistant is increasingly employed to support children with special educational needs in mainstream classrooms.
    (a)   How do you as classroom teacher view their role?
    (b)   What tasks will be assigned to the special needs assistant?
    (c)   How does the work of the special needs assistant and teacher differ?
5   How important are staff attitudes in developing whole-school approaches to special educational needs provision?

Chapter 15
Conclusion: Mapping the Road Ahead

Responding to special educational needs involves not just additional knowledge, skills and resources. It is a response that incorporates a lively and open-minded willingness to examine and reappraise attitudes; to challenge the barriers imposed by established structures, systems and routines; and a commitment to continual efforts at communication and collaboration among colleagues, parents and professional partners.

In this final chapter we will attempt to evaluate our progress so far in responding to the challenge of special educational needs. We have tracked the path of where we have come from to where we are now and we will indicate some salient pointers towards a more effective road map in the world of special education for the children and young people who remain in the greatest need.

In the past, people with disabilities were on the periphery of society and had very limited control over their lives. This is hard for us to imagine but vital for us to understand as we attempt to develop inclusive learning environments. Empathising with people who have been excluded from meaningful participation in society is obviously important, but it is not enough. It is clearly no substitute for ensuring that we develop the structures to ensure that people who have been marginalised are respected and included within all aspects of society. As a society, we have moved to an appreciation of our responsibility for marginalising particular groups and individuals and consequently our responsibility to redress the situation. Globally there has been an emergence of key concepts such as human and civil rights that in turn has led to a consideration of the equalisation of opportunities for people from marginalised groups. People with disabilities have been to the forefront of this campaign and express this view cogently and forcefully: 'Disability is a human rights issue! I repeat: disability is a human rights issue. Those of us who happen to have a disability are fed up being treated by the society and our fellow citizens as if we did not exist or as if we were aliens from outer space. We are human beings with equal value, claiming equal rights ...' (Quinn and Degener et al. 2002: 9). The human rights model aims 'to build societies that are genuinely inclusive, societies that value difference and respect the dignity and equality of all human beings regardless of difference' (Quinn and Degener et al. 2002: 10). For people with disabilities, this will involve a review of the accessibility of the physical environment, housing and transportation, education and work opportunities, social and health services and cultural and social life.

Education is obviously of critical importance if children and young people with disabilities are to become meaningful participants in society. The central concerns of learning are described by Hogan (1995: 249): 'Emergent identity, the uncovering of its individuality and promise, its search for meaning and acknowledgement ... constitute some of the central concerns of learning.' He continues by highlighting the right of everyone to develop their potential through education: 'These concerns identify important responsibilities but they also alert us to rights and affirmations which are in a crucial sense inviolable – in particular the right to become what our inherent potentials might enable us to become when these are addressed in a learning climate which is the most conducive to their nourishment and disciplined realisation' (p. 249). As educators, we have a crucial role to play in creating the learning environments that enable children and young people to fulfil their potential and are accessible to all. Within this learning environment, special educational provision can become an integral element in the education continuum that is available to all children.

Within an Irish context, we have seen significant changes in special education policy and practice. Until comparatively recently, special education existed on the margins of the general education system. Government support was limited and there appeared to be an attitude characterised by the phrase 'out of sight, out of mind'. To an increasing extent today, special education is treated as a central concern of the whole education community. It is no longer solely the responsibility of a small group of dedicated professionals, parents and organisations. The general education system has begun the process of owning special education and seeing how special education has relevance within all schools. There is evidence of this policy shift at a number of levels.

At policy level, special education concerns are included in general education policy documents. The process of developing curricula is increasingly informed by the requirement to include schools which have specified responsibilities towards providing an education service for children and young people with special educational needs. Parents are more centrally involved in decision-making processes around their child and this involvement is mandated by legislation. As educators, we are beginning to engage with our understanding of how children learn and how difficulties in learning arise.

It is difficult to detach ourselves from the traditional deficit model approaches to special educational needs. Our natural inclination on encountering a difficulty in learning will be to ask what is wrong with this child that s/he cannot grasp this basic concept. However, the answer to this type of question, while perhaps giving an indication of some of the causal factors involved, fails to address the complex nature of difficulties in learning. Our assessment process tended to reinforce the deficit model approach, with the emphasis on determining whether the child fitted into a pre-existing category of special educational need deemed eligible for special educational provision. In practice, it has proved difficult to divorce the provision of special education resources from the categorisation process. Our understanding of what constitutes a 'special educational need' has evolved and become more sophisticated. However, the equation of disability with special educational needs remains and our funding mechanisms are essentially based on categories of disability. Despite its flaws, the general allocation system represents a step away from this position and recognition that all schools will have pupils who require support for learning. Many countries face the same dilemma as Ireland – the targeting of resources for children and young people who require support while at the same time avoiding categorisation that may stigmatise the very children who are being supported.

In Ireland, we are beginning to develop the infrastructure required to create inclusive learning environments. However, we face many questions and critical concerns. What does an appropriate education for children and young people with special educational needs involve? What academic/social outcomes are achieved by children and young people with special educational needs? What level of resources should be committed to provide for the education of children and young people with special educational needs? Is full inclusion a realistic or even desirable goal? What is needed to develop inclusive learning environments? What types of support do teachers, parents and children and young people with special educational needs require?

The Salamanca Statement (UNESCO 1994: 23) argues that as a society we should measure our success by the following criteria: 'We should be asking ourselves: How many young people and adults with disabilities have mastered the skills and competencies required to function effectively in society? How many have found good and rewarding jobs?' This represents a challenge not only for educators, but for the whole of society.

Apart from special educational needs, schools face many challenges, such as increased public accountability, compliance with legislative demands, parental expectations, improving standards in literacy and numeracy, ensuring that young people achieve examination success, responding to socio-economic disadvantage and appreciating all aspects of diversity. We would maintain that responding appropriately to special educational needs can enhance the educational opportunities of all children in the school. We can understand that any child may at some point experience some difficulty in learning and design our teaching to acknowledge this fact. In developing differentiated teaching strategies and ensuring curricular access, we will create an effective learning environment. Through facilitating the active participation of the child with special educational needs, we will be aware of the need for every child to be fully involved in our classrooms.

Society in general and schools in particular face the challenge of creating schools that welcome, foster, educate and support all children: 'The challenge now is to formulate requirements of a "school for all". All children and young people of the world ... have the right to education. It is not our education systems that have a right to certain types of children. It is the school system of a country that must be adjusted to meet the needs of all children' (Lindqvist, UNESCO 1994: 28).

In 1978 the Warnock Report (para. 14, p. 5) stated that 'the purpose of education for all children is the same; the goals are the same. But the help that individual children need in progressing towards them will be different. Whereas for some the road they have to travel towards the goals is smooth and easy, for others it is fraught with obstacles.' Almost 30 years later, we are still discussing how best to provide an appropriate education that will enable children and young people with special educational needs to overcome obstacles to learning.

We believe that now is the time to smooth the path for all children, guarantee curricular access and move towards a reality of a flexible, responsive special education system that enables school personnel to create inclusive learning environments.

References

Ainscow, M. (1996), 'Towards inclusive schooling', *REACH: Journal of Special Needs Education in Ireland*, 9/2, 67–75.

Ainscow, M., Booth, T. and Dyson, A. (2006), *Improving Schools, Developing Inclusion*, London: Routledge.

Ainscow, M., Howes, A., Farrell, P. and Frankham, J. (2003), 'Making sense of the development of inclusive practices', *European Journal of Special Needs Education*, 18/2, 227–242.

Alban-Metcalf, J. and Alban-Metcalf, J. (2001), *Managing Attention Deficit-Hyperactivity Disorder in the Inclusive Classroom*, London: David Fulton.

Altman, B. (2001), 'Disability definitions, models, classification schemes, and applications' in G.L. Albrecht, K.D. Seelman and M. Bury (eds.), *Handbook of Disability Studies*, London: Sage, pp. 97–122.

Armstrong, D. and Kane, G. (2010), 'A Survey of Parental Attitudes to and Experiences of Local and National Special Education Services in Ireland', Presentation at National Council for Special Education Seminar, 24 November 2010.

ASTI (2005), *ASTI Policy Paper: Task Force on Student Behaviour in Second Level Schools, ASTI Written Submission, March 2005*, Dublin: ASTI.

Avramidis, E. and Norwich, B. (2002), 'Teachers' attitudes towards integration/inclusion: A review of the literature', *European Journal of Special Needs Education*, 17/2, 129–147.

Baldwin, S. and Carlisle, J. (1994), *Social Support for Disabled Children and Their Families: A Review of the Literature*, London: HMSO.

Ball, M., Hughes, A. and McCormack, W. (2006), *Dyslexia: An Irish Perspective*, Dublin: Blackhall Publishing.

Banks, J. and McCoy, S. (2011, forthcoming), *SEN Prevalence in Ireland*, National Council for Special Education.

Barkley, R.A. (1997), *ADHD and the Nature of Self-Control*, New York: Guildford Press.

Barnes, C. (1991), *Disabled People in Britain and Discrimination: A Case for Anti-discrimination Legislation*, London: Hurst and Co.

Barton, L. (2000), 'Profile: Len Barton' in P. Clough and J. Corbett, *Theories of Inclusive Education: A Students' Guide*, London: Paul Chapman Publishing, pp. 51–53.

Beaton, A.E., Mullis, I.V.S., Martin, M.O., Gonzalez, E.J., Kelly, D.L. and Smith, T.A. (1996), *Mathematics Achievement in the Middle School Years: IEA's Third International Mathematics and Science Study (TIMMS)*, Chestnut Hill, MA: TIMMS International Study Center, Boston College.

Beckman, P.J. and Beckman Boyes, G. (eds.) (1993), *Deciphering the System: A Guide for Families of Young Children with Disabilities*, Cambridge, MA: Brookline.

Bereiter, C. (1968), *Arithmetic and Mathematics*, San Rafael, CA: Dimensions.

Beveridge, S. (1999), *Special Educational Needs in Schools*, 2nd edn., London: Routledge.

Birkett, D. (2000), 'There was nothing in my list about this...' in P. Murray and J. Penman (eds.), *Telling our Own Stories – Reflections on Family Life in a Disabling World*, Sheffield: Parents with Attitude, pp. 118–126.

Booth, T. (1998), 'The poverty of special education: Theories to the rescue?' in C. Clark, A. Dyson and A. Millward (eds.), *Theorising Special Education*, London: Routledge, pp. 79–89.

Booth, T. (2000), 'Reflection: Tony Booth' in P. Clough and J. Corbett, *Theories of Inclusive Education: A Students' Guide*, London: Paul Chapman Publishing, pp. 59–64.

Booth, T., Ainscow, M., Black-Hawkins, K., Vaughan, M. and Shaw, L. (2000), *The Index for Inclusion*, Bristol: Centre for Studies on Inclusive Education.

Braddock, D.L. and Parish, S.L. (2001), 'An institutional history of disability' in G.L. Albrecht, K.D. Seelman and M. Bury (eds.), *Handbook of Disability Studies*, London: Sage, pp. 11–68.

Brosnahan, S. (1952), *Irish School Weekly*, Dublin: Irish National Teachers' Organisation (INTO).

Burke, A. (1992), 'Teaching: Retrospect and prospect', *Oideas*, 39.

Byers, R. and Rose, R. (1996), *Planning the Curriculum for Pupils with Special Educational Needs*, London: David Fulton.

Byrne, M. (1980), 'Educational provision for the mentally handicapped in Ireland, 1869–1926' in J. Coolahan (ed.), *Proceedings of the Fifth Annual Education Conference of the Educational Studies Association of Ireland*, Limerick: ESAI.

Campbell, J.R., Kelley, D.L., Mullis, I.V.S., Martin, M.O. and Sainsbury, M. (2001), *Framework and Specifications for PIRLS Assessment 2001*, Chestnut Hill, MA: PIRLS International Study Center, Boston College.

Carey, D. (2005), *The Essential Guide to Special Education in Ireland*, Dublin: Primary ABC.

Carpenter, B. (2000), 'Sustaining the family: Meeting the needs of families of children with disabilities', *British Journal of Special Education*, 27/3, 135–144.

Carpenter, B. and Shevlin, M. (2004), 'Creating an inclusive curriculum' in P. Noonan Walsh and H. Gash (eds.), *Lives and Times: Practice, Policy and People with Disabilities*, Bray, Co. Wicklow: Rathdown Press, pp. 81–92.

Carpenter, B., Ashdown, R. and Bovair, K. (1996), *Enabling Access: Effective Teaching and Learning for Pupils with Learning Difficulties*, London: David Fulton.

Clough, P. and Corbett, J. (2000), *Theories of Inclusive Education: A Students' Guide*, London: Paul Chapman Publishing.

Clough, P. and Nutbrown, C. (2003), 'The index for inclusion: Personal perspectives from early years educators' in M. Nind, K. Sheehy and K. Simmons (eds.), *Inclusive Education: Learners and Learning Contexts*, London: David Fulton, pp. 85–93.

Coffey, A. (2004), 'Accessing the curriculum: A case study of pupils with special educational needs in a mainstream Irish primary school', *REACH: Journal of Special Needs Education in Ireland*, 17/2, 93–103.

Coolahan, J. (1994), *Report on the National Education Convention*, Dublin: The National Education Convention Secretariat.

Copeland, S. and Hughes, C. (2000), 'Acquisition of a picture prompt strategy to increase independent performance', *Education and Training in Mental Retardation and Developmental Disabilities*, 35, 294–305.

Corbett, J. (2001), *Supporting Inclusive Education: A Connective Pedagogy*, London: Routledge Falmer.

Corcoran, T. (1928), *Education Systems in Ireland from the Close of the Middle Ages*, Dublin: University College, Dublin.

Cornwall, J. (1997), *Access to Learning for Pupils with Disabilities*, London: David Fulton.

Craig, A. (2006), 'Teacher–special needs assistant partnership: A school's response', *REACH: Journal of Special Needs Education in Ireland*, 19/2, 67–80.

Croll, P. (2001), 'Teacher contact with parents of children with special educational needs: a comparison over two decades', *Journal of Research in Special Educational Needs*, 1/2, available online at www.nasen.uk.com/ejournal (accessed October 2006).

Crow, L. (2003), 'Including all our lives: Renewing the social model of disability' in M. Nind, J. Rix, K. Sheehy and K. Simmons (eds.), *Inclusive Education: Diverse Perspectives*, London: David Fulton, pp. 135–149.

Crowther Report (1959), *Fifteen to Eighteen*, London: HMSO Central Advisory Council for Education.

Crowther, D., Dyson, A. and Millward, A. (2001), 'Supporting pupils with special educational needs: Issues and dilemmas for special needs co-ordinators in English primary schools', *European Journal of Special Needs Education*, 16/2, 85–97.

CSIE (2002), *The Inclusion Charter*, Bristol: Centre for Studies on Inclusive Education.

Culligan, B. (1997), *Improving Children's Spelling*, Dublin: Culligan.

Davidson, T. (1900), *The History of Education*, London: Archibald Constable.

Davis, P. and Florian, L. (2004), *Teaching Strategies and Approaches for Pupils with Special Educational Needs: A Scoping Study. Research Report 516*, London: DfES.

Day, T. (2005), 'In-class support for children with special educational needs in mainstream schools', *REACH: Journal of Special Needs Education in Ireland*, 18/2, 79–87.

Department for Children, Schools and Families (2009), *Lamb Inquiry: Special Educational Needs and Parental Confidence*, London: Stationery Office.

Department for Education (DfE) (1994), *Code of Practice on the identification and assessment of special educational needs*, London: HMSO.

Department of Education (1983), *The Education and Training of Severely and Profoundly Mentally Handicapped Children in Ireland*, Dublin: The Stationery Office.

Department of Education (1988), *Guidelines on Remedial Education*, Dublin: The Stationery Office.

Department of Education (1993), *Report of the Special Education Review Committee*, Dublin: The Stationery Office.

Department of Education and Science (1999), *Primary School Curriculum*, Dublin: The Stationery Office.

Department of Education and Science (2000), *Learning-Support Guidelines*, Dublin: The Stationery Office.

Department of Education and Science (2001), *The Report of the Task Force on Autism: Educational Provision and Support for Persons with Autistic Spectrum Disorders*, Dublin: The Stationery Office.

Department of Education and Science (2002a), *Circular SP. ED. 08/02. Applications for full-time or part-time resource teacher support to address the special educational needs of children with disabilities.*

Department of Education and Science (2002b), *Report of the Task Force on Dyslexia*, Dublin: The Stationery Office.

Department of Education and Science (2005a), *Circular SP. ED. 02/05, Organisation of Teaching Resources for Pupils who need Additional Support in Mainstream Primary Schools.*

Department of Education and Science (2005b), *Delivering Equality of Opportunity in Schools: An Action Plan for Educational Inclusion*, Dublin: The Stationery Office.

Department of Education and Science (2007), *Inclusion of Students with Special Educational Needs: Post-Primary Guidelines*, Dublin: The Stationery Office.

Department of Education and Science (England and Wales) (1978), *Report of the Committee of Enquiry into the Education of Handicapped Children and Young People*, London: HMSO.

Department of Education and Skills (2010), *Better Literacy and Numeracy for Children and Young People: A Draft National Plan to Improve Literacy and Numeracy in Schools*, Dublin: Department of Education and Skills.

Department of Education NI/Department of Education and Science/Irish Society for Autism/Parents and Professionals Autism Northern Ireland (2004), *Autism: An Introduction* (videotape and booklet), The Stationery Office/HMSO.

Department of Education Northern Ireland (DENI) (2006), *The Future Role of the Special School*, Belfast: DENI.

Department of Health (1965), *Report of the Commission of Inquiry on Mental Handicap*, Dublin: The Stationery Office.

Desforges, M. and Lindsay, G. (2010), *Procedures used to Diagnose a Disability and to Assess Special Educational Needs: An International Review*, Trim: National Council for Special Education.

Devecchi, C. and Nevin, A. (2010), 'Leadership for inclusive schools and inclusive school leadership', in Normore, A. (ed.), *Global Perspectives on Educational Leadership Reform: The Development and Preparation of Leaders of Learning and Learners of Leadership (Advances in Educational Administration, Volume 11)*, Bingley: Emerald Group Publishing Limited, pp. 211–241.

DfES (Department for Education and Skills) (2001), *Special Educational Needs Code of Practice*, London: HMSO.

DoH/DfES (Department of Health/Department for Education and Skills) (2003), *Together from the Start: Practical Guidance for Professionals Working with Young Disabled Children (Birth to Third Birthday) and Their Families*, Nottingham: DfES Publications.

Douglas, G., Mc Call, S., Mc Linden, M., Pavey, S., Ware, J. and Farrell, A. M. (2009), *International Review of the Literature of Evidence of Best Practice Models and Outcomes in the Education of Blind and Visually Impaired Children*, Trim, Co. Meath: National Council for Special Education.

Doyle, A. (2003), 'Disability policy in Ireland' in S. Quin and B. Redmond (eds.), *Disability and Social Policy in Ireland*, Dublin: UCD Press, pp. 10–27.

Dreikurs, R. and Grey, L. (1968), *The New Approach to Discipline: Logical Consequences*, New York: Plume.

Dreikurs, R. and Cassel, P. (1972), *Discipline without Tears*, 2nd edn., New York: Plume.

Dreikurs, R. (1990), *Children: The Challenge*, New York: Penguin Plume.

Drudy, S. and Kinsella, W. (2009), 'Developing an inclusive system in a rapidly changing European society', *International Journal of Inclusive Education*, 13/6, 647–663.

Duncan, N. (2003), 'Awkward customers? Parents and provision for special educational needs', *Disability and Society*, 18/3, 341–656.

Dunn, L.M. (1968), 'Special education for the mildly retarded – is much of it justifiable?', *Exceptional Children*, 35 (September), 5–24.

Educable (2000), *No Choice: No Chance. The Educational Experiences of Young People with Disabilities*, Belfast: Save the Children & Disability Action.

Eivers, E., Close, S., Shiel, G., Millar, D., Clerkin, A., Gilleece, L. and Kiniry, J. (2010), *The 2009 National Assessments of Mathematics and English Reading*, Dublin: Stationery Office.

Elliott, J. (2000), 'The psychological assessment of children with learning difficulties', *British Journal of Special Education*, 27/2, 59–66.

Emanuelson, I. (2001), 'Reactive versus proactive support co-ordinator roles: An international comparison', *European Journal of Special Needs Education*, 16/2, 133–142.

Enright, B.E. and Choate, J.S. (1997), 'Mathematical problem solving: Authentic mathematics' in J.S. Choate (ed.), *Successful Inclusive Teaching*, Boston: Allyn and Bacon.

Eyre, D. (1997), *Able Children in Ordinary Schools*, London: David Fulton.

Farmer, D. (1996), 'Curriculum Differentiation', http://www.austega.com/gifted/provisions/curdifferent.htm (accessed 26.2.2007).

Fernald, G.M. (1943), *Remedial Techniques in Basic School Subjects*, New York: McGraw Hill.

Fitzgerald, E. (2004), *Counting Our Children: An Analysis of Official Data Sources on Children and Childhood in Ireland*, Dublin: Children's Research Centre.

Flatman-Watson, S. (2009), 'Barriers to inclusive education in Ireland: the case for pupils with a diagnosis of intellectual and/or pervasive developmental disabilities', *British Journal of Learning Disabilities*, 37/4, 277–284.

Fletcher, W. (2001), 'Enabling students with severe learning difficulties to become effective target setters' in R. Rose and I. Grosvenor (eds.), *Doing Research in Special Education: Ideas into Practice*, London: David Fulton, pp. 18–29.

Florian, L., Hollenweger, J., Simeonson, R., Wedell, K., Riddell, S., Terzi, L. and Holland, A. (2006), 'Cultural perspectives on the classification of children with disabilities: Part 1. Issues in the classification of children with disabilities', *Journal of Special Education*, 40, 36–45.

Florian, L., Rose, R. and Tilstone, C. (1998), 'Pragmatism not dogmatism: Promoting more inclusive practice' in C. Tilstone, L. Florian and R. Rose (eds.), *Promoting Inclusive Practice*, London: Routledge.

Flutter, J. and Rudduck, J. (2004), *Consulting Pupils: What's in it for schools?* Abingdon, Oxon, UK: Routledge.

Fraser, D. (2005), 'Collaborating with parents/caregivers and whanau' in D. Fraser, R. Molten and K. Ryba (eds.), *Learners with Special Needs in Aotearoa New Zealand*, Melbourne, Australia: Thomson Dunmore Press, pp. 128–154.

Frederickson, N. and Cline, T. (2002), *Special Educational Needs, Inclusion and Diversity: A Textbook*, Buckingham: Open University Press.

Frith, U. (1985), 'Beneath the surface of developmental dyslexia' in K.E. Patterson, J.C. Marshall and M. Coltheart (eds.), *Surface Dyslexia*, London: Routledge and Kegan Paul.

Frith, U. (1989), *Autism: Explaining the Enigma*, Oxford: Blackwell.

Gaden, G. (1993), 'Integrated education, mental disability and respect for persons', *Irish Educational Studies*, 12, 57–72.

Gannon, B. and Nolan, B. (2004), *Disability and Social Inclusion in Ireland*, Dublin: The Equality Authority and National Disability Authority.

Gardner, H. (1983), *Frames of Mind: Theory of Multiple Intelligences*, New York: Basic Books.

Gardner, H. (1999), *Intelligence Reframed*, New York: Basic Books.

Garner, P. (1998), 'Who needs all this book learning?', *REACH: Journal of Special Needs Education in Ireland*, 12/1, 27–33.

Garnett, J. (1992), 'Marking written work: Marking and correcting children's written work to provide a record of individual learning and achievement', *Differentiating the Secondary Curriculum Package*, Trowbridge: Wiltshire Education Support and Training.

Gartner, A. and Joe, T. (1987), *Images of the Disabled, Disabling Images*, New York: Praeger.

Gash, H. (1993), 'A constructivist attempt to change attitudes towards children with special needs', *European Journal of Special Needs Education*, 8, 106–125.

Gash, H. (1996), 'Changing attitudes towards children with special needs', *European Journal of Special Needs Education*, 11, 286–297.

Gash, H., Illan Romeu, N. and Lopez Pina, J. (2004), 'Spanish and Irish images of special needs: Perceptions of inclusion' in P. Noonan Walsh and H. Gash (eds.), *Lives and Times: Practice, Policy and People with Disabilities*, Bray, Co. Wicklow: Rathdown Press, pp. 180–223.

Glasser, W. (1969), *Schools without Failure*, New York: Harper & Row.

Glendenning, D. (1999), *Education and the Law*, Dublin: Butterworth.

Goffman, E. (1963), *Stigma: Notes on a Spoiled Identity*, Englewood Cliffs, NJ: Prentice-Hall.

Government of Ireland (1965), *Report of the Commission of Inquiry on Mental Handicap*, Dublin: Stationery Office.

Government of Ireland (1980), *White Paper on Educational Development*, Dublin: The Stationery Office.

Government of Ireland (1984), *Towards a Full Life: Green Paper on Services for Disabled People*, Dublin: The Stationery Office.

Government of Ireland (1991), *Needs and Abilities: A Policy for the Intellectually Disabled. Report of the Review Group on Mental Handicap Services*, Dublin: The Stationery Office.

Government of Ireland (1995), *Government White Paper on Education: Charting Our Education Future*, Dublin: The Stationery Office.

Government of Ireland (1996), *A Strategy for Equality: Report of the Commission on the Status of People with Disabilities*, Dublin: The Stationery Office.

Government of Ireland (1998), Education Act.

Government of Ireland (2000), Education (Welfare) Act.

Government of Ireland (2000), Equal Status Act.

Government of Ireland (2004), Education for Persons with Special Educational Needs Act.

Government of Ireland (2005), Disability Act.

Government of the United States of America (1975), Individuals with Disabilities Education Act.

Grandin, T. (1995), *Thinking in Pictures: And Other Reports from My Life with Autism*, New York: Bantam Books.

Grey, C. (2006), *Writing Social Stories* (VHS video with workbook), Kentwood, MN: The Grey Center.

Griffin, S. (2006), 'Teaching for enjoyment: David Manson and his "play school" of Belfast', *Irish Educational Studies*, 24/2, 133–143.

Griffin, S. and Shevlin, M. (2007), *Responding to Special Educational Needs: An Irish Perspective*, 1st edn., Dublin: Gill and Macmillan.

Grogan, M. and Offaly Centre for Independent Living (2001), *Partners in Education: A Handbook on Disability Awareness and Inclusive Policies and Practices for Students with Disabilities*, Tullamore, Co. Offaly: Offaly Centre for Independent Living.

Gross, J. (2002), *Special Educational Needs in the Primary School: A Practical Guide*, 3rd edn., Buckingham, UK: Open University Press.

Hardiman, S., Guerin, S. and Fitzsimons, E. (2009), 'A comparison of the social competence of children with moderate intellectual disability in inclusive versus segregated school settings', *Research in Developmental Disabilities*, 30, 397–407.

Hart, S. (1996), *Beyond Special Needs*, London: Paul Chapman Publishing.

Hayes, J. (2003), 'Problem solving abilities in mathematics of pupils with spina bifida and hydrocephalus', *REACH: Journal of Special Needs Education in Ireland*, 17/10, 44–53.

Hayes, J. (2004), 'Visual annual reviews: How to include pupils with learning difficulties in their educational reviews', *Support for Learning*, 19/4, 175–180.

Hegarty, S. (1993a), *Educating Children and Young People with Disabilities: Principles and the Review of Practice*, Paris: UNESCO.

Hegarty, S. (1993b), 'Reviewing the literature on integration', *European Journal of Special Needs Education*, 8/3, 194–200.

Herbert, E. and Carpenter, B. (1994), 'Fathers – the secondary partners: Professional perceptions and a father's reflections', *Children and Society*, 8/1, 31–41.

Hill, M. (2005), *The Public Policy Process*, 4th edn., Harlow, UK: Pearson Education Ltd.

Hinshaw, S.P. (1994), *Attention Deficits and Hyperactivity in Children*, London: Sage.

Hogan, P. (1995), *The Custody and Courtship of Experience: Western Education in Philosophical Perspective*, Dublin: The Columba Press.

Horgan, G. (2003), 'Educable: Disabled young people in Northern Ireland challenge the education system' in M. Shevlin and R. Rose (eds.), *Encouraging Voices: Respecting the Insights of Young People Who Have Been Marginalised*, Dublin: National Disability Authority, pp. 100–120.

Hornby, G. (1994), *Counselling in Child Disability: Skills for Working with Parents*, London: Chapman & Hall.

Hornby, G. and Witte, C. (2008), 'Looking back on school – the views of adult graduates of a residential special school for children with emotional and behavioural difficulties', *British Journal of Special Education*, 35/2, 102–107.

Horne, P. and Timmons, V. (2009), 'Making it work: teachers' perspectives on inclusion', *International Journal of Inclusive Education*, 13/3, 273–286.

Howley, M. (2006), 'Structured teaching for pupils with autistic spectrum disorders: Meaningful or meaningless?', *REACH: Journal of Special Needs Education in Ireland*, 19/2, 94–101.

Hughes, M. (2000), 'Towards a new era: A review of policy documents relating to general learning disabilities, 1960–1990', *REACH: Journal of Special Needs Education in Ireland*, 13/2, 66–75.

Humphreys, T. (1993), *A Different Kind of Teacher*, Cork: Humphreys.

IALS (1995), *Literacy, Economy and Society: Results of the First International Adult Literacy Survey*, Paris: OECD.

Inspectorate, Department of Education and Science (2006a), *An Evaluation of Educational Provision for Children with Autistic Spectrum Disorders*, Dublin: The Stationery Office.

Inspectorate, Department of Education and Science (2006b), *An Evaluation of Special Classes for Pupils with Specific Speech and Language Disorder*, Dublin: The Stationery Office.

Inspectorate, Department of Education and Science (2007), *Inclusion of Students with Special Educational Needs: Post-Primary Guidelines*, Dublin: The Stationery Office.

Irish National Teachers' Organisation (INTO) (2000), *The Visiting Teacher Service for Special Needs*, Dublin: INTO.

Irish National Teachers' Organisation (INTO) (2003), *Supporting Special Education in the Mainstream School*, Dublin: INTO.

Jelly, M., Fuller, A. and Byers, R. (2000), *Involving Pupils in Practice: Promoting Partnership with Pupils with Special Educational Needs*, London: David Fulton.

Johnson, D.W. and Johnson, R.T. (2004), 'Implementing the "Teaching Students to be Peacemakers Program"', *Theory into Practice*, 43/1, 68–79.

Johnstone, D. (1998), *An Introduction to Disability Studies*, London: David Fulton.

Keller, H. (1961), *The Story of My Life*, New York: Dell.

Kelly, Á., Carey, S. and McCarthy, S. (2004), *A Nationwide Study of Challenging Behaviour in Special Schools in Ireland*, Dublin: St John of God Hospital Services.

Kenny, M., McNeela, E. and Shevlin, M. (2003a), 'Living and learning: The school experiences of some young people with disabilities' in M. Shevlin and R. Rose (eds.), *Encouraging Voices: Respecting the Insights of Young People Who Have Been Marginalised*, Dublin: National Disability Authority, pp. 138–158.

Kenny, M., McNeela, E., Noonan Walsh, P. and Shevlin, M. (2003b), *In the morning the dark opens: A study of the experience of parents of children with Down Syndrome and other learning disabilities in mainstream schools: why this choice was made, how it was achieved, and hopes for the future*, Dublin: Centre for Disability Studies, University College Dublin.

Kenny, M., McNeela, E., Shevlin, M. and Daly, T. (2000), *Hidden Voices: Young People with Disabilities Speak about Their Second Level Schooling*, Cork: South West Regional Authority.

Kenward, H. (1997), *Integrating Pupils with Disabilities in Mainstream Schools: Making it Happen*, London: David Fulton.

Kinsella, W. and Senior, J. (2008), 'Developing inclusive schools: a systematic approach', *International Journal of Inclusive Education*, 12/5/6, 651–665.

Kitchin, R., Shirlow, P. and Shuttleworth, I. (1998), 'On the margins: Disabled people's experience of employment in Donegal, West Ireland', *Disability and Society*, 13/5, 785–806.

Laevers, F., Cuvelier, N., Moons, J. and Debue, A. (2005), *A House Full of Feelings and Emotions* (materials, booklet and CD), Leuven, Belgium: CEGO (Centre for Experiential Learning) Publications.

Lawlor, L. and Cregan, A. (2003), 'The evolving role of the special needs assistant: Towards a new synergy', *REACH: Journal of Special Needs Education in Ireland*, 16/2, 82–93.

LeFanu, E. (1860), *Life of Dr. C.H.H. Orpen*, London: Charles Westerton.

Leithwood, K. A. and Riehl, C. J. (2003), 'What do we already know about successful school leadership?' AERA Division: A Task Force on Developing Research in Educational Leadership, Chicago, IL: AERA.

Lerner, J. (1981), *Learning Disabilities: Theories, Diagnosis and Teaching Strategies*, 3rd edn., Boston: Houghton Mifflin.

Lewis, A. (1995), *Children's Understanding of Disability*, London: Routledge.

Lewis, A. and Norwich, B. (2005), *Special Teaching for Special Children?: Pedagogies for Inclusion*, Maidenhead, Berkshire: Open University Press.

Lodge, A. and Lynch, K. (eds.) (2004), *Diversity at School*, Dublin: The Equality Authority.

Logan, A. (2006), 'The role of the special needs assistant supporting pupils with special educational needs in Irish mainstream primary schools', *Support for Learning*, 21/2, 92–99.

Lowe, P. and Reynolds, C.R. (2000), 'Attention-deficit-hyperactivity disorder' in C.R. Reynolds and E. Fletcher-Janzen (eds.), *Encyclopaedia of Special Education*, 2nd edn., New York: Wiley.

Lynch, K. (1999), *Equality in Education*, Dublin: Gill & Macmillan.

MacGiolla Phádraig, B. (2007), 'Towards inclusion: the development of provision for children with special educational needs in Ireland from 1991–2004', *Irish Educational Studies*, 25/2, 289–300.

MacNamara, J. (1966), *Bilingualism and Primary Education: A Study of Irish Experience,* Edinburgh: Edinburgh University Press.

McCallister, W.J. (1931), *The Growth of Freedom in Education*, London: Constable.

McCarthy, O. and Kenny, M. (2006), *Special Schools in Transition: Concerns and Hopes Among Teachers in the Sector*, Dublin: Irish Association of Teachers in Special Education (IATSE).

McCausland, D. (2005), *International Experience in the Provision of Individual Education Plans for Children with Disabilities*, Dublin: National Disability Authority.

McConkey, R. and McCormack, R. (1983), *Breaking Barriers: Educating People about Disability*, London: Souvenir Press.

McCormack, B. (2004), 'Trends in the development of Irish disability services' in P. Noonan Walsh and H. Gash (eds.), *Lives and Times: Practice, Policy and People with Disabilities*, Bray, Co. Wicklow: Rathdown Press, pp. 7–29.

McCormack, W. (2002), *Lost for Words: Dyslexia at Second Level and Beyond – A Practical Guide for Parents and Teachers*, 2nd edn., Dublin: Tower Press.

McDonnell, P. (2000), 'Inclusive education in Ireland: Rhetoric and reality' in F. Armstrong, D. Armstrong and L. Barton (eds.), *Inclusive Education: Policy, Contexts and Comparative Perspectives*, London: David Fulton.

McDonnell, P. (2003a), 'Education policy' in S. Quin and B. Redmond (eds.), *Disability and Social Policy in Ireland*, Dublin: UCD Press, pp. 28–44.

McDonnell, P. (2003b), 'Developments in special education in Ireland: deep structures and policy making', *International Journal of Inclusive Education*, 7/3, 259–269.

McGee, P. (2004), 'Reflections on Irish special education over four decades', *REACH: Journal of Special Educational Needs in Ireland*, 17/2, 67–80.

McManus, A. (2002), *The Irish Hedge School and Its Books, 1695–1831*, Dublin: Four Courts Press.

McNamara, S. and Moreton, G. (1997), *Changing Behaviour: Teaching Children with Emotional and Behavioural Difficulties in Primary and Secondary Classrooms*, London: David Fulton.

McPhillips, T. (2003), *The Learning Support Teacher: A Practical Handbook*, Dublin: Blackrock Education Centre.

Maker, C.J. (1982), *Curriculum development for the gifted*, Rockville, MD: Aspen.

Malone, G. and Smith, D. (1996), *Learning to Learn*, Tamworth: NASEN.

Manuel, P. (1996), 'A parent's perspective', paper presented at the National Children's Bureau Conference, London, 16 December.

Marschark, M. and Spencer, P. E. (2009a), *Evidence of Best Practice Models and Outcomes in the Education of Deaf and Hard-of-Hearing Children: An International Review*, Trim, Co. Meath: National Council for Special Education.

Marschark, M. and Spencer, P. E. (2009b), *Evidence of Best Practice Models and Outcomes in the Education of Deaf and Hard-of-Hearing Children: An International Review – Executive Summary*, Trim, Co. Meath: National Council for Special Education.

Martin, M. (2006), *Report of the Task Force on Student Behaviour in Second Level Schools: School Matters*, Dublin: Department of Education and Science.

Meaney, M., Kiernan, N. and Monahan, K. (2005), *Special Educational Needs and the Law*, Dublin: Thomson Round Hall.

Meijer, C.J.W. and Pijl, S.J. (1994a), 'Framework, Methods and Procedures' in C.J.W. Meijer, S.J. Pijl and S. Hegarty (eds.), *New Perspectives in Special Education: A six country study of integration*, London: Routledge, pp. 1–8.

Meijer, C.J.W. and Pijl, S.J. (1994b), 'Analysis of Findings' in C.J.W. Meijer, S.J. Pijl and S. Hegarty (eds.), *New Perspectives in Special Education: A six country study of integration*, London: Routledge, pp. 109–118.

Mitchell, D.T. and Snyder, S.L. (2001), 'Representation and its discontents: The uneasy home of disability in literature and film' in G.L. Albrecht, K.D. Seelman and M. Bury (eds.), *Handbook of Disability Studies*, London: Sage, pp. 195–218.

Morgan, M. and Martin, M. (1993), *ALCE Evaluation: Volume 3. Literacy Problems among Irish 14-Year-Olds*, Dublin: Educational Research Centre.

Morgan, M., Hickey, B. and Kellaghan, T. (1997), *International Adult Literacy Survey: Results for Ireland*, Dublin: The Stationery Office.

Mosley, J. (2005), *Turn Your School Around*, London: LDA.

Mosley, J. and Tew, M. (1999), *Quality Circle Time in the Secondary School: A Handbook of Good Practice*, London: David Fulton.

Mulrooney, M. and Harrold, M. (2004), 'Parents' voices' in P. Noonan Walsh and H. Gash (eds.), *Lives and Times: Practice, Policy and People with Disabilities*, Bray, Co. Wicklow: Rathdown Press, pp. 44–62.

Murphy, T. (2008), 'Responding to school disaffection: insights from the Republic of Ireland', *The International Journal on School Disaffection*, 6/1: 35–39.

National Behaviour Support Service (2006), *School Matters: The Report of the Task Force on Student Behaviour in Second Level Schools*, Navan, Co. Meath: National Behaviour Support Service.

National Behaviour Support Service (2009), *A Model of Support for Behaviour Improvement in Post Primary Schools*, Navan, Co. Meath: National Behaviour Support Service.

National Council for Curriculum and Assessment (1999), *Special Educational Needs: Curriculum Issues*, Dublin: National Council for Curriculum and Assessment.

National Council for Curriculum and Assessment (2002), *Draft Guidelines for Teachers of Students with General Learning Disabilities*, Dublin: The Stationery Office.

National Council for Curriculum and Assessment (2005), *Interim Report on the Developmental Initiative in Assessment for Learning in Junior Cycle*, Dublin: National Council for Curriculum and Assessment.

National Council for Curriculum and Assessment (2006), *Assessment for Learning* information leaflet, Dublin: National Council for Curriculum and Assessment.

National Council for Curriculum and Assessment (2007), *Exceptionally Able Students: Draft Guidelines for Teachers*, Dublin: National Council for Curriculum and Assessment.

National Council for Curriculum and Assessment (2007), *Guidelines for Teachers of Students with General Learning Disabilities*, Dublin: National Council for Curriculum and Assessment.

National Council for Curriculum and Assessment (2009), 'Junior Cycle Curriculum Framework for Students with General Learning Disabilities: Towards a Discussion Paper', Dublin: National Council for Curriculum and Assessment.

National Council for Special Education (2006), *Guidelines on the Individual Education Plan Process*, Trim, Co. Meath: National Council for Special Education.

National Council for Special Education (2006), *Implementation Report: Plan for the Phased Implementation of the EPSEN Act 2004*, Trim, Co. Meath: National Council for Special Education.

National Council for Special Education (2009), *Annual Report*, Trim, Co. Meath: National Council for Special Education.

National Disability Authority (2002), *Public Attitudes to Disability in the Republic of Ireland*, Dublin: National Disability Authority.

National Educational Psychological Service (2007a), *Special Educational Needs: A Continuum of Support (Guidelines for Teachers)*, Dublin: The Stationery Office.

National Educational Psychological Service (2007b), *Special Educational Needs: A Continuum of Support (Resource Pack for Teachers)*, Dublin: The Stationery Office.

National Educational Psychological Service (2010a), *A Continuum of Support for Post-Primary Schools: Guidelines for Teachers*, Dublin: The Stationery Office.

National Educational Psychological Service (2010b), *A Continuum of Support for Post-Primary Schools: Resource Pack for Teachers*, Dublin: The Stationery Office.

National Educational Psychological Service (2010c), *Behavioural, Emotional and Social Difficulties: A Continuum of Support (Guidelines for Teachers)*, Dublin: The Stationery Office.

National Educational Welfare Board (2008), *Developing a Code of Behaviour: Guidelines for Schools*, Dublin: The Stationery Office.

Norris, C. and Closs, A. (2003), 'Child and parent relationships with teachers in schools responsible for the education of children with serious medical conditions' in M. Nind, K. Sheehy and K. Simmons (eds.), *Inclusive Education: Learners and Learning Contexts*, London: David Fulton, pp. 21–30.

Norris, C. and Lloyd, G. (2000), 'Parents, professionals and ADHD: What the papers say', *European Journal of Special Needs Education*, 15/2, 123–137.

Norwich, B., Griffiths, C. and Burden, B. (2005), 'Dyslexia-friendly schools and parent partnership: Inclusion and home–school relationships', *European Journal of Special Needs Education*, 20/2, 147–165.

Nugent, M. (2002), 'Teachers' views of working with Individual Education Plans in an Irish school', *REACH: Journal of Special Needs Education in Ireland*, 15/2, 98–112.

Oakshott, M. (1972), 'Education: The engagement and its frustration' in R.F. Dearden et al. (eds.), *Education and the Development of Reason*, London: Routledge Kegan Paul.

O'Brien, T. (1998), *Promoting Positive Behaviour*, London: David Fulton.

O'Brien, T. and Guiney, D. (2001), *Differentiation in Teaching and Learning: Principles and Practice*, London and New York: Continuum.

O'Donnell, M. (2003), 'Transfer from special to mainstream: The voice of the pupil' in M. Shevlin and R. Rose (eds.), *Encouraging Voices: Respecting the Insights of Young People Who Have Been Marginalised*, Dublin: National Disability Authority, pp. 228–253.

O'Donoghue, J. (2002), 'Numeracy and mathematics', *Irish Mathematics Society Bulletin*, 48, 47–55.

OECD (1994), *The Integration of Disabled Children into Mainstream Education: Ambitions, Theories and Practices*, Paris: Organisation for Economic Co-operation and Development.

O'Flynn, S. and Kennedy, H. (2000), *Conflict and Confrontation in the Classroom: Reflections on Current Practice*, Cork: Paradigm Press.

O'Hara, J., Byrne, S.J. and McNamara, G. (2000), *Positive Discipline: An Irish Educational Appraisal and Practical Guide*, Dublin: School of Education Studies, Dublin City University.

O'Keefe, P. (2004), 'The special school in an age of inclusion', *REACH: Journal of Special Needs Education in Ireland*, 18/1, 3–15.

O'Leary, K. (2006), 'Outside the box?', *Prospero*, 12, 32–34.

Oliver, M. (1995), 'Does special education have a role to play in the 21st century?', *REACH: Journal of Special Needs Education in Ireland*, 8/2, 67–76.

Ó Murchú, E. (1996), 'What is special about education?', *Irish Educational Studies*, 15, 252–270.

Ó Murchú, E. and Shevlin, M. (1995), 'The SERC Report: A basis for change', *REACH: Journal of Special Needs Education in Ireland*, 8/2, 85–94.

O'Neill, Á. and Rose, R. (2008), 'The changing roles of teaching assistants in England and special needs assistants in Ireland: A comparison', *REACH, Journal of Special Needs Education in Ireland*, 22/1, 48–58.

O'Riordan, M., Plaisted, K., Driver, J. and Baron-Cohen, S. (2001), 'Superior visual search in autism', *Journal of Experimental Psychology: Human Perception and Performance*, 27, 719–730.

Parsons, S., Guldberg, K., Mac Leod, A., Jones, G., Prunty, A. and Balfe, T. (2009), *International Review of the Literature of Evidence of Best Practice Provision in the Education of Persons with Autistic Spectrum Disorders*, Trim, Co. Meath: National Council for Special Education.

Peck, C., Donaldson, J. and Pezzoli, M. (1990), 'Some benefits non-handicapped adolescents perceive for themselves from their social relationships with peers who have severe handicaps', *JASH (The Journal of the Association for Persons with Severe Handicaps)*, 15/4, 241–249.

Peer, L. (2003), 'Dyslexia and its manifestations in the secondary school' in L. Peer and G. Reid (eds.), *Dyslexia – Successful Inclusion in the Secondary School*, London: David Fulton in association with the British Dyslexia Association, pp. 1–9.

Perkins, R., Moran, G., Cosgrove, J. and Shiel, G. (2010), *PISA 2009: The Performance and Progress of 15-year-olds in Ireland: Summary Report*, Dublin: Educational Research Centre, St Patrick's College.

Piaget (1952), *The Origin of Intelligence in Children*, New York: International Universities Press.

Pinkus, S. (2005), 'Bridging the gap between policy and practice: Adopting a strategic vision for partnership working in special education', *British Journal of Special Education*, 32/4, 184–187.

PISA Study (2000), *Programme for International Student Assessment*, Paris: OECD.

Pollard, R. (2006), *The Avenue: A History of the Claremont Institute*, Dublin: Denzille Press.

Porter, J. (2005), 'Severe learning difficulties' in A. Lewis and B. Norwich (eds.), *Special Teaching for Special Children?: Pedagogies for Inclusion*, Maidenhead, Berkshire: Open University Press.

Powell, S. (ed.) (2000), *Helping Children with Autism to Learn*, London: David Fulton.

Pressley, M. (1994), 'State-of-the-science primary grades reading instruction or whole language?', *Educational Psychologist*

Purdie, N., Hattie, J. and Carroll, A. (2002), 'A review of the research on interventions for attention deficit hyperactivity disorder: What works best?', *Review of Educational Research*, 72, 61–99.

Quinn, F. (2001), 'Parents as partners: Parents' perceptions of partnership in Northern Ireland', *Journal of Research in Special Educational Needs*, 1/2, available online at www.nasen.uk.com/ejournal (accessed October 2006).

Quinn, G. and Degener, T. with Bruce, A., Burke, C., Castellino, J., Kenna, P., Kilkelly, U. and Quinlivan, S. (2002), *Human Rights and Disability: The Current Use and Future Potential of United Nations Human Rights Instruments in the Context Of Disability*, New York and Geneva: United Nations.

Ring, E. and Travers, J. (2005), 'Barriers to inclusion: A case study of a pupil with severe learning difficulties in Ireland', *European Journal of Special Needs Education*, 20/1, 41–56.

Robertson, P., Hamill, P. and Hewitt, C. (1994), *Effective Support for Learning: Themes from the RAISE Project, Interchange 27*, Edinburgh: Research and Intelligence Unit, Department of Education.

Robins, J. (1986), *Fools and Mad: A History of the Insane in Ireland*, Dublin: Institute of Public Administration.

Rogers, B. (1994), *Behaviour Recovery: A Whole-School Program for Mainstream Schools*, London: Longman.

Rooney, N. (2003), 'Creating a culture of change: Exploring the perspectives of young people with hearing impairments' in M. Shevlin and R. Rose (eds.), *Encouraging Voices: Respecting the Insights of Young People Who Have Been Marginalised*, Dublin: National Disability Authority, pp. 159–177.

Rose, R. and Howley, M. (2007), *Special Educational Needs in Inclusive Primary Classrooms*, London: Paul Chapman.

Rose, R. and Shevlin, M. (2004), 'Encouraging voices: listening to young people who have been marginalised', *Support for Learning*, 19/4, 155–161.

Rose, R. and Shevlin, M. (2010), *Count Me In: Ideas for Actively Engaging Students in Inclusive Classrooms*, London: Jessica Kingsley Publishers.

Rose, R., Shevlin, M., Winter, E. and O'Raw, P. (2010), 'Special and inclusive education in the Republic of Ireland: reviewing the literature from 2000 to 2009', *European Journal of Special Needs Education*, 25/4, 359–373.

Royal Commission on the Care and Control of the Feebleminded, 8/117 (1908).

Rudduck, J. and McIntyre, D. (2007), *Improving Learning through Consulting Pupils*, London: Routledge.

Russell, F. (2005), 'Starting school: The importance of parents' expectations', *Journal of Research in Special Educational Needs*, 5/3, 118–126, available online at www.nasen.uk.com/ejournal (accessed October 2006).

Scanlon, G. and McGilloway (2006), 'Managing children with special needs in the Irish education system: A professional perspective', *REACH: Journal of Special Needs Education in Ireland*, 19/2, 81–93.

ScoilNet, Official education portal of the Department of Education and Science in Ireland, www.scoilnet.ie.

Scott, I. (2009), 'Developing a whole school approach to including children with autistic spectrum disorders in a mainstream primary school', *REACH, Journal of Special Needs Education in Ireland*, 22/2, 113–121.

Serfontein, G. (1990), *The Hidden Handicap*, Australia: Simon & Schuster.

Shawe, S. and Hawes, T. (1998), *Effective Teaching and Learning in the Primary Classroom: A Practical Guide to Brain Compatible Learning*, Leicester: The Services Ltd.

Shevlin, M. and Flynn, P. (2011), 'Leadership and Special Educational Needs' in O'Sullivan, H. and West-Burnham, J. (eds) (2011) (in press), *Leadership and Management in Schools: An Irish Perspective*, London: Sage Publications Sage.

Shevlin, M. and Rose, R. (eds.) (2003), *Encouraging Voices: Respecting the Insights of Young People who have been Marginalised*, Dublin: National Disability Authority.

Shevlin, M., Noonan Walsh, P., Kenny, M., McNeela, E. and Molloy, R. (2003), 'Experiencing mainstream education: Exploring the perspectives of parents of young people who have Down syndrome', *REACH: Journal of Special Needs Education in Ireland*, 17/1, 3–11.

Shiel, G. and Morgan, M. with Larney, R. (1998), *Study of Remedial Education in Irish Primary Schools: Summary Report*, Dublin: The Stationery Office.

Siegel, L.S. (1992), 'An evaluation of the discrepancy definition of dyslexia', *Journal of Learning Disabilities*, 25, 618–629.

Simpson, J., Hornby, G., Davies, L. and Murray, R. (2005), 'Positive parent–professional relationships: Allies who emancipate one another' in P. O'Brien and M. Sullivan (eds.), *Allies in Emancipation: Shifting from Providing Service to Being of Support*, Melbourne, Australia: Thomson Dunmore Press, pp. 199–211.

Slavin, R., Madden, N., Dolan, L. and Wasik, B. (1996), *Every Child Every School: Success for All*, Thousand Oaks, CA: Corwin Press Inc.

Special Education Support Service (2008), *Meeting the Learning and Teaching Needs of Students with Special Educational Needs: Signposts (A Resource Pack for Teachers)*, Cork: Special Education Support Service.

Special Education Support Service (2008), *Science Differentiation in Action: Practical Strategies for Adapting Learning and Teaching in Science for Students with Diverse Needs and Abilities*, Cork: Special Education Support Service.

Spelman, B.J. and Griffin, S. (1994), *Special Educational Needs – Issues for the White Paper (Conference Proceedings)*, Dublin: Education Department, University College, Dublin and Educational Studies Association of Ireland.

Stahl, S.A., Osborn, J. and Lehr, F. (1990), *Beginning to Read: Thinking and Learning about Print. A Summary*, Urbana-Champaign, IL: University of Illinois Center for the Study of Reading.

Stauffer, R.G. (1980), *The Language Experience Approach to the Teaching of Reading*, New York: Harper & Row.

Stenhouse, L. (1975), *An Introduction to Curriculum Research and Development*, London: Heinemann.

Strain, M., Dennison, B., Ouston, J. and Hall, V. (eds.) (1998), *Policy, Leadership and Professional Knowledge in Education*, London: Paul Chapman.

Swain, J. and French, S. (2003), 'Towards an affirmation model of disability' in M. Nind, J. Rix, K. Sheehy and K. Simmons (eds.), *Inclusive Education: Diverse Perspectives*, London: David Fulton, pp. 150–164.

Swain, J., French, S. and Cameron, C. (2003), *Controversial Issues in a Disabling Society*, Buckingham, UK: Open University Press.

Thomas, C. (2002), 'Disability theory: Key ideas, issues and thinkers' in C. Barnes, M. Oliver and L. Barton (eds.), *Disability Studies Today*, Blackwell: Cambridge.

Thomas, G. and Loxley, A. (2001), *Deconstructing Special Education and Constructing Inclusion*, Buckingham: Open University Press.

Thomas, G. and O'Hanlon, C. (2004), 'Series editors' preface' in G. Thomas and M. Vaughan, *Inclusive Education: Readings and Reflections*, Maidenhead, Berkshire: Open University Press.

Thomas, G. and Vaughan, M. (2004), *Inclusive Education: Readings and Reflections*, Maidenhead, Berkshire: Open University Press.

Tilstone, C., Lacey, P., Porter, J. and Robertson, C. (2000), *Pupils with Learning Difficulties in Mainstream Schools*, London: David Fulton.

Tod, J., Castle, F. and Blamires, M. (1998), *Individual Education Plans: Implementing Effective Practice*, London: David Fulton.

Tomlinson, S. (1982), *The Sociology of Special Education*, London: Routledge and Kegan Paul.

Toolan, D. (2003), 'Shaped identities' in M. Shevlin and R. Rose (eds.), *Encouraging Voices: Respecting the Insights of Young People Who Have Been Marginalised*, Dublin: National Disability Authority, pp. 91–99.

Travers, J., Balfe, T., Butler, C., Day, T., Dupont, M., McDaid, R., O'Donnell, M. and Prunty, A. (2010), *Addressing the Challenges and Barriers to Inclusion in Irish Schools. Report to Research and Development Committee of the Department of Education and Science*, Dublin: St Patrick's College, Drumcondra.

Tregaskis, C. (2004), *Constructions of Disability: Researching the Interface between Disabled and Non-disabled People*, London: Routledge.

Turner, E. (2003), 'Dyslexia and English' in L. Peer and G. Reid (eds.), *Dyslexia – Successful Inclusion in the Secondary School*, London: David Fulton in association with the British Dyslexia Association, pp. 64–71.

Twachtmann-Cullen, D. (2004), 'Hyperlexia: A language treatment perspective', *Autism Asperger's Digest*, (May–June), 12–15.

UNESCO (UN Education, Social and Cultural Organisation) (1994), *Salamanca Statement and Framework for Action on Special Needs Education*, available at http://unesdoc.unesco.org/images/0009/000984/098427eo.pdf.

UNESCO (UN Education, Social and Cultural Organization) (2005), *Guidelines for inclusion: Ensuring access to education for all*, Paris: UNESCO.

United Nations (1989), *Convention on the Rights of the Child*, New York and Geneva: UN.

United Nations (1993), *Standard Rules on the Equalization of Opportunities for Persons with Disabilities*, New York and Geneva: UN.

United Nations (2006), Draft Convention on the Rights of Persons with Disabilities.

UPIAS (1976), *Fundamental Principles of Disability*, London: Union of the Physically Impaired against Segregation.

Visser, J. (1993), *Differentiation: Making it Work*, Tamworth: NASEN Publications.

Voeltz, L., Hemphill, N.J., Brown, S., Kishi, G., Klein, R., Royal Fruehling, G., Levy, J.C. and Kube, C. (1983), *The Special Friends Program: A Trainer's Manual for Integrated School Settings* (Revised Edition), Honolulu: College of Education, University of Hawaii Department of Special Education.

Vygotsky, L.S. (1962), *Thought and Language*, Boston: The MIT Press.

Walsh, L. (1997) 'Educators and clinicians: Conflict or collaboration?', *REACH: Journal of Special Needs Education in Ireland*, 10/2, 91–92.

Ware, J. (2005), 'Profound and multiple learning disabilities' in A. Lewis and B. Norwich, *Special Teaching for Special Children?: Pedagogies for Inclusion*, Maidenhead, Berkshire: Open University Press.

Ware, J., Balfe, T., Butler, C., Day, T., Dupont, M., Harten, C., Farrell, A. M., McDaid, R., O'Riordan, M., Prunty, A. and Travers, J. (2009), *Research Report on the Role of Special Schools and Special Classes in Ireland*, Trim: National Council for Special Education.

Ware, J., Julian, G. and McGee, P. (2005), 'Education for children with severe and profound general learning disabilities in Ireland: factors influencing teachers' decisions about teaching these pupils', *European Journal of Special Needs Education*, 20/2, 179–194.

Watson, N. (1998), 'Enabling identity: Disability, self and citizenship' in T. Shakespeare (ed.), *The Disability Reader: Social Science Perspectives*, London: Cassell, pp. 147–162.

Watson, N., Shakespeare, T., Cunningham-Burley, S., Barnes, C., Corker, M., Davis, J. and Priestley, M. (1999), *Life as a Disabled Child: A Qualitative Study of Young People's Experiences and Perspectives, Final Report*, Swindon: Economic and Social Research Council (ESRC), Research Programme.

Wentworth, R. and Lubienski, A. (1999), *Montessori for the New Millenium*, New Jersey: Lawrence Erlbaum Associates.

Westwood, P. (1997), *Commonsense Methods for Children with Special Needs: Strategies for the Regular Classroom*, London: Routledge Falmer.

Westwood, P. (2003), *Commonsense Methods for Children with Special Educational Needs: Strategies for the Regular Classroom*, 4th edn., London: Routledge Falmer.

Whyte, G. (2002), *Social Inclusion and the Legal System: Public Interest Law in Ireland*, Dublin: Institute of Public Administration (IPA).

Williams, G. (2001), 'Theorizing disability' in G.L. Albrecht, K.D. Seelman and M. Bury (eds.), *Handbook of Disability Studies*, London: Sage, pp. 123–144.

Wilson, C. and Jade, R. (1999), *Whose Voice Is It Anyway?: Talking to Disabled Young People at School*, London: The Alliance for Inclusive Education.

Wing, L. and Gould, J. (1979), 'Severe impairments of social interaction and associated abnormalities in children: Epidemiology and classification', *Journal of Autism and Developmental Disorders*, 9, 11–29.

Winter, E. and Kilpatrick, R. (2001), 'Special needs resource roles: A cross-jurisdictional comparison', *Journal of Instructional Psychology*, 28/1: 61–67.

Winter, E. and O'Raw, P. (2010), *Literature Review of the Principles and Practices Relating to Inclusive Education for Children with Special Educational Needs* (prepared in conjunction with the 2007–2009 NCSE Consultative Forum), Trim, Co. Meath: National Council for Special Education.

Winter, E., Fletcher-Campbell, F., Connolly, P. and Lynch, P. (2006), *Resource Requirements for the Diagnosis and Assessment of Special Educational Needs in Ireland, Research Report*, (Unpublished), Trim, Co. Meath: National Council for Special Education.

Wolfgang, C.H. (2001), *Solving Discipline and Classroom Management Problems*, New York: John Wiley & Sons.

Wood, D.J. (1998), *How Children Think and Learn: The Social Context of Cognitive Development*, 2nd edn., Oxford: Blackwell.

Zentall, S.S. (1995), 'Activity- and novelty-based curriculum for teachers of students with ADHD', Paper presented at the annual convention of the Council for Exceptional Children, Indianapolis, IN.

Glossary

Introduction

The definitions for particular types of special educational needs provided here are of necessity brief and limited in scope. Unfortunately, most of our official definitions tend to focus on the deficit aspect, as children and young people with special educational needs are compared unfavourably with the 'norm'. These definitions are intended purely as a reference or beginning point and the important thing for us all to remember is that each label provides us with limited information about the child so labelled and we cannot make assumptions about the learning capacity of the child based solely on the assigned label.

Autism/autistic spectrum disorders

Autism is usually described as covering a spectrum from mild to severe and involving a triad of impairments: social interaction, social communication and social imagination.

Asperger syndrome

Asperger syndrome is sometimes known as higher functioning autism (HFA). The child will likely have above-average intellectual ability but at the same time may experience great difficulties in ordinary social interaction.

General learning disability

The category of general learning disability is usually subdivided into the categories of borderline mild, mild, moderate and severe/profound, indicating the level of difficulty in learning experienced along a continuum. Children and young people with a general learning disability usually function at an intellectual level where they find all aspects of learning difficult.

- **Borderline mild general learning disability** refers to children and young people who are capable of living independent lives but experience significant barriers to learning, including delayed conceptual development and slow speech and language development.
- **Mild general learning disability** refers to children and young people who have significantly below-average intellectual functioning and their adaptive development (motor development, speech and language skills and daily living skills) will be significantly underdeveloped compared to their age peers.
- **Moderate general learning disability** refers to children and young people who have significant intellectual impairments and may also have difficulties in motor skills, communication and the acquisition of self-help skills. These

children and young people use a variety of methods to communicate, including signs and symbols, and others will be able to hold conversations.

- **Severe/profound general learning disability** refers to children and young people who are learning at a very early developmental level and may experience associated impairments in motor skills and communication.

Down syndrome

Down syndrome is a genetic condition where children are born with an extra chromosome and is the most common cause of a learning disability. These children will have individual learning profiles that will range across a continuum from mild to moderate to severe learning difficulties. It has been reported that these children will often have strengths in visual processing and visual memory.

Specific learning disability/dyslexia

Specific learning disability/dyslexia is a generic term used to refer to a range of difficulties associated with reading, writing, number and motor coordination. Children and young people with dyslexia process written information differently from their peers and as a result can experience significant difficulties in reading, writing and numbers.

- **Dyscalculia** refers to significant difficulties a child or young person experiences in relation to numbers/maths.
- **Dysgraphia** refers to significant difficulties a child or young person experiences in relation to writing.
- **Dyspraxia** is sometimes known as Developmental Co-ordination Disorder (DCD) and refers to significant difficulties experienced in relation to coordination and physical movement.

Social, emotional and behavioural disturbance

Social, emotional and behavioural disturbance refers to a continuum of conditions that can affect the child or young person. This continuum includes neurotic behaviour, anti-social behaviour and sometimes, in a minority of situations, psychotic behaviour. These children and young people may require interventions by a range of professionals including psychiatrists, psychologists and counsellors. Attention disorders such as Attention Deficit Disorder and Attention Deficit Hyperactivity Disorder are included in this continuum.

- **Attention Disorder:** Children and young people with Attention Disorder experience extreme difficulty in concentrating or staying on-task for a reasonable length of time.
- **Attention Deficit Disorder (ADD):** Children and young people with ADD experience significant difficulties in maintaining concentration for any period of time, they are usually easily distracted, may be disorganised and forgetful.

- **Attention Deficit Hyperactivity Disorder (ADHD):** Children and young people with Attention Deficit Hyperactivity Disorder will usually experience extreme levels of restlessness, impulsiveness and over-activity.
- **Specific Speech and Language Disorder:** Children and young people with Specific Speech and Language Disorder will have significant difficulties involving impaired receptive or expressive language skills.

Gifted/exceptionally able

Children and young people who are gifted or exceptionally able will demonstrate outstanding ability in one or more of the following areas: intellectual ability, specific subject attainment, creative thinking, the arts, sports and mechanical aptitude.

Assessment

Assessment is a systematic process that gathers all available information about the child or young person with special educational needs in order to develop appropriate educational provision.

Assessment can involve various types of assessment, including summative, formative informal and/or formal and involve the use of norm-referenced and criterion-referenced tests.

Summative assessment consists of testing an individual's knowledge according to a national standard within a formal setting, e.g. Junior Certificate and Leaving Certificate.

The purpose of **formative assessment** is to check on an individual's progress in learning, usually in an informal setting, e.g. providing feedback on homework.

Informal assessment is usually conducted by a teacher and/or parents and involves observation of the child or young person's capacity to cope with classroom learning tasks. This may involve the use of behavioural/cognitive checklists and helps to determine the types of difficulties in learning experienced by the child and/or young person.

Formal assessment can consist of the use of norm-referenced/standardised/criterion-referenced tests and/or a psychological assessment.

Norm-referenced/standardised tests involve the development of what is considered the norm (expected level of proficiency) for this population of children of a particular age. These include tests in reading, spelling and/or mathematics and the individual's performance can be compared nationally to other children of the same age or class level who have taken the same test.

Criterion-referenced tests are devised to find out whether the individual has achieved a set of learning objectives or mastered a particular task. Success is not measured in relation to the individual's peer group or age cohort, but in relation to the achievement of specific goals set for the individual.

A **psychological assessment** is carried out by an educational psychologist to establish intellectual functioning; strengths and difficulties in learning; social, speech and language and motor skills.

The **Individual Education Plan** (IEP) is one important outcome of the formal assessment process. The IEP consists of a written document that specifies learning goals/targets for a child or young person who has special educational needs.

The **Individual Profile and Learning Programme** (IPLP) is a programme designed for any child or young person selected for additional support in school. These children or young people will usually have difficulties in learning that may not warrant a psychological assessment and will generally receive learning support. Like the IEP, it involves the setting of individual goals for the learner and a review of learning outcomes.

Support personnel and equipment

A learning support teacher will generally focus on helping children and young people who experience serious difficulties in literacy and numeracy.

A resource teacher will generally work with children and young people who have 'low incidence' disabilities and require more intensive support to make progress in learning. Low incidence disabilities include, for example, autism, Down syndrome, Attention Deficit Disorder and Attention Deficit Hyperactivity Disorder.

A special needs assistant is employed to attend to children and young people who have specific care and/or social and behavioural needs.

Speech and language therapy supports children and young people who have Specific Speech and Language Disorder. Speech and language therapy aims to enable these children and young people to improve their communication skills in order to access the curriculum.

Occupational therapy focuses principally on motor, sensory, perceptual, social, emotional and self-care skills of children and young people with severe physical and/or sensory disabilities. Occupational therapists will advise on appropriate equipment for the child and any environmental adaptations required.

Assistive technology

Assistive technology refers to any device or programme that enables people with disabilities to improve their functional capacities. This technology is often used, but by no means exclusively so, in relation to people with severe physical and/or sensory disabilities. Examples include specialist keyboard, switch or touch screen or software, including screen-reading and voice recognition.

System supports to schools, children, young people and their families

National Council for Special Education (NCSE) was established under the Education for Persons with Special Educational Needs Act 2004. The NCSE has responsibility for coordinating the provision of resources and supports to schools. The council also provides policy advice to the minister in relation to the education of children and others with special educational needs.

A **special Educational Needs Organiser (SENO)** is employed by the National Council for Special Education and coordinates educational services for children and young people with special educational needs at local level.

Visiting Teacher Service was initially established to provide support for children and young people who have sensory (visual/hearing) impairments. The service supports children and young people with sensory impairments through from pre-school, primary and post-primary up to higher education.

Special Education Unit is part of the Department of Education and Science and until the establishment of the National Council for Special Education was responsible for the organisation and delivery of special educational provision nationally. In future, the remit of the Special Education Unit will include policy development in relation to special education.

The Inspectorate of the Department of Education and Science had established a section to deal specifically with special education. The restructuring of the Inspectorate has resulted in a focus on policy development in special education and monitoring and reviewing special educational provision through whole-school evaluation.

Special Education Support Service (SESS) was established by the Department of Education and Science in 2003 to provide opportunities for the professional development of teachers involved in special educational provision and to enable schools to create effective support mechanisms for children and young people with special educational needs.

National Educational Psychological Service (NEPS) was established by the Department of Education and Science in 1999 to provide a psychological service to schools. Priority has been given to children and young people with special educational needs and NEPS has been involved in providing psychological assessments and advice to schools.

National Council for Curriculum and Assessment (NCCA) was established to advise on curriculum and assessment issues and develop appropriate curricular programmes. The NCCA has developed Draft Guidelines for teachers of children and young people who have general learning disabilities.

Index

A Continuum of Support for Post-Primary Schools: Guidelines for Teachers (2010a), see National Educational Psychological Service (2010a)

A Continuum of Support for Post-Primary Schools: Resource Pack for Teachers (2010b), see National Educational Psychological Service (2010b)

A House Full of Feelings and Emotions, 207

A Model of Support for Behaviour Improvement in Post Primary Schools (2009), 71

A Strategy for Equality: Report of the Commission on the Status of People with Disabilities, (1996), 50, 87

able pupils, 104–5

Accredited Long-Term Professional Development, 70

ADD, *see* Attention Deficit Disorder (ADD), 68

ADHD, *see* Attention Deficit Hyperactivity Disorder (ADHD)

Adler, Alfred, 195, 204

Ainscow, M., 75.

Ainscow, M., Booth, T. and Dyson, A., 115

Ainscow, M., Howes, A., Farrell, P. and Frankham, J., 85

Alban-Metcalf, J. and Alban-Metcalf, J., 213

alphabetic stage in the teaching of reading, 183

Altman, B., 17

amadán, 32

America, 13, 76

American Individuals with Disabilities Act (IDEA) (1975), 54

Americans with Disabilities Act (ADA) (1990), 13–14

An Evaluation of Educational Provision for Children with Autistic Spectrum Disorders, see Education and Science (DES), Department of, Inspectorate (2006a)

An Evaluation of Special Classes for Pupils with Specific Speech and Language Disorder, see Education and Science (DES), Department of, (DES 2006b)

anger, *see* behavioural difficulties, revenge

Applied Behaviour Analysis (ABA), 235

Armstrong, D. and Kane, G., 241

ASD, *see* autistic spectrum disorder (ASD)

Asperger syndrome (AS)/high-functioning autism (AS/HFA), 63, 146, 218, 219, 221–22

assessment for learning, 127, 130

Assessment for Learning information leaflet, *see* National Council for Curriculum and Assessment (2006)

assessment in an Irish context, *see under* Ireland

Association for Parents of Mentally Backward Children, 40

ASTI Policy Paper: *Task Force on Student Behaviour in Second Level Schools, ASTI Written Submission, (2005),* 195

asylums and workhouses, 36–37

Attention Deficit Disorder (ADD), 68

Attention Deficit Hyperactivity Disorder (ADHD), 68, 145, 212–13, 215, 216, 232–34, 248

attention seeking/needs, *see under* behavioural difficulties

autism, 49, 53, 54–55, 57, 62–64, 67, 101, 139, 258

autistic spectrum disorder (ASD), 6, 62–65, 70, 101, 143, 215, 216, 218–22, 232

strategies for learners with, 219–20
structured teaching, 220–22
Avramidis, E. and Norwich, B., 81

Baldwin, S. and Carlisle, J., 23
Ball, M., Hughes, A. and McCormack, W., 101, 226
Banks, J. and McCoy, S., 99
Barkley, R.A., 232
Barnes, C., 19
Barr, Justice, 56
Barton, L., 86
Beaton, A.E., Mullis, I.V.S., Martin, M.O., Gonzalez, E.J., Kelly, D.L. and Smith, T.A., 260
Beckman, P.J. and Beckman Boyes, G., 243
Behaviour and primary needs: Understanding behaviour difficulties, 198–200
behavioural difficulties, 195–98
    attention seeking/needs, 200–3
    goals of misbehaviour, 200
    making rules, 212
    positive discipline and whole school approach, 211
    power seeking, 203–5, 206
    recognition needs, 201–3
    revenge, 205–8
    self-esteem, 210–11
    withdrawal, 208–10
behavioural objectives approach to curricular design and teaching strategies in special education, 140–41
Behavioural, Emotional and Social Difficulties: A Continuum of Support (Guidelines for Teachers), see National Educational Psychological Service (2010c)
Belfast, 32
Belgium, 79
Benicasa Special School for Emotionally Disturbed Children, 41
Bereiter, C., 191
Better Literacy and Numeracy for Children and Young People: A Draft National Plan to Improve Literacy and Numeracy in

Schools, see Education and Science, (DES 2010)
Beveridge, S., 77, 96, 97, 98, 122, 128, 129, 140, 141, 252
Birkett, D., 239
blindness, 66, 67
bóbre, 32
Booth, T., 85, 99
Booth, T., Ainscow, M., Black-Hawkins, K., Vaughan, M. and Shaw, L., 85
Braddock, D.L. and Parish, S.L., 12, 13, 17
Brehon Laws, 31, 36
Britain, 43, 44
British Deaf and Dumb Association, 12
British Psychological Society (1999), 222–23
Brosnahan, S., 39
bullying in schools, 24, 26
Burke, A., 117
Byers, R. and Rose, R., 155
Byrne, M., 35, 36

Cabra school for the deaf and dumb, 38
caeptha, 32
Cameron, Colin, 15
Campbell, J.R., Kelley, D.L., Mullis, I.V.S, Martin, M.O. and Sainsbury, M., 174
Canada, 82
Carey, D., 101, 240
Carmelite Brothers, school for the blind, 38
Carpenter, B., 243
Carpenter, B., Ashdown, R. and Bovair, K., 165
Carpenter, B. and Shevlin, M., 82
Carrigoline, 37
categorical approach to facilitating learning, 265
Census of Ireland 1851, 1901, 37
Centre for Studies of Inclusive Education (CSIE, 2002), 84
cerebral palsy, 17, 148, 232
challenging behaviour in special schools, 70
change, the challenge of, 6–7
change, tracing the origins of, 76–78
charity model of disability, 19, 247

Charting Our Education Future (Government of Ireland, 1995), 49–50, 53, 56, 57, 155–56
children and young people with disabilities, *see under* disabilities
Children, Schools and Families, Department of, (2009), *see* Lamb Inquiry
civil rights, 20, 54
civil rights movement, 74, 76, 77, 267
Claremont Institute, Glasnevin, 34–35
Classroom Support (NEPS three-stage model), 131–33
classroom-based assessment, 129
Clifford, Louis, 39
Clough, P. and Corbett, J., 73, 74
Clough, P. and Nutbrown, C., 86
Code of Practice (UK) 1994, 147
Code of Practice on the identification and assessment of special educational needs, see Education (UK), Department for, DfE, 1994
Code of Practice, DfES (UK) 2001, *see* Education and Skills (UK), Department for (DfES, 2001)
Coffey, A., 87, 157, 158
Collins, Thomas, 34–35
Commission on the Status of People with Disabilities (Report 1996), *see A Strategy for Equality*
Commissioners of National Education, 37
communication for understanding, 217
concentric model of differentiation, 161
content modification, and curriculum differentiation, 163–64
Coolahan, J., 259
Coombe Hospital, 36
cooperative learning, 33–34, 80
Copeland, S. and Hughes, C., 231
Corbett, J., 159
Corcoran, Father Timothy, 38
Corcoran, T., 32
Cork, 37
Cornwall, J., 24, 27
corporal punishment, 195
Costello, Declan, 39–40
Costello, John A. Taoiseach, 40

CPD (Continuing Professional Development), 88
Craig, A., 264
Croll, P., 248
Crow, L., 18
Crowther Report (1959), Fifteen to Eighteen, 189
Crowther, D., Dyson, A. and Millward, A., 265
Culligan, B., 186, 187
curricular approaches perspective, 74, 75
curriculum access, 155–56
    translating policy into practice, 157–58
curriculum differentiation, 162–64
curriculum-based assessment, 126–27
    and individual education planning, 140–41

Davidson, T., 32
Davis, P. and Florian, L., 136
Day, T., 87, 262
deafness, 12, 65–66, 67
deficit model, 107, 126
Delivering Equality of Opportunity in Schools: An Action Plan for Educational Inclusion, see Education and Science, Department of, (DES 2005b)
Denmark, 13, 43, 79
DES 1998, 2002a, 2005b, 2006b, 2010, *see under* Education and Science (DES), Department of
DES Circular SP. ED. 02/05, *see* Education and Science, Department of, (DES 2005a)
DES Circular SP. ED. 07/02, *see under* Education and Science, Department of
DES Circular SP. ED. 08/02, *see* Education and Science, Department of, (DES 2002a)
DES Inspectorate report, *DES 2006a, see* Education and Science (DES), Department of, Inspectorate (2006a)
DES, England and Wales, 1978, 97
DES, *see* Education and Science (DES), Department of
Desforges, M. and Lindsay, G., 91, 135

Devecchi, C. and Nevin, A., 115
Developing a Code of Behaviour:
    Guidelines for Schools (National
    Education and Welfare Board
    2008), see National Educational
    Welfare Board (2008)
differentiation, 158–71
    in assessment, 168–69
    differentiating resources, 166–68
    information communication
        technology usage, 166–68
    'learning things differently', 165
    marking written work, 169–71
    models of, 160–61
    principles of teaching and learning,
        159–60
    'watering down' the curriculum?,
        165–66
    see also curriculum differentiation
disabilities,
    changing attitudes to people with, 36
    children and young people with,
        23–27, 34, 41, 58, 75,
        100–1, 267
        curriculum and syllabus
            requirements, 71
        educational and service needs,
            67, 258
        international research studies
            on, 24–25, 27
        legislation, 57
    definitions of, 5–6, 17, 19–20, 60,
        62, 242
    high incidence, 67–68
    historical perspective, 11–14
    international classifications of, 18
    learning difficulties/disabilities, 31,
        98–99, 106–10, 122–23,
        124–25
        children with, 34, 39, 54–55,
            98, 190, 192
        see also general learning
            disabilities
    low incidence, 67
        resource allocation model, 69
    movement, 20
    studies critique, 74, 75–76
disabilities and/or special educational
    needs, 99
    children with, and human rights, 83

children with, equitable educational
    opportunities, 75, 83
    see also special educational needs
Disability Act (Government of Ireland
    2005), 49, 50, 62
disability: an Irish perspective, 20–23, 29
disabled person/people,
    and employment, 23
    institutionalisation of, 12, 13, 41, 76
    and labelling, *see* labelling
    and language definition negativity,
        16–17
    public policy in relation to, 48
Disabled People's International, 19
distinct learning needs, 161–62
District Lunatic Asylums in Ireland, 37
diversity, children and special education,
    3
Dixon, Janet, 254
DoH/DfES, (UK Department of
    Health/Department for Education
    and Skills) (2003), 245
Donegal, 22
Douglas, G., Mc Call, S., Mc Linden,
    M., Pavey, S., Ware, J. and
    Farrell, A.M., 50, 66, 90
Down syndrome, 15–16, 23, 32, 89,
    229, 230, 243, 244, 246, 258
Down Syndrome Association, 244
Doyle, A., 48, 49
Draft Convention on the Rights of
    Persons with Disabilities, see
    United Nations (2006)
Draft Guidelines for Teachers of
    Students with General Learning
    Disabilities, see National Council
    for Curriculum and Assessment
    (NCCA 2002a, 2007 and 2009)
Draft Guidelines for Teachers of
    Students with Severe and
    Profound General Learning
    Disabilities: Primary, see
    National Council for Curriculum
    and Assessment (NCCA 2002b)
Dreikurs, R. and Cassel, P., 204
Dreikurs, R. and Grey, L., 204
Dreikurs, R., 195, 203, 206
Drudy, S. and Kinsella, W., 88
drúth, see fool
Duncan, N., 245, 246

Dunn, L.M., 76
dyscalculia, 101, 189, 190
dysgraphia, 101, 186
dyslexia, 5, 32, 49, 50, 62–64, 67, 70,
   101, 105, 123, 145, 146, 216,
   232, 248
   indicators for identifying, 223–24
   strategies for post-primary level
         learners, 225–27
   strategies for primary level learners,
         224–25
   understanding, 222–23
dyspraxia, 5, 68, 101, 232

early childhood care and education
      (ECCE), 173
ecological perspective approach to
      curricular design and teaching
      strategies in special education,
      140–41
Educable (2000), 26
education, as a fundamental human
      right, 3–4
Education, Department of, 41, 42, 43,
      44, 48–50, 54
Education, Department of (1983), 44,
      231
Education, Department of (1988), 259,
      260
Education, Department of (1993), 1, 31,
      38, 49, 50, 114, 156
Education (1995), see Charting Our
      Education Future (Government
      of Ireland, 1995)
Education Act (Government of Ireland
      1998), 1, 37, 45, 49, 50, 57–58,
      60, 87, 130, 240, 255–56
Education Act 1981 (UK), 43
Education Act 1944 (UK), 96
Education and Science (DES),
      Department of, 51, 53, 58, 60,
      61, 67, 69, 70, 88, 262
   and children with ASDs, 63, 218
   (DES 1998), 260
   (DES 1999), 157
   (DES 2000), 256, 259, 260–62
   (DES 2001), 50, 62–64, 101, 221
   (DES 2002a), 262
   (DES 2002b), 50, 62–64, 222–24
   (DES 2005a), 67–68, 131

(DES 2005b), 182
(DES 2006b), 103
(DES 2007), 88–89, 91, 116,
      256–58, 263
(DES 2010), 172, 174
DES Circular SP. ED. 07/02, 263
In-Career Development Unit, 70
Inspectorate, 58, 61, 63, 103, 116
Inspectorate (2006a), 63, 64
Education and Skills, Department of,
      and terminology, 5
Education and Skills (UK), Department
      for (DfES, 2001), 122–23, 129
Education for All, 124
Education for All Handicapped Children
      Act (USA) 1975, 57
Education for Persons with Special
      Educational Needs (EPSEN) Act
      (Government of Ireland 2004), 2,
      4, 49, 50, 57, 67, 68, 100, 104,
      150
   challenges in implementing, 61
   Consultative Forum, 91
   definition of disability, 60
   and IEPs, 138, 139, 141, 239, 261
   and inclusive education/environment,
         59, 87, 114, 131, 256
   parents and identification and
         assessment of their child's
         learning difficulties, 239,
         240
   within-child factors, 100
Education Northern Ireland (DENI),
      Department of, 218
DENI 2006, 114
Education (UK), Department for, DfE,
      1994, 147
Education (Welfare) Act (Government of
      Ireland 2000), 49, 50, 57, 59
educational assessments, 124
Educational Development (Government
      of Ireland 1980), White Paper on,
      44, 48
Educational Development (1995), White
      Paper on, see Charting Our
      Education Future
educational integration, 51
Educational invisibility and state neglect
      (1922–1952), 38
educational model, 233

Educational Provision and Support for Persons with Autistic Spectrum Disorders, see Education and Science, Department of, (DES 2001)

Educationally Sub-Normal (ESN) Mild/Moderate schools, *see* United Kingdom, schools for disadvantaged

Eivers, E., Close, S., Shiel, G., Millar, D., Clerkin, A., Gilleece, L. and Kiniry, J., 172, 173

Elliott, J., 125, 126

Emanuelson, I., 265

emerging approach to facilitating learning, 265

England, 79, 122, 189

Enright, B.E. and Choate, J.S., 193

environmental demands approach, 98

epilepsy, 12

EPSEN Act, *see* Education for Persons with Special Educational Needs (EPSEN) Act 2004

Equal Status Act (Government of Ireland 2000), 49, 50, 57, 59

Equality Authority, 59

equality of opportunity, as a fundamental right, 3–4, 53–54, 56

ESN, 97

EU Council of Ministers Charter, 44

eugenics movement, 13

Europe, 12, 36

European Community, 43, 47, 48

Evidence of Best Practice Models and Outcomes in the Education of Deaf and Hard-of-Hearing Children: An International Review, 50, 65–66

Exceptionally Able Students: Draft Guidelines for Teachers (2007), 104

experience and literacy, 176–77

extended objectives approach to curricular design and teaching strategies in special education, 140–41

Eyre, D., 105–6

failure to learn, 106–10

families, *see* parents and families

Farmer, D., 163

Farrell, Patricia, 39–40

Fernald, G.M., 184–85

Fitzgerald, E., 20, 21

Flatman-Watson, S., 89–90

Fletcher, W., 147–48

Florian, L., Hollenweger, J., Simeonson, R., Wedell, K., Riddell, S., Terzi, L. and Holland, A., 135

Florian, L., Rose, R. and Tilstone, C., 84, 85

Flutter, J. and Rudduck, J., 108

fool, 31–32

Framework for Action, 83

France, 34

Fraser, D., 242, 244, 245, 251, 252, 254

Frederickson, N. and Cline, T., 85, 86, 98, 99, 106, 126, 127

Frith, U., 183, 219

functional integration, 77, 78

Fundamental Principles of Disability, see Union of the Physically Impaired against Segregation and the Disability Alliance (UPIAS), 1976

future, planning for, 56–57

Gaden, G., 113

Gaelicisation policy, 29, 38, 42

Gannon, B. and Nolan, B., 20

Gardner, H., 210, 216

Garner, P., 210

Garnett, J., 170

Gartner, A. and Joe, T., 15

Gash, H., 24

Gash, H., Illan Romeu, N. and Lopez Pina, J., 24

general allocation scheme, 67

general learning disabilities, 5, 12, 15–17, 23–24, 139, 165, 180, 183, 216, 228

changing attitudes towards, 36–37

curriculum guidelines for teachers, 71, 157, 228

and eugenics movement, 13

in mainstream schools, 71, 80, 183

mild, 52, 68–69, 71, 101, 102, 114, 157, 168

strategies for, 190, 229–30

understanding, 174, 228–29
moderate, 42, 71, 82, 102, 104, 148,
    157, 194
    strategies for, 166, 230–31
    understanding, 21, 229–30
severe/profound, 54–56, 67, 71, 82,
    102, 103, 157, 215
    strategies for, 231–32
    understanding, 231
special schools, 38, 39–43, 52
teaching strategies, 35–36, 189–90,
    215–16, 231
George IV, King, 35
Germany, 79
gifted pupils, see able pupils
Glasser, William, 195, 198–99
Glendenning, D., 57
Goffman, E., 76
Grandin, T., 219
Great Famine, 38
Greece, 12
Green Paper on Services for Disabled
    People (Government of Ireland
    1984), see Towards a Full Life
Grey, C., 219
Griffin, S. and Shevlin, M., 87
Griffin, S., 33
Grogan, M., 24–25
Gross, J., 121, 122, 123, 128, 129–30
Growing Up in Ireland, 99
Guidelines for Teachers of Students with
    General Learning Disabilities, see
    National Council for Curriculum
    and Assessment (2002a, 2007
    and 2009)
Guidelines on Remedial Education, see
    Education, Department of (1988)
Guidelines on the Individual Education
    Plan Process (2006), see National
    Council for Special Education
    (2006)

Hardiman, S., Guerin, S. and Fitzsimons,
    E., 90
Hart, S., 99
Hayes, J., 148, 190
Health, Department of, 43, 44, 48, 54,
    55
Health, Department of, Commission,
    29

Health, Department of (1965), 29, 30,
    41, 114
health assessments, 124
Hegarty, S., 3, 80, 81, 82
Herbert, E. and Carpenter, B., 243
high incidence needs, see under
    disabilities
higher functioning autism (HFA), see
    Asperger syndrome
Hill, M., 47
Hinshaw, S.P., 233
historical perspective, see under
    disabilities
Hogan, P., 268
holistic assessment, 126
Horgan, G., 26, 242
Hornby, G. and Witte, C., 109
Horne, P. and Timmons, V., 116
Howley, M., 220
Hughes, M., 44
human rights, 267
Humphreys, Joseph, 34–35
Humphreys, T., 211

IALS (International Adult Literary)
    Survey (1995), 189
idiot, 4, 12, 17, 31, 36, 37
imbecile, 4, 17, 36, 37
impairment, 18–20
Implementation Report: Plan for the
    Phased Implementation of the
    EPSEN Act 2004, 99
in-class support models, 262
inclusion in Ireland, see under Ireland
Inclusion Ireland, 5
inclusion movement, 82–86
Inclusion of Students with Special
    Educational Needs: Post-Primary
    Guidelines, see Education and
    Science, Department of, (DES
    2007)
inclusion process/policy, 24–25, 72, 73,
    74, 75–76
inclusive learning environments, 2, 59,
    67–68, 77, 84, 115–17, 131, 256
Index for Inclusion, 85–86
Individual Education Plan(s) (IEP),
    138–42, 239, 240, 261, 263
    definition of, 139–40

Individual Education Process (2006), 139–40
  issues, 150
  tracking progress and evaluating interventions, 149–50
  writing, implementing and reviewing, 143–44
  who designed for, 138–39
Individual Education Programme (IEP), 54
individual model of support, 266
Individual Profile and Learning Programme, 260–62
Individuals with Disabilities Education Act (Government of the United States of America, 1975), *see* American Individuals with Disabilities Act (IDEA)
Information Communication Technology (ICT), 66, 99, 166, 213, 224, 232
institutionalisation of people with disabilities, *see under* disabled person/people
integration, 84
integrated education, benefits to children with/without disabilities, 79
integrated education, moral issue, 78–79, 81
integration/inclusion, teachers' attitudes to, 81
integration/mainstreaming special education policy, 74, 77–82
Intelligence Quotient (IQ) tests, 125–26
Interim Report on the Developmental Initiative in Assessment for Learning in Junior Cycle, see National Council for Curriculum and Assessment (2005)
International Adult Literacy Survey (IALS) 1995, 259
International Classification of Impairment, Disabilities and Handicaps, 18
international research studies on children with disabilities, *see under* disabilities
International Review of the Literature of Evidence of Best Practice Models and Outcomes in the Education of Blind and Visually

Impaired Children, 50, 66
International Review of the Literature of Evidence of Best Practice Provision in the Education of Persons with Autistic Spectrum Disorders, 50, 64–65
International Year of the Disabled 1981, 48
Investment in Education (1966), 42
Ireland, 24, 35, 36, 43, 44
  assessment in an Irish context, 130–36
  and autism, 219
  blind and visually impaired children, 66
  curricular access policy developments in, 156–57
  District Lunatic Asylums, *see* District Lunatic Asylums in Ireland
  education of children, 57
  and IEPs, 138
  and inclusion, 54, 87–91, 219, 269
  Irish system of SEN assessment, 135
  and mental handicap, 5, 228
  national system of education establishment, 36, 38
  post-primary schools special education, 134
  special education in, 29–45, 49, 87–90 , 115, 117, 268
    historical timeline, 30
    policy and practice, 268–69
  spelling difficulties, 186
Irish Association of Teachers in Special Education, 42
Irish Christian Brothers, 38
Irish Hospital Sweepstake, 39
Irish National Teachers' Organisation (INTO), 30, 38, 42, 71
Irish perspective on disability, 20–23, 53
Irish Society for Autism 2004, 218
Irish Times, 39
Italy, 43, 79
Itard, Jean-Marc–Gaspard, 34
'Items for Learning' framework for marking written work, 170–71

Jelly, M., Fuller, A. and Byers, R., 109, 148

Johnson, D.W. and Johnson, T., 80
Johnstone, D., 20
Jordan, Nancy, 40–41
Junior Certificate curriculum, 157
Junior Cycle Framework, 157
Justice, Department of, 54

Keller, Helen, 174–75
Kelly, A., Carey, S. and McCarthy, S.,
    195–96
Kenny, M., McNeela, E. and Shevlin,
    M., 90
Kenny, M., McNeela, E., Noonan
    Walsh, P. and Shevlin, M., 243,
    244, 236
Kenny, M., McNeela, E., Shevlin, M.
    and Daly, T., 25, 26–27
Kenward, H., 24
Kidd, George, 36
King, William, 32
Kinsella, W. and Senior, J., 87
Kitchin, R., Shirlow, P. and
    Shuttleworth, I., 22

labelling, 14–16, 77
Laevers, F., Cuvelier, N., Moons, J. and
    Debue, A., 207
Lamb Inquiry (Department for Children,
    Schools and Families 2009), 241
LAMH signs, 231
language arts hierarchy, 175–76
language experience approach (LEA),
    188–89
Lawlor, L. and Cregan, A., 264
leadership and special educational needs,
    115–17
learning difficulties/disabilities, see
    under disabilities
learning disability (LD), see dyslexia,
    understanding
learning environment, focus on, 127
    and curriculum differentiation, 163
learning helplessness, 109
learning priorities, setting of, 144–48
learning styles, 216
learning support, 258–62
    teachers, 67, 258, 261, 262
Learning-Support Guidelines (DES
    2000), see Education and Science,
    Department of, (DES 2000)

LeFanu, E., 35
left-handedness, 186
legislation, parents role, 240, 246
legislation: enabling significant change,
    57–59
Leithwood, K.A. and Riehl, C.J., 115
Lerner, J., 175
Lewis, A., 82
Lewis, A. and Norwich, B., 112, 222,
    228
Lindqvist, B., UNESCO, 269
listening and literacy, 177–80
listening, teaching strategies, 178–80
literacy,
    defining, 174
    difficulties, 172–89
    receptive and expressive skills, 176
Literacy, Economy and Society: Results
    of the First International Adult
    Literacy Survey, Paris: OECD,
    189
Local Initiatives Scheme, 70
locational integration, 77, 79, 80,
    139, 165, 166, 174, 180, 183,
    190, 216
Locke, John, 32, 33
Logan, A., 87
Lodge, A. and Lynch, K., 59
logographic stage in the teaching of
    reading, 183
London, 40
Lost for Words, 235
low incidence needs, see under
    disabilities
Lowe, P. and Reynolds, C.R., 232
Lucan, 36
lunatics, 37
Lynch, K., 257

MacGiolla Phádraig, B., 87
Macnamara, J., 42
mainstream education, principles of, 3
Maker, C.J., 162–63
Malone, G. and Smith, D., 217
Mansion House, Dublin, 40
Manson, David, 32–34
Manuel, P., 253
Marschark, M. and Spencer, P.E., 50,
    65–66, 90
Martin, M., 196

Mary Immaculate College of Education, Limerick, *see* PASSPORT Programme

mathematics, *see* numeracy

McCallister, W.J., 33

McCarthy, O. and Kenny, M., 115

McCausland, D., 143–44, 150

McConkey, R. and McCormack, R., 21

McCormack, B., 41

McCormack, Wyn, 235

McDonnell, P., 74, 87, 228

McGee, P., 42, 43, 44, 114

McManus, A., 38

McNamara, S. and Moreton, G., 165, 199, 205, 212

McPhillips, T., 182, 184, 191, 262

Meaney, M., Kiernan, N. and Monahan, K., 58, 61

meaning-emphasis approach to reading, 184

medical model of disability, 17–19, 34, 41, 55, 58, 60, 96, 215, 233

medical profession, and disabilities, 12

Meeting the Learning and Teaching Needs of Students with Special Educational Needs: Signposts (A Resource Pack for Teachers) (2008), 70

Meijer, C.J.W. and Pijl, S.J., 78, 79

mental handicap, 5, 21, 29
  policy development, 41–42

mental illness, 5, 12, 31
  and learning disability, 31

MGLD (mild general learning disability) schools, 114–15

military model of school life, 111

miscue analysis, 129–30

Mitchell, D.T. and Snyder, S.L., 15

Montessori, Maria, 33, 40

Montessori College, Blackrock, 41

Montessori Method and special education, 40–41, 185–86

Morgan, M. and Martin, M., 259

Morgan, M., Hickey, B. and Kellaghan, T., 259

Mosley, J., 181

Mosley, J. and Tew, M., 181, 201

Mulrooney, M. and Harrold, M., 243, 245

multi-sensory approaches towards mastery in reading, 184–85

Murphy, T., 90

NAMHI (National Association of Mentally Handicapped Ireland), *see* Inclusion Ireland

naming the world, 14–16

National Assessments of Mathematics and English Reading 2009, 173

National Behaviour Support Service (NBSS), 70–71

National Centre for Technology in Education (NCTE), 224–25

National Council for Curriculum and Assessment (NCCA), 53, 58, 60, 71, 104–5, 135, 156, 157
  (NCCA 1999), 119, 156–57
  (NCCA 2002), 159, 228, 230, 232
  (NCCA 2002a, 2007 and 2009), 157, 229
  (NCCA 2002b), 232
  (NCCA 2005), 135
  (NCCA 2006), 119

National Council for Special Education (NCSE), 49, 59, 60–61, 67, 90, 91, 99, 139, 240
  (NCSE 2006), 139, 141, 142, 144, 145, 146, 147, 149–50
  NCSE Implementation Report (2006): Plan for the Phased Implementation of the EPSEN Act 2004, 99
  research reports, 64–65

National Council for Special Education Annual Report (2009), 68–69

National Disability Authority survey (2002), 21

National Education Convention (1994), 56

National Educational Welfare Board, 59, 196

National Educational Psychological Service (NEPS), 53, 60, 61, 69, 131, 196, 197
  (NEPS 2007), 132
  (NEPS 2007a/2007b), 131
  (NEPS 2010a/2007b), 131, 134
  (NEPS 2010c), 196–98

National Educational Psychological
    Service (NEPS), three-stage
    model, 131–36
National Institution for the Education
    of the Deaf and Dumb, *see*
    Claremont Institute
national plan on literacy and numeracy,
    173–74
National Reading Initiative, 181–82
National Survey of Reading (1993), 260
Nazi Germany, 13
NBSS, *see* National Behaviour Support
    Service (NBSS)
NCSE, *see* National Council for Special
    Education (NCSE)
Needs and Abilities: A Policy for the
    Intellectually Disabled
    (Government of Ireland 1991),
    48, 49, 50
NEPS, *see* National Educational
    Psychological Service (NEPS)
Netherlands, 79
New Curriculum (*Curaclam na*
    mBunscoile 1971), 42
New York, 38
No Choice: No Chance. The
    Educational Experiences of
    Young People with Disabilities,
    see Educable (2000)
normalisation principles, 76
Norman, Connolly, 37
Norris, C. and Closs, A., 245, 247
Norris, C. and Lloyd, G., 248
North Carolina, University of, 220
Northern Ireland, 26, 248
Norwich, B., Griffiths, C. and Burden,
    B., 248, 253
Nugent, M., 150
numeracy, defining, 189
    learning difficulties, 189–91
        see also dyscalculia
    teaching strategies, 190–93

Ó Murchú, E., 112–13
Ó Murchú, E. and Shevlin, M., 113
O'Brien, T, and Guiney, D., 159–61
O'Donnell, M., 25, 26
O'Donoghue court case (1993), 45, 49,
    50, 51, 55
O'Donoghue, J., 189

O'Flynn, S. and Kennedy, H., 198, 199,
    205, 208, 210
O'Hanlon, Justice, 55
O'Keefe, P., 114
O'Leary, K., 23
O'Rourke, Mary, 44
O'Brien, T., 211
O'Hara, J., Byrne, S.J. and McNamara,
    G., 211
O'Neill, A. and Rose, R., 87
O'Riordan, M., Plaisted, K., Driver, J.
    and Baron-Cohen, S., 219
Oakshott, M., 113
OECD, 47
Offaly Centre for Independent Living
    (2001), 24–25
óinseach, 32
Oliver, M., 75, 117
Organisation for Economic Co-operation
    and Development (OECD 1994),
    78
Organisation of Teaching Resources for
    Pupils who need Additional
    Support in Mainstream Primary
    Schools, see Education and
    Science, Department of, (DES
    2005a)
organisational skills, 216–17
Orpen, Charles, 34, 35
orthographic stage in the teaching of
    reading, 183

Palmerstown, 36
parental experiences of disability,
    243–245
parental reaction to assessment of
    special educational need, 248–49
parental struggle for support services,
    245–46
parents and families,
    building collaborative relationships,
        249–50
    creating responsive parent-teacher
        relationships, 252
    developing collaborative
        relationships with,
        239–40, 241
    guidelines for beginning teachers,
        252–53
    home-school relationships, 246–48

parents' attitudes to special education
  provision, 240–43
principles of effective partnership,
  250–52
reaction and adaption to disability,
  242–43
Paris, 12
Parsons, S., Guldberg, K., Mac Leod,
  A., Jones, G., Prunty, A. and
  Balfe, T., 50, 64, 65, 90
PASSPORT Programme by Curriculum
  Development Unit, Mary
  Immaculate College of Education,
  Limerick, 194
Pathfinders, 26
Peck, C., Donaldson, J. and Pezzoli, M.,
  79
peer tutoring, 80–81
Peer, L., 226
Perkins, R., Moran, G., Cosgrove, J.
  and Shiel, G., 172
Pestalozzi, Johann Heinrich, 34, 35
phonological awareness in reading
  teaching, 183–84
physical/sensory disability, children
  with, 2
physical/sensory disability, official
  government policy, 2
Piaget, Jean, 1952, 174
Pim, Jonathan, 36
Pinkus, S., 250
PISA 2009 report, 172
Pisa Study 2000, 189
Pollard, R., 35
Poor Relief Act (1838), 37
Porter, J., 231
Post-Primary Guidelines (2007), see
  Education and Science,
  Department of, (DES 2007)
Powell, S., 219
power seeking, see under behavioural
  difficulties
Pressley, M., 183
Primary School Curriculum (DES 1999),
  see Education and Science,
  Department of, (DES 1999)
process model, 141
process modification, and curriculum
  differentiation, 163, 164
Proclamation of the Republic, 38

product modification, and curriculum
  differentiation, 163, 164
Programme for International Student
  Assessment (PISA), 173
provision, see under special education
psychiatric illness, see mental illness
psycho-educational assessments, 124
psycho-medical legacy/perspective, 74
psychological assessment, 120, 123,
  125–26, 159
Public Attitudes to Disability in the
  Republic of Ireland, see National
  Disability Authority survey
  (2002)
Public Law 94–142 1975, 77
Purdie, N., Hattie, J. and Carroll, A.,
  233

Quinn, F., 248, 249
Quinn, G. and Degener, T. with Bruce,
  A., Burke, C., Castellino, J.,
  Kenna, P., Kilkelly, U. and
  Quinlivan, S., 267

Radcliffe College, 175
Rathmines, 40
reading, strategies for teaching, 183–85
reading and literacy, 177–78, 181–83
reading difficulties, see dyslexia
recognition needs in schools, see under
  behavioural difficulties
Reid (Lewis and Norwich 2005), 222
relational approach to facilitating
  learning, 265
remedial teaching, see learning support
Report of the Commission of Inquiry on
  Mental Handicap 1965, see
  Health, Department of, (1965)
Report of the Commission on the Status
  of People with Disabilities
  (1996), 1, 49, 50, 53–54
Report of the Committee of Enquiry
  into the Education of
  Handicapped Children and
  Young People, see Warnock
  Report
Report of the Special Education Review
  Committee (1993), see Education,
  Department of, (1993)

*Report of the Task Force on Autism
    (2001), see* Education and Science
    (DES), Department of, (DES
    2001)
*Report of the Task Force on Dyslexia
    (2002b), see* Education and
    Science (DES), Department of,
    (DES 2002b)
*Report of the Task Force on Student
    Behaviour in Second Level
    Schools,* 196
*Report on the National Education
    Convention (1994),* 259
Reports of the Claremont Institute, 35
resource teaching, 262–63
revenge, *see under* behavioural
    difficulties
Ring, E. and Travers, J., 87
Robertson, P., Hamill, P. and Hewitt,
    C., 228
Robins, J., 31, 39
Rogers, B., 212
Rome, 12, 40
Rooney, N., 25
Rose, R. and Howley, M., 99, 108,
    220, 230, 252
Rose, R. and Shevlin, M., 90, 109–10
Rose, R., Shevlin, M., Winter, E. and
    O'Raw, P., 87, 90
Roundwood, 35
Royal Commission 1908, 37
RRCC strategy, 190
Rudduck, J. and McIntyre, D., 108–9
Russell, F., 249

Salamanca Statement (UNESCO 1994),
    83, 269
Scandinavia, 41, 74, 76
Scanlon, G. and McGilloway, 264
*School Matters: The Report of the Task
    Force on Student Behaviour in
    Second Level Schools (2006),* 70
School Psychological Service, 52
School Support Plus, *see* National
    Educational Psychological Service
    (NEPS), three-stage model
schools,
    banding, 257
    effectiveness strategies, 75
    improvement strategies, 74, 75

leadership, *see* leadership and special
    educational needs
resource teachers, 258, 263
streaming, 257
supplementary teaching, 258
whole-school approaches, 255–58,
    261, 262–63
Schweigert, P., 232
*Science Differentiation in Action:
    Practical Strategies for Adapting
    Learning and Teaching in Science
    for Students with Diverse Needs
    and Abilities (2008),* 70
ScoilNet, 224–25
Scotland, 5
Scott, I., 87
Second World War, *see* World War Two
segregated provision in special
    education policy, 74, 77, 79, 81
Séguin, Édouard, 34, 36
self-esteem, *see under* behavioural
    difficulties
SEN, *see* special educational needs (SEN)
senile dementia, 31
SENO, *see* Special Educational Needs
    Organiser (SENO)
Serfontein, G., 212
*Services for Disabled People (1984),
    Green Paper on,* 48–49, 50
SESS, *see* Special Education Support
    Service (SESS)
Shawe, S. and Hawes, T., 216
Shevlin, M. and Flynn, P., 116–17
Shevlin, M., Noonan Walsh, P., Kenny,
    M., McNeela, E. and Molloy, R.,
    89
Shiel, G. and Morgan, M. with Larney,
    R., 259, 260
Siegel, L.S., 223
Simpson, J., Hornby, G., Davies, L. and
    Murray, R., 242, 245
Sinnott court case (2000), 49, 50, 55, 56
Sion Hill, Blackrock, 40
Slavin, R., Madden, N., Dolan, L. and
    Wasik, B., 106
SMART approach to individual
    education planning, 145
social and educational model of
    disability, 19–20, 34, 54, 55, 96
social integration, 51, 77, 78

social policy and disability issues, 48
Social Stories, 219
Social Welfare, Department of, 44
sociological response perspective, 74–75
Solity, J., 98
Sopko, K., 150
spastic, 4, 17
speaking, 180–81
   teaching strategies, 181
special education, 112–13
   historical evolution in an Irish
      cultural context, 29–33
   in Ireland, *see under* Ireland
   knowledge and practice, 6
   and mainstream education, 2, 156
   and mainstream schools, 6–7, 56,
      72, 82, 102–3
     see also schools
   policy and practice, 1, 2–3, 6, 47–48,
      49–50, 78
   provision, 67, 72
   recommending changes, 50–53
   route map, 7–8
   whole-school approaches, *see under*
      schools
Special Education Review Committee
     (SERC) Report, 1993, 31, 38, 45,
     47, 49, 50, 51–53, 54, 56, 87,
     100, 114
   deficiencies in curricular provision,
      156
   and dyslexia, 222
   'special educational needs' definition,
      100, 104, 259
Special Education Support Service (SESS)
     (2008), 70, 165
special educational discourse (current),
     58
Special Educational Needs: A
     Continuum of Support (Guide-
     lines for Teachers) (2007a), see
     National Educational
     Psychological Service (2007a)
Special Educational Needs: A
     Continuum of Support (Resource
     Pack for Teachers) (2007b), see
     National Educational
     Psychological Service (2007b)
Special Educational Needs: Curriculum
     Issues (1999), see National

Council for Curriculum and
     Assessment (1999)
Special Educational Needs Code of
     Practice (DfES, 2001), see
     Education and Skills (UK),
     Department for (DfES, 2001)
Special Educational Needs Organiser
     (SENO), 60–61, 67, 68
special educational needs (SEN), 70, 112
   assessment process, 120–21, 122,
     124–30, 131
   children with, categorisation of, 78,
     242
     curriculum access for, *see*
      curriculum access
     education programmes for, 58,
      70, 72, 79–80, 89
     educational and service needs,
      67, 72, 108–10
     learning opportunities, 76,
      85, 108–10, 234
     organisational skills, 216–17
     participation in society, 4,
      131
     strengths and needs, 142–44
   concepts, 96–99
   definition of, 5–6, 51, 60, 77, 95, 97,
     99–101, 104, 138–39
   identifying and assessing, 119–36
   responding to, 60, 267
   special needs assistants (SNAs),
     263–65
   special needs coordinator (SENCO),
     249
   special schools, 103–4
     see also schools
   support roles in facilitating learning,
     265
   see also disabilities
special educational needs and/or
     disabilities, and schools and
     teachers, 1–2, 81–82, 108–9,
     122, 127, 258,
special educational provision, principles
     of, 3
Special Friends programme for
     integrated education, 80
special schools, 25
   and classes, role of, 114–17

obstacles to progress and provision, 42–43
speech and language disorders, 67, 103
spelling, strategies for teaching, 187–88
spelling in language skills development, 186–87
Spelman, B.J. and Griffin, S., 45
spina bifida, 23
SQ3R Comprehension Strategy: Survey, Question, Read, Recall and Review, 184
St Michael's House, 39–40
St Patrick's College of Education, Dublin, 41
St Ultan's Infant Hospital, 40
St Vincent's Home for Mentally Defective Children, 38
Stahl, S.A., Osborn, J. and Lehr, F., 182
Standard Rules on the Equalization of Opportunities for Persons with Disabilities 1993, see United Nations (1993)
State Examination Commission, 60
Statistical and Social Inquiry Society of Ireland, 35–36
Stauffer, R.G., 189
Stenhouse, L., 141
Stewart's Institute, 35–36
Stewarts School and Residential Centre, see Stewart's Institute
Strain, M., Dennison, B., Ouston, J. and Hall, V., 8, 221
Strategy for Support Provision, 70
Success for All programme, 106
Sullivan Anne, 174–75
Support for All, 134
Supporting Special Education in the Mainstream School (2003), 263
Survey of Learning Disability (1943), 39
Swain, J. and French, S., 14, 15, 16
Swain, J., French, S. and Cameron, C., 14, 17, 19
Sweden, 13, 79
Switzerland, 34
Synge, J.M., 35
Synge, John, 35

target setting process, 148
teachers,
    cycle of failure, 110–11
    education, 7
    and the learning process, 126–27, 128–30, 132–33
learning support and resource teachers, 258
teaching methods and strategies to achieve learning targets, 149
Teachers of Students with General Learning Disabilities, guidelines for, 157
terminology, 4–6
The Education and Training of Severely and Profoundly Mentally Handicapped Children in Ireland, see Education, Department of, (1983)
The Future Role of the Special School, see Education Northern Ireland (DENI), Department of, (2006)
The Inclusion Charter, CSIE 2002, 84
The National Education Convention Report, 1994, 49, 50
theory of mind, 218
Third International Mathematics and Science study (TIMMS), 260
Thomas, C., 18
Thomas, G. and Loxley, A., 97–98
Thomas, G. and O'Hanlon, C., 84
Thomas, G. and Vaughan, M., 73, 78
Tilstone, C., Lacey, P., Porter, J. and Robertson, C., 124, 126, 127, 145
Tod, J., Castle, F. and Blamires, M., 148
Together from the Start (UK), 245
Together from the Start: Practical Guidance for Professionals Working with Young Disabled Children (Birth to Third Birthday) and Their Families, see DoH/DfES (UK 2003)
Tomlinson, S., 75
Toolan, D., 21–22
Tourette syndrome, 37
Towards a Full Life: Green Paper on Services for Disabled People, (Government of Ireland 1984), 48–50

travellers, 24
Travers, J., Balfe, T., Butler, C., Day, T.,
    Dupont, M., McDaid, R.,
    O'Donnell, M. and Prunty, A.,
    87
Treatment and Education for Autistic
    and related Communication
    handicapped Children
    (TEACCH), 220
Tregaskis, C., 19
Trifling Club, 33
Turner, E., 225
Twachtmann-Cullen, D., 219
Tyneside Disability Arts, 15, 16

UN Convention on the Rights of the
    Child, 1989, 44, 83
UNESCO, 47, 82, 83
UNESCO 2005 report, 91
Union of the Physically Impaired against
    Segregation and the Disability
    Alliance (UPIAS, 1976), 19
United Kingdom, 24, 43, 85, 96, 100,
    228, 264
    schools for disadvantaged, 4–5, 74
    special educational provision, 77,
    241
United Kingdom Spastics Society, 17
United Nations, 47, 48, 82
United Nations Declaration on the
    Rights of Disabled Persons
    (1975), 48
United Nations Draft Convention on
    the Rights of Persons with
    Disabilities (2006), 20
United Nations Educational Scientific
    and Cultural Organisation, see
    UNESCO
United Nations General Assembly,
    New York, 83
United Nations (1993), 83
United Nations (2006), 20
United States (US), 13, 41, 79, 82,
    85,106, 222, 264, see also
    America
Universal Newborn Hearing Screening
    (UN HS), 66

visiting teacher service, 71–72

Visser, J., 160
visual impairment, see blindness
Voeltz, L., Hemphill, N.J., Brown, S.,
    Kishi, G., Klein, R., Royal
    Fruehling, G., Levy, J.C. and
    Kube, C., 80
Vygotsky, Lev, 127, 174

Wales, 79, 122
Walsh, L., 247
Ware, J., 2005
Ware, J., Balfe, T., Butler, C., Day, T.,
    Dupont, M., Harten, C., Farrell,
    A.M., McDaid, R., O'Riordan,
    M., Prunty, A. and Travers, J.,
    91, 114, 115
Ware, J., Julian, G. and McGee, P., 87
Warnock Committee, 51
Warnock Report, 43–44, 51, 52, 57, 77,
    78, 96–97, 98, 270
Watson, N., 15
Watson, N., Shakespeare, T.,
    Cunningham-Burley, S., Barnes,
    C., Corker, M., Davis, J. and
    Priestley, M., 24
Wentworth, R. and Lubienski, A., 33
Westminster Catechism, 32
Westwood, P., 106, 107, 108, 165, 166,
    168, 184, 185, 187, 189, 192,
    213, 222, 228, 229, 232
White Paper on Educational
    Development (Government of
    Ireland, 1980), 44, 48
Whyte, G., 55, 56
Wild Boy of Aveyron, 34
Wilde, Oscar, 35
Wilde, Sir William, 35–36
Williams, G., 18
Wilson, C. and Jade, R., 24
Wing, L. and Gould, J., 218
Winter, E. and Kilpatrick, R., 116
Winter, E. and O'Raw, P., 89, 91, 116
Winter, E., Fletcher-Campbell, F.,
    Connolly, P. and Lynch, P., 135
withdrawal, see under behavioural
    difficulties
Wolfgang, C.H., 202, 203, 204
Wood, D.J., 169
workhouses, see asylums
World Health Organisation, 18

World War Two, 19, 40
writing,
    in language skills development,
        185–86
    strategies for teaching, 188

writing difficulties, *see* dysgraphia
written expression, 188

Zentall, S.S., 233
zone of potential development, 127